A
FIELD GUIDE
TO
REPTILES
AND THE LAW

SECOND REVISED EDITION

BY

JOHN P. LEVELL

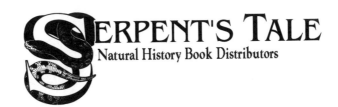

SERPENT'S TALE
Natural History Book Distributors

A Field Guide to Reptiles and the Law
by John P. Levell

From A Declaration Of Principles Jointly Adopted By A Committee Of The American Bar Association And A Committee Of Publishers:

This publication is designed to provide accurate and authoritative information in regard to the subject matter covered. It is sold with the understanding that the publisher is not engaged in rendering legal, accounting, or other professional service. If legal advice or other expert assistance is required, the services of a competent professional person should be sought.

Second Edition, Revised 1997

Credits:
Cover Design and Book Production: Sang Froid Press, Inc.
Front Cover Photography: Barney Oldfield
Back Cover Photography: William B. Love/Blue Chameleon Ventures

ISBN: Softcover: 1-885209-06-1
       Hardcover: 1-885209-07-X

Published by:

SERPENT'S TALE
Natural History Book Distributors

403 Parkway Avenue North
P.O. Box 405
Lanesboro, MN 55949
Telephone: 507-467-8734
Fax: 507-467-8735
email: zoobooks@ptel.net

Printed in Canada

This book is dedicated to
Victor P. Hauser and John "Sunny" Levell

Both of whom provided inspiration throughout the duration of this project,
in two very different, yet never the less special ways.
I miss them both.

Contents

Second Edition Comments

What can be said about this second edition of *A Field Guide to Reptiles and the Law*? At 270 pages in length, 30 more than the original, it has obviously gotten bigger. But for what reason? Can amphibian and reptile legislation in the United States really have changed enough in the past two years to account for this growth?

Unfortunately, the answer to the preceding question is both yes and no. For example, and contrary to "popular belief," in the majority of U.S. States little to no substantial change has occurred in the legal status of amphibians and reptiles during the past two years. Despite this fact, however, virtually every state's account has been modified in some way from that of the previous edition. Obviously, typographical errors and other inconsistencies have been corrected as much as possible. More importantly, and largely a reflection of greater confidence and efficiency in data gathering activities, a number of previously omitted regulations have been subsequently "discovered" and added where necessary.

While undoubtedly a contributing factor, a few inadvertently omitted regulations cannot possibly account for all 30 of this title's additional pages. Indeed, the vast majority of the book's increase in size is a direct result of actual changes in existing herpetological law. Although relatively few in number, those agencies which have modified their state's amphibian and reptile regulations have often done so dramatically. Some have developed extensive lists of permit exempt/permit required species, and restrictions on how amphibians and reptiles may be collected and housed have also become much more prevalent.

Naturally, it would be nice to believe that all regulatory change represents actual improvement in the overall quality of amphibian and reptile legislation in the United States, but in far too many instances this is simply not the case. In fact, some of the more recent legislative modification appears to have been created with little or no regard for either clarity, accuracy, or established scientific fact and the value of much to the long term conservation of amphibians and reptiles is highly questionable at best. At the same time, relatively little has been done to rectify previously made mistakes, and incorrectly spelled, misused, or non-existent scientific names are now more common than ever.

Not all of the more recent legislative manipulation is totally without merit, however, and much (including some regulations containing plainly obvious errors) is clearly a step in the right direction. Other agencies have done well in simply leaving existing herpetological law alone. Not surprisingly, in those agencies with sensible or improving amphibian and reptile legislation, it is normally one or two key individuals who are largely responsible for its existence. These individuals not only work hard and do an exceptional job, but usually have an interest in amphibians and reptiles as well.

Thankfully, many of these same individuals are among this book's greatest supporters. The continued cooperation of people like New Mexico's Charlie Painter, Tennessee's Walter Cook, Kevin Enge of Florida, Mike Pinder of Virginia, Fred Krause of the Hawaii Department of Land and Natural Resources, South Carolina's Walt Rhodes, Bob Arini of Massachusetts, Minnesota's Rich Baker, and Andrew Price of Texas Parks and Wildlife, in the completion of this project is truly gratifying and is something that is most sincerely appreciated. Other individuals not associated with any government wildlife agency also deserving special mention include Susan George of the Defenders of Wildlife, Dr. Joseph Mitchell of the University of Richmond, New Mexico's Dr. Roger Conant, Dr. J. Whitfield Gibbons of the Savannah River Ecology Lab, and Joseph Collins of the University of Kansas Museum of Natural History. My gratitude for the contributions of all these individuals, as well as that of others too numerous to mention, to this project's successful completion can never be adequately expressed.

Unfortunately, this same degree of professionalism is not always evident among all of this country's wildlife regulatory agencies. Quite the contrary, in still far too many instances written requests for information are routinely and completely ignored and "voice mail messages" are seldom if ever returned. More frustrating still is the difficulty in obtaining answers to even the most basic of questions, whether through a genuine inability or, worse, an unwillingness of agency personal to do so. These facts, in combination with others, have forced an obvious reassessment on how data for this compilation may best be collected and much less reliance can be placed in the input of these agencies in the future. Hopefully, this situation will also soon improve as any and all assistance will always be most welcome in the completion of this project.

John P. Levell
Lanesboro, Minnesota
July 4, 1997

In late November 1993, initial plans for the creation of a guidebook to all amphibian and reptile wildlife legislation in the United States were first formulated. With a dramatic increase in the popularity of these animals in the pet trade, the explosion of herpetoculture, the continuing interest in herpetology among academic and zoological institutions, and a growing concern among state regulatory agencies regarding not only the conservation of native species, but the suitability of certain amphibians and reptiles as captives as well, the need for such a publication was evident. Work on the project began in earnest in early December 1993, with a primary goal of synthesizing all pertinent legislation into a single source-book which would prove useful to everyone with an interest in amphibians and reptiles including students, herpetologists, hobbyists, breeders, commercial dealers, and to the personnel of the various wildlife regulatory and law enforcement agencies.

As a means of determining the feasibility of producing such a guidebook, two previous publications on the subject, *State Regulations for Collecting Reptiles and Amphibians* by Adrian F. Czajka and Max A. Nickerson (1974) and *State Lists of Endangered and Threatened Species of Reptiles and Amphibians* by William B. Allen (1987), were consulted early in the preparatory stages of the project. During this preliminary period, the conclusion was somehow reached that the process of producing a new legislative guide would be a simple matter of combining and updating the information of these two earlier publications. Initial responses to preliminary information requests, however, clearly demonstrated that this conclusion was quite erroneous.

To begin with, substantial changes in virtually all the wildlife legislation has occurred since the pioneering work of Czajka and Nickerson (1974), so much so that any hope of utilizing information from their publication was completely eliminated. Secondarily, the reality of the situation regarding the amphibian and reptile legislation of most states is much more complex than eluded to in either the publication of Czjaka and Nickerson or in Bill Allen's 1984 title. While a few states have developed what may possibly be termed "model legislation" specifically regulating various activities involving amphibians and reptiles, wildlife legislation regarding these animals in the majority of states is scattered through a complicated maze of separate statutes and regulations, many of which are poorly written (from a readability stand-point at least) and/or difficult to understand. To compound these problems further, in several states conflicting interpretations of statutes and regulations exist even within the respective government agencies.

Although the above mentioned factors forced an obvious reevaluation of the difficulty inherent to the project, the need for a comprehensive guide to amphibian and reptile legislation became considerably more apparent. Information regarding each individual state's statutes and regulations was gathered from a variety of sources including various state wildlife and agriculture departments, the University of Minnesota law library, and from interested individuals in the private sector. Information on C.I.T.E.S. and federal regulations was obtained through the offices of the U.S. Department of the Interior. This data was subsequently interpreted and compiled in preliminary draft form and then forwarded to the respective government agencies for comment and review. Corrections and additions noted in these reviews were incorporated into the final revised draft of each individual account.

Throughout this process the majority of state agencies demonstrated a remarkable degree of interest in the project, sharing the conviction that a comprehensive legislation guide was a much needed publication, and many proved more than willing to participate in its production. A few state agencies (which here shall remain unidentified), however, proved quite resistant to the concept of cooperation. Hopefully, this is a situation that can be resolved in the very near future as, given the constantly changing nature of wildlife law within the United States, frequent revision will obviously be necessary if this publication is to remain accurate and up-to-date. The speed and efficiency with which such revisions can be made will be greatly enhanced with the full input and cooperation of all respective government agencies. At the same time, the fact remains that the personnel of all government entities are, in reality, public servants entrusted with the duty of not only enforcing the various rules and regulations of their respective departments, but in providing information on these laws in an understandable and readily available manner as well. Simply put, it's impossible to obey laws which are unknown.

In attempting to compile all the pertinent legislation concerning amphibians and reptiles into a single volume, it is the author's sincere hope that a document has been produced which will prove useful to those state wildlife departments interested in developing and enforcing regulations which effectively conserve wild populations of native amphibians and reptiles. At the same time, however, it must be stressed that all government regulatory agencies need to develop fair and equitable legislation which preserves the right of responsible individuals and institutions to work with and enjoy these remarkable animals, both in the wild and in captivity. Conversely, the necessity for all individuals and institutions to operate strictly within the confines of existing wildlife legislation at all times cannot be too strongly emphasized. As wildlife rules and regulations are subject to change without notice, prior consultation with respective regulatory agencies regarding the legality of any proposed activity is highly recommended.

While every attempt has been made to insure the completeness and accuracy of this title's contents, omissions and mistakes are probably inevitable in any publication of this type. Ideally, problems of this nature can be rectified in future editions and, with this thought in mind, interested readers are encouraged to point out any and all discrepancies to the author and/or publisher at the address on the title page. Despite the limitations of this particular edition, the goal of creating a comprehensive standard reference to all existing amphibian and reptile legislation in the United States is now one step closer to becoming reality. With the cooperation of all government agencies, and the input and contributions of as many interested individuals and institutions as possible, this publication will eventually achieve this goal.

John P. Levell

Several people deserve special mention for their generous contributions to the completion of this project. First and foremost among these friends and colleagues are Dr. Jeff Lang of the University of North Dakota and Dr. James Grier of North Dakota State University whose support for this project during a somewhat difficult period is most sincerely appreciated. Likewise, the patience and cooperation demonstrated by Joseph T. Collins of the University of Kansas Museum of Natural History, for answering my numerous questions regarding nomenclature, must be gratefully acknowledged. Additionally, the input and effort of numerous other fine folks including; AFH Legislative Action Coordinator Galyon L. Holmes from the beautiful State of Wyoming, Theron E. Magers of the Louisiana Amphibian and Reptile Task Force, John Moriarty of Minnesota's Hennepin County Parks Dept., Michigan's Theresa Moran, and Attorneys at Law Curt Harbsmeier of Florida and Glen "Jake" Jacobsen of Minnesota contributed greatly to the quality and accuracy of this publication. While not participating in the production of this book directly, the continuous kind words of encouragement and often not so subtle prodding of Dr. Hobart M. Smith undoubtedly contribute greatly toward the completion of every project I undertake.

Thanks are also due the various individuals involved with the actual physical production end of this project, in particular my publisher, Eric Thiss, of Serpent's Tale Natural History Books. His constant faith in my ability to see this project through to it's completion is a testament of his patience, although not necessarily his common sense, and for this I shall be forever grateful. The tediously mundane task of data entry and word processing was made infinitely easier through the considerable skills of Sharon Helm, and the expertise demonstrated by Mark Stratman of Sang Froid Press in turning the final manuscript into a "finished" product was amazing.

Lastly, but by no means least, I must extend my heartfelt and sincere thanks to my wife, and best friend, Connie. The patience, understanding, and tolerance she exhibited throughout the exceedingly long duration of this project was tremendous, especially considering the type of expletives which were likely to issue from my direction. If not for her constant encouragement, and occasional "kicks in the rear", this project would have ground to a halt on numerous occasions. As for just plain taking care of business she went far beyond the call of duty, for which I shall forever remain happily indebted. Without her, this book simply wouldn't exist!

In addition, the gracious assistance of the following government agencies, and the respective personnel associated with each, is most sincerely appreciated. Their patient cooperation in answering my numerous requests for information was instrumental in the production of this publication, and without their support this project could never have been completed. To all these individuals and agencies, Thanks.

Alabama Dept. of Conservation and Natural Resources	William E. Boone
Alaska Division of Fish and Game	Mark Schwan
Arizona Game and Fish Department	Jim Bidle, John Conneally, Jeff Howland and Tim Wade
Arkansas Game and Fish Commission	Belinda Ederington
California Department of Fish and Game	John Brode and Celeste Cushman
Colorado Division of Wildlife	John Smeltzer
Connecticut Department of Environmental Protection	Julie Victoria
Delaware Department of Agriculture	Bob Moore
Delaware Division of Fish and Wildlife	Lisa Gelvin-Innvaer
Florida Game and Fresh Water Fish Commission	Henry P. Cabbage and Kevin M. Enge
Florida Department of Environmental Protection	
Georgia Department of Natural Resources	Haven Barnhill and Maggie Beacham
Hawaii Department of Land and Natural Resources	Fred Krause and Randy Harr
Hawaii Department of Agriculture	Charles Christensen and Fred Helm
Idaho Fish and Game Department	Frank Lundburg and Ray Lyons

Illinois Department of Agriculture .... David R. Bromwell Chief Veterinarian
Illinois Department of Conservation .... Glen Kruse
Indiana Department of Natural Resources .... Tina Nichols
Iowa Department of Natural Resources .... Daryl Howell
Kansas Department of Wildlife and Parks .... Kevin L. Couillard and Mark E. Johnson
Kentucky Department of Fish and Wildlife Resources .... Theresa Anderson, Paul Oliver and Dave Yancy
Louisiana Department of Wildlife and Fisheries .... Steve Shively, John Tarver and Jeff Boundy
Maine Department of Inland Fisheries and Wildlife .... Mark McCollough, Henry Hilton and Alan
                                                                  Hutchinson

Maryland Department of Natural Resources .... Mary Jo Scanlan
Massachusetts Division of Fisheries and Wildlife .... Bob Arini
Michigan Department of Natural Resources .... Ned Fogel
Minnesota Department of Natural Resources .... Carol Dorff Hall, Rich Baker, and Roy Johannes
Mississippi Department of Wildlife, Fisheries, and Parks .... Robert L. Jones
Missouri Department of Conservation .... Dennis Figg and Tom R. Johnson
Montana Department of Fish, Wildlife, and Parks .... Dennis L. Flath
Nebraska Game and Parks Commission .... Frank Andelt and Daylan Figgs
Nevada Division of Wildlife .... Steve Albert
New Hampshire Fish and Game Department .... John J. Kanter
New Jersey Division of Fish, Game and Wildlife .... Paul Kalka
New Mexico Department of Game and Fish .... John Crenshaw and Charlie Painter
New York Department of Environmental Conservation .... Al Breisch, Patrick P. Martin and Chris von
                                                                  Schilgen

North Carolina Wildlife Resources Commission .... Randall C. Wilson
North Dakota Game and Fish Department .... Bruce Burkett
Ohio Department of Natural Resources .... Bill Page
Oklahoma Department of Wildlife Conservation .... Mark D. Howery
Oregon Department of Fish and Wildlife .... Dale Nelson
Pennsylvania Fish and Boat Commission .... Andrew L. Sheils
Rhode Island Department of Environmental Management...... Christopher J. Raithel
South Carolina Wildlife and Marine Resources Dept. .... Walt Rhodes
South Dakota Department of Game, Fish, and Parks .... Steve W. Thompson
Tennessee Wildlife Resources Agency .... Walter Cook, Robert M. Hatcher and Larry
                                                                  Marcum

Texas Parks and Wildlife Department .... Harold D. Oates and David Sinclair
Utah Department of Natural Resources .... Sue Skrobiszewski and Jane Perkins
Vermont Department of Fish and Wildlife .... Roger Wickham
Virginia Department of Game and Inland Fisheries .... Michael J. Pinder
Washington Department of Fish and Wildlife .... Kelly R. McAllister
West Virginia Division of Natural Resources .... J. Scott Butterworth
Wisconsin Department of Natural Resources .... Maya P. Cole and Robert Hay
Wyoming Game and Fish Commission .... Terry Cleveland and Scott Talbot

Special thanks are also due all the personnel of the U.S. Fish and Wildlife Service, in particular Chuck Kjos and Kate Windsor of the Twin Cities Regional District, who quickly and efficiently provided much needed information.

How to Use This Book

To better facilitate the use of this publication, it is recommended that this introductory chapter be read completely at least once before proceeding on to other portions of the book. General facts applicable to virtually all of the individual regulation accounts of the following pages will be discussed in this introduction, many, if not all, of which are vitally important to the proper interpretation of this title's contents. Most of these general facts will not be repeated elsewhere in the text. In addition, a basic review of the book's overall format has been provided, which may prove useful in better utilizing the information contained in this title.

The vast majority of this book is devoted to individual accounts of the amphibian and reptile legislation of the Convention on International Trade in Endangered Species (C.I.T.E.S.), the federal government of the United States, and for each of the fifty U.S. states. These individual accounts incorporate all the legislation pertinent to amphibians and reptiles, and an attempt has been made to organize the various statutes and regulations into the categories reviewed later in this introduction. In numerous instances, however, individual statutes and regulations are applicable to more than one category, and in such cases annotations have been utilized to cross-reference areas of overlap. In addition, several categories are not applicable to the legislation of C.I.T.E.S. and/or the federal government, and these categories have therefore been omitted from those accounts. Due to space limitations, substantial summarization has been necessary for the majority of statutes and regulations reproduced in this publication, but complete source citations and reference numbers have been provided for all reviewed legislation to help facilitate further inquiry and research.

Before proceeding further, it must be noted that only legislation at the state and federal level is covered in this publication, and no attempt has been made to compile information on the rules and regulations of any lower governmental unit. As numerous counties, townships, and municipalities have local wildlife ordinances, particularly regarding the type and number of animals that may be maintained in captivity, interested readers are advised to consult with the appropriate government agency regarding the legality of any proposed activity. Similarly, as all legislation is subject to change at anytime a cut off date of April 1, 1997 was established for any and all revisions. Readers are again advised to contact the appropriate government agency regarding possible changes in the status and/or interpretation of all statutes and regulations since that date.

Throughout the text scientific names for amphibian and reptile species occurring in the United States have been brought into conformity with those listed in the fourth edition of *Standard Common and Current Scientific Names for North American Amphibians and Reptiles* by Joseph T. Collins (1997). This has been done purely to help eliminate confusion, and does not necessarily represent an endorsement of any one taxonomic name over another on the part of the author of this publication. All changes in nomenclature from that specified in the actual government document concerned have been annotated via footnotes.

The remaining portion of this introduction will review the arrangement and content of the various categories utilized in formatting the individual regulation accounts of the following pages. Throughout the format review, general facts applicable to all the individual accounts will be discussed within the context of each respective category. As stated previously, many of these general facts are extremely important to the proper interpretation of this title's contents, and most will not be repeated elsewhere in the text.

Endangered, Threatened, and Special Concern Species

While compiling information for inclusion in this publication, it soon became apparent that endangered species legislation in the United States was a much more complex issue than originally anticipated. To begin with, the level of endangered species legislation is extremely variable among the states, ranging from very sophisticated laws similar in concept to the U.S. Endangered Species Act all the way through no endangered species legislation at all. A multitude of terminology, categories, and degrees of protection complicate matters further. For instance, species listed as "Special Concern" or "In Need of Management" are fully protected in some states, but totally unprotected in others. At the opposite extreme, the wildlife laws of several states allow for the full legal protection of species not officially included in any designation normally associated with endangered species legislation.

In light of these facts, basic explanations of the status of endangered species legislation in all states are included in each respective account. Only those amphibians and reptiles which are fully legally protected are included in the species listings under this heading. For example, if permits are required to collect and/or possess all specimens of species designated "In Need of Management," those species are included in the fully protected lists of this publication. If permits are not required to collect and/or possess species designated as "Special Concern," those species are not listed. State wildlife status designations are provided where applicable. Nomenclature changes, special rules, etc. are annotated via footnotes. Dates in ( ) indicate the last official state revision of each respective list. Permit requirement and application information is also provided whenever possible.

Native Wildlife Regulations

Statutes and regulations pertaining to the collection and subsequent possession of amphibians and reptiles taken from wild populations of each state for non-commercial or recreational purposes are covered under this heading. Topics covered include: open seasons, bag and possession limits, minimum size restrictions, legal collecting methods, and permit and/or license requirements. Information on specially regulated or prohibited species, and on other regulations pertinent to the subject have also been provided. Annotations and/ or footnotes have been used to help clarify areas of uncertainty. Here it must be pointed out that the various statutes and regulations contained within this heading are not applicable to specially protected lands and waters administered by state and federal agencies such as State and National Parks, Wildlife Refuges, State

Fish Hatcheries, etc. In addition, numerous states specifically prohibit hunting and fishing activities on private property without the express permission of the respective landowners. Prior consultation with the appropriate government agency is recommended before participating in any collection activities anywhere.

Importation and Commercial Trade Regulations

Information regarding restrictions regulating the commercial exploitation of native species taken from wild populations, and statutes and regulations governing the importation, possession, and sale of both native and non-native species are included in this category. Complete listings of prohibited, restricted, and/or unregulated species are provided when included among the legislation of the respective state or federal agencies. While no concerted effort has been made to standardize the scientific names of amphibian and reptile species not native to the United States in the current edition of this guide, the publication *A Complete Guide to Scientific and Common Names of Reptiles and Amphibians of the World* by Norman Frank and Erica Ramus (1995) has proven invaluable in correcting instances of obviously misspelled or misused nomenclature. As always, annotations via footnotes are included as needed. In addition, all included species listings have been rearranged on the basis of major taxonomic group (i.e. salamanders, frogs, crocodilians, etc.) when necessary. License and/ or permit requirements and fees have been provided when applicable and available.

Captive Maintenance Regulations

Any statutes and regulations relevant to the captive possession of amphibians and reptiles which are not included among the previous sections are covered under this heading. Additionally, brief reviews of all captive possession restrictions are provided for each individual account. All restrictions covered under this heading are applicable to the captive possession of live amphibians and reptiles only, and do not specifically address collection and/or importation regulations covered elsewhere.

History

The Convention on International Trade in Endangered Species of Wild Fauna and Flora (C.I.T.E.S.) is a multinational agreement in which participating nations agree to cooperate in the worldwide conservation of rare, vulnerable, and in many cases, valuable plant and animal species. Originally drafted during a 1973 convention of about 80 countries held in Washington D.C., the treaty is based upon an earlier document developed by the International Union for the Conservation of Nature (IUCN). Treaty provisions became effective in 1975, and the complete document including English, French, Spanish, Chinese, and Russian text, was published in Volume 27 of U.S. Treaties and International Agreements (reference: 27 UST TIAS 8249).

Established to regulate international trade in listed species among participating nations, C.I.T.E.S. in itself is a political agreement only. Practical enforcement of any treaty provisions remains largely the responsibility of each individual country, and the actual level of enforcement for the regulations of C.I.T.E.S. may vary widely among the participating nations. U.S. legislation enforcing all the provisions of C.I.T.E.S., as specified in title 50, section 23, of the Code of Federal Regulations (reference: 50 CFR 23), became law in 1977.

Since its inception in 1973, well over 130 nations have ratified the C.I.T.E.S. treaty agreement. A current (February 1997) alphabetical listing of these countries is provided below.

Afghanistan	Cote d' Ivorie	India
Algeria	Cuba	Indonesia
Argentina	Cyprus	Iran
Australia	Czech Republic	Israel
Austria	Denmark	Italy
Bahamas	Djibouti	Japan
Bangladesh	Dominica	Jordan
Barbados	Dominican Republic	Kenya
Belarus	Ecuador	Korea
Belgium	Egypt	Latvia
Belize	El Salvador	Liberia
Benin	Equatorial Guinea	Liechtenstein
Bolivia	Eritrea	Luxembourg
Botswana	Estonia	Madagascar
Brazil	Ethiopia	Malawi
Brunei Darussalem	Finland	Malaysia
Bulgaria	France	Mali
Burkina Faso	Gabon	Malta
Burundi	Gambia	Mauritius
Cameroon	Georgia	Mexico
Canada	Germany	Monaco
Central African Republic	Ghana	Mongolia
Chad	Greece	Morocco
Chile	Guatemala	Mozambique
China	Guinea	Namibia
Colombia	Guinea-Bissau	Nepal
Comoros	Guyana	Netherlands
Congo	Honduras	New Zealand
Costa Rica	Hungary	Nicaragua

Niger	St. Vincent & the Grenadines	Tanzania
Nigeria	Saudi Arabia	Thailand
Norway	Senegal	Togo
Pakistan	Seychelles	Trinidad and Tobago
Panama	Sierra Leone	Tunisia
Papua New Guinea	Singapore	Turkey
Paraguay	Slovakia	Uganda
Peru	Somalia	United Arab Emirates
Philippines	South Africa	United Kingdom
Poland	Spain	United States
Portugal	Sri Lanka	Uruguay
Romania	Sudan	Vanuatu
Russian Federation	Suriname	Venezuela
Rwandese Republic	Swaziland	Viet Nam
St. Lucia	Sweden	Zaire
St. Kitts and Nevis	Switzerland	Zambia
		Zimbabwe

C.I.T.E.S. Treaty Provisions

Conceived as a conservation tool providing for multi-national participation in standardized protective measures for the world's rare or vulnerable wildlife, C.I.T.E.S. primarily establishes guideline regulations restricting the international trade in designated plant and animal species. Regulated species are classified into one of three Appendices, of which the first provides the most protection. Generally prohibited activities include; the international trade in Appendix I species for primarily commercial purposes, the importation and exportation of Appendix I species without permit, the exportation of Appendix II and III species without permit, the re-exportation of any C.I.T.E.S. listed species without permit, and the possession of specimens traded in violation of treaty provisions.

While in principal, participating nations agree to adhere to C.I.T.E.S. guidelines prohibiting or restricting international trade in regulated species, actual commitment to the provisions of the treaty varies from country to country. For example, the continued commercial exploitation of endangered sea turtles by Japan is permitted through a "Reservation" provision of the C.I.T.E.S. agreement allowing any participating nation to exempt itself from treaty restrictions pertaining to individual species. In addition, several species are included in more than one Appendix on the basis of permitted commercial ranching and farming activities, or the variable status of individual populations within a species geographic range. This is particularly evident among the listed crocodilians, and actual trade restrictions on individual specimens is dependent upon the Appendix classification of the population from which the specimen in question originates. The inclusion of a particular taxon in any of the Appendices of C.I.T.E.S. automatically includes all lower taxonomic units (i.e. Gopherus sp. = all species in the genus Gopherus) unless otherwise specified.

In general, U.S. enforcement regulations virtually mirror all provisions of the C.I.T.E.S. treaty agreement, and these restrictions, as currently interpreted by the U.S. Fish and Wildlife Service, are summarized below. Here it should be noted that C.I.T.E.S. regulations only apply to the international importation or exportation of listed species, and lawfully imported specimens may be traded within the confines of the United States and it's territories without further C.I.T.E.S. restriction. It must also be noted that numerous species regulated by the treaty are also protected by the U.S. Endangered Species Act, and in such instances the more restrictive federal regulations pertaining to the interstate transportation of endangered and threatened species take precedence (see U.S. Federal Regulations). In either case, the acquisition and maintenance of acceptable documentation of the legality of all specimens of listed species is recommended.

C.I.T.E.S. Appendix I

Animals and plants listed in Appendix I are those species deemed to be presently threatened with extinction, and which are currently, or may be in the future, adversely affected by international trade. International trade in Appendix I species, including parts or derivatives, shall only be allowed if all specimens have been lawfully obtained and trade activities are not detrimental to the survival of the species in question. Appendix I species may not enter international trade for primarily commercial purposes. Both import and export/re-export permits are required for all international trade activities involving Appendix I species. Importation permits are also required to import any specimens of Appendix I species taken from the sea beyond the jurisdiction of any country. The following amphibian and reptile families, genera, species, subspecies, and/or populations are included in the current (December 1996) list of Appendix I wildlife.

Andrias (= *Megalobatrachus*) *davidianus* .... Chinese Giant Salamander
Andrias (= *Megalobatrachus*) *japonicus* .... Japanese Giant Salamander

Atelopus varius zeteki .... Panamanian Golden Frog
Bufo periglenes .... Golden Toad
Bufo superciliaris .... Cameroon Toad
Dyscophus antongilii .... Tomato Frog
Nectophrynoides spp. .... African Viviparous Toads

Alligator sinensis .... Chinese Alligator
Caiman crocodilus apaporiensis .... Apaporis River Caiman
Caiman latirostris .... Broad-snouted Caiman
Crocodylus acutus .... American Crocodile
Crocodylus cataphractus .... Slender-snouted Crocodile
Crocodylus intermedius .... Orinoco Crocodile
Crocodylus moreletii .... Morelet's Crocodile
Crocodylus niloticus [1] .... Nile Crocodile
Crocodylus novaeguineae mindorensis .... Philippine Crocodile
Crocodylus palustris .... Mugger Crocodile
Crocodylus porosus [1] .... Saltwater Crocodile
Crocodylus rhombifer .... Cuban Crocodile
Crocodylus siamensis .... Siamese Crocodile
Gavialis gangeticus .... Gavial, Gharial
Melanosuchus niger [1] .... Black Caiman
Osteolaemus tetraspis .... Dwarf Crocodile
Osteolaemus tetraspis osborni .... Dwarf Crocodile
Osteolaemus tetraspis tetraspis .... Dwarf Crocodile
Tomistoma schlegelii .... Tomistoma, False Gavial

Batagur baska .... River Terrapin, Tuntong
Cheloniidae spp. .... Sea Turtles, all species
Clemmys muhlenbergii .... Bog Turtle
Dermochelys coriacea .... Leatherback Sea Turtle

Geochelone (= Testudo) nigra (= elephantopus)........ Galapagos Tortoise
Geochelone (= Testudo) radiata .... Madagascar Radiated Tortoise
Geochelone (= Testudo) yniphora .... Angulated Tortoise
Geoclemys (= Damonia) hamiltonii .... Spotted Pond Turtle
Gopherus flavomarginatus .... Bolson Tortoise
Kachuga tecta .... Indian Sawback Turtle
Melanochelys (= Geoemyda) tricarinata .... Three-keeled Asian Turtle
Morenia ocellata .... Burmese Peacock Turtle
Psammobates (= Testudo) geometricus .... Geometric Tortoise
Pseudemydura umbrina .... Short-necked Swamp Turtle
Terrapene coahuila .... Aquatic Box Turtle
Testudo kleinmanni .... Russian Tortoise
Trionyx ater .... Cuatro Cienegas Softshell Turtle
Trionyx gangeticus .... Indian Softshell Turtle
Trionyx hurum .... Peacock Softshell Turtle
Trionyx nigricans .... Black Softshell Turtle

Sphenodon spp. .... Tuataras, all species

Brachylophus spp. .... Fiji Iguanas, all species
Cyclura spp. .... Ground Iguanas, all species
Gallotia simonyi .... Hierro Giant Lizard
Sauromalus varius .... San Esteban Island Chuckwalla
Varanus bengalensis .... Indian Monitor, Bengal Monitor
Varanus flavescens .... Yellow Monitor
Varanus griseus .... Desert Monitor
Varanus komodoensis .... Komodo Dragon

Acrantophis spp. .... Madagascar Boas, all species
Boa constrictor occidentalis .... Argentine Boa Constrictor
Bolyeria multocarinata .... Round Island Burrowing Boa
Casarea dussumieri .... Round Island Ground Boa
Epicrates inornatus .... Puerto Rican Boa
Epicrates monensis .... Mona Boa
Epicrates subflavus .... Jamaican Boa
Python molurus molurus .... Indian Python
Sanzinia madagascariensis .... Madagascar Tree Boa
Vipera ursinii [2] .... Orsini's Viper

[1] Except those populations listed in Appendix II.

[2] Except those populations in the U.S.S.R. (not listed in Appendix I or II).

C.I.T.E.S. Appendix II

Animals and plants listed in Appendix II are those species which are deemed to be not currently threatened with extinction but which may become so if international trade is not regulated. Appendix II species may be traded internationally, including for primarily commercial purposes, if all specimens are legally obtained and trade activities will not be detrimental to the survival of the species in question. Normally only export/re-export permits are required to import

Appendix II species into the U.S., but importation permits are required in the case of specimens taken from the sea beyond the jurisdiction of any country. Export permits (in the case of native species) or re-export permits (in the case of previously imported or captive produced specimens of non-native species) are required to export any Appendix II wildlife from the United States. The following amphibian and reptile families, genera, species, subspecies, and/or populations are included in the current (December 1996) list of Appendix II wildlife.

Ambystoma dumerilii .... Lake Patzcuaro Salamander
Ambystoma mexicanum .... Axolotl

Bufo retiformis .... Sonoran Green Toad
Dendrobates spp. .... Poison Dart Frog
Mantella aurantiaca .... Golden Toad
Phyllobates spp. .... Poison Arrow Frogs
Rana hexadactyla .... Asian Bullfrog
Rana tigerina .... Indian Bullfrog
Rheobatrachus spp. .... Platypus Frog

Alligatoridae spp. [1] .... Alligators and Caimans
Alligator mississippiensis .... American Alligator
Caiman crocodilus crocodilus .... Common Caiman
Caiman crocodilus fuscus [2] .... Brown Caiman
Caiman crocodilus yacare (= *C. yacare*) .... Yacare
Crocodylidae spp. [1] .... Crocodiles
Crocodylus johnsoni .... Johnston's Crocodile
Crocodylus niloticus [3] .... Nile Crocodile
Crocodylus novaeguineae [4] .... New Guinea Crocodile
Crocodylus porosus [5] .... Saltwater Crocodile
Melanosuchus niger [6] .... Black Caiman
Paleosuchus trigonatus .... Smooth-fronted Caiman

Chersina (= *Testudo*) spp. .... Bow-sprint Tortoises
Clemmys insculpta .... Wood Turtle
Dermatemys mawii .... Central American River Turtle
Erymnochelys madagascariensis .... Madagascar Turtle
Geochelone spp. [7] .... Land Tortoises
Gopherus spp. [7] .... Gopher Tortoises
Homopus spp. .... African Parrot-beaked Tortoises
Kinixys spp. .... Hinged-back Tortoises
Lissemys punctata .... Indian Flap-shell Turtle
Malacochersus spp. .... Pancake Tortoise
Peltocephalus dumeriliana .... Big-headed Amazon River Turtle
Podocnemis spp. .... South American Sideneck Turtles
Pyxis spp. .... Madagascar Spider Tortoises
Terrapene spp. [1] .... American Box Turtles
Testudinidae spp. [1] .... Land Tortoises
Testudo spp. [1] .... Eurasian Land Tortoises

Amblyrhynchus cristatus .... Galapagos Marine Iguana
Bradypodion spp. .... Chameleons
Chamaeleo spp. .... Chameleons
Cnemidophorus hyperythrus .... Orange-throated Whiptail Lizard
Conolophus spp. [1] .... Land Iguanas
Conolophus pallidus .... Barrington Island Land Iguana
Conolophus subcristatus .... Galapagos Land Iguana
Cordylus spp. .... Girdled Lizards
Corucia zebrata .... Prehensile-tailed Skink
Crocodilurus lacertinus .... Dragon Lizard
Cyrtodactylus serpensinsula .... Serpent Island Gecko
Dracaena spp. .... Caiman Lizards
Heloderma spp. .... Gila Monster and Beaded Lizards
Iguana spp. .... Iguanas
Phelsuma spp. .... Day Geckos
Phrynosoma coronatum [8] .... Coastal Horned Lizards
Phrynosoma coronatum blainvillei .... San Diego Horned Lizard
Podarcis lilfordi .... Lilford's Wall Lizard
Podacris pityusensis .... Ibiza Wall Lizard
Pseudocordylus spp. .... Crag Lizards
Shinisaurus crocodilurus .... Chinese Crocodile Lizard
Tupinambis spp. .... Tegu Lizards
Uromastyx spp. .... Spiny-tailed Lizards
Varanus spp. [1] .... Monitor Lizards

Boa (= *Constrictor*) *constrictor* .... Boa Constrictor
Boidae spp. [1] .... Boas and Pythons
Clelia (= *Pseudoboa*) *clelia* .... Mussurana
Cyclagras (= *Hydrodynastes*) *gigas* .... South American False Water Cobra
Elachistodon westermanni .... Indian Egg-eating Snake
Epicrates cenchria cenchria .... Rainbow Boa
Eunectes notaeus .... Yellow Anaconda
Hoplocephalus bungaroides .... Broad-headed Snake
Naja naja .... Indian Cobra
Ophiophagus hannah .... King Cobra
Pytas mucosus .... Oriental Rat Snake, Whipsnake
Python spp. [1] .... Pythons
Vipera wagneri .... Wagner's Viper

[1] All species in family or genus except those listed in Appendix I or with earlier date in Appendix II.

[2] Includes *Caiman crocodilus chiapasius*.

[3] Populations in Madagascar and Uganda subject to export quota provisions, populations of Botswana, Ethiopia, Kenya, Malawi, Mozambique, South Africa, Zambia and Zimbabwe subject to ranching provisions, and the population of Tanzania subject to ranching and annual export quota provisions as described by the C.I.T.E.S. Secretariat only. All other populations listed in Appendix I.

[4] Except for subspecies listed in Appendix I.

[5] Populations in Australia and Papua New Guinea, and the population in Indonesian subject to ranching provisions as described by the C.I.T.E.S. Secretariat only. All other populations listed in Appendix I.

[6] Population in Ecuador subject to annual export quota provisions as described by the C.I.T.E.S. Secretariat only. All other populations listed in Appendix I.

[7] All species except those listed in Appendix I.

[8] All subspecies except those with an earlier date in Appendix II.

C.I.T.E.S. Appendix III

Animals and plants included in Appendix III are species which have been identified as subject to trade restrictions within the confines of individual nations for which multi-national cooperation is required to regulate international trade. Export/re-export permits are required for all specimens of Appendix III wildlife originating from within the country which listed the species in question. Certificates of Origin are required for specimens of Appendix III wildlife originating from outside the jurisdiction of the country listing the species in question. The nations specified have included the following amphibians and reptiles in the current (January 1996) list of Appendix III species.

Species	Common Name	Country
Pelomedusa subrufa	Helmeted Terrapin	Ghana
Pelusios adansonii	Adanson's Hinged Terrapin	Ghana
Pelusios castaneus	Brown Hinged Terrapin	Ghana
Pelusios gabonensis	Gabon Hinged Terrapin	Ghana
Pelusios niger	Black Hinged Terrapin	Ghana
Trionyx triunguis	Three-clawed Softshell Turtle	Ghana
Agkistrodon bilineatus	Cantil	Honduras
Atretium schistosum	Olive Keelback Water Snake	India
Bothrops asper	Terciopelo	Honduras
Bothrops nasutus	Rainforest Hognosed Pit-viper	Honduras
Bothrops nummifer	Jumping Pit-viper	Honduras
Bothrops ophryomegas	Slender Hognosed Pit-viper	Honduras
Bothrops schlegelii	Eyelash Palm Pit-viper	Honduras
Cerberus rhynchops	Dog-faced Water Snake	India
Crotalus durissus	Tropical Rattlesnake	Honduras
Micrurus diastema	Atlantic Coral Snake	Honduras
Micrurus nigrocinctus	Black-banded Coral Snake	Honduras
Vipera russellii	Russell's Viper	India
Xenochrophis (= *Natrix*) *piscator*	Checkered Keelback Water Snake	India

Fiji Island Banded Iguana, *Brachylophus fasciatus* - One of two Iguanine lizards of the genus *Brachylophus* found in Fiji and listed as C.I.T.E.S. Appendix I wildlife. Both are included in the list of U.S. endangered and threatened species as well. Photograph courtesy of William B. Love.

C.I.T.E.S. Permit Information

Importation

Importation permits must be issued prior to the importation of any Appendix I species into the United States. Export/re-export permits are also required. C.I.T.E.S. certified captive produced specimens of Appendix I amphibians and reptiles may be imported without an importation permit if accompanied by a Captive-bred Certificate for primarily non-commercial purposes only. The importation of captive produced specimens of Appendix I species for commercial purposes requires both import and export/re-export permits. Export or re-export permits for specimens of C.I.T.E.S. listed species imported into the United States are issued by the country from which wildlife shipments originate. Documentation similar in content to standard export/re-export permits are required to import specimens of C.I.T.E.S. listed species originating in nations not participating in the treaty agreement. Shipments of C.I.T.E.S. listed wildlife may only enter the country through designated "U.S. Ports of Entry" (see U.S. Importation and Commercial Trade Regulations), and all required permits and or documents must be present before U.S. Customs will release shipments.

Exportation

Export permits, in the case of native species, or re-export permits, in the case of previously imported non-native species, are required prior to the exportation from the United States of any Appendix I or Appendix II amphibian or reptile species. Re-export Certificates or a Certificate of Origin are required to export all amphibians and reptiles currently included in Appendix III of the treaty. Applications for all required U.S. permits, including C.I.T.E.S. import permits, may be obtained from the U.S. Fish and Wildlife Service's Office of Management Authority (address in the first Appendix of this publication). There is a $25.00 non-refundable fee for all permit applications.

Scientific Exchange Certificates

Scientific Exchange Certificates may be issued to recognized scientific institutions authorizing the non-commercial loan, exchange, or donation of C.I.T.E.S. listed species without importation or exportation permits. There is currently no fee for Scientific Exchange Certificates.

Galapagos Tortoise, *Geochelone nigra* (=*G. elephantopus*, =*Chelonoidis elephantopus*, =*Testudo nigrita*, =etc., etc.) - Despite sometimes reaching a weight in excess of 500 pounds (225 kilos) and being known to science for several hundred years, this species is still of uncertain taxonomic designation. Photograph by J.P. Levell.

U.S. Federal Regulations

U.S. Endangered and Threatened Species

In an effort to prevent the extinction of imperiled species of animals and plants, the government of the United States passed the "U.S. Endangered Species Act" (ESA) in late December of 1973. An elaboration of two previous acts, the "Endangered Species Preservation Act" of 1966 and the "Endangered Species Conservation Act" of 1969, the current ESA provides for the protection of rare animals and plants, including both native and non-native species. The U.S. act has served as the model for the individual endangered species acts of numerous states, and protects populations of listed species occurring in the few states without regional endangered species legislation.

Plants and animals protected by the ESA are classified into one of two categories of wildlife, endangered or threatened, based upon the population status of each species in the world. By official definition endangered species are those currently in danger of extinction throughout all or a significant portion of their range. Threatened species are those likely to become endangered in the foreseeable future. ESA provisions allow specific populations and/or subspecies of the same species to be evaluated on an individual basis, and in many cases a particular species is only protected within a portion of it's total geographic range. In order to protect listed species, similar appearing species which are not actually threatened or endangered with extinction may also be listed. In addition, "Critical Habitat" provisions of the current act allow for governmental protection and/or acquisition of areas vital to the survival of listed species.

Extensive regulations enforcing the various protective provisions of the ESA are specified in title 50, part 17, of the Code of Federal Regulations (reference: 50 CFR 17). Generally, prohibited activities include; the taking of endangered or threatened species within the territorial limits of the United States or from the high seas without permit, the importation or exportation of listed species without permit, interstate and international trade of endangered or threatened wildlife for commercial purposes without permit, and the possession, transportation, purchase, and/or sale of any unlawfully obtained specimens.

The amphibians and reptiles included in the current (January 1997) list of U.S. endangered and threatened species are listed below. As stated previously, permits issued by the U.S. Fish and Wildlife Service (USFWS) are required for virtually all activities involving any of these species. To facilitate use of the following list, all species have been arranged first by major taxonomic group (i.e. salamanders, frogs, etc.) and secondly alphabetically by genus. In cases where the protective status of individual populations of the same species varies, the most restrictive wildlife designation is provided in the list below. Clarification of the variable status of individual species is provided via footnotes, as is other relevant information.

In a further attempt at clarification, several common names for turtles have been substituted for those utilized in the official U.S. Department of Interior list. The species affected by these changes, and their respective common names as published in the official U.S. list are; *Batagur baska*, River Terrapin, *Kachuga tecta tecta*, Indian Sawback, *Podocnemis expansa*, Tartaruga, *Podocnemis unifilis*, Trajaca, and *Psammobates geometricus*, Geometric Turtle. In addition, the term "slider" rather than the more generic "turtle" is utilized as the common name for all turtles in the genus Trachemys in the following list. Common names have also been provided for two species of snake for which this information is lacking in the official U.S. document. These snake species are *Bolyeria multocarinata* and *Casarea dussumieri*. Reference sources for the substitute common names of turtles are Ernst and Barbour (1989) and Pritchard (1979). Substitute common names for the two snakes are from Frank and Ramus (1995).

Species	Common Name	Status
Ambystoma macrodactylus croceum	Santa Cruz Long-toed Salamander	Endangered
Andrias davidianus davidianus	Chinese Giant Salamander	Endangered
Andrias davidianus japonicus	Japanese Giant Salamander	Endangered
Batrachoseps aridus	Desert Slender Salamander	Endangered
Eurycea nana [1]	San Marcos Salamander	Threatened
Phaeognathus hubrichti	Red Hills Salamander	Threatened
Plethodon nettingi	Cheat Mountain Salamander	Threatened
Plethodon shenandoah	Shenandoah Salamander	Endangered
Typhlomolge rathbuni	Texas Blind Salamander	Endangered
Atelopus varius zeteki	Panamanian Golden Frog	Endangered
Bufo baxteri [2]	Wyoming Toad	Endangered
Bufo californicus [3]	Arroyo Toad	Endangered
Bufo houstonensis	Houston Toad	Endangered
Bufo periglenes	Monte Verde Toad	Endangered
Bufo superciliaris	Cameroon Toad	Endangered
Conraua goliath	Goliath Frog	Threatened
Discoglossus nigriventer	Israel Painted Frog	Endangered
Eleutherodactylus jasperi	Golden Coqui	Threatened
Leiopelma hamiltoni	Stephen Island Frog	Endangered
Nectophrynoides spp.	African Viviparous Toads	Endangered
Peltophryne lemur	Puerto Rican Crested Toad	Threatened
Rana aurora draytonii	California Red-legged Frog	Threatened
Alligator mississippiensis [4]	American Alligator	S/A
Alligator sinensis	Chinese Alligator	Endangered
Caiman crocodilus apaporiensis	Aparoris River Caiman	Endangered
Caiman crocodilus yacare	Yacare Caiman	Endangered
Caiman latirostris	Broad-snouted Caiman	Endangered
Crocodylus acutus	American Crocodile	Endangered
Crocodylus cataphractus	African Slender-snouted Crocodile	Endangered
Crocodylus intermedius	Orinoco Crocodile	Endangered
Crocodylus moreletti	Morelet's Crocodile	Endangered
Crocodylus niloticus [1]	Nile Crocodile	Threatened
Crocodylus novaeguineae mindorensis	Philippine Crocodile	Endangered
Crocodylus palustris kimbula	Ceylon Mugger Crocodile	Endangered
Crocodylus palustris palustris	Mugger Crocodile	Endangered
Crocodylus porosus [5]	Saltwater Crocodile	Endangered
Crocodylus rhombifer	Cuban Crocodile	Endangered
Crocodylus siamensis	Siamese Crocodile	Endangered
Gavialis gangeticus	Gavial	Endangered
Melanosuchus niger	Black Caiman	Endangered
Osteolaemus tetraspis tetraspis	African Dwarf Crocodile	Endangered
Osteolaemus tetraspis osborni	Congo Dwarf Crocodile	Endangered
Tomistoma schlegelii	Tomistoma	Endangered
Batagur baska	Common Batagur	Endangered
Caretta caretta [1]	Loggerhead Sea Turtle	Threatened
Chelonia mydas [6]	Green Sea Turtle	Threatened

Dermatemys mawii	Central American River Turtle	Endangered
Dermochelys coriacea	Leatherback Sea Turtle	Endangered
Eretmochelys imbricata	Hawksbill Sea Turtle	Endangered
Geochelone elephantopus	Galapagos Tortoise	Endangered
Geochelone radiata	Radiated Tortoise	Endangered
Geochelone yniphora	Angulated Tortoise	Endangered
Geoclemys hamiltonii	Indian Spotted Pond Turtle	Endangered
Gopherus agassizii [7]	Desert Tortoise	Threatened
Gopherus flavomarginatus	Bolson Tortoise	Endangered
Gopherus polyphemus [8]	Gopher Tortoise	Threatened
Graptemys flavimaculata	Yellow-blotched Sawback	Threatened
Graptemys oculifera	Ringed Sawback	Threatened
Kachuga tecta tecta	Indian Roofed Turtle	Endangered
Lepidochelys kempii	Atlantic Ridley Sea Turtle	Endangered
Lepidochelys olivacea [9]	Pacific Ridley Sea Turtle	Threatened
Melanochelys tricarinata	Asian Three-keeled Turtle	Endangered
Morenia ocellata	Burmese Peacock Turtle	Endangered
Phrynops hogei	Brazilian Sideneck Turtle	Endangered
Podocnemis expansa	South American River Turtle	Endangered
Podocnemis unifilis	Yellow-spotted Sideneck	Endangered
Psammobates geometricus	Geometric Tortoise	Endangered
Pseudemydura umbrina	Western Swamp Tortoise	Endangered
Pseudemys alabamensis	Alabama Redbelly Turtle	Endangered
Pseudemys rubriventris bangsi	Plymouth Redbelly Turtle	Endangered
Sternotherus depressus [10]	Flattened Musk Turtle	Threatened
Terrapene coahuila	Aquatic Box Turtle	Endangered
Trachemys scripta callirostris	South American Red-lined Slider	Endangered
Trachemys stejnegeri malonei	Inagua Island Slider	Endangered
Trachemys terrapen	Cat Island Slider	Endangered
Trionyx ater	Cuarto Cienegas Softshell	Endangered
Trionyx gangeticus	Indian Softshell	Endangered
Trionyx hurum	Peacock Softshell	Endangered
Trionyx nigricans	Black Softshell	Endangered
Sphenodon punctatus	Tuatara	Endangered
Amevia polops	St. Croix Ground Lizard	Endangered
Anolis roosevelti	Culebra Island Giant Anole	Endangered
Brachylophus fasciatus	Fiji Banded Iguana	Endangered
Brachylophus vitiensis	Fiji Crested Iguana	Endangered
Cnemidophorus vanzoi	Maria Island Ground Lizard	Endangered
Conolophus pallidus	Barrington Land Iguana	Endangered
Cyclura carinata bartschi	Mayaguana Iguana	Threatened
Cyclura carinata carinata	Turks and Calicos Iguana	Threatened
Cyclura collei	Jamaican Iguana	Endangered
Cyclura cychlura cychlura	Andros Island Ground Iguana	Threatened
Cyclura cychlura figginsi	Exuma Island Iguana	Threatened
Cyclura cychlura inornata	Allen's Cay Iguana	Threatened
Cyclura nubilia caymanensis	Cayman Brac Ground Iguana	Threatened

Cyclura nubilia lewisi	Grand Cayman Ground Iguana	Endangered
Cyclura nubilia nubilia [11]	Cuban Ground Iguana	Threatened
Cyclura pinguis	Anegada Ground Iguana	Endangered
Cyclura rileyi cristata	White Cay Ground Iguana	Threatened
Cyclura rileyi nuchalis	Acklins Ground Iguana	Threatened
Cyclura rileyi rileyi	Watling Island Ground Iguana	Endangered
Cyclura stejnegeri	Mona Ground Iguana	Threatened
Cyrtodactylus serpensisnula	Serpent Island Gecko	Threatened
Eumeces egregius lividus [1]	Bluetail Mole Skink	Threatened
Gallotia simonyi simonyi	Hierro Giant Lizard	Endangered
Gambelia silus	Blunt-nosed Leopard Lizard	Endangered
Leiolopisma telfairi	Round Island Skink	Threatened
Neoseps reynoldsi [1]	Sand Skink	Threatened
Phelsuma edwardnewtoni	Day Gecko	Endangered
Phelsuma guentheri	Round Island Day Gecko	Endangered
Podacris pityusensis	Ibiza Wall Lizard	Threatened
Sauromalus varius	San Estaban Island Chuckwalla	Endangered
Sphaerodactylus micropithecus	Monito Gecko	Endangered
Uma inornata [12]	Coachella Valley Fringe-toed Lizard	Threatened
Varanus bengalensis	Bengal Monitor	Endangered
Varanus flavescens	Yellow Monitor	Endangered
Varanus griseus	Desert Monitor	Endangered
Varanus komodoensis	Komodo Monitor	Endangered
Xantusia riversiana	Island Night Lizard	Threatened
Bolyeria multocarinata	Round Island Burrowing Boa	Endangered
Casarea dussumieri	Round Island Boa	Endangered
Crotalus unicolor	Aruba Island Rattlesnake	Threatened
Crotalus willardi obscurus	New Mexican Ridge-nosed Rattlesnake	Threatened
Drymarchon couperi [13]	Eastern Indigo Snake	Threatened
Epicrates inornata	Puerto Rican Boa	Endangered
Epicrates monensis granti	Virgin Islands Tree Boa	Endangered
Epicrates monensis monensis	Mona Boa	Threatened
Epicrates subflavus	Jamaican Boa	Endangered
Liophus ornatus	Maria Island Snake	Endangered
Nerodia clarki taeniata	Atlantic Salt Marsh Snake	Threatened
Nerodia erythrogaster neglecta [14]	Copperbelly Water Snake	Threatened
Nerodia paucimaculata	Concho Water Snake	Threatened
Python molurus molurus	Indian Python	Endangered
Thamnophis gigas	Giant Garter Snake	Threatened
Thamnophis sirtalis tetrataenia [15]	San Francisco Garter Snake	Endangered
Vipera latifii	Lar Valley Viper	Endangered

[1] Special rules apply to this species (see below).
[2] Listed as *Bufo hemiophrys baxteri* by the U.S. Department of the Interior.
[3] Listed as *Bufo microscaphus californicus* by the U.S. Department of the Interior.
[4] Listed as threatened due to "Similarity of Appearance" for law enforcement purposes only, biologically American Alligators are not currently considered endangered or threatened. In addition, special rules apply to this species (see below).
[5] Population in Papua New Guinea not classified as threatened or endangered. Population in Australia listed as threatened. All other populations listed as endangered. In addition, special rules apply to this species (see below).

6 Breeding populations in Florida and on the Pacific coast of Mexico listed as endangered, all other populations classified as threatened. In addition, special rules apply to this species (see below).

7 Populations in Mexico and in Arizona south and east of the Colorado river classified as "Threatened due to Similarity of Appearance" for law enforcement purposes only, all other populations classified as threatened.

8 Threatened status applies to populations west of the Mobile and Tombigbee Rivers in Alabama, Louisiana, and Mississippi only. Other populations are not classified as threatened or endangered.

9 Breeding population on the pacific coast of Mexico listed as endangered, all other populations classified as threatened. In addition, special rules apply to this species (see below).

10 Threatened status applies to the Alabama population in the Black Warrior River System upstream from the Bankhead Dam, other populations not listed as threatened or endangered.

11 Threatened status does not apply to the introduced population in Puerto Rico.

12 Not listed in Collins (1997). Currently considered an invalid taxonomic designation.

13 Listed as *Drymarchon corais couperi* by the U.S. Department of the Interior.

14 Threatened status applies to those populations in Michigan, Ohio, and north of 40 degrees latitude north in Indiana.

15 Subspecies not listed in Collins (1997).

Special Rules

ESA provisions allow for the establishment of "Special Rules" which eliminate normal permit requirements for designated threatened species in certain specific instances. Special Rules may not be established for any wildlife designated as an endangered species. The special rules applicable to amphibians and reptiles, as specified in the Code of Federal Regulations, are summarized below.

Eurycea nana, San Marcos Salamanders may be taken without federal permit in accordance with applicable State law of Texas. Violations of any State law also constitute violations of the ESA (50 CFR 17.42a).

Alligator mississippiensis, American Alligators, including wild caught and captive produced specimens, may be taken, possessed, transported, purchased, sold, imported, and exported in accordance with the laws and regulations of the State of taking. Federally approved tags for hides and/or parts are required. International import/export activities must comply with general U.S. wildlife importation and exportation regulations (see U.S. Importation and Commercial Trade Regulations), or established C.I.T.E.S. permit procedures. Accurate records of all import/export transactions are required (50 CFR 17.43a).

Crocodylus niloticus, Nile Crocodiles originating from populations listed in Appendix II of C.I.T.E.S. and *Crocodylus porosus*, Saltwater Crocodiles originating from Australia may be imported/re-exported directly into/from the United States without required ESA permits under the following conditions. Live animals,

scientific specimens, whole skins, meat, parts and eggs may be imported/re-exported. All specimens or parts must be tagged or otherwise identified as having been removed from designated populations in accordance with the laws of the Country of origin and C.I.T.E.S. Appendix II wildlife requirements. Compliance with the general wildlife importation regulations of the United States (see U.S. Importation and Commercial Trade Regulations) is also required. The importation into the United States of any specimens originating from populations other than those specified above for commercial purposes is prohibited (50 CFR 17.42c).

Caretta caretta, Loggerhead Sea Turtle, *Chelonia mydas*, Green Sea Turtle, and *Lepidochelys olivacea*, Olive Ridley Sea Turtle take restrictions of the ESA do not apply to the accidental capture during fishing activities by vessels in compliance with established U.S. National Marine Fisheries Service (NMFS) regulations regarding Turtle Excluder Devices (see NMFS regulations below). *Chelonia mydas*, Green Sea Turtles may be taken for legitimate subsistence purposes as specified in the marine reptile regulations of NMFS (see NMFS regulations below). These exemptions do not apply to populations of the above marine turtles classified as endangered species (50 CFR 17.42b).

Eumeces egregius lividus, Bluetail Mole Skink and *Neoseps reynoldsi*, Sand Skink may be taken in accordance with applicable State fish and wildlife laws and regulations for educational and scientific purposes, the enhancement or survival of the species, zoological exhibition, and other conservation purposes consistent with the ESA (50 CFR 17.42d).

National Marine Fisheries Service Regulations

Regulations enforcing ESA provisions protecting sea turtles are administered by both the USFWS and the NMFS, with the Fish and Wildlife Service having jurisdiction only while marine turtles are ashore. As these animals spend practically all their lives at sea, NMFS administers the vast majority of ESA restrictions regulating sea turtles. While standard ESA take and possession restrictions are included, the bulk of the NMFS's sea turtle legislation regulates the incidental take of sea turtles by vessels engaged in fishing activities targeting other species. Due to the extreme length (well over 20 pages) of this legislation, only the most basic review is possible here.

Incidental Capture permits are required by fishing vessels operating in areas where the accidental capture of sea turtles is likely to occur. Vessels must be in compliance with established operational, net tow time, and basic equipment criteria while engaged in fishing activities. Turtle Excluder Device (TED) requirements must be met where applicable, and acceptably designed TEDs are specified and illustrated. All accidentally captured sea turtles must be returned to the water, and explicit requirements and procedures for the release of living, the disposal of dead, and the resuscitation of comatose sea turtles are provided (50 CFR 222.50 and 227.72).

Chelonia mydas, Green Sea Turtles may be taken in waters seaward of mean low tide for personal consumption by residents of the Trust Territory of the Pacific Islands if such taking is customary, traditional, and necessary for the sustenance of such resident and his immediate family. Sea turtles so taken cannot be transferred to non-residents or sold (50 CFR 227.72f).

* The preceding NMFS permit requirement exemption has been provided for the sake of completeness.

Endangered and Threatened Species Permit Information

The ESA contains provisions allowing for the issuance of permits authorizing normally prohibited activities, including the collection, possession, importation, exportation, and propagation of protected species. In general, permits authorizing these activities involving wildlife designated as endangered species will only be issued for the following purposes; legitimate scientific research, enhancement of propagation, survival of the species, or incidental take. Threatened species permits may be issued for zoological exhibition, educational,

and other special purposes, as well as for the purposes listed previously. ESA and C.I.T.E.S. import/export permits are required for individual species regulated by both documents. A single application meeting ESA permit requirements will also fulfill C.I.T.E.S. permit application requirements of the United States. All import/export activities involving ESA species must be done through U.S. Customs designated "Ports of Entry" (see U.S. Importation and Commercial Trade Regulations).

In addition, Captive Bred Wildlife permits authorizing commercial trade of live specimens of non-native endangered and threatened species, propagated in captivity within the United States, may be issued to qualified individuals. All commercial transactions involving captive bred wildlife must be for enhancement of propagation purposes, and all parties participating in such transactions must be properly registered for the species being traded. Prominent notice of ESA permit requirements must be displayed wherever endangered and threatened species are offered for sale.

It should be noted that the ESA only regulates commercial transactions at the interstate level. Commercial activities involving legally acquired endangered and threatened species which take place entirely within one state are not prohibited by the ESA. Individual state governments may restrict these activities, however, and applicable state agencies should be consulted regarding the legality of commercial trade in federally listed endangered and threatened wildlife. In all cases proper documentation, such as photocopies of original ESA permits and sales receipts, which demonstrates the legality of the specimens in question should be obtained.

Further information on permit requirements and applications for all required permits, except for the incidental capture of marine turtles, may be obtained from the U.S. Fish and Wildlife Service's Office of Management Authority (address in Appendix I). ESA permits are issued at the discretion of the U.S. Fish and Wildlife Service, and all permit applications are evaluated on an individual case by case basis. There is a $25.00 non-refundable fee for each permit application. Please be advised that ESA permits are not issued for keeping or breeding endangered and threatened species for primarily pet purposes. Incidental capture permit requirements and applications are obtained from the National Marine Fisheries Service (address in Appendix I).

U.S. Importation and Commercial Trade Regulations

Extensive regulations restricting the importation and exportation of all animals and plants are included among the wildlife legislation of the USFWS. These regulations apply to any wildlife import/export activities, including shipments of species not protected by C.I.T.E.S. or the ESA. While the majority of this legislation is applicable to all types of wildlife in general, specific amphibian and reptile import/export conditions are included in the importation and transportation of "Injurious Wildlife" regulations of the USFWS. The portions of the USFWS import/export regulations pertinent to amphibians and reptiles are summarized below.

Designated Ports of Entry

The importation or exportation of any wildlife at any place other than one of the following designated ports of entry is prohibited, unless otherwise specified (50 CFR 14.11 and 14.12):

Los Angeles, California
San Francisco, California
Atlanta, Georgia
Miami, Florida
Honolulu, Hawaii
Chicago, Illinois
New Orleans, Louisiana
Baltimore, Maryland
Boston, Massachusetts
Portland, Oregon
Newark, New Jersey
New York, New York
Dallas/Fort Worth, Texas
Seattle, Washington

Except for species otherwise requiring a permit, wildlife whose country of origin is Canada or the United States may be imported or exported at the following U.S. Customs Border Ports of Entry (50 CFR 14.16a):

Alaska	Alcan
Idaho	Eastport
Maine	Calais, Houlton, and Jackman
Massachusetts	Boston
Michigan	Detroit, Port Huron, and Sault St. Marie
Minnesota	Grand Portage, International Falls, and Minneapolis/St. Paul
Montana	Raymond and Sweetgrass
New York	Buffalo/Niagara Falls and Champlain
North Dakota	Dunseith, Pembina, and Portal
Ohio	Cleveland
Vermont	Derby Line and Highgate Springs
Washington	Blaine and Sumas

Except for species otherwise requiring a permit, wildlife whose country of origin is Mexico or the United States may be imported or exported at the following U.S. Customs Border Ports of Entry (50 CFR 14.16b):

Arizona	Lukeville and Nogales
California	Calexico and San Diego/San Ysidro
Texas	Brownsville, El Paso, and Laredo

Except for species otherwise requiring a permit, wildlife lawfully taken by U.S. residents in the United States, Canada, or Mexico may be imported or exported for non-commercial purposes at any U.S. Customs Port of Entry (50 CFR 14.16c).

Permits authorizing the importation or exportation of wildlife at non-designated ports of entry may be issued for scientific purposes, to minimize deterioration or loss, or to alleviate economic hardship (50 CFR 14.31, 14.32, and 14.33).

Clearance of Wildlife Shipments

All imported or exported wildlife shipments are subject to inspection by USFW Service officers and customs officers. Imported wildlife shipments must be authorized clearance by USFW Service officers prior to being released by U.S. Customs. To obtain clearance, importers shall make available all shipping documents, all required U.S. permits and licenses, all required foreign permits, licenses or documents, and the wildlife being imported (50 CFR 14.51 to 14.55).

A completed and signed Declaration of Importation or Exportation of Wildlife form must be filed with the USFWS at the time and place where clearance is requested, except under specified conditions of exemption (50 CFR 14.61 to 14.64).

Marking of Shipping Containers

All containers or packages used to import, export, and/or transport wildlife must be labeled as to content, origin, and destination of shipment. Conspicuously marking the outside of each container with the appropriate term such as "wildlife" or "reptiles", and providing a readily accessible invoice, packing list, bill of lading, or similar document stating the name and address of both the exporter and importer, total number of packages in the shipment, and type and number of specimens of each species being shipped shall constitute compliance with this requirement (50 CFR 14.81 and 14.82).

Commercial Importation and Exportation

Import/Export Licenses are required for commercial activities involving the importation and exportation of wildlife in which the total declared value of wildlife traded exceeds $25,000 annually. Commercial wildlife import/export businesses include; animal dealers, animal brokers, pet dealers and suppliers, laboratory research suppliers, the tanning, manufacture, and sale of hides, skin and/or leather dealers and brokers, finished product wholesalers, retailers, distributors, and/or brokers, and taxidermy. Import/export activities in excess of $25,000 annually by public museums, scientific or educational institutions, and circuses are exempt from license requirements provided imported wildlife is not resold. Federal, State, or municipal government agencies are also exempt from import/export license requirements (50 CFR 14.91 to 14.93).

Injurious Wildlife

The importation or transportation of live wildlife or eggs deemed injurious or potentially injurious to; the health and welfare of the general public, forestry, agricultural, and/or horticultural interests, and the wildlife or wildlife resources of the United States is prohibited, except as expressly allowed by permit. Injurious wildlife permit requirements are in addition to all other permit or license requirements (50 CFR 16.1 to 16.3).

All species of amphibians and their eggs may be imported, transported and possessed in captivity for scientific, educational, medical, exhibition, or propagation purposes without injurious wildlife permit. Written notification of the District Director of U.S. Customs at the applicable designated port of entry is required prior to importation activities. Live amphibians, or their progeny or eggs, may not be released into the wild except as authorized by the state wildlife agency having jurisdiction of the area of release (50 CFR 16.14).

The importation, transportation, and/or acquisition of any live specimens or eggs of the Brown Tree Snake, *Boiga irregularis* without an injurious wildlife permit is prohibited (50 CFR 16.15a).

All other reptile species and their eggs may be imported, transported, and possessed in captivity for scientific, educational, medical, exhibition, or propagation purposes without injurious wildlife permit. Written notification of the District Director of U.S. Customs at the applicable designated port of entry is required prior to importation activities. Live reptiles, or their progeny or eggs, may not be released into the wild except as authorized by the state wildlife agency having jurisdiction of the area of release (50 CFR 16.15b).

License and Permit Information

Wildlife import/export licenses are issued on a yearly basis, at a fee of $50.00 per application or renewal. In addition to any license fees, importers/exporters are also subject to inspection fees of $55.00 per wildlife shipment. The USFWS may also charge reasonable additional fees when importer/exporters request inspections at times other than normal hours of operation. These "per shipment" inspection fees are applicable whether import/export licenses are required or not. Import/export license applications are obtained from the USFWS Special Agent in charge of the Regional District (see USFWS Regional District Map below) having jurisdiction over the area in which the designated port of entry occurs (addresses in Appendix I). Injurious Wildlife permits are issued, subject to stringent conditions, to qualified individuals and institutions for legitimate scientific, zoological, educational, or medical purposes only. Further information on Injurious Wildlife permits may be obtained from the USFW Service's Office of Management Authority (address in Appendix I).

Special Turtle Regulations

In addition to the general import/export restrictions of the USFWS, the legislation of two other federal agencies, the U.S. Food and Drug Administration (FDA) and the U.S. Public Health Service (PHS), regulate the importation and transportation of turtles under 4 inches in carapace length. Restrictions on the foreign importation of these animals into the United States are specified in the PHS regulations in title 42, part 71 of the Code of Federal Regulations (reference: 42 CFR 71). Interstate and intrastate transportation and commercial trade restrictions are included among the regulations of the FDA, as specified in title 21, part 1240, of the Code of Federal Regulations (reference: 21 CFR 1240). Each of these two regulations are summarized below.

Live turtles less than 4 inches in carapace length, and/or viable turtle eggs may not be imported into the United States except as otherwise specified in this regulation. The term "turtle" includes all animals of the order Testudinata, class Reptilia, commonly known as turtles, tortoises, or terrapins, except marine turtles. Shipments of six or less turtles and turtle eggs (total specimens of turtles and eggs combined) are exempt from this restriction provided that the importation is for non-commercial purposes. The importation of shipments containing seven or more turtles and/or turtle eggs may be authorized by permit for legitimate scientific, educational, or exhibition purposes (42 CFR 71. 52).

Live turtles under 4 inches in carapace length, or viable turtle eggs, may not be sold, held for sale, or offered for any type of public distribution except as otherwise specified in this regulation. The term "turtle" includes all animals of the order Testudinata, class Reptilia, commonly known as turtles, tortoises, or terrapins except marine turtles. Exceptions to this prohibition include; the sale, holding for sale, and distribution of live turtles and viable eggs for bona fide scientific, educational or exhibition purposes other than use as pets, and the sale, holding for sale, and distribution of turtles and turtle eggs for export purposes only. Any live turtles or viable turtle eggs confiscated in violation of the provisions of this regulation are subject to humane destruction by officials of the FDA (21 CFR 1240.62).

Permit Information

Further information on these regulations and applications for any required permits may be obtained from the respective government agency (addresses in Appendix I).

Hatchling Red-eared Slider, *Trachemys scripta elegans* - If judged solely upon the amount of legislation regulating the possession and sale of hatchling turtles, these animals would surely have to be considered among the most dangerous reptiles in the United States. Photograph courtesy of Richard D. Bartlett.

ALABAMA

ENDANGERED, THREATENED, AND SPECIAL CONCERN SPECIES

Rare, threatened, and endangered species of amphibians and reptiles in Alabama are legally protected by Part 1 of the state's Nongame Species Regulation, as specified in the Regulations of the Alabama Department of Conservation and Natural Resources. This regulation specifically prohibits the collection, possession, and sale of designated protected non-game species (reference: 97-AL GFR 16 220-2-.92-1). In addition, the Flattened Musk Turtle, *Sternotherus depressus*, is fully protected by Alabama statutory law, as specified in title 9 of the Code of Alabama (reference: ALC 9-11-269).

The following species are the amphibians and reptiles currently (1997) included in Alabama's list of legally protected non-game animals. Permits are required for any activities involving these species. In addition, a permit issued by the U.S. Department of the Interior is required for several of Alabama's listed species (see U.S. Endangered and Threatened Species).

Species	Common Name
Ambystoma cingulatum	Flatwoods Salamander
Aneides aeneus	Green Salamander
Cryptobranchus alleganiensis alleganiensis [1]	Eastern Hellbender
Desmognathus monticola	Seal Salamander
Gyrinophilus palleucus	Tennessee Cave Salamander
Phaeognathus hubrichti	Red Hills Salamander
Hyla andersonii	Pine Barrens Treefrog
Rana capito sevosa	Dusky Gopher Frog
Gopherus polyphemus	Gopher Tortoise
Graptemys barbouri	Barbour's Map Turtle
Graptemys pulchra	Alabama Map Turtle
Macrochelys temminckii [2]	Alligator Snapping Turtle
Malaclemys terrapin pileata	Mississippi Diamondback Terrapin
Pseudemys alabamensis	Alabama Red-bellied Turtle
Sternotherus depressus [3]	Flattened Musk Turtle
Drymarchon couperi [4]	Eastern Indigo Snake
Heterodon simus	Southern Hognose Snake
Masticophis flagellum flagellum [5]	Eastern Coachwhip
Nerodia clarkii clarkii [6]	Gulf Salt Marsh Snake
Pituophis melanoleucus lodingi	Black Pine Snake
Pituophis melanoleucus mugitus	Florida Pine Snake

[1] Listed as *Cryptobranchus alleganiensis* by Alabama.
[2] Listed as *Macroclemys temminicki* by Alabama.
[3] Listed as *Sternotherus minor depressus* by Alabama.
[4] Listed as *Drymarchon corais couperi* by Alabama.
[6] Listed as *Masticophis flagellum* by Alabama.
[7] Listed as *Nerodia fasciata clarkii* by Alabama.

Protected Species Permit Information

Permits allowing for the scientific collection and possession of Alabama's protected species may be issued to qualified institutions and individuals. Alabama does not have specific permit application forms, and all permit requests should be directed to the Alabama Department of Conservation and Natural Resources (address in Appendix I).

AL

NATIVE WILDLIFE REGULATIONS

Relatively few restrictions on the collection or possession of native amphibians and reptiles are included among the fish and game regulations of the Alabama Department of Conservation and Natural Resources (reference: AL GFR 16). With the exception of designated protected non-game species, a few turtles, and the American Alligator, all of Alabama's native amphibians and reptiles are currently unprotected and may be collected and possessed within the state without license or restriction. Alligators are classified as game animals, but there is no legal open season for the taking of alligators in Alabama at the present time (reference: AL GFR 16 220-2-.01). Additional regulations pertaining to American Alligators are included among Alabama's wildlife laws as well. The following is a brief summarization of Alabama's restrictions on the non-commercial collection and possession of amphibians and reptiles wild caught within the state.

Turtles

Terrapene carolina, Box Turtles, including box turtle parts or reproductive products, may not be collected, offered for sale, sold, or traded for anything of value except by permit (AL GFR 16 220-2-.92-2).

* As currently interpreted by the Alabama Department of Conservation and Natural Resources, the preceding regulation does not prohibit possession of Box Turtles legally obtained from outside of Alabama.

It is unlawful to collect, harvest, possess, offer for sale, sell or trade for anything of value any of the following turtles with a carapace length of less than eight inches. These species may be taken while controlling "nuisance animals" on private property provided they are not sold or traded for anything of value (AL GFR 16 220-2-.92-3):

Chelydra serpentina	Common Snapping Turtle
Apalone ferox	Florida Softshell
Apalone mutica mutica [1]	Midland Smooth Softshell
Apalone mutica calvata [1]	Gulf Coast Smooth Softshell
Apalone spinifera spinifera [2]	Eastern Spiny Softshell
Apalone spinifera aspera [2]	Gulf Coast Spiny Softshell

[1] Listed as *Apalone muticus* by Alabama.
[2] Listed as *Apalone spinferus* by Alabama.

Alligators

Alligator mississippiensis, American Alligators or the skins, meat, eggs or parts thereof, may not be possessed, taken, captured, or killed except as otherwise permitted by rule or regulation. Legally obtained alligator meat or other alligator products may be possessed without permit. There is currently no open season for the taking of American Alligators (AL GFR 16 220-2-.01, 220-2-.95-2b and 220-2-.97).

Nuisance alligators may only be removed by the Alabama Department of Conservation and Natural Resources or by a hunter licensed by that agency (AL GFR 16 220-2-.95).

* Numerous conditions and restrictions are included in the Nuisance Alligator Control Regulation and the complete text of this regulation is several pages in length.

Permit and License Information

License and permit requirements and the full text of the Nuisance Alligator Control Regulation may be obtained from the Law Enforcement Section of the Alabama Department of Conservation and Natural Resources (address in Appendix I).

IMPORTATION AND COMMERCIAL TRADE REGULATIONS

Native Species
Restrictions on the sale of specific species of native amphibians and reptiles not protected by Part 1 of the Nongame Species Regulation are included among the wildlife laws of Alabama (reference: AL GFR 16). The following is a brief review of these regulations.

Turtles
Terrapene carolina, Box Turtles, including box turtle parts or reproductive products, may not be collected, offered for sale, sold, or traded for anything of value except by permit (AL GFR 16 220-2-.92-2).

Chelydra serpentina, Common Snapping Turtles under eight inches in carapace length may not be sold (AL GFR 16 220-2-.92-3).

Apalone sp., Softshell Turtles (all native species) under eight inches in carapace length may not be sold (AL GFR 16 220-2-.92-3).

Alligators
Alligator mississippiensis, American Alligators legally obtained outside of Alabama may only be imported by permit. American Alligators may be possessed, raised, and sold by licensed alligator farming operations. Living alligators at least four feet in length, as well as alligator meat, hides, and parts may be sold (AL GFR 16 220-2-.96).

* The complete text of the alligator farming regulation, which includes numerous recommendations and requirements, is several pages in length.

Exotic Species
With the exception of the following summarized rules included in Alabama's alligator farming and nuisance alligator control regulations, the State of Alabama does not currently restrict the importation, possession and sale of any non-native amphibian or reptile.

It is unlawful to use the word "alligator" or "gator" in connection with the sale of any other crocodilian species, or other crocodilian skins, parts, or products (AL GFR 16 220-2-.95-5a).

A permit is required to buy, sell, take, or possess any alligator or crocodile including parts, nests, or eggs. Legally obtained crocodilian trophies or hide products may be possessed without permit. (AL GFR 16 220-2-.96-1).

License and Permit Information
Fees for Alligator Farming licenses are $1000 annually. The complete text of the alligator farming regulation, and information and/or applications for any required permits or licenses of this section may be obtained from the Alabama Department of Conservation and Natural Resources (address in Appendix I).

CAPTIVE MAINTENANCE REGULATIONS

Restrictions on the possession of both native and exotic amphibian and reptile species are included among the preceding regulations. The following is a brief review of these restrictions.

a. Permits are required to possess any protected species.
b. *Chelydra serpentina*, Common Snapping Turtles and *Apalone* sp., Softshell Turtles (all native species) under eight inches in carapace length may not be possessed except as specified.
c. Permits are required to possess any living crocodilian.

(b above see Native Wildlife Regulations).
(c above see Importation and Commercial Trade Regulations).

ALASKA

ENDANGERED, THREATENED, AND SPECIAL CONCERN SPECIES

AK

Endangered species in Alaska are legally protected by the Alaska Endangered Species Act, as specified in Article 4 of Alaska Statutes (reference: AS 4-16.20.180-.210). None of Alaska's few species of amphibians and reptiles are included in the current (September 1993) list of State Endangered Species. Despite not being listed as threatened or endangered, however, permits are still required for many activities involving any species of amphibian or reptile occurring in Alaska (see Native Wildlife Regulations).

Although not included in Alaska's official list of endangered wildlife, the following two species of federally protected marine turtles have occasionally been reported from Alaskan waters, and a permit issued by the U.S. Department of the Interior is required for any activities involving these species (see U.S. Endangered and Threatened Species).

Species	Common Name
Chelonia mydas	Green Sea Turtle
Dermochelys coriacea	Leatherback Sea Turtle

NATIVE WILDLIFE REGULATIONS

Regulations governing the collection and possession of amphibians and reptiles wild caught in Alaska are somewhat complex and confusing. The following review of these regulations is an attempt to summarize these restrictions as simply and accurately as possible.

Amphibians

The State of Alaska defines fish as any species of aquatic finfish, invertebrate, or amphibian, in any stage of its life cycle, found in or introduced into the state, and includes any part of such aquatic finfish, invertebrate, or amphibian (reference: AS 16.05.940-10). Because of their status as fish, any restrictions pertaining to fish are equally applicable to amphibians. Alaska strictly regulates the taking of all species occurring in the state, whether native or introduced, and a fish resource permit is required to collect and possess any amphibian taken from the wild in Alaska (reference: AS 16.05. 930). In addition, a fish transport permit is required to possess and transport any amphibians in the State of Alaska, as specified in the Alaska Annotated Code (reference: 5 AAC 41.005).

Reptiles

On the basis of a few fairly reliable records from the extreme southeastern corner of the state, the Common Garter Snake, *Thamnophis sirtalis*, is the only terrestrial reptile included among the indigenous herpetofauna of Alaska. All reptiles are classified as game animals by the State of Alaska, and the collection or possession of Common Garter Snakes without a scientific or educational permit is prohibited (reference: 5 AAC 92.029).

License and Permit Information

Several different types of permits are issued by the State of Alaska and in some instances more than one state permit is required for activities involving amphibians and reptiles occurring in the natural environment of the state. Permit requirements apply to introduced species as well as to native wildlife and at least one amphibian, the Pacific Chorus Frog, *Hyla regilla*, is believed to have been introduced and now established in Alaska. Due to the multitude of available permits, it is recommended that interested parties contact the Alaska Department of Fish and Game (address in Appendix I) for the complete list of state permit requirements and permit applications.

IMPORTATION AND COMMERCIAL TRADE REGULATIONS

As with Alaska's Native Wildlife Regulations, restrictions on the importation and/or commercial trade of amphibians and reptiles in the state are often vague and confusing. Once again, the following review is an attempt to summarize these regulations as simply and accurately as possible.

Native Species

Specimens of any wildlife collected under the authority of a state fish resource permit or state scientific or educational permits may not be bartered or sold. As these permits are required to collect or possess any amphibian or reptile occurring in the state, the sale of any specimens wild caught in Alaska is prohibited (AS 16.05.930).

* What effect this legislation has on the sale of specimens of native species originating from another state and imported into Alaska is unclear at this time.

Amphibians

In addition to any fish resource permits, a fish transport permit may be required to possess any live amphibian, including native species lawfully obtained from outside the State of Alaska (5 AAC 41.005).

Reptiles

Live game possession permits may be required to possess living specimens of the Common Garter Snake, *Thamnophis sirtalis*, including specimens legally acquired from outside the state (5 AAC 92. 029).

Exotic Species

Restrictions on the importation, possession, and sale of non-native species of wildlife are included among the fish and game legislation of the Alaska Annotated Code (reference: 5 AAC) and in Alaska Statutes (reference: AS). As with other aspects of Alaska's wildlife law, these restrictions are often difficult to interpret and the following review is an attempt to simplify this legislation as accurately as possible.

Amphibians

Although restrictions on the importation, possession, and sale of non-native amphibian species are not specifically included among Alaska's wildlife importation statutes and regulations, all state fish import/export legislation is equally applicable to amphibians due to the classification of these animals as fish by the State of Alaska. As fish, multiple permits, including fish transport permits, may be required to import, sell, and/or possess non-native amphibians in Alaska (5 AAC 41.005). State fish resource permits may also be required (AS 16.05.930).

Reptiles

Any non-venomous reptile may be imported, possessed, sold, and/or traded without permit (5 AAC 92.029B).

* What effect, if any, the preceding regulation has on the importation, possession, or sale of *Thamnophis sirtalis* is uncertain at this time.

License and Permit Information

Due to the complexity of Alaska's permit requirements, particularly regarding amphibians, it is highly recommended that the Alaska Department of Fish and Game be contacted regarding exactly which permits may be required prior to the importation of any species of amphibian into the State of Alaska. Permits authorizing the importation and possession of venomous reptiles are issued to qualified individuals and institutions for legitimate research or exhibition purposes only. Further information on Alaska's permit requirements and permit applications may be obtained from the Alaska Department of Fish and Game (address in Appendix I).

CAPTIVE MAINTENANCE REGULATIONS

As is clearly evident in the preceding sections, exactly what type of permits are required to maintain amphibians and reptiles in captivity within Alaska is often an exceedingly complex issue. For instance, while permits are definitely required to possess any venomous reptile in Alaska, it is uncertain whether or not permits are required to possess all specimens of the Common Garter Snake, *Thamnophis sirtalis*, including those animals lawfully obtained from outside the state. Permits may, likewise, also be required to possess both native and non-native species of amphibians in Alaska. To complicate matters further, multiple permits may sometimes be required for specific animal species. For example, in addition to any required state scientific, educational, fish resource, fish transport, and live game possession permits, fish and game propagation licenses or permits may also be required to possess, propagate and/or trade each individual amphibian and restricted reptile species. As in the previous sections, interested parties are directed to the Alaska Department of Fish and Game for further information on the state's permit requirements and for any required permit applications (address in Appendix I). In addition to the restrictions included among the legislation of the preceding sections, the following summarized regulation is also applicable to the captive maintenance of both native and non-native amphibians and reptiles within Alaska.

The release of any wildlife into the natural environment of Alaska without permit is prohibited (5 AAC 92.029).

Captive Maintenance Regulations Review

The following is a brief review of Alaska's regulations concerning the captive maintenance and propagation of amphibians and reptiles.

a. Permits are required to possess both native and introduced Alaskan amphibian species.
b. Fish transport permits may be required to possess non-native amphibian species.
c. Scientific, educational, or live game possession permits may be required to possess Common Garter Snakes, *Thamnophis sirtalis*.
d. Venomous reptiles may not be possessed without permit.
e. Non-venomous, non-native reptile species may be possessed without permit.

(a above see Native Wildlife Regulations).
(b, d, and e above see Importation and Commercial Trade Regulations).
(c above see Native Wildlife Regulations and Importation and Commercial Trade Regulations).

ARIZONA

ENDANGERED, THREATENED, AND SPECIAL CONCERN SPECIES

Categorized as either Extripated, Endangered, Threatened, or Candidate species, various members of Arizona's herpetofauna are included in the state's list of "Threatened Native Wildlife." Although officially listed, Arizona does not have any endangered species legislation, and the inclusion of a species among one of the four categories of Threatened Native Wildlife does not necessarily mean that particular species is protected. However, the collection and possession of certain species of native amphibians and reptiles without a scientific collecting permit is prohibited through various rules and regulations of the Arizona Game and Fish Department.

The following amphibian and reptile species are currently (January 1997) legally protected in Arizona, as specified in Orders 41 and 43 of the Arizona Game and Fish Commission (reference: AZ GFC 41F and 43F). A permit is required to collect and/or possess these species.

Species	Common Name
Rana blairi	Plains Leopard Frog
Rana chiricahuensis	Chiricahau Leopard Frog
Rana onca [1]	Relict Leopard Frog
Rana pipiens	Northern Leopard Frog
Rana subaquavocalis	Ramsey Canyon Leopard Frog
Rana tarahumarae	Tarahumara Frog
Rana yavapaiensis	Lowland Leopard Frog
Gopherus agassizii	Desert Tortoise
Heloderma suspectum	Gila Monster
Phrynosoma mcallii	Flat-tailed Horned Lizard
Crotalus lepidus	Rock Rattlesnake
Crotalus pricei	Twin-spotted Rattlesnake
Crotalus willardi	Ridgenosed Rattlesnake
Sistrurus catenatus	Massasauga

[1] Possibly extinct in Arizona

Protected Species Permit Information

Scientific collection permits are issued to qualified institutions and individuals for legitimate research purposes. The actual application for this permit is 14 pages in length and includes an extensive list of permit conditions and requirements. There is no fee for a scientific collection permit. Permits allowing for the possession of legally obtained specimens of Arizona's protected species for educational or exhibition purposes may also be issued on occasion. Permit applications, including a complete list of permit requirements, may be obtained from the Permits Coordinator of the Arizona Game and Fish Department (address in Appendix I).

NATIVE WILDLIFE REGULATIONS

Restrictions on the collection and possession of unprotected native amphibian and reptile species for non-commercial purposes are specified in section 17 of the Revised Statutes of Arizona (reference: ARS 17) or in the rules or orders of the Arizona Game and Fish Commission (reference: AZ GFC). The following is a summarization of these regulations.

Amphibians

A valid fishing or combination hunting/fishing license is required to take amphibians (ARS 17-331). Amphibians may be taken day or night and the use of artificial light is permitted. Amphibians may be legally taken by; minnow trap, crawfish net, angling, hand, or hand held, non-motorized implement which does not discharge a projectile (AZ GFC R12-4-313).

Unless otherwise specified, the open season for taking those species of native amphibians which may be taken is from January 1 through December 31st. The yearly bag and possession limit is 10 of each species live or dead, unless otherwise specified (AZ GFC 41A).

*No amphibians may be collected from restricted areas except as specified (see Restricted Areas below).

Salamanders

Larval salamanders (waterdogs) may be taken and possessed alive for use as bait (AZ GFC R12-4-316), except in the portion of Santa Cruz County east and south of State Highway 82 or the portion of Cochise County west of the San Pedro River and south of State Highway 82 (AZ GFC R12-4-313B).

Ambystoma tigrinum, Tiger Salamanders, larval or adult, may be taken throughout the year in unlimited numbers live or dead, except for those portions of Santa Cruz and Cochise counties specified above (AZ GFC 41D).

Frogs

The following frogs may be taken throughout the year with a daily bag limit and possession limit of 10 per species live or dead (AZ GFC 41B and 41C):

Bufo cognatus	Great Plains Toad
Bufo punctatus	Red-spotted Toad
Bufo woodhousii	Woodhouse's Toad
Scaphiopus couchii	Couch's Spadefoot Toad
Spea multiplicata	New Mexico Spadefoot Toad

Rana catesbeiana, Bullfrogs may be taken throughout the year in unlimited numbers, dead frogs only (AZ GFC 41E). Bullfrogs may be taken by the following methods; minnow trap, crawfish net, angling, hand, hand held implement, bow and arrow, crossbow or slingshot (AZ GFC R12-2-313E).

Reptiles

Unless otherwise specified, the open season for taking those species of native reptiles which may be taken is from January 1 through December 31st. The yearly bag and possession limit is four of each species live or dead (AZ GFC 43A). A valid hunting or combination hunting and fishing license is required (ARS 17-331).

Turtles

Apalone spinifera, Spiny Softshells may be taken throughout the year in unlimited numbers except from the Colorado River, where the possession limit is five live or dead (AZ GFC 43E). Softshells may not be taken from restricted areas except as specified (see Restricted Areas below).

* Softshells are considered aquatic wildlife in Arizona, and a valid fishing or combination hunting/fishing license is required for their collection.

Lizards

The following lizards may be taken throughout the year with a daily bag limit and a possession limit of 20 in aggregate (AZ GFC 43D):

Callisaurus	Zebra-tailed Lizard
Cnemidophorus spp.	Whiptail Lizards, (all species)
Coleonyx	Banded Gecko
Cophosaurus	Greater Earless Lizard
Holbrookia	Lesser Earless Lizard
Sceloporus undulatus	Fence Lizard
Urosaurus spp.	Tree Lizards, (all species)
Uta (*stansburiana*)	Side-blotched Lizard

* With the exception of comments enclosed within (), the preceeding list is reproduced exactly as provided by the State of Arizona.

Snakes

The following snakes have a daily bag limit and a possession limit of four of each species live or dead (AZ GFC 43B):

Crotalus atrox	Western Diamondback Rattlesnake
Crotalus scutulatus	Mojave Rattlesnake

The following snakes have a yearly bag limit of two of each species and a possession limit of four of each species live or dead (AZ GFC 43C):

Lampropeltis pyromelana	Sonoran Mountain Kingsnake
Lichanura trivirgata	Rosy Boa
Senticolis triaspis	Green Rat Snake

The following snakes have a daily bag limit and a possession limit of 20 in aggregate live or dead (AZ GFC 43D):

Hypsiglena torquata	Night Snake
Leptotyphlops spp.	Blind Snakes, all species
Sonora semiannulata	Ground Snake
Tantilla hobartsmithi	Southwestern Blackheaded Snake

Restricted Areas

Amphibians and softshell turtles may not be taken from the following areas at any time unless otherwise specified (AZ GFC 41 and 43):

1. Posted boundaries of state and federal fish hatcheries.
2. Posted boundary of the Region 1 regional headquarters in Pinetop.
3. The Colorado River 1/2 mile upstream and 1/2 mile downstream of its confluence with the Little Colorado River.
4. That portion of the Colorado River lying within Grand Canyon National Park.
5. Lee Valley Creek above Lee Valley Reservoir.
6. Gap Creek between Honeymoon cabin and its confluence with the Verde River.
7. Mineral Creek (Apache County) upstream of the Apache Sitgreaves National Forest Boundary.
8. Posted areas immediately above the dams at Upper Lake Mary, Alamo Lake, and Lake Mead.
9. Posted areas immediately below Davis, Hoover, Glen Canyon, Waddell (Lake Pleasant), Roosevelt, Horse Mesa, and Mormon Flat dams.
10. Posted Spawning Pond Number 1 and Spawning Pond Number 2 located along the Salinity Canal North of Yuma..

11. Luna Lake Wildlife Area from April 1 through July 31.
12. Posted portions of Alamo lake.
13. Posted portions of the Tonto Arm of Roosevelt Lake from January 1 through February 15 and from November 15 through December 31.
14. Posted portions of Mittry Lake from January 1 through the second Monday in February and from November 15 through December 31.
15. Posted portions of Becker Lake are closed to all public entry from April 1 through July 31.
16. Posted portions of Lake Mead.
17. Posted portions of Powers Butte are closed to entry for the purposes of taking wildlife.
18. Posted portions of Bog Hole Wildlife Area.
19. Posted portions of Lake Havasu.

License and Permit Information

Hunting and fishing licenses are available from bait shops, sporting goods stores, and other retail outlets. Hunting license fees are $18.00 for residents and $85.50 for non-residents. Combination hunting/fishing licenses are available at a cost of $34.00 for residents and $137.50 for non-residents. Annual fees for fishing licenses are residents $12.00 and non-residents $38.00 Short term non-resident fishing licenses are also available at a reduced cost.

IMPORTATION AND COMMERCIAL TRADE REGULATIONS

Restrictions on the importation, possession, and sale of both native and non-native amphibian and reptile species are included among the Revised Statutes of Arizona and the Rules of the Arizona Game and Fish Commission. The following is a brief summary of these regulations.

Native Species

Amphibians and reptiles legally taken from the wild in Arizona may be possessed, transported, placed on educational display, propagated, or killed for personal use (AZ GFC R12-4-404A).

Amphibians and reptiles and their progeny legally taken from the wild in Arizona may only be disposed of by gift or as directed by the Arizona Game and Fish Department. Lawfully possessed live wildlife may be exported (AZ GFC R12-4-404B).

The combined total specimens of each species of amphibian or reptile and their offspring shall not exceed the possession limit for that species, except that the progeny of amphibians and reptiles may be held in captivity in excess of the possession limit for 12 months from the date of birth. The captive produced offspring shall be disposed of by gift or as directed by the Arizona Game and Fish Department (AZ GFC R12-4-404C).

Exotic Species

No person shall import or transport into Arizona or sell, trade, release, or possess within the state any live wildlife except as authorized (ARS 17-306).

Lawfully possessed amphibians and reptiles not included in the list of Restricted Live Wildlife (see R12-4-406 below) may be imported, purchased, possessed, exhibited, transported, propagated, traded, rented or leased, given away, sold, exported, and killed without a license (AZ GFC R12-4-405).

* R12-4-405 allows for the sale of specimens of native amphibians and reptiles legally obtained from outside of Arizona, as well as unrestricted non-native species. Proper documentation is required.

AZ

Restricted Live Wildlife

Arizona regulates the importation and possession of non-native amphibian and reptile species determined to be potentially injurious to the state's indigenous wildlife or a threat to public safety. Any species included in the list of Restricted Live Wildlife may not be imported or possessed without a permit from the Arizona Game and Fish Department (AZ GFC R12-4-401).

The following amphibian and reptile species, genera, or families are included in the Restricted Live Wildlife list of the Arizona Game and Fish Commission (reference: AZ GFC R12-4-406):

Bufo horribilis	Giant Toad
Bufo marinus	Marine Toad
Bufo paracnemis	Giant Toad
Xenopus spp.	Clawed Frogs, all species
Crocodylia	Crocodilians, all species
Chelydridae	Snapping Turtles, all species
Gopherus	Gopher & Desert Tortoises, all species
Helodermatidae	Beaded Lizards, all species
Atractaspidae	Mole Vipers, all species
Dispholidus typus	Boomslang
Elapidae	Cobras, Coral Snakes, etc., all species
Hydrophiidae	Sea Snakes, all species
Rhabdophis spp.	Keelbacks, all species
Thelotornis kirtlandii	Twig Snake
Viperidae	Vipers, Pit Vipers, all species

License and Permit Information

Requirements and applications for any required permits of this section may be obtained from the Permits Coordinator of the Arizona Game and Fish Department (address in Appendix I).

CAPTIVE MAINTENANCE REGULATIONS

Restrictions on the possession of native and non-native amphibians and reptiles are included among the previous regulations. The following is a review of the restrictions on the captive maintenance of amphibians and reptiles in Arizona.

a. A permit is required to possess any species for which there is no open season (see Endangered, Threatened, and Special Concern Species).
b. *Ambystoma tigrinum*, Tiger Salamanders may be possessed in unlimited numbers.
c. Possession limit for all other open season native amphibians is 10 per species.
d. *Apalone spinifera*, Spiny Softshell Turtles may be possessed in unlimited numbers.
e. Lizards and snakes of AZ GFC 43D have a possession limit of 20 in aggregate, (all species combined).
f. Possession limit for all other unprotected native reptiles is four per species.
g. *Rana catesbeiana*, Bullfrogs may not be possessed alive unless legally obtained prior to January 1, 1996.
h. Giant exotic toads (i.e., *Bufo marinus*, etc.) may not be possessed without a permit.
i. *Xenopus* spp., Clawed Frogs may not be possessed without a permit.
j. Crocodilians may not be possessed without a permit.
k. *Heloderma* spp., Beaded Lizards may not be possessed without a permit.
l. Non-native venomous snakes, including some rear fanged colubrids, may not be possessed without a permit.

(b, c, d, e, f, and g, see Native Wildlife Regulations).
(h, i, j, k and l, see Importation and Commercial Trade Regulations).

ARKANSAS

ENDANGERED, THREATENED, AND SPECIAL CONCERN SPECIES

As the Arkansas State Legislature does not have the authority to regulate the taking of any wildlife in the state, no official endangered species act exists in Arkansas. Instead, the management and protection of the state's wildlife resources are the responsibility of the Arkansas Game and Fish Commission, and the Commission has the sole administrative authority to regulate the taking of wildlife, as specified in Amendment 35 of the Arkansas State Constitution. Although legislation protecting endangered species is included among the rules and regulations of the Arkansas Game and Fish Commission Code (reference: AGFC 18.20), only species included in the federal endangered and threatened species list are officially included in the state list.

The following species is the only reptile or amphibian included in the current (November 1993) endangered and threatened species list of Arkansas. Permits are required for activities involving this species.

Species	Common Name	Status
Alligator mississippiensis	American Alligator	Threatened S/A

* American Alligators are listed as threatened due to similarity of appearance by the U.S. Department of the Interior for law enforcement purposes only. Populations in the wild are not currently considered endangered or threatened. Although the possession of specimens wild caught in Arkansas is prohibited, various activities are allowed under the authority of permits (see Native Wildlife Regulations and Importation and Commercial Trade Regulations).

Protected Species Permit Information

Scientific collection permits are apparently required for any activity involving American Alligators occurring in the wild in Arkansas. These permits are issued to qualified individuals and institutions for legitimate research or educational purposes. Permit applications and requirements may be obtained from the Arkansas Game and Fish Commission (address in Appendix I).

NATIVE WILDLIFE REGULATIONS

Restrictions on the collection and possession of amphibians and reptiles wild caught in Arkansas for personal use are included among the regulations of the Arkansas Game and Fish Commission Code. The following is a summarization of these regulations.

It is unlawful to take fish or wildlife by the use of deadfalls, drugs, poisons. chemicals, or explosives (AGFC 18.07).

Taking or attempting to take or locate any wildlife from a boat during the hours of darkness is prohibited unless otherwise specified (AGFC 18.05).

It is unlawful to take any wildlife when and where a license, permit, tag, or stamp is required without first obtaining such license, permit, tag, or stamp (AGFC 03.01).

* As currently interpreted by the Arkansas Game and Fish Commission, licenses are only required to collect native frogs and turtles. Other native amphibians and reptiles may be collected within specified possession limits without license.

Unless otherwise specified, the possession limit for native amphibians and reptiles wild caught in Arkansas is six of each species. Specimens may be taken by hand only (AGFC 18.17).

Salamanders

The following salamander species may not be taken from the wild at any time (AGFC 18.17B).

Cryptobranchus alleganiensis	Hellbender
Typhlotriton spelaeus [1]	Grotto Salamander

[1] This species is not specifically included by name in the regulations of the Arkansas Game and Fish Commission. It is protected, however, by virtue of being a troglodytic (cave dwelling) species as specified in regulation 18.17B.

Frogs

A valid fishing license is required to collect frogs in Arkansas (AGFC 03.02).

Rana catesbeiana, Bullfrogs may be taken from 12 o'clock noon April 15 through December 31, with a daily bag limit of 18 and a possession limit of 36 frogs. Bullfrogs may be taken by hand, hand nets, hook and line, gig, spear, or long bow and arrow (AGFC 36.01 and 36.02). Bullfrogs may be taken at night during the open season (AGFC 18.05-1).

Alligators

Alligator mississippiensis, American Alligator. It is unlawful to take, attempt to take, or possess alligators or any part thereof (AGFC 18.14).

* Legally obtained alligators and alligator products may be possessed; proper documentation and permits are required.

Turtles

A valid fishing license is required to collect turtles in Arkansas (AGFC 39.01).

Turtles may be taken by 1/4 inch mesh hoop net traps with a maximum slot opening of one inch by three feet or by box traps measuring not more than four feet by four feet by four feet, which are incapable of taking fish. A portion of all traps must remain above the water's surface. Turtle trap tags are required. Aquatic turtles may not be taken by use of chemicals or explosives (AGFC 39.02 and 39.03).

Macrochelys temminckii, Alligator Snapping Turtles, eggs, or parts may not be taken from the wild in Arkansas (AGFC 39.01A).

* Listed as *Macroclemys temminckii* by Arkansas.

Terrapene ornata, Ornate Box Turtles may not be taken or possessed from the wild in Arkansas (AGFC 18.17B).

License and Permit Information

Fishing licenses are available from numerous retail outlets, including bait and sporting goods stores, at an annual fee of $11.50 for residents and $30.00 for non-residents. Fourteen-day, seven-day, and three-day non-resident licenses are also available at a cost of $20.00, $15.00, and $8.00 respectively.

IMPORTATION AND COMMERCIAL TRADE REGULATIONS

Native Species

Restrictions on the sale of native amphibian and reptile species are included among the regulations of the Arkansas Game and Fish Commission. The following is a summary of these regulations.

It is unlawful to purchase, sell, offer for sale, barter or trade any species of wildlife or portions thereof, unless otherwise specified (AGFC 18.03).

* Does not apply to non-native species legally acquired outside of Arkansas.

It is unlawful to possess for commercial purposes captive Arkansas native or naturalized species without a commercial nongame breeder's permit (AGFC 15.05).

Frogs

Rana catesbeiana, Bullfrogs taken from the waters of the state may not be purchased or sold except as specified (AGFC 36.03).

Rana catesbeiana, Bullfrogs may be taken and sold in unlimited numbers by licensed fish farmers under the authority of a bullfrog permit. The taking of bullfrogs for commercial purposes is limited to those ponds, impoundments, and drainages where legitimate fish farming operations are occurring. Sales invoices recording the date, number of frogs sold or shipped, and the Bullfrog permit number are required for each transaction (AGFC 36.02 to 36.04).

Alligators

Alligator mississippiensis, American Alligators may be propagated, raised, and sold by licensed alligator farmers. Alligators may not be taken from the wild in Arkansas to stock an alligator farming operation. All applicable U.S. Department of the Interior, U.S. Department of Agriculture. and Arkansas State Health Department requirements apply to the purchase and/or sale of American Alligators, alligator eggs, or parts (AGFC 40.01 and 40.02).

Turtles

A commercial fishing license and tackle tags are required to take turtles for commercial purposes in Arkansas. Licensed fish farmers may take turtles from waters where legitimate fish farming operations are occurring without a commercial license or tags. Turtles may be taken commercially only from those waters of the state open to commercial turtling. Only residents of the state may harvest turtles in Arkansas (AGFC 39.01 to 36.06).

* As currently interpreted by the Arkansas Game and Fish Commission, the residency requirement of the preceding regulation only applies to commercial turtle collection activities.

Exotic Species

With the exception of the following summarized regulation, the State of Arkansas does not currently restrict the importation, possession, or sale of non-native amphibian and reptiles species.

The release of any imported or domesticated species of wildlife into the natural environment of Arkansas without permit is prohibited (AGFC 18.12).

License and Permit Information

Commercial nongame breeder's permits are required to sell native amphibians and reptiles in Arkansas, except as specified for bullfrogs, alligators, and turtles above. All specimens in excess of the possession limit for that species (see Native Wildlife Regulations) must have either been produced in captivity or legally obtained from outside of Arkansas. Commercial nongame breeder's permits cost $25.00. Bullfrog permits authorizing the sale of farm raised frogs cost $25.00 plus an additional $25.00 for the required fish farmer permit. Alligator farmer permit fees are $500.00 annually with additional fees of $4.00 for each alligator tag. Resident commercial fishing permits (required to take turtles commercially) have an annual fee of $25.00. The cost for any required turtle trap tags is $2.00 each. Applications for the commercial nongame breeder's permit, as well as the requirements and applications for the other licenses and permits of this section may be obtained from the Arkansas Game and Fish Commission (address in Appendix I).

CAPTIVE MAINTENANCE REGULATIONS

Restrictions on the possession of amphibians and reptiles are included among the previous regulations. The following is a brief review of these restrictions.

a. *Alligator mississippiensis*, American Alligators may not be possessed without permit.

b. The following species may not be possessed if taken from the wild in Arkansas. Specimens legally obtained from outside of Arkansas may be possessed; proper documentation is required.

Cryptobranchus alleganiensis	Hellbender
Typhlotriton spelaeus	Grotto Salamander
Macrochelys temminckii	Alligator Snapping Turtle
Terrapene ornata	Ornate Box Turtle

c. *Rana catesbeiana*, Bullfrogs have a possession limit of 36 specimens; a valid fishing license is required.

d. The possession limit for all other native species wild caught in the state is six of each species. All specimens in excess of this limit must be legally obtained with proper documentation.

e. No restrictions on the possession of non-native amphibian and reptiles species.

(b, c, and d above see Native Wildlife Regulations).

CALIFORNIA

ENDANGERED, THREATENED, AND SPECIAL CONCERN SPECIES

Endangered and threatened species of California's fauna and flora are legally protected by the California Endangered Species Act, as specified in Chapter 1.5 of the California Fish and Game Code (reference: CAC FG 1.5 2050-2098). Easily among the strongest in the nation, California's Endangered Species Act does contain both critical habitat and recovery plan provisions, two features normally lacking in the endangered wildlife laws of other states. In addition to any species officially protected by the state's endangered species legislation, California also prohibits the collection and possession of several other native wildlife species including a number of amphibians and reptiles. As with state endangered and threatened animals and plants, permits are required to collect or possess any designated protected species, including specimens lawfully obtained from outside of California, as specified in the fish and wildlife legislation of title 14, chapter 5 California Code of Regulations (reference: CAR 14 5-40.0 to 42.5). Habitat impact and mitigation procedures of the state's endangered species legislation, however, do not apply to designated protected species.

The amphibians and reptiles included in California's current (March 1997) list of legally protected are listed below. The collection or possession of any of these species without a permit is prohibited. In addition to those species officially designated as protected by the state of California, five federally protected marine turtles have been recorded from the state's coastal waters and these species are also included in the following list. As always, permits issued by the U.S. Department of the Interior are required for required for all activities involving any sea turtles (see U.S. Endangered and Threatened Species).

Species	Common Name	Status
Ambystoma californiense	California Tiger Salamander	Protected
Ambystoma macrodactylum croceum	Santa Cruz Long-toed Salamander	Endangered
Batrachoseps aridus	Desert Slender Salamander	Endangered
Batrachoseps campi	Inyo Mountains Salamander	Protected
Batrachoseps simatus	Kern Canyon Slender Salamander	Threatened
Batrachoseps stebbinsi	Tehachapi Slender Salamander	Threatened
Hydromantes brunus	Limestone Salamander	Threatened
Hydromantes platycephalus	Mount Lyell Salamander	Protected
Hydromantes shastae	Shasta Salamander	Threatened
Plethodon elongatus	Del Norte Salamander	Protected
Plethodon stormi	Siskiyou Mountains Salamander	Threatened
Rhyacotriton olympicus	Olympic Salamander	Protected
Ascaphus truei	Tailed Frog	Protected
Bufo alvarius	Colorado River Toad	Protected
Bufo canorus	Yosemite Toad	Protected
Bufo exsul	Black Toad	Threatened
Bufo microscaphus	Southwestern Toad	Protected
Rana aurora [1]	Red-legged Frog	Protected
Rana boylii	Foothill Yellow-legged Frog	Protected
Rana cascadae	Cascade Frog	Protected
Rana muscosa	Mountain Yellow-legged Frog	Protected
Rana pretiosa	Spotted Frog	Protected
Rana yavapaiensis	Lowland Leopard Frog	Protected
Spea hammondii [2]	Western Spadefoot Toad	Protected

Caretta caretta	Loggerhead Sea Turtle	Threatened
Chelonia mydas	Green Sea Turtle	Threatened
Clemmys marmorata	Western Pond Turtle	Protected
Dermochelys coriacea	Leatherback Sea Turtle	Endangered
Eretmochelys imbricata	Hawksbill Sea Turtle	Endangered
Gopherus agassizii	Desert Tortoise	Threatened
Kinosternon sonoriense	Sonoran Mud Turtle	Protected
Lepidochelys olivacea	Pacific Ridley	Threatened
Anniella pulchra nigra	Black Legless Lizard	Protected
Cnemidophorus hyperythrus	Orangethroat Whiptail	Protected
Coleonyx switaki	Switak's Barefoot Gecko	Threatened
Elgaria panamintina [3]	Panamint Alligator Lizard	Protected
Gambelia sila	Bluntnose Leopard Lizard	Endangered
Heloderma suspectum cinctum	Banded Gila Monster	Protected
Phrynosoma coronatum	Coast Horned Lizard	Protected
Phrynosoma mcallii	Flat-tailed Horned Lizard	Protected
Phyllodactylus nocticolus [4]	Leaf-toed Gecko	Protected
Uma inornata [5]	Coachella Valley Fringe-Toed Lizard	Endangered
Xantusia henshawi	Granite Night Lizard	Protected
Xantusia riversiana	Island Night Lizard	Protected
Lampropeltis zonata pulchra	San Diego Mountain Kingsnake	Protected
Lichanura bottae [6]	Rubber Boa	Threatened
Masticophis flagellum ruddocki	San Joaquin Coachwhip	Protected
Masticophis lateralis euryxanthus	Alameda Striped Racer	Threatened
Thamnophis gigas	Giant Garter Snake	Threatened
Thamnophis hammondii	Two-striped Garter Snake	Protected
Thamnophis sirtalis tetrataenia [7]	San Francisco Garter Snake	Endangered

[1] No subspecies specified by California. The exact legal status of non-native subspecies is uncertain at this time.
[2] Listed as *Scaphiopus hammondii* by California.
[3] Listed as *Gerrhonotus panamintinus* by California.
[4] Listed as *Phyllodactylus xanti* by California.
[5] Not listed in Collins (1997).
[6] Listed as *Charina bottae umbratica* by California. No subspecies listed in Collins (1997).
[7] Subspecies not listed in Collins (1997).

Protected Species Permit Information

Permits allowing for the collection and possession of protected species may be issued for specific purposes. All permit requests are evaluated on an individual basis, and the State of California is extremely selective about what types of activities will be authorized. In general, permits will only be issued to qualified individuals or institutions for purposes of legitimate scientific research, or for pre-project surveys required by California's Environmental Quality Act. Several categories of permits are available and individual permit fees are variable. More information on permit requirements and any required permit applications may be obtained from the Wildlife Protection Division of the California Department of Fish and Game (address in Appendix I).

NATIVE WILDLIFE REGULATIONS

As is true of the state's endangered species legislation, fish and wildlife law in California is among the most comprehensive in the country. In most aspects California's legislation is completely explicit, establishing specific collection, possession, and sales restrictions on virtually all of the native and introduced indigenous wildlife species of the state. In addition, nearly identical species take and possession restrictions are often included among a multitude of separate regulations of both the California Fish and Game Code (reference: CAC FG) and the California Code of Regulations (reference: CAR 14). Despite the overall high quality of California's fish and wildlife laws, however, a few truly bizarre amphibian and reptile regulations do exist among the state's wildlife legislation. Those portions of California wildlife law regulating the non-commercial collection and possession of amphibians and reptiles are summarized below.

It is unlawful to take any amphibian and reptile except as otherwise specified by law. Possession of an amphibian or reptile in the field with collecting equipment is prima facie evidence of take (CAC FG 2000).

It is unlawful to take or possess any native amphibian or reptile unless otherwise specified (CAR 14 5-40.0a).

Amphibians

Unless otherwise specified, unprotected amphibians may be taken any time of the day or night throughout the year. The bag and possession limit is four of each species. The collection of amphibians from state designated ecological reserves, State Parks, or National Parks and Monuments without permit is prohibited. The following are the legal methods for taking amphibians: hand, hand-held dip net, or hook and line, unless specified otherwise. A valid sport fishing license is required (CAR 14 5-41.5).

Salamanders

Batrachoseps spp., Slender Salamanders (all species) may not be collected from Inyo and Mono Counties, or from the Santa Rosa Mountains in Riverside County (CAR 14 5-41.5e).

Hydromantes spp., Web-footed Salamanders (all species) may not be from Inyo and Mono Counties (CAR 14 5-41.5e).

Frogs

It is unlawful to take frogs by the use of firearms of any caliber or type (CAC FG 6854).

The California Department of Fish and Game may issue a permit to take and dispose of frogs under prescribed limitations, when, in the department's judgment, such frogs are polluting the water supply in any area or otherwise constitute a nuisance (CAC FG 6855).

* Applies to all frog species. The exact purpose of this regulation is uncertain at this time.

Rana catesbeiana, Bullfrogs may be taken throughout the year in unlimited numbers. There are no minimum size requirements. Bullfrogs may be legally taken by the following methods: spears, gigs, grabs, paddles, hook and line, dip net, bow and arrow fishing tackle, or hand. The use of artificial light is permitted. A valid fishing license is required (CAR 14 2-5.05).

* *Rana catesbeiana* is a non-native, introduced species in California.

Frog Jumping Contests

As used in this article, "frog-jumping contest" means a contest generally and popularly known as a frog-jumping contest which is open to the public and is advertised or announced in a newspaper. Frogs to be used in frog-jumping contests shall be governed by this article only. Frogs to be so used may be taken at anytime and without a license or permit. If the means used for taking such frogs can, as normally used, seriously injure the frog, it shall be conclusively presumed the taking is not for purposes of a frog-jumping contest. Any person may possess any number of live frogs to use in frog-jumping contests, but if a frog dies or is killed it must be destroyed as soon as possible, and may not be eaten or otherwise used for any purpose. A frog which is not kept in a manner which is reasonable to preserve its life is not within the coverage of this article. The commission has no power to modify the provisions of this article by any order, rule, or regulation (CAC FG 6880 to 6885).

* The preceding regulation has been reproduced without modification.

Reptiles

Unless otherwise specified, unprotected native reptiles may be taken any time of the day or night throughout the year. The possession limit is two of each species. The collection of reptiles from state designated ecological reserves, State Parks, or National Parks and Monuments without permit is prohibited. Reptiles may not be injured and may only be taken by the following methods unless otherwise specified: hand, lizard nooses, snake tongs, snake hooks. A valid sport fishing license is required (CAR 14 5-42.5).

It is unlawful to use any method of collecting which involves the breaking apart of rocks, granite flakes, logs, or other shelters in or under which reptiles may be found (CAR 14 5-425).

Turtles

In addition to the other legal methods of taking reptiles, turtles may be taken by hook and line. A valid fishing license is required (CAR 14 5-42.5b).

Apalone spinifera, Spiny Softshell Turtles have a bag and possession limit of five specimens (CAR 14 2-5.70).

* Listed as *Trionyx spiniferus* by the State of California. Softshell Turtles are not native to California.

Gopherus spp., It is unlawful to harm, take, possess, or transport any tortoise of the genus *Gopherus* without permit, or to shoot any projectile at a tortoise, genus *Gopherus* (CAC FG 5000).

* No species specified by California.

Malaclemys spp.,, Diamondback Terrapins may not be taken at any time (CAC FG 5020).

* Why the previous restriction is included among California's wildlife legislation is currently unknown. *Malaclemys* does not naturally occur anywhere on the western coast of the United States and viable, reproducing Diamondback Terrapin populations are not known to exist within the State of California at this time.

Lizards

Anniella pulchra, California Legless Lizards have a bag and possession limit of one specimen (CAR 14 5-442.5b).

The following lizard species have a possession limit of 25 in aggregate (CAR 14 5-42.5b):

Eumeces skiltonianus	Western Skink
Sceloporus graciosus	Sagebrush Lizard
Sceloporus occidentalis	Western Fence Lizard
Uta stansburiana	Side-blotched Lizard
Xantusia vigilis	Desert Night Lizard

Snakes

Crotalus, spp., Rattlesnakes may be taken by any method (CAR 14 5-42.5d).

Rattlesnakes of the genera *Crotalus* and *Sistrurus* may be taken by California residents without a sport fishing license (CAC FG 7149.3).

* Snakes of the genus *Sistrurus* are not native to California.

Lampropeltis zonata, California Mountain Kingsnakes have a possession limit of one specimen. California Mountain Kingsnakes may not be taken in San Diego or Orange Counties or in Los Angeles County west of Interstate Highway 5 (CAR 14 5-42.5b and 42.5e).

Thamnophis sirtalis spp., Common Garter Snakes may not be taken in Los Angeles, Orange, Riverside, San Diego, or Ventura Counties (CAR 14 5-442.5e).

The following snakes have a possession limit of four wild caught specimens per species (CAR 14 5-42.5b):

Lampropeltis getula [1]	Common Kingsnake
Pituophis catenifer [2]	Gopher Snake

[1] Listed as *Lampropeltis getulus* by the State of California.
[2] Listed as *Pituophis melanoleucus* by the State of California.

License and Permit Information

A valid sport fishing license is required to collect any amphibians and reptiles except rattlesnakes in California. Fishing licenses are available from many retail outlets including bait shops and sporting goods stores. Sport fishing license fees change annually, but currently average about $25 for residents and $70 for non-residents. One day sport fishing licenses are also available at a cost of about $10 for both residents and non-residents.

IMPORTATION AND COMMERCIAL TRADE REGULATIONS

Restrictions on the sale of both native and non-native amphibians and reptiles are included among the wildlife legislation of the California Fish and Game Code (reference CAC FG) and in the California Code of Regulations (reference: CAR 14). In general, the sale of all native species, particularly specimens wild caught within the state, is prohibited. Captive produced specimens of a few native species may be commercially tradedw by permit, however. With the exception of a few "prohibited" species (see Exotic Species below), the State of California does not currently restrict the importation, possession, or commercial trade of non-native amphibians and reptiles. Those portions of California's wildlife legislation restricting commercial activities involving native and introduced indigenous amphibian and reptile species are summarized below.

Native Species

The collection, possession, purchase, sale, propagation, transportation, import or export of any native amphibian and reptile is prohibited unless otherwise specified. Except for processed reptile skins, it is unlawful to display native amphibians and reptiles which may not be sold in locations where animals are offered for sale (CAR 14 5-40).

Permits allowing for the sale of native amphibians and reptiles by biological supply houses to scientific and educational institutions may be issued by the California Department of Fish and Game (CAR 14 5-40e).

Institutions and organizations engaged in the legitimate scientific study or public exhibition of native wildlife may possess and sell, purchase, or exchange native amphibians and reptiles between organizations without permit (CAR 14 5-40).

Albinos

Captive bred native amphibians and reptiles lacking normal body pigment and having red or pink eyes may be possessed, propagated, imported, purchased, or sold without permit (CAR 14 5-43).

Captive Propagation Permits

Certain species of native amphibians and reptiles may be possessed, propagated, and sold through the authorization of a captive propagation permit. Authorized species may be possessed in unlimited numbers provided that the number of specimens wild caught within California does not exceed the bag and possession limit specified for that species (see Native Wildlife Regulations). The captive produced offspring of authorized species may be sold. Properly licensed pet shops are exempt from captive propagation permit requirements provided all species are obtained from a lawful source and all sales are sold from the premises. The following native species are currently authorized for possession and sale under the authority of this permit (CAR 14 5-43):

Lampropeltis getula californiae	California Kingsnake
Lichanura trivirgata gracia	Desert Rosy Boa
Lichanura trivirgata roseofusca	Coastal Rosy Boa
Pituophis catenifer affinis [1]	Sonoran Gopher Snake
Pituophis catenifer annectens [1]	San Diego Gopher Snake
Pituophis catenifer catenifer [1]	Pacific Gopher Snake
Pituophis catenifer deserticola [1]	Great Basin Gopher Snake

[1] Listed as *Pituophis melanoleucus* by the State of California.

The California Fish and Game Commission may authorize the possession, propagation, and sale of other species not included in the above list. However, no species in the genus Crotalus will be authorized by the Commission (CAR 14 185.5C).

Amphibians

It is unlawful to possess any amphibian which may not be sold in any restaurant or other eating establishment unless the possession is by the person who lawfully took or otherwise legally possessed the amphibian. This does not prohibit the preparation for consumption by the individuals who have lawfully possessed amphibians (CAC FG 2015).

Frogs

The commercial collection, possession, sale, transportation, or export of frogs for human consumption is prohibited. This restriction does not apply to frogs raised by registered aquaculturists or lawfully imported into the state. Records of all transactions involving frogs for human consumption must be maintained for a period of one year from the date of receipt of the frogs (CAR 14 5-41.7).

Rana catesbeiana, Bullfrogs may be harvested from the wild for use in developing domesticated aquacultural brood stock only as specified by California Department of Fish and Game permit (CAR 14 243).

Exotic Species

Restrictions on the importation, possession, and sale of non-native amphibians and reptiles are included in California's wildlife legislation. The following is a brief review of these regulations.

Except as otherwise prohibited by state or federal law, non-native amphibian and reptile species may be imported, exported, transported, possessed, propagated, purchased, or sold without permit (CAR 14 5-40f).

Prohibited Species

Non-native species determined to be detrimental to the native wildlife, agricultural interests, or public health and safety may not be imported, transported, or possessed except by special permit issued by the California Department of Fish and Game. In general, these permits will only be issued to recognized zoos, aquariums, and universities, or to properly accredited and qualified individuals and other private institutions for legitimate research, propagation, or exhibition purposes.

The following amphibian and reptile species, genera, or families are included in California's list of prohibited wildlife and California Department of Fish and Game permits are required to possess any species included in this list (CAR 14 671):

Bufo horribilis [1]	Giant Toad
Bufo marinus	Marine Toad
Bufo paracnemis	Cururu Giant Toad
Bufo spp.	All large Mexican, Central and South American species
Xenopus [2]	Clawed Frogs, all species in genus
Crocodilia	Crocodilians, all species
Chelydridae	Snapping Turtles, all species
Heloderma suspectum suspectum	Reticulated Gila Monster
Crotalidae	Pit Vipers, all species except:

	Crotalus atrox [3]	Western Diamondback Rattlesnake
	Crotalus cerastes [3]	Sidewinder
	Crotalus mitchellii [3]	Speckled Rattlesnake
	Crotalus ruber [3]	Red Diamondback Rattlesnake
	Crotalus scutulatus [3]	Mojave Rattlesnake
	Crotalus viridis [3]	Western Rattlesnake

Dispholidus typus	Boomslang
Elapidae	Cobras, Coral Snakes, Mambas, Kraits, etc., all species
Thelotornis kirtlandii	Twig Snake
Viperidae	Vipers, all species

[1] Species not listed in Frank and Ramus (1995).
[2] Species included in the introduced, non-native indigenous herpetofauna of California.
[3] Species included among the native herpetofauna of California.

Salamanders

Ambystoma tigrinum spp., Tiger Salamanders (Waterdogs) legally obtained non-native species may be possessed and used as bait, except where prohibited by regulation. All salamanders used as bait must be at least three inches in length (CAR 14 3-4.00e).

Turtles

Gopherus spp., It is unlawful to sell, purchase, possess, or transport any tortoise, genus *Gopherus*, or parts thereof (CAC FG 5000).

* No species specified by California. What effect, if any this legislation has on the possession and sale of non-native species of the genus *Gopherus* in California is uncertain at this time.

Crocodilians

No permits will be issued or renewed for the operation of an alligator or crocodile farm if the animals are kept for the use and sale of their meat and hides (CAC FG 5062).

License and Permit Information

Permits for the commercial sale of native amphibians and reptiles by biological supply houses are available for a $50 annual fee. Captive propagation permit fees are $62 annually. Several different types of permits are available for species prohibited as detrimental wildlife, most of which have an annual fee of $260. There is also an annual inspection fee of $100 for all facilities maintaining specimens of designated prohibited wildlife. Numerous conditions and restrictions are associated with each of these permits, and a complete list of requirements and permit applications may be obtained from the Wildlife Protection Division of the California Department of Fish and Game (address in Appendix I).

CAPTIVE MAINTENANCE REGULATIONS

In addition to the restrictions on the possession of native and non-native amphibian and reptile species included among the legislation of the previous sections, the following summarized statutes and regulations are also applicable to the captive maintenance of amphibians and reptiles.

The release into the wild of any wild animal not native to California, including domestically reared stocks of such animal, without permit is prohibited (CAR 14 671.6).

Native amphibians and reptiles which have been in captivity, including both wild caught and captive produced individuals and offspring, may not be released into the wild (CAR 14 5-40d).

Progeny resulting from pregnant native amphibians and reptiles collected from the wild must be transferred to another person or to a scientific or educational institution within 45 days of birth or hatching. Individuals receiving such progeny must comply with specified bag and possession limits established for that species (CAR 14 5-40c).

Caging Requirements for Prohibited Non-native Species

The possession and public exhibition of all designated prohibited non-native amphibian and reptile species is subject to the following minimum caging requirements. In addition, all animals held in captivity must be maintained in a humane manner with the proper food, water, handling, veterinary care, and cage cleaning and disinfection procedures necessary to insure the health and well being of the captive. A written log documenting the health care of all prohibited species held in captivity is also required (CAR 14 671.2).

CA

Amphibians - General Requirements

All enclosures must be maintained within a closed and locked building which has covers over all drains and openings to prevent the escape of amphibians and all building doors must be equipped with sweeps. Containers or exhibits housing amphibians must be labeled with the identification of the species and the number of specimens contained inside. Any substrate used must be non-abrasive and kept clean. Any transfer containers must have locked tops and shall be constructed in a manner which prevents the likelihood of escape.

Giant Toads - Family Bufonidae

For one animal an enclosure equivalent in size to one standard ten-gallon commercial aquarium. For each additional animal add 3/4 of one square foot. At least 1/3 of the bottom of the enclosure shall be covered with water and 2/3 shall be dry. Animals shall be maintained at temperatures between 60 to 80 degrees Fahrenheit.

Clawed Frogs - Family Pipidae

For one animal an enclosure equivalent in size to one standard ten-gallon commercial aquarium. For each additional animal increase available floor space by 50 percent. Water of at least 1 foot in depth must cover the required minimum floor space for each animal housed in the container. Animals shall be maintained at temperatures between 60 to 80 degrees Fahrenheit.

Crocodilians - Order Crocodilia

For one animal an enclosure measuring in length and width at least 1 1/2 times by 1 1/2 times the total length of the animal. For two animals double the minimum size requirement. For each additional animal thereafter increase by a factor of 2/3 the minimum enclosure size. At least 1/3 of the minimum enclosure space shall be water of a sufficient depth for the animal to immerse itself. If more than one animal is present, the pool must be of sufficient size for all animals to immerse themselves simultaneously. Pool surfaces must be constructed of a non-abrasive material and must have a drain. The portion of the enclosure not occupied by water shall be covered in non-abrasive material such as dirt or grass.

Crocodilians, except alligators and caimans less than 4 feet in length, shall be confined in a totally enclosed building or exhibit which precludes their coming in contact with the public. The walls of an open pen for other crocodilians shall be equivalent to at least 1 foot in height for every foot in length of the largest animal housed up to a maximum of 6 feet. If walls are made of a climbable material such as fencing, the 1 1/2 feet of wall shall be constructed of slippery, non-climbable material for all crocodilians except alligators. The walls of enclosures for all species must be buried deep enough to prevent escape by digging, or a buried apron shall be used. Walls of open alligator pens must be at least 4 feet high and the corners shall be covered to prevent climbing. The upper 1/2 of the enclosure walls shall be constructed of concrete, concrete block, or 9 gauge chain link or welded wire with a mesh size of 2 inches by 4 inches or less. Concrete or concrete block must be used for the bottom 1/2 of the enclosure. All chain link or welded wire fencing edges shall be smoothly secured in a manner to prevent injury to the animals.

Alligators may be kept outdoors if an external heat source is provided, and the pool is maintained above freezing. The pool is at least 3 feet deep; and the nighttime air temperature does not fall below freezing for more than 2 consecutive nights.

Crocodilians other than alligators may be maintained outdoors between sunrise and sunset if the air temperature is above 65 degrees Fahrenheit. Crocodilians other than alligators may not be confined outdoors between sunset and sunrise.

Snapping Turtles - Family Chelydridae

The container or exhibit must be labeled with the common and scientific name of the species and subspecies, if known, and the number of animals contained inside. Each turtle must be provided with a minimum floor space equal to 5 times the size of the animal. At least 1/2 of the enclosure shall be covered in water of sufficient depth to immerse the turtle.

Venomous Snakes - Families Colubridae, Crotalidae, Elapidae, and Viperidae

Containers or exhibits housing venomous snakes shall be labeled with the common and scientific name of the species and subspecies, if known, and the number of specimens contained inside. The label shall be legibly marked with the warning "Poisonous" or "Venomous." In addition, each enclosure shall be clearly and conspicuously labeled with the appropriate antivenin for the species contained. The perimeter measurements of enclosures for snakes less than 6 feet in length shall be 1 1/2 times the length of the snake. Perimeter measurements for enclosures for snakes over 6 feet in length shall be twice the length of the snake.

All venomous snakes shall be kept in locked exhibits or containers which shall be located within a locked building, compound, or enclosure. At least two fully trained people shall be present when any occupied enclosure is opened or when venomous snakes are handled. A record of the names of trained handlers must be filed with the California Department of Fish and Game. Written animal escape "emergency procedures" shall be clearly and conspicuously posted in buildings housing venomous snakes and a copy of these procedures must be submitted to the California Department of Fish and Game at the time initial permit applications are submitted. A clearly and conspicuously posted notice providing the location of the nearest readily available source of appropriate antivenins and a written hospital venomous snakebite treatment plan notice is also required.

Captive Maintenance Regulation Review

The following is a brief review of California's restrictions on the captive maintenance of amphibians and reptiles.

a. A permit is required to possess any species listed as endangered, threatened, or protected.

b. Possession of unprotected native amphibians without permit limited to four of each species unless otherwise specified.

c. *Rana catesbeiana*, Bullfrogs may be possessed in unlimited numbers without permit.

d. Possession of unprotected native reptiles without permit is limited to two of each species unless otherwise specified.

e. *Apalone spinifera*, Spiny Softshell Turtle possession limit is five without permit.

f. *Anniella pulchra*, California Legless Lizard possession limit is one without permit.

g. Possession limit without permit for the following lizards is 25 specimens in aggregate (all species combined):

Eumeces skiltonianus	Western Skink
Sceloporus graciosus	Sagebrush Lizard
Sceloporus occidentalis	Western Fence Lizard
Uta stansburiana	Side-blotched Lizard
Xantusia vigilis	Desert Night Lizard

h. *Crotalus* spp., Rattlesnakes native to California may be possessed without permit, possession limit two of each species.

i. *Lampropeltis zonata*, California Mountain Kingsnake possession limit is one without permit.

j. *Lampropeltis getula*, Common Kingsnake possession limit is four without permit. Albino specimens produced in captivity may be possessed in unlimited numbers.

k. *Pituophis catenifer*, Gopher Snake possession limit four without permit. Albino specimens produced in captivity may be possessed in unlimited numbers.

l. *Ambystoma tigrinum*, Tiger Salamanders varieties not native to California may be possessed without permit.

m. Permits required to possess any non-native amphibian or reptile designated a prohibited detrimental species, including all crocodilians and non-native venomous snakes.

(b through i above see Native Wildlife Regulations).

(j and k above see Native Wildlife Regulations and Importation and Commercial Trade regulations).

(l and m above see Importation and Commercial Trade regulations).

CA

Copulating California Kingsnakes, *Lampropeltis getula californiae* - Kingsnakes are easily and routinely reproduced in captivity. In fact, captive produced examples of this subspecies (in a variety of color phases) are now available in such large numbers that there is little reason to collect specimens from the wild. Photograph courtesy of William B. Love.

1994 National Reptile Breeder's Expo in Orlando, Florida - An ever increasing assortment of captive produced amphibian and reptile species, including a truly astounding number of Kingsnakes, are readily available at reptile swap-meets and in pet stores throughout the United States. Several thousand people regularly attend the annual 2 day Breeder's Expo in Orlando. Photograph courtesy of William B. Love.

COLORADO

ENDANGERED, THREATENED, AND SPECIAL CONCERN SPECIES

Endangered and threatened animal species in Colorado are legally protected through the State's Nongame, Endangered, or Threatened Species Conservation Act, as specified in title 33 of Colorado's revised Statutes (reference: CRS 33-2-101 to 33-2-114). This legislation prohibits the harassment, taking, or possession of any listed species without a permit issued by the Colorado Division of Wildlife.

The following amphibian species are included in Colorado's current (November 1993) list of endangered and threatened wildlife, as specified in the regulations of the Colorado Wildlife Commission (reference: CWCR 10-II-1002 and 10-III-1003). As stated above, permits are required for all activities involving these species.

Species	Common Name	Status
Bufo boreas boreas	Boreal Toad	Endangered
Rana sylvatica	Wood Frog	Threatened

Protected Species Permit Information

Scientific collecting licenses are issued for legitimate research purposes to qualified institutions and individuals. Special purposes licenses allow for the possession of state threatened or endangered species for zoological, educational, or propagation purposes. Permits allowing for the possession of specimens of state threatened and endangered species legally obtained from outside of Colorado are also available. Applications, requirements, and more information on these permits may be obtained from the Colorado Division of Wildlife (address in Appendix I).

NATIVE WILDLIFE REGULATIONS

With the exception of Tiger Salamanders, *Ambystoma tigrinum*, Bullfrogs, *Rana catesbeiana*, and Snapping Turtles, *Chelydra serpentina*, all of Colorado's native amphibians and reptiles are classified as nongame species, and restrictions on their collection and possession are included among the nongame wildlife regulations of the Colorado Wildlife Commission (reference: CWCR 10). Restrictions on the collection and possession of Tiger Salamanders, Bullfrogs, and Snapping Turtles are specified in the Colorado Wildlife Commission's hunting and fishing regulations (reference: CWCR 1). The following is a summary of the restrictions on the non-commercial collection and possession of amphibians and reptiles wild caught within Colorado.

Unless otherwise specified, six of each species of amphibian and reptile may be collected and maintained in captivity (CWCR 10-I-1000A-6).

A valid fishing license is required to collect amphibians for personal use (CWCR 1-I-105A-1).

Salamanders

Ambystoma tigrinum, Tiger Salamanders may be taken throughout the year. The daily bag and possession limit for larval specimens (five inches or less in length) is 20. The possession limit for terrestrial adult Tiger Salamanders is six. Larval salamanders may be taken by the following methods: fishing, hand, traps, seines, or nets. A fishing license is required (CWCR 1-IV-111).

Frogs

Rana catesbeiana, Bullfrogs may be taken throughout the year with a daily bag and possession limit of 10 frogs. A valid Colorado fishing license is required. Bullfrogs may be taken by the following methods: fishing, archery, hand, gig, or net. The use of artificial light is permitted (CWCR 1-IV-110).

Turtles

Chelydra serpentina, Snapping Turtles may be taken in unlimited numbers and maintained alive. A valid fishing license may be required to take snapping turtles (CWCR 1-XI-015B).

Snakes

The following snake species may not be collected from the wild in Colorado (CWCR 10-I-1000-6c and 6d).

Crotalus viridis concolor	Midget Faded Rattlesnake
Sistrurus catenatus	Massasauga

* Does not prohibit the possession of specimens legally acquired outside of Colorado, proper documentation of legal acquisition is required. Importation and possession permits are also required (see Importation and Commercial Trade Regulations).

License and Permit Information

Fishing licenses may be obtained from sporting goods stores, bait shops, and other retail outlets at an annual fee of $20.25 for residents and $40.25 for non-residents. One day non-resident fishing licenses at a cost of $5.25 and five day non-resident licenses at a cost of $18.25 are also available. Scientific collecting licenses, required to capture or possess Midget Faded Rattlesnakes or Massasaugas wild caught within the state, are available from the Colorado Division of Wildlife (address in Appendix I).

IMPORTATION AND COMMERCIAL TRADE REGULATIONS

Restrictions on the importation, sale, and possession of both native and non-native amphibians and reptiles are included among the wildlife legislation of Colorado's Revised Statutes (reference: CRS) and among the regulations of the Colorado Wildlife Commission (reference: CWCR). In general, these statutes and regulations prohibit the sale without permit of virtually all amphibian and reptile species native to Colorado, including specimens legally obtained from outside the state. Importation permits are required to import both native and non-native amphibians and reptiles into the state as well, and all wildlife shipments entering Colorado are subject to state veterinary health certification requirements. In addition, the possession of a wide variety of non-native amphibians and reptiles is also expressly prohibited without permit. The following is a summarization of these statutes and regulations.

Native Species

The sale of native amphibian and reptile species wild caught in the state of Colorado is prohibited, except as otherwise specified by regulation (CRS 33-6-113).

Salamanders

Ambystoma tigrinum, Tiger Salamander larvae harvested within Colorado may be sold under the authority of a commercial fishing license. Statewide bag limits apply (see Native Wildlife Regulations). The sale of wild caught adult Tiger Salamanders is prohibited (CWCR 1-I-105A 2 and 1-I-105B 4).

* The sale of other lawfully acquired specimens of *Ambystoma tigrinum* is also permitted (see Native and Exotic Species below).

Frogs

Rana catesbeiana, Bullfrogs may be harvested and sold. Statewide bag limits apply (see Native Wildlife Regulations) and a valid commercial fishing license is required (CWCR 1-I-105A 2 and 1-I-105B 4).

Native and Exotic Species

The transportation within the state or the export from Colorado of any wildlife is prohibited, unless otherwise specified (CRS 33-6-114-1).

Importation licenses and valid health certification is required to import any wildlife into Colorado unless otherwise specified (CRS 33-6-114-2).

Detrimental Wildlife

Wildlife determined to be detrimental to existing native wildlife and their habitat may not be released, transported, imported, sold, bartered, traded, or possessed in Colorado without permit. Detrimental wildlife species may be transported out of Colorado in accordance with state and federal regulations). The following amphibian is included in Colorado's current (November 1995) list of detrimental terrestrial wildlife species (CWCR 11-VIII-008B):

Rana clamitans	Green Frog

Unregulated Wildlife

Animals designated as unregulated wildlife may be sold, bartered, traded, transferred, possessed, propagated and transported in Colorado without license. Importation permits are apparently still required to import unregulated species, however, and all state health certification requirements also apply. The following amphibian and reptile orders, families, and species are included in Colorado's current (May 1995) list of unregulated wildlife and no license is required for their possession, propagation, or sale. Licenses are required to possess, propagate or sell any species not specifically included in the following list, including native amphibians and reptiles legally obtained from outside the state (CWCR 11-II-1103B).

Gymnophiona	Caecilians
Urodela	Salamanders and Newts
Ambystoma tigrinum [1]	Tiger Salamander

All Tropical and subtropical frogs and toads in the families:

Atelopodidae [2]	Stub-footed Toads
Bufonidae	True Toads
Centrolenidae	Glass Frogs
Dendrobatidae	Poison dart Frogs
Hylidae	Treefrogs
Leptodactylidae	Tropical Frogs
Microhylidae	Narrow-mouthed Toads
Pelobatidae	Spadefoot Toads
Pelodytidae	Parsley Frogs [3]
Phrynomeridae [2]	Snake-necked Frogs
Pipidae	Surinam Toads and Clawed Frogs
Pseudidae	Harlequin Frogs
Ranidae	True Frogs
Rhacophoridae	Flying Frogs
Rhinophrynidae	Cone-nosed Frogs
Bombina orientalis	Oriental Fire-bellied Toad
Rana pipiens [1]	Leopard Frog

Caimans [4]   Caimans

All tropical and subtropical turtles in the following families:
  Carettochelyidae New Guinea Softshell Turtles
  Dermatemyidae   Central American River Turtles
  Kinosternidae   Mud and Musk Turtles
  Testudinidae   Tortoises
  Trionychidae   Softshell Turtles
  Trachemys scripta Red-eared Slider

  Amphisbaenia   Worm Lizards

All tropical and subtropical lizards in the Suborder Sauria, including but not limited to the following families:
  Agamidae   Agamids
  Anelytropsidae [2] Snake Lizards
  Anguidae   Glass and Alligator Lizards
  Chamaeleonidae   True Chameleons
  Cordylidae   Girdle-tailed Lizards
  Corytophanidae [2] Casquehead Lizards
  Crotaphytidae [2] Collared and Leopard Lizards
  Dibamidae   Blind Lizards
  Eublepharidae [2] Eyelid Geckos
  Feyliniidae [2]   African Snake Skinks
  Gekkonidae   Geckos
  Helodermatidae   Gila Monster and Beaded Lizards
  Iguanidae   Iguanids
  Lacertidae   Wall Lizards
  Lanthanotidae [2] Earless Monitor
  Phrynosomatidae [2] Horned Lizards
  Polychridae [2]   Anoles
  Pygopodidae [2] Australian Snake Lizards
  Scincidae   Skinks
  Teiidae   Whiptails
  Tropiduridae [2]   Neotropical Ground Lizards
  Varanidae   Monitor Lizards
  Xantusiidae   Night Lizards
  Xenosauridae   Knob-scaled Lizards

All non-native snakes in the families:
  Acrochordidae   File Snakes
  Aniliidae   Pipe Snakes
  Boidae [5]   Boas and Pythons
  Colubridae   Modern Snakes (except venomous species)
  Uropeltidae   Shield-tailed Snakes
  Xenopeltidae   Sunbeam Snakes

---

[1] Acquired from lawful out-of-state source or instate commercial producer. There are currently no instate commercial producers of this species within Colorado.
[2] Problematical taxonomic designation, may or may not constitute an actual family.
[3] Listed as Spadefoot Toads by Colorado.
[4] No genera specified by Colorado.
[5] Listed as Bolidae and Giant Snakes by Colorado.

License and Permit Information

Importation permits or importation permit numbers must be obtained from the Colorado State Veterinarians Office prior to the importation of any wildlife for which these permits are required. Veterinary health certification must accompany each shipment of imported live wildlife and this certification is obtained from an accredited veterinarian in the state or country from which the wildlife shipment originates. Further information on importation permits and health certification, and importation permit applications may be obtained from the Colorado State Veterinarians Office (address in Appendix I). Licenses authorizing the possession and public exhibition, but not the propagation or sale, of non-exempt or prohibited wildlife species include Wildlife Exhibitors Park and Zoological Park licenses. The propagation and sale of non-exempt wildlife requires a Wildlife Producers Park license. The fee for each of these three licenses is $100 annually. Licenses applications and further information on license requirements may be obtained from the Colorado Division of Wildlife (address in Appendix I).

CAPTIVE MAINTENANCE REGULATIONS

In addition to the restrictions on the possession of amphibians and reptiles included among the previous regulations, the following summarized statute is applicable to the captive maintenance of these animals.

It is unlawful to release, or knowingly allow the escape of, any native or non-native species of wildlife in Colorado without permit (CRS 33-6-114-2).

Captive Maintenance Regulations Review

The following is a brief review of Colorado's restrictions on the captive possession of both native and non-native amphibians and reptiles.

a. Permits are required to possess state threatened and endangered species.

b. Unless otherwise specified, six of each native species wild caught in Colorado may be possessed without permit. Specimens in excess of state possession limits must be legally acquired outside of Colorado. Proper documentation is required.

c. *Ambystoma tigrinum*, Tiger Salamander larvae (five inches or less in length) have a possession limit of 20 specimens. A valid fishing license is required.

d. *Rana catesbeiana*, Bullfrog possession limit is 10 specimens. A valid fishing license is required.

e. *Chelydra serpentina*, Snapping Turtles may be possessed in unlimited numbers. A fishing license may be required.

f. A license is required to possess the following snake species, including specimens legally obtained outside of Colorado:

Crotalus viridis concolor	Midget Faded Rattlesnake
Sistrurus catenatus	Massasauga

g. Licenses are required to possess any non-native amphibian or reptile not included on Colorado's list of unregulated wildlife.

CONNECTICUT

ENDANGERED, THREATENED, AND SPECIAL CONCERN SPECIES

Connecticut lists various species of the state's herpetofauna as either endangered, threatened, or as species of special concern. Although species of special concern are included in the list of Connecticut's endangered and threatened wildlife, special concern species receive no official protection by the state's endangered species legislation. Only species designated as endangered or threatened are legally protected by the Connecticut Endangered Species Act, as specified in chapter 495 of Connecticut General Statutes (reference: CTGS 495 89-224). Established in 1989, this law is similar in concept to the U.S. Endangered Species Act and contains provisions for the protection of all federally listed endangered and threatened species. In addition to state listed threatened and endangered species, Connecticut also prohibits the collection and possession of all specimens of the Wood Turtle, *Clemmys insculpta*, through a variety of separate but related regulations.

The following species are the amphibians and reptiles which are currently (1993) officially protected by Connecticut's Endangered Species Act, or are otherwise fully protected by law. A scientific collection permit or a special purposes permit is required for all activities involving these species. In addition to the permits required by the State of Connecticut, U.S. Endangered Species permits are required for several animals in the following list (see U.S. Endangered and Threatened Species).

Species	Common Name	Status
Ambystoma laterale [1]	Blue-spotted Salamander	Threatened
Gyrinophilus porphyriticus	Northern Spring Salamander	Threatened
Plethodon glutinosus	Slimy Salamander	Threatened
Scaphiopus holbrookii	Eastern Spadefoot Toad	Endangered
Caretta caretta	Loggerhead Sea Turtle	Threatened
Chelonia mydas	Green Sea Turtle	Threatened
Clemmys insculpta [2]	Wood Turtle	Protected
Clemmys muhlenbergii	Bog Turtle	Endangered
Dermochelys coriacea	Leatherback Sea Turtle	Endangered
Lepidochelys kempii	Atlantic Ridley Sea Turtle	Endangered
Eumeces fasciatus	Five-lined Skink	Threatened
Crotalus horridus	Timber Rattlesnake	Endangered

[1] Diploid populations only, other species, subspecies, and hybrids of the *jeffersonianum/laterale* complex are listed as Special Concern Species and their collection from the wild is prohibited (see Native Wildlife Regulations).
[2] See Native Wildlife Regulations, Importation and Commercial Trade Regulations, and Captive Maintenance Regulations.

* Connecticut is currently revising the state's list of endangered and threatened species. When this revision will be complete is uncertain at this time.

Protected Species Permit Information

Scientific collection permits will be issued at a cost of $10.00 to qualified institutions or individuals for purposes of legitimate research or for the salvage of usable dead specimens. Special purposes permits allowing for the importation and possession of legally obtained protected species for educational purposes are also issued on occasion. Applications for both these permits may be obtained from the Wildlife Division of the Connecticut Department of Environmental Protection (address in Appendix I).

NATIVE WILDLIFE REGULATIONS

Restrictions on the non-commercial collection and possession of wild caught native amphibians and reptiles not protected by Connecticut's endangered species legislation are specified in chapter 490, section 26, of Connecticut's General Statutes (reference: CTGS 490-26). The following is a summarization of these regulations.

The hunting of amphibians and reptiles is prohibited except as authorized (CTGS 490 26-70).

Salamanders
The following salamanders, in any developmental stage, may not be taken at any time (CTGS 490 26-66 13A).

Ambystoma jeffersonianum	Jefferson's Salamander
Ambystoma tremblayi [1]	Tremblay's Salamander
Ambystoma platineum [1]	Silvery Salamander

[1] Not listed in Collins (1997). Currently considered hybrid members of the *Ambystoma jeffersonianum/laterale* complex.

The following salamanders (adult only) may be taken by hand or hand-held implement, from May 1 through August 31. There is a daily and seasonal bag limit of three of each species. The use of seine nets is prohibited (CTGS 490 26-66-13B):

Ambystoma maculatum	Spotted Salamander
Ambystoma opacum	Marbled Salamander

Notophthalmus viridescens, Red-spotted Newts adults may be taken by hand or hand-held implement throughout the year. There is no daily or seasonal bag limit. The use of seine nets and minnow traps is prohibited (CTGS 490 26-66-13C).

*The collection of eggs and juveniles of all salamanders is prohibited in Connecticut.

Frogs
Rana pipiens, Northern Leopard Frogs adults may be taken by hand or hand-held implement throughout the year. There is no daily or seasonal bag limit. The use of seine nets and head lamps is prohibited (CTGS 490 26-66-13D).

Turtles
Clemmys insculpta, Wood Turtles may not be collected at any time in any developmental stage (CTGS 490 26-66-14A).

Terrapene carolina, Eastern Box Turtles adults may be taken from July 1 through August 31. Box Turtles may only be collected by hand or hand-held implement. The daily and seasonal bag limit is one specimen. Box turtle eggs or juveniles may not be collected at any time (CTGS 490 26-66-14B).

Malaclemys terrapin, Diamondback Terrapins may be taken from August 1 through April 30. Only specimens having a straight line carapace length between four and seven inches inclusive may be collected. Diamondback Terrapins may be taken by hand, dip net, seine net, or traps that insure the turtles are captured alive. The possession limit is five. Eggs may not be taken at any time (CTGS 490 26-66-14D).

Snakes
Elaphe obsoleta obsoleta, Black Rat Snakes may be taken by hand or hand-held implement from May 1 through August 31. The daily and seasonal bag limit is one specimen. Eggs may not be collected at any time (CTGS 490 26-66-14C).

License and Permit Information
Apparently a hunting or fishing license is not required to collect unprotected amphibians and reptiles in Connecticut.

IMPORTATION AND COMMERCIAL TRADE REGULATIONS

Restrictions on the importation, exportation, transportation, and sale of native and exotic species are also included in chapter 490, section 26 of the Connecticut General Statutes (reference: CTGS 490 26). The following is a brief review of these regulations.

Native Species
The sale of native amphibians and reptiles taken from the wild in Connecticut is prohibited (CTGS 490 26-78).

* *Chelydra serpentina*, Snapping Turtles are exempt from this regulation.

Transportation within the state or transportation out of the state of any native amphibian or reptile for which there is a closed season is prohibited, except by permit (CTGS 490 26-57).

Native and Exotic Species
A permit is required for the importation and possession of amphibians and reptiles. This restriction apparently applies to imported specimens of native species legally obtained from outside of Connecticut, as well as to exotic species (CTGS 490 26-55).

Permitted Species
The Department of Environmental Protection maintains a list of amphibians and reptiles which may be imported by the above permit. With the exception of all crocodilians, venomous lizards, and venomous snakes, virtually every species normally offered for sale appears on this list. Giant boids and large monitor lizards are included and may be imported. Special permits are required for any species not specifically included in the following list.

Species	Common Name
Ambystoma tigrinum	Tiger Salamander
Ambystoma tigrinum	Waterdogs
Amphiuma tridactylum	Congo Eel
Batrachoseps sp.	Oregon Newt
Cynops pyrrhogaster	Firebelly Newt
Necturus maculosus	Mudpuppy
Notophthalmus	Common Newt
Notophthalmus viridescans	Eastern Newt
Gymnopis multiplicata	Caecilian Worm
Afrixaluss spp.	Clown Treefrog
Bombina orientalis	Firebelly Toad
Bufo sp.	Lemon Toad
Bufo terrestris or *marina* [1]	Common Toad
Ceratophrys ornata or *cranwelli*	Argentine Horned Frog
Hyla avivoca	Bird-voiced Treefrog
Hyla cinerea	Green Treefrog
Hyla gratiosa	Barking Treefrog
Hyla vasta	Giant Treefrog
Hyla sp.	Philippine Treefrog
Hyla sp.	Red-eyed Treefrog
Hymenochirus curtipes	Dwarf African Clawed Frog

Litoria caerulea [2]	White's Treefrog
Litoria infrafrenata	White-lipped Treefrog
Osteopilus septentrionalis	Cuban Treefrog
Phrynomantis bifasciata [3]	Red and Black Walking Frog
Pyxicephalus adspersis	Pixie Frog
Rana catesbeiana	Frog Tadpole (Bullfrog)
Rana clamitans clamitans	Bronze Frog
Rana pipiens	Leopard Frog
Xenopus laevis	African Clawed Frog
Chelus fimbriata	Mata Mata
Chelydra serpentina	Common Snapping Turtle
Chinemys reevesii	Reeve's Turtle
Chrysemys picta	Painted Turtle
Clemmys guttata	Spotted Turtle
Clemmys insculpta	American Wood Turtle
Cuora amboinensis	Asian Box Turtle
Cuora trifasciata	Chinese Box Turtle
Cyclemys mouhotii [4]	Jagged Shell Turtle
Deirochelys reticularia	Chicken Turtle
Geochelone chilensis	Red Foot Tortoise
Geochelone denticulata	Yellow Foot Tortoise
Geochelone elegans	Star Tortoise
Geochelone pardalis	Leopard Tortoise
Geomyda spengleri	Vietnamese Wood Turtle
Graptemys geographica	Map Turtle
Kinixys belliana	Bell's Hingeback Tortoise
Kinosternon subrubrum	Mud Turtle
Malaclemys terrapin	Diamondback Terrapin
Peltocephalus tracaxa [5]	African Sideneck Turtle
Platysternon megacephalum	Chinese Bighead Turtle
Pseudemys concinna	River Cooter
Pseudemys rubriventris	Redbelly Turtle
Rhinoclemmys punctalaria [6]	South American Wood Turtle
Sternotherus odoratus	Common Musk Turtle
Terrapene carolina maior	Gulf Coast Box Turtle
Terrapene ornata	Ornate Box Turtle
Trachemys scripta elegans [7]	Red-eared Slider
Trionyx sp.	Florida Softshell Turtle
Ablepharus sp.	Oscillated Skink
Acanthosaura mormorata [4]	Mountain Horned Agama
Agama nupta [4]	Red Head Agama
Agama sp.	Dwarf Agama
Agama sp.	Toad Headed Agama
Ameiva ameiva	Green Ameiva
Ameiva sp.	Rainbow Ameiva
Anolis carolinensis	American Anole
Anolis equestris	Knight Anole
Anolis roquet	Blue Anole
Anolis sagrei	Bahamian Anole
Anolis sp.	Crested Anole
Basiliscus plumifrons	Green Basilisk

CT

Basiliscus vittatus	Brown Basilisk
Callisaurus	Zebratail Lizard
Callopistes maculatus	Dwarf Tegu
Calotes emma	Bloodsucker
Calotes sp.	Green Calote
Chamaeleo calyptratus	Veiled Chameleon
Chamaeleo dilepis	Flapneck Chameleon
Chamaeleo gracilis	Gracillis Chameleon
Chamaeleo jacksonii	Jackson's Chameleon
Chamaeleo johnstoni	Johnson's Chameleon
Chameleo melleri	Giant Chameleon
Chamaeleo pardalis	Panther Chameleon
Chamaeleo parsonii	Parson's Chameleon
Chamaeleo senegalensis	Senegal Chameleon
Cnemidophorus tesselatus	Checkered Whiptail
Coleonyx variegatus	Banded Gecko
Cordylus jonesii [4]	Jone's Armadillo Lizard
Corucia zebrata	Prehensile Tail Skink
Corytophanes cristatus	Forest Chameleon
Crotaphytus collaris	Collared Lizard
Ctenosaura similis	Spiny Iguana
Dasia dasia [4]	Green Dasia
Dipsosaurus	Desert Iguana
Draco spp.	Flying Dragon
Eublepharis macularius	Leopard Gecko
Eumeces	Blue Tail Skink
Eumeces fasciatus	Five-lined Skink
Eumeces laticeps	Broadhead Skink
Eumeces obsoletus [8]	Great Plains Skink
Eumeces schneideri	Schneider's Skink
Eumeces sp.	Yellow-sided Skink
Gambelia wislizenii	Leopard Lizard
Gekko gecko	Tokay Gecko
Gerrhosaurus mason [4]	Plated Lizard
Gerrhosaurus flavigularis [9]	Yellow-throated Plated lizard
Hemidactylus brookii	Brook's Gecko
Hemidactylus sp.	Crocodile Gecko
Hemidactylus sp.	White-spotted Gecko
Hemidactylus sp.	Zebra Throat Gecko
Hemidactylus sp.	Mediterranean Gecko
Hemidactylus sp.	House Gecko
Hemitheconyx caudicinctus [10]	Fat-tailed Gecko
Hydrosaurus weberi [11]	Sailfin Lizard
Iguana iguana	Green Iguana
Japalura sp.	Mountain Lizard
Lacerta muralis [4]	Wall Lizard
Lacerta viridis	Emerald Lacerta
Laemanctus iguanidae [4]	Casquehead Iguana
Leiocephalus carinatus	Curly Tail Lizard
Leiocephalus sp.	Peruvian Curly Tail Lizard
Leiolepis belliana	Butterfly Agama
Liolaemus alter [4]	Midnight Swift
Liolaemus bimaculatus [4]	Snow Swift

CT

Liolaemus chiliensis	Longtail Swift
Liolaemus kuhlmanni	Mutlicolor Swift
Liolaemus leopardinas	Leopard Swift
Liolaemus pictus	Pictus Swift
Liolaemus punctatisimus [4]	Jewel Swift
Liolaemus rufescens [4]	Firebelly Swift
Liolaemus sp.	Black-sided Swift
Liolaemus sp.	Black Throat Swift
Liolaemus sp.	Copper-sided Swift
Liolaemus sp.	Monticola Swift
Liolaemus sp.	Orange Belly Swift
Liolaemus sp.	Red Back Swift
Liolaemus sp.	Rosey Swift
Liolaemus sp.	Salt and Pepper Swift
Liolaemus	Sunset Swift
Mabuya striata	Red-sided Skink
Ophisaurus spp.	Glass Lizard
Oplurus sp.	Clubtail Iguana
Pachydactlus bibronii	Bibron's Gecko
Phelsuma lineata	Lined Day Gecko
Phelsuma madagascariensis	Giant Day Gecko
Phelsuma quadriocellata	Spotted Day Gecko
Phrynosoma platyrhinos	Desert Horned Lizard
Physignathus cocincinus	Green Water Dragon
Physignathus sp.	Brown water Dragon
Plica umbra [12]	Green Tree Climber
Pogona barbata [13]	Bearded Dragon
Ptychzoon kuhli	Flying Gecko
Sauromalus obesus	Chuckwalla
Sauromalus sp.	Chilean Chuckwalla
Sceloporus clarkii	Clark's Spiny Lizard
Sceloporus magister	Desert Spiny Lizard
Sceloporus orcutti	Granite Spiny Lizard
Sceloporus poinsettii	Blue Spiny Lizard
Scincopus fasciatus	Sandfish
Scincus spp.	Sand Skink
Tiliqua	Blue Tongue Skink
Tropidurus torguatus	Collared Swift
Tropidurus sp.	Velvet Collared Swift
Tupinambis nigropunctatus	Black and White Tegu
Tupinambis tequixin	Gold Tegu
Uranoscodon supercillus	Mophead Iguana
Uromastyx aegypticus	Uromastyx
Varanus dumerilli	Dumerill's Monitor
Varanus exanthematicus	Savanna Monitor
Varanus indicus	Indo-pacific Monitor
Varanus kordensis [4]	Tree Monitor
Varanus niloticus	Nile Monitor
Varanus rudicollis	Roughneck Monitor
Varanus salvator	Water Monitor

CT

Acrantophis dumerili	Dumeril's Boa
Arizona elegans spp.	Glossy Snake
Boa constrictor spp.	Boa Constrictor
Bogertophis subocularis [14]	Trans Pecos Ratsnake
Candoia carinata paulsoni	Solomon Island Ground Boa
Carphophis amoenus	Worm Snake
Cemophora coccinea	Scarlet Snake
Charina bottae	Rubber Boa
Chionactis occipitalis spp.	Western Shovel-nosed Snake
Chondropython viridis	Green Tree Python
Clonophis kirtlandii	Kirtland's Snake
Coluber constrictor spp.	Racer
Contia tenuis	Sharp-tailed Snake
Corallus caninus	Emerald Tree Boa
Corallus enydris spp.	Tree Boa
Diadophis punctatus spp.	Ringneck Snake
Drymobius margaritiferus	Speckled Racer
Elaphe bimaculata	Chinese Twin-spotted Rat Snake
Elaphe carinata	Chinese King Rat snake
Elaphe climacophora spp.	Japanese Green Rat Snake
Elaphe dione	Steppe Rat Snake
Elaphe flavirufa	Central American Rat Snake
Elaphe guttata spp.	Corn Snake
Elaphe helenae	Trinket Snake
Elaphe mandarinus	Mandarin Rat Snake
Elaphe moellendorffi	100 Flower Snake
Elaphe obsoleta spp.	Common Rat Snake
Elaphe quatuorlineata quatuorlineata	Four-lined Rat Snake
Elaphe quatuorlineata sauromates	Bulgarian Blotched Rat Snake
Elaphe schrenckii anomola [15]	Korean Rat Snake
Elaphe schrenckii schrenckii [15]	Russian Rat Snake
Elaphe taeniura spp.	Tawian Beauty Snake
Elaphe tinorei [4]	Black Tail Rat Snake
Elaphe triaspis	Green Rat Snake
Elaphe vulpina	Fox Snake
Epicrates cenchria spp.	Rainbow Boa
Epicrates striatus	Haitian Boa
Eryx spp.	Sand Boa
Eunectes murinus	Green Anaconda
Eunectes notaeus	Yellow Anaconda
Farancia abacura	Mud Snake
Farancia erytrogramma	Rainbow Snake
Gonyosoma oxycephalum	Red-tailed Green Rat Snake
Heterodon nasicus spp.	Western Hognose Snake
Heterodon platirhinos	Eastern Hognose Snake
Heterodon simus	Southern Hognose Snake
Lampropeltis alterna	Gray-banded Kingsnake
Lampropeltis calligaster spp.	Prairie Kingsnake
Lampropeltis getula spp. [16]	Common Kingsnake
Lampropeltis mexicana spp.	San Luis Potosi Kingsnake
Lampropeltis pyromelana ssp.	Sonoran Mountain Kingsnake
Lampropeltis ruthveni	Ruthven's Kingsnake
Lampropeltis triangulum ssp.	Milk Snake

CT

Lampropeltis zonata spp.	California Mountain Kingsnake
Lamprophis fuliginosus spp.	African House Snake
Leptodeira septentrionalis spp.	Cat-eyed Snake
Leptotyphlops dulcis spp.	Texas Blind Snake
Leptotyphlops humilis spp.	Western Blind Snake
Liasis albertisii	White-lipped Python
Liasis mackloti	Macklot's Python
Lichanura trivirgata spp.	Rosy Boa
Liochlorophis vernalis [17]	Smooth Green Snake
Masticophis flagellum spp.	Coachwhip
Morelia amethistina	Amethystine Python
Morelia spilota spp.	Carpet Python
Nerodia spp.	American Water Snakes
Opheodrys aestivus	Rough Green Snake
Phyllorhynchus spp.	Leaf-nosed Snake
Pituophis melanoleucus spp. [18]	Pine/Bull/Gopher Snakes
Python curtus spp.	Blood Python
Python molurus bivittatus	Burmese Python
Python regius	Ball Python
Python reticulatus	Reticulated Python
Python sebae	African Rock Python
Regina spp.	Crawfish/Queen Snake
Rhadinaea flavilata	Pine Woods Snake
Rhinocheilus lecontei spp.	Long-nosed Snake
Salvadora spp.	Patch-nosed Snake
Seminatrix pygaea spp. [19]	Swamp Snake
Sonora semiannulata	Ground Snake
Spalerosophis diadema spp.	Egyptian Rat Snake
Spalerosophis diadema spp.	Royal Diadem Rat Snake
Spilotes pullatus	Tiger Rat Snake
Storeria dekayi spp.	Brown Snake
Storeria occipitomaculata spp.	Redbelly Snake
Tantilla spp.	Crowned Snake
Thamnophis spp.	Garter/Ribbon Snake
Virginia spp.	Earth Snake

[1] *Bufo marina* is not listed in Frank and Ramus (1995).
[2] Listed as *Hyla caerulea* by Connecticut.
[3] Listed as *Phrynomenus bifasciata* by Connecticut.
[4] Not listed in Frank and Ramus (1995).
[5] The genus *Peltocephalus* is found in South America and is not an African Sideneck. Species *tracaxa* unknown.
[6] Listed as *Rhynoclemys punctalaria* by Connecticut.
[7] Listed as *Pseudemys scripta elegans* by Connecticut.
[8] Listed as *Eumeces gigas* by Connecticut.
[9] Listed as *Gerrhosaurus* and Yellow Stripe Plated Lizard by Connecticut.
[10] Listed as *Hemitheconyx hemichadinctus* by Connecticut.
[11] Listed as *Hydrosaurus niberi* by Connecticut.
[12] Listed as *Plica ambra* by Connecticut.
[13] Listed as *Pogana barbatus* by Connecticut.
[14] Listed as *Elaphe subocularis* by Connecticut.
[15] Listed as *Elaphe schrenki* by Connecticut.
[16] Listed as *Lampropeltis getulus* by Connecticut.
[17] Listed as *Opheodrys vernalis* spp. by Connecticut. No subspecies listed in Collins (1997).
[18] Includes *Pituophis melanoleucus* and *Pituophis catenifer*.
[19] Listed as *Seminatrix pigaea* by Connecticut.

CT

Special Turtle Regulations

Additional stipulations regulating the sale of live turtles within the State of Connecticut are specified in Public Act No. 94-29 (reference: CTPA 94-29) and in the regulations of the Connecticut Department of Public Health (reference: CTDPH 19a-36-A46). This legislation is included below.

CTPA 94-29

a) "Turtle" means any reptiles commonly known as turtles, tortoises, or terrapins but shall not include a turtle used solely for agricultural, scientific or educational purposes.

b) No turtle with a carapace length of less than 4 inches or viable turtle eggs may be sold in this state.

c) No person may sell a live turtle with a carapace length of 4" or greater unless;

(1) A caution notice must be posted by the seller which warns that the transmission of salmonella disease by turtles is possible.

(2) At the time of sale, the seller must furnish the buyer with a copy of the caution notice and information obtained from a veterinarian regarding the proper care and feeding of the species being sold.

(3) The buyer must sign a form stating that he has read the caution notice. If the buyer is less than 16 years of age, the form must be signed by a parent or guardian.

(4) The turtle to be sold must not be a species identified by the Commissioner of Environmental Protection as endangered, threatened or of special concern.

(5) The seller must receive and keep on file for inspection by the Commissioner of Agriculture, written verification that such turtle was bred at a licensed commercial fish farm or aquaculture facility and was not collected from the wild.

(6) If turtles are to be imported into Connecticut from another state, a permit must be obtained from the Department of Environmental Protection.

CTDPH 19a-36-A46

1. No live turtle shall be sold in Connecticut until examination in the laboratory of the State Department of Health of three specimens of water from the tank in which the turtle is kept, taken not less than 48 hours apart by a representative of either a local health department or state department of health, fails to show the presence of *Salmonella* organisms.

2. Should a single such examination show the presence of salmonella organisms, all turtles in the tank shall be destroyed.

3. Persons who import, purchase, sell, exchange, barter, give away or otherwise deal in turtles shall keep records of such transactions embodying information required by the State Department of Health for a minimum period of two years which records shall be open for inspection by a representative of the local director of health or the State Department of Health.

4. In any location where turtles are offered for sale the vendor shall post warnings which adequately inform the public that the transmission of salmonella disease by turtles is possible.

* As far as can be determined, both of the previous regulations are currently still in effect.

License and Permit Information

Information and applications for any required permits, including the importation and possession permit, can be obtained from the Connecticut Department of Environmental Protection (address in Appendix I).

CAPTIVE MAINTENANCE REGULATIONS

In addition to any restrictions included in the importation and possession permit regulation, Connecticut limits the possession of some species native to the state with the following summarized regulations.

No more than three specimens of each species of the following salamanders may be possessed at any time (CTGS 490 26-55-3):

Ambystoma maculatum	Spotted Salamander
Ambystoma opacum	Marbled Salamander

Clemmys insculpta, Wood Turtle may not be possessed at any time without permit (CTGS 490 26-55-3c).

* Connecticut has not yet developed permit criteria for the possession of Wood Turtles.

Terrapene carolina carolina, Eastern Box Turtles have a possession limit of one specimen at any time (CTGS 490 26-55-3).

Captive Maintenance Regulations Review

The following is a brief review of the restrictions on the captive maintenance of amphibians and reptiles included among Connecticut's regulations.

a. Permits are required to possess endangered and threatened species.
b. Possession without permit limited on certain native species of amphibians and reptiles.
c. *Clemmys insculpta*, Wood Turtle may not be possessed without permit.
d. Importation Permit required for non-native species.
e. Special Permit required for all crocodilian species.
e. Special Permit required for all venomous reptiles.

(b and c above see Captive Maintenance Regulations).
(d, e, and f above see Importation and Commercial Trade Regulations).

CT

DELAWARE

ENDANGERED, THREATENED, AND SPECIAL CONCERN SPECIES

Species designated as endangered and threatened by the Delaware Division of Fish and Wildlife are legally protected by the endangered species legislation included among the state's conservation statutes, as specified in title 7, chapter 6 of the Delaware Code (reference: DEC CS 7-6-601 to 604). As is the case with the endangered species laws of most states, Delaware's legislation also protects all species included in the U.S. list of threatened and endangered species.

The following species are the amphibians and reptiles included in the current (February 1994) list of threatened and endangered animals in Delaware. Permits are required for all activities involving these species. In addition to any required state permits, a permit issued by the U.S. Department of the Interior is required for activities involving any species included in the federal list of endangered and threatened species (see U.S. Endangered and Threatened Species).

Species	Common Name	Status
Ambystoma tigrinum	Tiger Salamander	Endangered
Hyla chrysoscelis	Cope's Gray Treefrog	Endangered
Hyla gratiosa	Barking Treefrog	Endangered
Caretta caretta	Loggerhead Sea Turtle	Threatened
Chelonia mydas	Green Sea Turtle	Threatened
Clemmys muhlenbergii	Bog Turtle	Endangered
Dermochelys coriacea	Leatherback Sea Turtle	Endangered
Eretmochelys imbricata	Hawksbill Sea Turtle	Endangered
Lepidochelys kempii	Atlantic Ridley Sea Turtle	Endangered

* The State of Delaware is currently in the process of revising their endangered and threatened species list. When this revision will be complete is uncertain at this time.

DE

Protected Species Permit Information

Permits authorizing the collection and/or possession of state listed endangered and threatened species may be issued for zoological, educational, scientific, or propagation purposes. Permits allowing for the importation and possession of specimens of protected amphibian and reptile species legally obtained outside of Delaware may also be issued. Further information on these permits may be obtained from the Delaware Department of Natural Resources and Environmental Control, Division of Fish and Wildlife (address in Appendix I).

NATIVE WILDLIFE REGULATIONS

Restrictions on the non-commercial collection and possession of native species of wildlife captured within Delaware are included among the conservation statutes of the Delaware Code (reference DEC CS) or in the Compiled Regulations of the Division of Fish and Wildlife, Delaware Department of Natural Resources and Environmental Control (reference: DE DFW CR). With the exception of the 3 species covered in the following summarized regulations, however, none of this legislation specifically regulates the collection and/or possession of amphibians and reptiles and any restrictions on the capture of these animals within the state must be "extracted" from among the general provisions of Delaware's wildlife law. Unfortunately, much of this environmental legislation is rather convoluted and vague, and Delaware's wildlife laws are easily among the more difficult to decipher in the country. For example, while the possession of any "protected wildlife" is clearly prohibited by statute (DEC CS 7-5-515), exactly which species are actually classified as "protected wildlife" is not adequately explained anywhere in the state's extensive wildlife legislation. As currently interpreted by Delaware's Division of Fish and Wildlife, "protected species" means those species listed as threatened and endangered or which are otherwise regulated by law (i.e. closed seasons, bag and possession limits, etc.). All other native amphibian and reptile species are considered "unprotected wildlife" and may be collected and possessed from private property (with landowner permission) without restrictions. As virtually everywhere in the United States, permits may be required to collect on certain lands administered by the state including Delaware State Parks, Game Refuges, and Fish Hatcheries. The following is a summarization of Delaware's restrictions affecting the non-commercial collection and possession of native amphibians and reptiles.

It is unlawful to needlessly destroy, break, or interfere with any nest, den, or lair of any animal protected by law, or to burn, bark, or in any way mutilate any tree, living or dead, stump or log, without the consent of the land owner or person in charge (DEC CS 7-7-706).

Frogs

Rana catesbeiana, Bullfrogs may be taken from May 1 to September 30. Frogs may be taken by hand, spear, gig, or hook. Hand held artificial lights may be legally used while hunting on foot. Daily bag limit is 24 frogs. Bullfrogs may be possessed alive after the close of the season for scientific or propagation purposes. A valid fishing or hunting license is required to collect frogs (DEC CS 7-7-792).

Turtles

Chelydra serpentina, Snapping Turtles may be taken from June 16 through May 14 of the following year. Minimum size requirement is eight inches in length, measured over the curvature of the carapace. Snappers may be taken by hand, gig, spear, or net. A valid hunting or fishing license is required (DE DFW CS 17.16).

Malaclemys terrapin, Diamondback Terrapins. It is unlawful to collect, destroy, or possess Diamondback Terrapin eggs harvested from the wild in Delaware. The use of dredges to take Diamondback Terrapins in the Indian River or Rehoboth Bay is prohibited. A valid hunting or fishing license is required to collect Terrapins. Nothing in these regulations shall prevent the raising of Diamondback Terrapins in private ponds. (DEC CS 7-7-781, 783, and 784).

Malaclemys terrapin, Diamondback Terrapin females may be taken from July 15 through October 1 (DE DFW CR 17.14).

* Delaware's legislature has recently repealed several portions of the state's Diamondback Terrapin regulations, including those sections establishing legal size limits for harvested specimens. The exact legal status of Diamondback Terrapin minimum size requirements, as well as any bag and/or possession restrictions regulating this species, within the State of Delaware is uncertain at this time.

License and Permit Information

Delaware fishing and hunting licenses are available from most bait and sporting goods stores. Annual fishing license fees are $8.50 for residents and $15.00 for non-residents. Non-resident seven-day fishing licenses are also available for a $5.20 fee. Hunting license costs are $12.50 for residents and $45.00 for non-residents. Non-resident licenses limited to three days are also available for a $15.00 fee. Information on collection permits for lands administered by the state may be obtained from the Delaware Department of Natural Resources and Environmental Control (address in Appendix I).

DE

IMPORTATION AND COMMERCIAL TRADE REGULATIONS

Native Species

Although not specifically included among the wildlife laws of Delaware, the sale of unprotected native amphibian and reptile species, whether wild caught or imported, is apparently not restricted. Portions of the legislation governing the harvest of Bullfrogs, *Rana catesbeiana*, Snapping Turtles, *Chelydra serpentina*, and Diamondback Terrapins, *Malaclemys terrapin*, specifically contain provisions allowing for the sale of those species. Naturally, the sale of any specimens of the two turtles mentioned above are subject to the size limit requirements specified for each species (see Native Wildlife Regulations). For the sake of completeness, those portions of Delaware's regulations pertaining to the sale of the previously mentioned species are summarized below.

Rana catesbeiana, Bullfrogs lawfully taken or killed may be bought, sold and possessed without limit (DEC CS 7-7-793).

Chelydra serpentina, Snapping Turtles may be purchased and sold during the lawful open season (DEC CS 7-7-715).

Malaclemys terrapin, Diamondback Terrapins lawfully taken and of legal size may be purchased and sold at any time (DEC CS 7-7-715).

Exotic Species

Restrictions on the importation, possession, and sale of non-native reptiles are included among the rules and regulations of both the Delaware Department of Natural Resources and Environmental Control and the Delaware Department of Agriculture. Department of Agriculture animal importation restrictions are specified in the agricultural statutes in title 3, chapter 72 of the Delaware Code (reference: DEC AS 3-72). The following is a brief summary of these regulations.

Alligators, crocodiles, or caimans, including raw and manufactured skins and bodies or body parts may not be sold or offered for sale within Delaware (DEC CS 7-6-601).

The importation, possession, sale, or exhibition of any live reptile not native to Delaware without a permit is prohibited. The Delaware Department of Agriculture may exempt from permit requirements those species that do not represent a significant threat to community interests (DEC AS 3-72-7201).

* Does not prohibit the importation, possession, or sale of non-native amphibian species.

Exempt Species

As of June 2, 1994, the Delaware Department of Agriculture considers the following reptiles to be exempt from the permit requirements of the preceding regulation. Except for corrections to obviously misspelled names, the following list of reptiles which do not require permits is reproduced here exactly as provided by the Delaware Department of Agriculture:

> Chameleons
> Geckos
> Swifts
> Iguanas
> Agamas
> Ameivas
> Skinks

* The complete text of rules and requirements promulgated under the authority of the above legislation, which also regulates the importation, possession, and sale of exotic mammals, is over seven pages in length.

License and Permit Information

There are two types of exotic species permits issued by the Delaware Department of Agriculture; individual permits and class permits. Individual permits are required for each animal maintained for pet purposes. Captive produced offspring of already permitted animals are exempt from individual permit requirements for a period of three months. Class permits (i.e., reptiles, primates, etc.) are issued to individuals and institutions possessing non-native species for resale, exhibition, or research purposes. Further information on permit requirements and permit applications may be obtained from the Delaware Department of Agriculture (address in Appendix I).

CAPTIVE MAINTENANCE REGULATIONS

Restrictions on the possession in captivity of amphibians and reptiles are included among the regulations of the previous sections. In addition, several sections of the rules and regulations promulgated pursuant to the authority of the exotic species legislation of chapter 72, title 3 of the Delaware Code relate directly or indirectly to the captive maintenance of amphibians and reptiles. Those portions of these regulations of particular interest are included below in their entirety.

"Reptile" means any cold blooded vertebrate of the class Reptilia including turtles, lizards, snakes, crocodilians and the tuatara (DEC AS 3-72-2e).

There must be two enclosures to house a subject creature: a primary enclosure and a secondary enclosure. Fastening or locking devices shall be required on both the primary and the secondary enclosures and must be tamper proof from the general public. If the subject creature is a reptile, the requirement for a secondary enclosure may be waived if, in the opinion of the state veterinarian or his or her designee, the primary enclosure provides adequate protection for the general public (DEC AS 3-72-3.01).

The subject creature or creatures must be receiving proper care, humane treatment, and veterinary treatment, if required. The state veterinarian may consult with the local Society for the Protection* of Cruelty to Animals (the "S.P.C.A.") to enforce the provisions of this rule (DEC AS 3-72-3.02).

* The word "Prevention" should apparently replace "Protection".

The subject creature must not be a public nuisance. A nuisance will be considered as including, but not limited to, a subject creature which creates excessive odors or noise, displays obnoxious behavior, or causes justifiable fear (DEC AS 3-72-3.03).

Captive Maintenance Regulations Review

a. Permits are required to possess endangered and threatened species.
b. *Rana catesbeiana*, Bullfrogs may be possessed in unlimited numbers.
c. *Chelydra serpentina*, Common Snapping Turtle minimum size requirement of eight inches may apply to captive specimens.
d. Permits are required to possess any non-native reptile species not included in the exempt species list.

(b and d above see Importation and Commercial Trade Regulations).
(c above see Native Wildlife Regulations).

FLORIDA

ENDANGERED, THREATENED, AND SPECIAL CONCERN SPECIES

Florida lists various members of the state's native fauna as endangered, threatened, or as species of special concern. All species listed as endangered or threatened and several species listed as special concern are fully protected by the Florida Endangered Species Act of 1979, as specified in article IV of the Florida Statutes Annotated (reference: FS 9-372.072). Some special concern species, however, may be legally possessed in limited numbers without a permit (see Native Wildlife Regulations).

The following amphibians and reptiles are the species which are currently (July 1996) fully protected by law in Florida. Permits are required for all activities involving any of these species, including their possession.

Species	Common Name	Status
Haideotrition wallacei	Georgia Blind Salamander	Special Concern
Hyla andersonii	Pine Barrens Treefrog	Special Concern
Rana capito aesopus [1]	Florida Gopher Frog	Special Concern
Rana capito sevosa [2]	Dusky Gopher Frog	Special Concern
Rana okaloosae	Florida Bog Frog	Special Concern
Caretta caretta	Loggerhead Sea Turtle	Threatened
Chelonia mydas	Green Sea Turtle	Endangered
Dermochelys coriacea	Leatherback Sea Turtle	Endangered
Eretmochelys imbricata	Hawksbill Sea Turtle	Endangered
Gopherus polyphemus	Gopher Tortoise	Special Concern
Kinosternon baurii [3]	Striped Mud Turtle	Endangered
Lepidochelys kempii	Atlantic Ridley Sea Turtle	Endangered
Alligator mississippiensis [4]	American Alligator	Special Concern
Crocodylus acutus	American Crocodile	Endangered
Eumeces egregius egregius	Florida Keys Mole Skink	Special Concern
Eumeces egregius lividus	Bluetail Mole Skink	Threatened
Neoseps reynoldsi	Sand Skink	Threatened
Diadophis punctatus acricus	Key Ringneck Snake	Threatened
Drymarchon couperi [5]	Eastern Indigo Snake	Threatened
Elaphe guttata guttata [6]	Red Rat Snake	Special Concern
Nerodia clarkii taeniata [7]	Atlantic Salt Marsh Snake	Threatened
Stilosoma extenuatum	Short-tailed Snake	Threatened
Storeria dekayi victa [3]	Florida Brown Snake	Threatened
Tantilla oolitica	Rim Rock Crowned Snake	Threatened
Thamnophis sauritus sackenii [3]	Florida Ribbon Snake	Threatened

[1] Listed as *Rana areolata aesopus* by Florida.
[2] Listed as *Rana areolata sevosa* by Florida.
[3] Lower Florida Keys population only. Does not prohibit the collection and possession of specimens of this species legally acquired from other portions of the state or from outside of Florida.

[4] Although officially listed and protected as a special concern species, licenses allowing for various activities involving American Alligators, including limited hunting, are readily issued by the State of Florida (see Native Wildlife Regulations and Importation and Commercial Trade Regulations).
[5] Listed as *Drymarchon corais couperi* by Florida.
[6] No subspecies recognized in Collins (1997). Lower Florida Keys population only. Does not prohibit the collection and possession of specimens of this species legally acquired from other portions of the state or from outside of Florida.
[7] Listed as *Nerodia fasciata taeniata* by Florida.

Protected Species Permit Information

Permits allowing for the collection and possession of Florida's fully protected amphibian and reptile species are issued to qualified individuals and institutions for legitimate research and conservation purposes only. Permit applications for activities involving protected terrestrial and freshwater species may be obtained from the Florida Game and Fresh Water Commission (address in Appendix I). Marine wildlife is managed by the Florida Department of Environmental Protection, and permit requirements and applications for activities involving all sea turtle species may be obtained by writing that agency (address in Appendix I). Additionally, several of Florida's endangered and threatened species are also protected by the U.S. Endangered Species Act, and any required federal permits must be obtained before any state permits will be issued (see U.S. Endangered and Threatened Species).

NATIVE WILDLIFE REGULATIONS

Restrictions on the non-commercial collection and possession of native amphibian and reptile species wild caught in the state are included among the Game and Fresh Water Fish Commission legislation of Florida's Statutes (reference: FS) and the Florida Administrative Code (reference: FAC). Easily among the most comprehensive in the Nation, these statutes and regulations define legal seasons and method of take, as well as specific possession limits and permit requirements for a variety of species of Florida's herpetofauna. In addition to this more typical wildlife legislation, various other portions of Florida's environmental law address issues important to the successful long-term conservation of sea turtles. Administered by the Florida Department of Environmental Protection, these regulations have been specifically designed to minimize the detrimental effects of human activities to marine turtle habitats and nesting sites. The following is a summary of all these regulations.

The use of gasoline or other chemical or gaseous substances to drive wildlife from their retreats is prohibited (FAC 39-4.001-2).

Amphibians
Amphibians other than frogs may be taken throughout the year in any manner, unless otherwise specified (FAC 39-26.002-2).

Frogs
Frogs may be taken throughout the year by gig, club, blow gun, hook and line or manually. The use of firearms is permitted during daylight hours (FAC 39-26.002-1).

* A license is not required provided captured frogs are not sold.

Reptiles
Reptiles may be taken throughout the year in any manner unless otherwise prohibited (FAC 39-25.002-13).

FL

Turtles

Freshwater turtles may be taken by hand, baited hook, bow, dip net, turtle trap so designed as to allow any captured freshwater fish to escape, or by spearing during daylight hours only. The use of bucket traps, snares, or firearms is prohibited (FAC 39-25.002-8).

Pseudemys concinna, River Cooter may not be taken from April 15th to July 31st (FAC 39-25.0002-8).

The following freshwater turtles have a possession limit without permit of two of each species (FAC 39-25.002-8):

Graptemys barbouri [1]	Barbour's Map Turtle
Graptemys ernsti	Escambia River Map Turtle
Malaclemys terrapin	Diamondback Terrapin
Pseudemys concinna [2]	River Cooter
Sternotherus minor	Loggerhead Musk Turtle
Terrapene carolina	Box Turtle

[1] Listed as a Species of Special Concern by Florida.
[2] *Pseudemys concinna suwanniensis* listed as a Species of Special Concern by Florida.

Macrochelys temminckii, Alligator Snapping Turtles have a possession limit without permit of one specimen (FAC 39-25.002-8).

* Listed as *Macroclemys temminckii* by Florida. Listed as a Species of Special Concern by Florida.

Marine Turtle Protection Act

It is unlawful to take, possess, disturb, mutilate, destroy, cause to be destroyed, sell, offer to sell, transfer, molest, or harass any marine turtle, marine turtle nest, or eggs at any time. This includes any activity which actually kills or injures marine turtles, including habitat modification or degradation that significantly impairs essential marine turtle behavioral patterns such as breeding, feeding, or sheltering. Activities that affect marine turtles, marine turtle nests, or habitats are subject to Florida Department of Environmental Protection permit requirements and conditions. The Department of Environmental Protection may condition the nature, timing, and sequence of permitted shoreline construction activities, including beach restoration, beach renourishment, or inlet sand transfer projects, to provide protection to nesting marine turtles, marine turtle hatchlings, and their habitat. The approval of any such construction activities is dependent upon the implementation of an active Marine Turtle Nest Relocation and Monitoring Program when necessary. Marine turtle nest relocation programs shall be conducted in a manner that ensures successful hatching. Special consideration will be given to beach preservation and nourishment projects that restore the habitat of endangered marine turtle species (FS 370.12).

* The preceding legislation provides the statutory authority by which the Florida Department of Environmental Protection can regulate activities affecting sea turtles, including organized "beach walks" to observe the nesting and hatching of these animals.

Beach and Shore Preservation

Coastal structure and construction criteria, as well as permit conditions and requirements for beach restoration, renourishment, or other shoreline protection and maintenance projects, are specified in the Beach and Shore Preservation legislation in chapter 161 of Florida Statutes Annotated (reference: FS 161.053 to 161.61). While mainly concerned with the establishment of "coastal construction control lines" designed to protect Florida's beach-dune ecosystems and the prevention of beach erosion, consideration of the conservation needs of sea turtles is never-the-less evident throughout the 20 pages of this legislation. Included among the stipulations of this legislation is the general requirement that all permitted activities adhere to the provisions of Florida's Marine Turtle Protection Act. All shoreline armoring or other coastal structures must be located and designed in a manner which protects marine turtles. Permitted construction activities and finished structures must not cause measurable interference with marine turtles or their nesting sites, and the nature, timing, and sequence of permitted construction activities shall provide protection to nesting sea turtles, sea turtle hatchlings, and their habitat. The creation of a state-wide beach restoration management plan which must identify beach areas utilized by marine turtles and develop strategies to protect turtles, turtle nests, and nesting locations is also mandated by this legislation. In addition, state funding is available to help cover the cost of projects which enhance marine turtle propagation.

* The complete version of this legislation may be obtained from the Florida Department of Environmental Protection (Address in Appendix I).

Special Model Lighting Ordinance for the Protection of Marine Turtles

In an effort to protect nesting and hatchling marine turtles, the Florida Department of Environmental Protection has developed a list of recommendations on beachfront lighting designed to minimize any detrimental effects artificial illumination may have on the nesting success of these species. These recommendations are in the form of a Model Lighting Ordinance included in chapter 16 of the Florida Administrative Code (reference: FAC 16B-55). As the successful completion of the life-cycle stages of nesting and hatching is critical to the conservation of these species, these recommendations will hopefully be adopted in all areas where sea turtles come ashore to lay their eggs. The following is a summarized review of the Florida Department of Environmental Protection's recommendations on beachfront lighting.

1. Exterior artificial light fixtures shall be designed and positioned so that the point source of light or any reflective surface of the light is not directly visible from the beach, areas seaward of the frontal dune are not directly or indirectly illuminated, and areas seaward of the frontal dune are not cumulatively illuminated.
2. Exterior artificial light fixtures within direct line of sight of the beach are considered appropriately designed if they are completely shielded downlight only fixtures or recessed fixtures having non-insect attractive yellow bulbs of 50 watts or less and non-reflective interior surfaces. Other fixtures that have appropriate shields, louvers, or cut-off features may also be used if they are in compliance with the recommendations of number 1 above and are mounted as low in elevation as possible through the use of low-mounted wall fixtures, low bollards, and ground-level fixtures.
3. Floodlights, uplights, or spotlights for decorative and accent purposes which are directly visible from, or indirectly or cumulatively illuminate the beach shall not be used.
4. Exterior lights used for safety or security purposes shall be limited in number and configuration to the minimum required to achieve their role. The use of motion detector switches which turn on lights for the minimum duration possible are preferred.
5. Only low intensity lighting shall be used in parking areas within line of sight of the beach. Such lighting shall be set on a base which raises the source of light no higher than 48 inches off the ground and shall be positioned or shielded so that light is cast downward and the source of the light or any reflective surface of the fixture does not directly or indirectly illuminate the beach.
6. Parking areas and roadways shall be designed and located to prevent vehicular headlights from directly or indirectly illuminating the beach.
7. Vehicular, parking area, and roadway lighting shall be shielded from the beach through the use of ground-level barriers. Ground level barriers must not interfere with emergence of nesting or hatching marine turtles, or cause short or long term damage to the beach/dune ecosystem.
8. Tinted glass, film or other window treatments (e.g., blinds, curtains) shall be used to eliminate the negative affects of interior lighting emanating from doors and windows within direct line of sight of the beach.

FL

9. Appropriately shielded low pressure sodium lamps and fixtures shall be preferred for high-intensity lighting applications such as parking areas, roadways, security, and safety.
10. Temporary construction lighting shall be restricted to the minimum amount necessary during the turtle nesting and hatching season and shall incorporate all the standards of the above recommendations.
11. Beach campfires and bonfires shall be prohibited during the marine turtle nesting and hatching season.
12. Except for authorized emergency, law enforcement, or research purposes, all motorized vehicles shall not be operated on the beach during the marine turtle nesting and hatching season.

Crocodilians

Well over twenty pages of Florida's Fish and Wildlife statutes and regulations specifically address the harvest and possession of American Alligators, *Alligator mississippiensis*, wild caught in the state. The following is a brief summarization of some of these restrictions.

It is unlawful to kill, injure, capture, or possess, or to attempt to kill, injure, capture, or possess any alligator or other crocodilian or their eggs, unless authorized by the rules and permits of the Florida Game and Fresh Water Fish Commission (FS 372.663-1).

The intentional feeding or enticing with feed of any wild American Alligator, *Alligator mississippiensis*, or American Crocodile, *Crocodylus acutus*, is prohibited except as authorized (FS 372.667).

Alligator mississippiensis, American Alligator eggs and hatchlings may be harvested from the wild by licensed alligator farmers. Alligator individual egg or hatchling collection permits are also required (FAC 39-25.031).

Alligator mississippiensis, American Alligators over four feet in length may be harvested from the wild by licensed alligator trappers. Valid alligator harvest permits and alligator harvest tags are also required. Alligators may only be taken from 1/2 hour before sunset to 1/2 hour after sunrise during the September harvest period specified in the harvest permit. Alligators may be taken by bait wooden pegs less than two inches in length attached to a hand-held restraining line, hand-held snare, harpoon, gig, snatch hook, manually operated spears, spearguns, crossbow, and bow with projectiles attached to a restraining line. The use of baited hooks, gig-equipped bang sticks, and firearms is prohibited. Bang sticks may be used to take alligators attached to a restraining line. All harvested alligators shall be killed and tagged with an alligator harvest tag placed within six inches of the tail tip immediately upon capture (FAC 39-25.042).

Nuisance alligators may only be taken, possessed, or killed by licensed nuisance alligator trappers (FAC 39-25.003).

Snakes

Pituophis melanoleucus mugitus, Florida Pine Snakes have a possession limit without permit of one specimen. Amelanistic (= albino) specimens are exempt from this restriction (FAC 39-25.002-12).

* As currently interpreted by the Florida Game and Fresh Water Fish Commission, amelanistic specimens of the Florida Pine Snake may be possessed without limit. Normal color phase specimens of *Pituophis melanoleucus mugitus* are included in the state list of special concern species.

Venomous snakes, including species native to Florida, may not be possessed without a venomous reptile license or permit (FS 372.86).

Organized poisonous reptile hunts must be registered with the Florida Game and Fresh Water Fish Commission. Organized reptile hunt participants are exempt from licensing requirements during the duration of the organized hunt (FS 372.912).

License and Permit Information

Alligator farming licenses allowing for the harvest of alligator eggs and hatchlings are available to Florida residents for a $250 annual fee. Individual egg permits and hatchling tags are also required. There is a fee of $5 per egg permit, with a minimum purchase of 35 permits. Individual hatchling tags cost $15. Alligator trapping licenses are available at a fee of $250 for residents and $1,000 for non-residents. Further information and applications for these and the other required permits of this section may be obtained from the Florida Game and Fresh Water Fish Commission (address in Appendix I).

IMPORTATION AND COMMERCIAL TRADE REGULATIONS

Native Species

Restrictions on the sale of native amphibians and reptiles are included among the wildlife laws of Florida. The following is a summarization of these statutes and regulations.

Amphibian and reptile species native to Florida may not be sold without a license to possess live wildlife for exhibition or pubic sale unless otherwise specified (FS 372.921).

Frogs

A commercial fishing license is required to harvest frogs for sale in Florida. Native frog species legally obtained from outside Florida may be imported and sold under the authority of a freshwater fish dealers license (FS 372.65).

Turtles

A commercial fishing license is required to harvest turtles for sale in Florida using commercial fishing devices (FAC 39-23.003-2a).

The following native turtle species may not be sold (FAC 39.25.002-8):

Graptemys barbouri [1]	Barbour's Map Turtle
Graptemys ernsti	Escambia River Map Turtle
Macrochelys temminckii [2]	Alligator Snapping Turtle
Malaclemys terrapin	Diamondback Terrapin
Pseudemys concinna [3]	River Cooter
Sternotherus minor	Loggerhead Musk Turtle
Terrapene carolina	Box Turtle

[1] Listed as a Species of Special Concern in Florida.
[2] Listed as *Macroclemys temminckii* by Florida. Listed as a Species of Special Concern in Florida.
[3] *Pseudemys concinna suwanniensis* listed as a Species of Special Concern by Florida.

Specimens of the following native turtles wild caught in Lake Okeechobee, Florida which measure less than eight inches in carapace length may not be sold (FAC 39-23.012):

Apalone ferox [1]	Florida Softshell Turtle
Chelydra serpentina osceola [2]	Florida Snapping Turtle
Pseudemys floridana peninsularis [3]	Peninsula Cooter
Pseudemys nelsoni [3]	Florida Redbelly Turtle

[1] Listed as *Trionyx ferox* by Florida.
[2] Listed as *Chelydra osceola* by Florida.
[3] Listed in the genus *Chrysemys* by Florida.

Crocodilians

Alligator mississippiensis, American Alligator may be possessed, propagated and sold by licensed alligator farmers. Alligator eggs and live alligators may only be sold to other licensed alligator farmers, licensed exhibitors, properly permitted individuals, individuals out of state, or as otherwise authorized by the Florida Game and Fresh water Fish Commission. Farm Alligator and Egg Transfer Documents are required. Alligator meat, hides, and products may also be sold, C.I.T.E.S. tag requirements apply (FAC 39-25.004).

The meat and hides of alligators over four feet in length harvested from the wild may be sold under the authority of an alligator trapping license (FS 372.6673).

* All commercial activities involving both farm raised and legally harvested wild alligators are subject to an extensive array of conditions and requirements. A complete list of these restrictions may be obtained from the Florida Game and Fresh water Fish Commission (Address in Appendix I).

Snakes

Pituophis melanoleucus mugitus Florida Pine Snakes may not be sold. Amelanistic (= albino) specimens are exempt from this restriction (FAC 39-25.002-12).

* A license to possess wildlife for exhibition or public sale is required to sell amelanistic specimens of the Florida Pine Snake. Normal color phase specimens of *Pituophis melanoleucus mugitus* are included in Florida's list of special concern species and may not be sold.

A venomous reptile license is required to possess venomous snakes, including native species, for commercial and non-commercial purposes. A license to possess wildlife for exhibition or public sale is also required (FS 372.86).

Exotic Species

The following is a summarization of Florida's regulations on the importation, possession, and/or sale of non-native amphibian and reptile species.

Non-native wildlife species may not be held in captivity for the purpose of public sale without a license to possess wildlife for exhibition or public sale (FS 372.921).

Frogs

A freshwater fish dealers license is required to import or export frogs for sale (FS 372.65).

Reptiles

Venomous reptiles, including non-native species, may not be possessed for commercial or non-commercial purposes without a venomous reptile license. A license to possess wildlife for exhibition or public sale is also required (FS 372.86).

License and Permit Information

Licenses to possess wildlife for exhibition or public sale are available for an annual fee of $5 for from one to ten animals, or $25 for more than ten animals. There is no fee for Amphibian and Reptile Product Dealer permits. The fee for a commercial freshwater fishing license is $25 for residents and $100 for non-residents. Freshwater fish dealers licenses cost Florida residents $40. Non-residents may purchase retail freshwater fish dealers licenses at an annual fee of $100, while the same license at the wholesale level is available for $500. Venomous reptile licenses cost $5 annually, and all applicants must be at least 18 years of age. Alligator farm license fees are $250 plus $50 for each additional authorized alligator farm agent. The complete list of requirements and applications for all the licenses and permits of this section may be obtained from the Florida Game and Fresh Water Fish Commission (address in Appendix I).

CAPTIVE MAINTENANCE REGULATIONS

In addition to the restrictions on the possession of amphibians and reptiles included among the previous regulations, several portions of Florida's wildlife legislation deal specifically with the captive maintenance of these animals. A review of these regulations follows.

It is unlawful to possess any native or non-native wildlife in captivity without permit unless otherwise specified (FAC 39-5.051).

A license to possess wildlife is required to possess any native or non-native amphibian or reptile for exhibition purposes (FS 372.921).

The possession of any turtle or tortoise to which paint has been applied to the shell or body parts is prohibited, except for water soluble, non-toxic identification markings used in turtle races (FAC 39-25.002-11).

Amphibians and reptiles not included in Florida's Class I or Class II wildlife lists may be possessed for personal use without permit unless otherwise specified (FAC 39-6.0022-2).

Class I Wildlife

Animals which may not be possessed as personal pets because of their nature, habits, or status are classified as Class I. Permits are required to possess any species included in the Class I wildlife list (FS 372.922). The following reptiles are included in the Class I wildlife list.

Crocodilidae	All species except *Osteolaemus tetraspis*
Gavialidae	Gavials
Melanosuchus niger	Black Caiman
Varanus komodoensis	Komodo Dragon

Class II Wildlife

Animals considered to present a real or potential threat to human safety are classified as Class II. Permits are required to possess any species included in the Class II wildlife list (FS 372.922). The following reptiles are included in Florida's Class II wildlife list.

Osteolaemus tetraspis	Dwarf Crocodile
Alligatoridae	All species except *Alligator mississippiensis*

Special Caging Requirements for Class I and Class II Wildlife

Outdoor facilities for Crocodiles, Gavials, Alligators, Caimans and Komodo Dragons must be bounded by a fence at least five feet high of not less than 11.5 gauge chain link or equivalent (FAC 39-6.003).

Class I and Class II Wildlife Permit Information

Permits allowing for the possession of Class I or Class II wildlife are only issued to qualified individuals, zoos, research institutions, etc. which have adequate facilities to maintain such wildlife. Further information on the permit requirements and applications may be obtained from the Florida Game and Fresh Water Fish Commission (address in Appendix I).

Venomous Reptiles

A license is required to possess any venomous reptiles (FS 372.86).

A $1,000 bond is required to possess venomous reptiles for public exhibition purposes (FS 372-88).

It us unlawful to house captive venomous reptiles in any manner not approved as safe, secure, and proper by the Florida Game and Fish Commission (FS 372.89).

Caging Requirements for Venomous Reptiles

The possession of any venomous reptile is subject to the following caging provisions (FAC 39-25.006).

Indoor Caging

1. Cages shall be fronted with 1/4 inch mesh hardware cloth or plate glass at least 1/4 inch thick.
2. Cages may be constructed of waterproof plywood at least 1/4 inch thick, concrete plastered over wire, sheet metal, 1/4 inch mesh hardware cloth, or interlocking lumber at least 3/4 inch in thick.
3. Cages are to be tightly closed at the top and all doors are to be tightly fitting and securely locked.

Outdoor Caging

The floors of outdoor cages or pits shall be of concrete or masonry construction at least two inches in thickness. Sides shall be of similar construction at least six inches in thickness, with a minimum height of four feet from the floor unless completely roofed over by close-meshed wire. The corners of all open topped pits shall be designed or guarded so as to prevent the escape of reptiles by climbing. Entrance doors accessible to the public shall be kept key locked.

All cages housing poisonous reptiles shall be maintained in good repair at all times.

General Reptile Caging Specifications

No captive wildlife shall be confined in any cage which contains more individuals, is smaller in dimension, or is not equipped as specified (FAC 39-6.0004).

1. Snakes — For up to four specimens, a cage having a perimeter 1-1/2 times the length of the longest confined snake, with a resting limb or ledge, a large rock, shade, and water. For each additional snake, increase cage floor area by 25 percent.
2. Lizards 2 to 6 inches in length — For one or two lizards, a cage 12 inches by 8 inches, 10 inches high, with branches and access to sun or ultraviolet light. For each two additional, increase cage size by two inches in length and width.
3. Lizards 7 to 12 inches in length — For one or two lizards, a cage 20 inches by 10 inches, 15 inches high, with branches and access to sun or ultraviolet light. For each two additional, increase cage size by four inches in length and width.
4. Lizards 13 to 24 inches in length — For one or two lizards, a cage 30 inches by 15 inches, 12 inches high, with branches and access to sun or ultraviolet light. For each two additional, increase cage size by six inches in length and width.
5. Lizards 2 to 4 feet in length — For one or two lizards, a cage 36 inches by 15 inches, 18 inches high, with branches and access to sun or ultraviolet light. For each two additional, increase cage size by 10 inches in

length and width.

6. Lizards 4 to 6 feet in length — For one or two lizards, a cage 6 feet by 3 feet, 4 feet high, with branches and access to sun or ultraviolet light. For each two additional, increase cage size by one foot in length and width.

7. Gila Monster and Beaded Lizards — For each lizard, a cage 24 inches by 18 inches, 15 inches high having rounded corners, with two rocks and access to sun or ultraviolet light. For each additional lizard, increase cage size by four inches in length and width.

8. Turtles and Terrapins — For one turtle, a cage with an area five times body size of which 50 percent shall be a pool, with sun and shade. For soft-shelled turtles, a non-abrasive pool bottom is required. The water area shall permit submersion of the largest turtle. For each additional turtle, increase cage area by five times body size.

9. Tortoises — For one tortoise, a cage with land area 10 times body size, with sun and shade, and a sloped pool for immersion. For each additional tortoise increase area seven times body size.

10. Crocodilians — For one animal, a cage of sufficient size to permit moving and turning both on land and in a pool of sufficient depth to permit submersion. For additional animals, the combined area covered by their bodies shall not exceed 50 percent of cage area.

* The above list of general cage specifications serves as an example of the minimum cage size requirements of captive reptiles.

Captive Maintenance Regulations Review

The following is a basic summary of Florida's restrictions on the captive possession of amphibians and reptiles.

a. Endangered and threatened species may not be possessed without permit.

b. Special concern species may not be possessed without permit unless otherwise specified.

c. The following turtles have a possession limit without permit of two specimens of each species.

Graptemys barbouri	Barbour's Map Turtle
Graptemys ernsti	Escambia River Map Turtle
Malaclemys terrapin	Diamondback Terrapin
Pseudemys concinna	River Cooter
Sternotherus minor	Loggerhead Musk Turtle
Terrapene carolina	Box Turtle

d. *Macrochelys temminckii*, Alligator Snapping Turtle possession limit without permit is one specimen.

e. *Pituophis melanoleucus mugitus*, Florida Pine Snake possession without permit limited to one specimen, except for amelanistic specimens which may be possessed without limit.

f. A license is required to possess all venomous reptile species.

g. *Alligator mississippiensis*, Alligators may not be possessed without a permit.

h. Permits are required to possess any reptile included in the lists of Class I or Class II wildlife.

(b, c, d and e above see Native Wildlife Regulations).
(f and g above see Native Wildlife Regulations and Importation and Commercial Trade Regulations).
(h above see Captive Maintenance Regulations).

RETURN BOTH COPIES
ALL INCOMPLETE APPLICATIONS WILL BE RETURNED

Florida Game and Fresh Water Fish Commission

620 South Meridian Street, Tallahassee, FL 32399-1600

(904) 488 - 3641

Application for

LICENSE TO POSSESS WILDLIFE FOR EXHIBITION OR PUBLIC SALE
[ ] **EPA-240 One to Ten Animals ......$ 5.00** Fee
[ ] **EPB-241 Eleven or More Animals ..$25.00** Fee

(Enter any changes here)

LICENSEE NAME
MAILING ADDRESS
CITY, STATE/ZIP

_____
_____
_____

New_____   Renewal_____

*FACILITY ADDRESS _____   City_____   State_____   Zip_____
County Of Facility_____   Business Phone (_____)____-_____
*If address is a rural route, provide directions to location of activity on separate page.

Applicant's Information: Date of Birth_____ Social Security #_____ Height____ Weight_____ Hair___ Sex__ Race__
(Information must pertain to the person (owner\manager) signing the application below and will be returned if incomplete)

COMMERCIAL ACTIVITY

____ Exhibit or Sell Exotic Bird	____ Importation Business	____ Capture and Sell Non-Venomous Reptiles
____ Wildlife Exhibit (Permanent)	____ Wildlife Broker	____ Capture and Sell Venomous Reptiles
____ Pet Shop		____ Other (give details on reverse)
____ Wildlife Lecture/Educational Service		____ Non-Profit Educational Organization
____ Traveling Exhibit or Circus Act (Attach a twelve month itinerary)		____ Wildlife Rehabilitator
	(for non-residents)	

List on a separate sheet of paper the <u>exact number by species</u> of wildlife you are applying for (ex. 50 parakeets, 3 cougars)

Do you currently possess these animals? Yes__ No__

For Class I or Class II: If Applying For the <u>First Time or For Any Species Not Previously Permitted for</u>

__ A statement must be attached that states that the construction of the Facility, its cages and enclosures, is not prohibited by
county ordinance and, if within a municipality, municipal ordinance.
AND
__ Two letters of reference documenting at least one year's experience to include no less than 1000 hours in the husbandry of the
species for which you are applying.

*The above information is true and correct. I agree to adhere to the provisions of Chapter
372, Florida Statutes, and the rules and regulations of the Game and Fresh Water Fish
Commission pertaining to the possession and the commercialization of wildlife. I understand
that my wildlife facilities are subject to inspection by Game and Fresh Water Fish
Commission personnel as required by Chapter 372.921 F.S.*

_____ (_____)_____ _____
Owner/Manager Name(Please Print)   Home Phone   Owner/Manager Signature/Date

Expires 12 months from the date of issuance.

FOR COMMISSION USE ONLY

Class I _____Class II _____ Class III_____
Approved By_____ Date _____
Denied_____ Date _____ Reason _____
GFC - # 341
Revised 05/94   **ADMINISTRATIVE COPY**

Sample Permit Application - Courtesy Florida Game and Fresh Water Fish Commission.

GEORGIA

ENDANGERED, THREATENED, AND SPECIAL CONCERN SPECIES

The Georgia Department of Natural Resources classifies various species of the state's fauna as Unusual, Rare, Threatened, or Endangered. Species in all four categories are legally protected by Georgia's Endangered Wildlife Act of 1973 as specified in the Georgia Annotated Code (reference: GA AC 27-3-130-133).

The following amphibians and reptiles are included in the current (October 1992) list of officially protected wildlife in Georgia. Scientific collection permits issued by the State of Georgia are required for all activities involving any of these species. In addition to any required state permits, a permit issued by the U.S. Department of the Interior must be obtained for any species included in the federal list of endangered and threatened wildlife (see U.S. Endangered and Threatened Species).

Species	Common Name	Status
Ambystoma cingulatum	Flatwoods Salamander	Rare
Amphiuma pholeter	One-toed Amphiuma	Rare
Aneides aeneus	Green Salamander	Rare
Cryptobranchus alleganiensis	Hellbender	Rare
Haideotriton wallacei	Georgia Blind Salamander	Threatened
Notophthalmus perstriatus	Striped Newt	Rare
Plethodon petraeus	Pigeon Mountain Salamander	Rare
Alligator mississippiensis [1]	American Alligator	S/A
Caretta caretta	Loggerhead Sea Turtle	Threatened
Chelonia mydas	Green Sea Turtle	Threatened
Clemmys guttata	Spotted Turtle	Unusual
Clemmys muhlenbergii	Bog Turtle	Threatened
Dermochelys coriacea	Leatherback Sea Turtle	Endangered
Eretmochelys imbricata	Hawksbill Sea Turtle	Endangered
Gopherus polyphemus	Gopher Tortoise	Threatened
Graptemys barbouri	Barbour's Map Turtle	Threatened
Graptemys geographica	Common Map Turtle	Rare
Graptemys pulchra	Alabama Map Turtle	Rare
Lepidochelys kempii	Atlantic Ridley Sea Turtle	Endangered
Macrochelys temminckii [2]	Alligator Snapping Turtle	Threatened
Drymarchon couperi [3]	Eastern Indigo Snake	Threatened

[1] Listed as threatened due to similarity of appearance for law enforcement purposes only. American Alligators are not biologically endangered or threatened in Georgia, and licensed alligator farming operations are allowed (see Importation and Commercial Trade Regulations).
[2] Listed as *Macroclemys temminckii* by Georgia.
[3] Listed as *Drymarchon corais couperi* by Georgia.

Protected Species Permit Information

Scientific collection permits may be issued to qualified individuals and institutions for legitimate research or educational purposes only. There is a $50 annual permit fee. Further information on permit conditions and applications for scientific collecting permits may be obtained from the Special Permit Unit of the Georgia Department of Natural Resources (address in Appendix I).

GA

NATIVE WILDLIFE REGULATIONS

Restrictions on the possession and collection of amphibians and reptiles wild caught in the state are included among the nongame wildlife regulations of the Georgia Annotated Code. The following is a summarization of these regulations.

It is unlawful to hunt, fish, trap, take, possess, or transport any nongame species of wildlife. With the exception of any species classified as unusual, rare, threatened, or endangered, the following amphibians and reptiles are exempt from this restriction (GA AC 27-1-28):

> Fresh-water Turtles
> Poisonous Snakes
> Frogs
> Spring Lizards (Salamanders)

* The Georgia Department of Natural Resources interprets this regulation as prohibiting the possession without permit of any native species of lizard or nonvenomous snake, including specimens legally obtained from outside of Georgia.

It is unlawful to disturb, mutilate, or destroy the dens, holes, or homes of any wildlife; or to blind wildlife with lights; or to use explosives, chemicals, electrical or mechanical devices, or smokers of any kind in order to drive such wildlife out of such habitats, provided that this code section shall not apply to poisonous snakes (GA AC 27-1-30).

License and Permit Information

Permits are required for all activities involving any lizard or nonvenomous snake species native to the state, as specified in regulation 27-1-28 of the Georgia Annotated Code. As stated above, the Georgia Department of Natural Resources considers the possession without permit of these species unlawful regardless of their origin including captive produced specimens. Native species of nonvenomous snakes and lizards may be possessed under the authorization of a wildlife exhibition permit for scientific or educational purposes only. There is a $59 annual fee for a wildlife exhibition permit. Scientific collection permits are required to collect lizards and nonvenomous snakes from the wild in Georgia. Requirements and applications for these permits may be obtained from the Georgia Department of Natural Resources' Special Permits Unit (address in Appendix I).

IMPORTATION AND COMMERCIAL TRADE REGULATIONS

Native Species

In addition to regulation 27-1-28 prohibiting the possession of native lizards and nonvenomous snakes which obviously affects the sale of those species, other restrictions on commercial activities involving native amphibian and reptile species are included among the wildlife regulations of the Georgia Annotated Code. The following is a summary of these regulations.

Alligators

A commercial alligator farming license is required to possess and propagate *Alligator mississippiensis*. Additional permits are required to import and to sell or transfer live American Alligators (GA AC 27-2-10).

Turtles

A commercial fishing license is required to harvest legal fresh-water turtles from the wild for commercial purposes (GA AC 27-2-23).

* Specimens of native turtle species legally obtained from outside of Georgia may be sold without a commercial fishing license. U.S.F.D.A restrictions apply (see U.S. Importation and Commercial Trade Regulations).

GA

Exotic Species

Restrictions on the importation, possession, and sale of specific types of animals are included among the wildlife regulations of Georgia. A summarization of these regulations and of the amphibian and reptile groups affected follows.

It is unlawful to import, transport, transfer, sell, purchase, or possess any of the following families, genera, or species without a wild animal license or wild animal permit. In addition, proof of adequate insurance in the amount of $40,000 per animal up to a maximum of $500,000 is required for any animal included in the following list categorized as "inherently dangerous" to humans (GA AC 7-5-4 and 27-5-5).

Bufo horribilis	Giant Toad
Bufo marinus	Marine Toad
Bufo paracnemis	Giant Toad
Crocodylidae [1]	Crocodiles and Gavials all species
Alligatoridae [1]	Alligators and Caimans all species
Helodermatidae [1]	Gila Monsters and Beaded Lizards
Colubridae [1]	All Poisonous Rear-fanged Species
Crotalidae [1]	Pit Vipers all species
Elapidae [1]	Cobras, Coral Snakes, etc. all species
Viperidae [1]	Vipers all species

[1] Listed as inherently dangerous to humans.

* Although the above regulation appears to prohibit without license or permit the possession and sale of all venomous reptiles including native species, the Georgia Department of Natural Resources interprets this regulation as pertaining only to exotic species and does not restrict activities involving any native venomous snake.

A wild animal auction license is required to conduct a public or private auction in which regulated wild animals are sold to the highest bidder (GA AC 27-5-11).

* Applies to those amphibians and reptiles requiring wild animal licenses and permits listed above.

License and Permit Information

Wild animal licenses are issued to qualified individuals engaged in the wholesale or retail sale of animals, or the exhibition of animals to the public. The fee for a wild animal license is $236 annually. Wild animal permits are issued for scientific or educational purposes only, and are free of charge. Wild animal auction licenses cost $5,000 and an additional $50,000 bond is required. Annual commercial fishing license fees are $12 for residents and $118 for non-residents. Further information and applications for all the required licenses and permits of this section may be obtained form the Special Permit Unit of the Georgia Department of Natural Resources (address in Appendix I).

CAPTIVE MAINTENANCE REGULATIONS

Restrictions on the possession of both native and non-native amphibian and reptile species are included among the regulations of the previous sections. The following is a brief review of Georgia's restrictions on the captive maintenance of amphibians and reptiles.

Captive Maintenance Regulations Review

a. Unusual, rare, threatened, and endangered species may not be possessed without a scientific collection permit.

b. Wildlife exhibition permits are required to possess any native lizard and nonvenomous snake species for exhibition purposes.

c. Permits are not required to possess native species of venomous snakes.

d. Giant toads of the genus *Bufo* may not be possessed without permit.

e. Permits are required to possess all species of crocodilians.

f. Permits are required to possess any non-native species of venomous reptile including rear-fanged colubrids.

(b and c above see Native Wildlife Regulations).
(d, e and f above see Importation and Commercial Trade Regulations).

Hatchling Gopher Tortoise, *Gopherus polyphemus* - One of 12 species of chelonians currently protected by law within the State of Georgia. Georgia's Gopher Tortoise population is not legally protected by the U.S. Endangered Species Act at this time. Photograph courtesy of James E. Gerholdt.

GA

HAWAII

ENDANGERED, THREATENED, AND SPECIAL CONCERN SPECIES

Of the 33 or so species of amphibians and reptiles currently inhabiting the Hawaiian Archipelago, only six marine species are actually naturally indigenous to the islands. Among the six native marine species all but one, the Yellow-bellied Sea Snake, *Pelamis platurus*, are considered endangered or threatened in Hawaii. The five endangered or threatened species, all sea turtles, are protected by the U.S. Endangered Species Act as well as by Hawaii's Endangered and Threatened Species legislation, as specified in title 12, chapter 195 of Hawaii Revised Statutes (reference: HRS 12 195D). An endangered and threatened species permit issued by the U.S. Department of the Interior is required for all activities involving any marine turtles.

The following marine turtles have been recorded in Hawaiian coastal waters, and are included in the U.S. Department of the Interior's current (January 1997) list of endangered and threatened wildlife. All five species are fully protected by the U.S. Endangered Species Act and by the endangered species legislation of the State of Hawaii. All regulations concerning marine turtles are vigorously enforced in Hawaii.

Species	Common Name	Status
Caretta caretta	Loggerhead Sea Turtle	Threatened
Chelonia mydas	Green Sea Turtle	Threatened
Dermochelys coriacea	Leatherback Sea Turtle	Endangered
Eretmochelys imbricata	Hawksbill Sea Turtle	Endangered
Lepidochelys olivacea	Pacific Ridley Sea Turtle	Threatened

Protected Species Permit Information

As stated above, an endangered and threatened species permit issued by the U.S. Department of the Interior is required for all activities involving any marine turtle species (see U.S. Endangered and Threatened Species) and no state permits will be issued until all federal permit requirements have been fulfilled. State scientific collection or educational permit applications and information may be obtained from the Hawaii Division of Aquatic Resources (address in Appendix I).

NATIVE WILDLIFE REGULATIONS

With the exception of the six Hawaiian marine species, all amphibians and reptiles in Hawaii have been introduced, either purposefully or accidentally, through the activities of humans. As non-native species, these introduced amphibians and reptiles are not protected and there are no restrictions on their collection, as specified in title 13, chapter 124 of Hawaii Administrative Rules (reference: HAR 13-124-3). Several of these unprotected introduced species are included in the restricted live wildlife lists of Hawaii, however, and individuals or institutions may not possess living specimens of these species without permit (see Importation and Commercial Trade Regulations). The introduced species which may not be possessed alive within Hawaii are listed below.

Anolis equestris	Knight Anole
Anolis sagrei	Brown Anole
Iguana iguana	Green Iguana
Phelsuma cepediana	Blue-tailed Day Gecko
Phelsuma guimbeaui	Orange Spotted Day Gecko
Phelsuma laticauda	Gold Dust Day Gecko

IMPORTATION AND COMMERCIAL TRADE

Having the largest number of endemic species of any geographic region in the world, the State of Hawaii is extremely concerned with preserving the native flora and fauna of the islands. The importation of any species of plant or animal into the state is strictly regulated, an action which is clearly necessary if Hawaii's unique endemic species are to be protected from the devastation which can be caused by introduced non-native wildlife. Permits issued by the Hawaii Department of Agriculture are required to import animals or plants of any type into the state and all wildlife shipments may additionally be subject to state quarantine requirements, as specified in title 4, chapter 71 of Hawaii Administrative Rules (reference: HAR 4-71-3 and 4-71-4). In addition, the Hawaii Department of Agriculture has established lists of prohibited, restricted, and conditionally approved wildlife species which may or may not require an additional live wildlife possession permit. These species listings are reviewed below.

Prohibited Species

Animals included in the list of designated prohibited species may not be imported or possessed in the State of Hawaii under any circumstances. Live possession permits will not be issued for any designated prohibited species. This restriction applies to zoos, universities, and all types of research institutions, as well as to private individuals. The following amphibian and reptile orders, families, genera and species are included in Hawaii's list of prohibited animals (HAR 4-71-6).

Amphiuma	Amphiumas, All species in genus
Necturus	Mudpuppies, All species in genus
Pseudobranchus striatus	Dwarf Siren
Siren intermedia	Lesser Siren
Siren lacertina	Greater Siren
Hyla septentrionalis [1]	Cuban Treefrog
Phyllobates	Golden Poison Frogs, All species in genus
Pipidae	Aquatic Frogs, All species in family except:
	Pipa pipa [2] Surinam Toad
	Xenopus laevis [2] African Clawed Frog
Heloderma	Gila Monster & Beaded Lizards, All species in genus
Serpentes [3]	Snakes, All species

[1] Species included among the non-native indigenous herpetofauna of Hawaii.

[2] *Pipa pipa*, Surinam Toad, and *Xenopus laevis*, African Clawed Frog, may be possessed by government approved zoos, research institutions, etc. (see Restricted Animal List Part A).

[3] Zoos may possess for exhibition two of each nonvenomous snake species provided that both specimens are males (reference: HI RS 150A-6-3).

Restricted and Conditionally Approved Species

In addition to the prohibited animals list, the Department of Agriculture maintains a list of species which may be legally imported into Hawaii. Species included in the list of animals which are permitted entry into the state are assigned to one of three categories on the basis of specific restrictions regarding their possession. Due to the length of Hawaii's list of Permitted Animals, the included species of each category have been arranged first by major taxonomic order (i.e., frogs, turtles, etc.) and then alphabetically by genus. Hawaii automatically considers any species not included in either the Restricted Animals List parts A and B or in the Conditionally Approved Animal List a prohibited species (HAR 4-71-6.5).

Restricted Animal List (Part A)

Species included in part A of the Restricted Animal List may only be imported and possessed by universities, research institutions, zoos, aquariums, etc., and these species may not be commercially traded. A special Possession Permit issued by the Hawaii Department of Agriculture is required. The following amphibian and reptile genera and species are included in part A of the Restricted Animal list.

Ambystoma jeffersonianum	Jefferson's Salamander
Ambystoma texanum	Smallmouth Salamander
Andrias japonicus	Japanese Giant Salamander
Andrias japonicus davidianus	Chinese Giant Salamander
Cryptobranchus alleganiensis	Hellbender
Echinotriton andersoni	Spiny Newt
Eurycea longicauda	Long-tailed Salamander
Notophthalmus viridescens	Red-spotted Newt
Agalychnis annae	Yellow-eyed Treefrog
Agalychnis callidryas	Red-eyed Treefrog
Bombina maxima	Giant Fire-bellied Toad
Bombina orientalis	Fire-bellied Toad
Bufo	Toads, all species in genus
Ceratophrys calcarata	Colombian Horned Frog
Ceratophrys ornata	Ornate Horned Frog
Kalouha mediolineata	Siamese Painted Toad
Kalouha pulchra	Malayan Painted Toad
Kassina maculata	Spotted Running Frog
Leptodactylus pentadactylus	South American Bullfrog
Megophrys nasuta montana	Siamese Horned Frog
Megophrys nasuta monticola	Asian Horned Frog
Pachymedusa dacnicolor	Mexican Giant Treefrog
Pipa pipa	Surinam Toad
Polypedates leucomystax	Bamboo Climbing Frog
Pyxicephalus adspersus	African Bullfrog
Similisca baudini	Mottled Treefrog
Xenopus laevis	African Clawed Frog
Alligator mississippiensis	American Alligator
Caiman crocodilus	Spectacled Caiman
Crocodylus	All species in genus
Gavialis gangeticus	Gavial
Chelydra serpentina	Snapping Turtle
Chelus fimbriatus	Mata Mata
Emydura albertisi	New Guinea Snake Neck Turtle
Heosemys grandis	Asian Temple Turtle
Macrochelys temminckii [1]	Alligator Snapping Turtle
Pelomedusa subrufa olivacera	Helmeted Turtle
Pelusios adansoni	African Side-neck Turtle
Podocnemis unifilis	Yellow-spotted Side-neck Turtle

Acanthosaura armata	Mountain Horned Agama
Agama agama	Common Agama
Agama atricollis	South African Agama
Amevia amevia	Jungle Runner
Anolis equestris	Knight Anole
Basiliscus basiliscus	Brown Basilisk
Basiliscus plumifrons	Green Basilisk
Basiliscus vittatus	Banded Basilisk
Brachylophus fasciatus	Fiji Island Iguana
Callisaurus draconoides	Zebratail Lizard
Callopistes maculatus	Monitor Tegu
Calotes calotes	Sawback Agama
Ceratophora stoderti	Horned Agama
Chamaeleo chamaeleon	Common Chameleon
Cnemidophorus tesselatus	Checkered Whiptail
Cnemidophorus tigris	Western Whiptail
Coleonyx elegans	Elegant Banded Gecko
Coleonyx variegatus	Western Banded Gecko
Cordylus cataphractus	Armadillo Lizard
Cordylus giganteus	Sun Gazer
Cordylus warreni	Warren's Girdletail Lizard
Corucia zebrata	Prehensile-tailed Skink
Corytophanes cristatus	Helmeted Iguana
Crotaphytus collaris	Collared Lizard
Cryptoblepharus boutoni	Snake-eyed Skink
Ctenophorus cristatus	Crested Dragon
Ctenophorus scutulatus	Lozenge Marked Dragon
Ctenosaura similis	Spiny-tailed Iguana
Cyclodomorphus branchialis	Australian Short-lined Skink
Cyclura macleayi	Cuban Iguana
Cyrtodactylus louisadensis	Naked-finger Gecko
Cyrtodactylus pulchellus	Malayan Banded Gecko
Delma impar	Smooth Scalyfoot Lizard
Diplodactylus spinigerus	Spiny-tailed Gecko
Diplosaurus dorsalis	Desert Iguana
Draco	Flying Dragons, all species in genus
Egernia cunninghami	Cunningham's Skink
Egernia stokesii	Gidgee Skink
Elgaria multicarinata	Southern Alligator Lizard
Emoia cyanura	Blue-tailed Skink
Enyaliosaurus quinquecarinatus	Club Tail Iguana
Eumeces obsoletus	Great Plains Skink
Eublepharis macularis	Leopard Gecko
Gambelia wislizenii	Long-nosed Leopard Lizard
Gehyra mutilata	Stump-toed Gecko
Gekko gekko	Tokay Gecko
Gekko stentor	Giant Gecko
Gerrhosaurus flavigularis	Yellow Throat Plated Lizard
Gerrhosaurus major	Tawny Plated Lizard

HI

Gerrhosaurus nigrolineatus	Black-lined Plated Lizard
Gonocephalus borniensis	Horn-headed Dragon
Gymnodactylus penguensis zebraic	Bent-toed Gecko
Hemidactylus frenatus	House Gecko
Hemidactylus garnoti	Indo-pacific Gecko
Hemiphyllodactylus typus	Tree Gecko
Hemitheconyx caudicinctus	African Fat-tailed Gecko
Holbrookia maculata	Lesser Earless Lizard
Homopholus walbergi	Walberg's Velvety Gecko
Hydrosaurus amboinensis	Sailfin Dragon
Iguana	Iguanas, all species in genus
Lacerta lepida	Jeweled Lacerta
Lacerta sicula	European Wall Lizard
Lacerta viridis	Green Lizard
Leiolepis belliana	Butterfly Agama
Leiolepis rubritaeniata	Giant Ground Agama
Leiolopisma metallicum	Metallic Skink
Lialis burtoni	Burton's Snake Lizard
Lipinnia noctua	Moth Skink
Mabuya capensis	South African Skink
Mabuya macularia	Orange Throat Skink
Moloch horridus	Thorny Devil
Oedura lesueuri	Lesueur's Velvety Gecko
Oedura marmorata	Velvet Gecko
Oedura robusta	Robust Velvet Gecko
Omolepida branchialis	Short-limbed Skink
Ophisaurus ventralis	Eastern Glass Lizard
Pachydactylus bibroni	Bibron's Gecko
Phelsuma abbotti	Aldabra Day Gecko
Phelsuma cepediana	Blue-tailed Day Gecko
Phelsuma guimbeaui [2]	Orange-spotted Day Gecko
Phelsuma laticauda [2]	Gold Dust Day Gecko
Phelsuma madagascariensis	Madagascar Day Gecko
Phelsuma ornata	Ornate Day Gecko
Phrynosoma	Horned Lizards, all species in genus
Phyllurus cornutus	Northern Leaf-tailed Gecko
Phyllurus platurus	Southern Leaf-tailed Gecko
Physignathus cocincinus	Malayan Water Dragon
Physignathus lesueuri	Brown Water Dragon
Pogona barbatus	Australian Bearded Dragon
Pogona nullarbor	Nullarbor Bearded Dragon
Pogona vitticeps	Inland Bearded Dragon
Ptychozoon kuhli	Kuhl's Flying Gecko
Ptychozoon lionotum	Common Flying Gecko
Pygopus lepidopodus	Common Scalyfoot Lizard
Sauromalus obesus	Chuckwalla
Sauromalus varius	Piebald Chuckwalla
Sceloporus clarkii	Clark's Spiny Lizard
Sceloporus jarrovii	Yarrow's Spiny Lizard

HI

Sceloporus magister	Desert Spiny Lizard
Sceloporus occidentalis	Western Fence Lizard
Sceloporus orcutti	Granite Spiny Lizard
Takydromus sexlineatus	Long-tailed Lizard
Thecadactylus rapicauda	Turnip-tailed Gecko
Tiliqua nigrolutes	Blotched Blue Tongue Skink
Tiliqua occipitalis	Australian Blue Tongue Skink
Tiliqua scincoides	Eastern Blue Tongue Skink
Trachysaurus rugosus	Shingle Back Skink
Tupinambis nigropunctatus	Golden Tegu
Tupinambis rufescens	Red Tegu
Tupinambis teguixin	Black Tegu
Underwoodsaurus mili	Turnip-tailed Gecko
Urosaurus ornatus	Tree Lizard
Uta stansburiana	Side-blotched Lizard
Varanus acanthurus	Spiny-tailed Monitor
Varanus bengalensis	Bengal Monitor
Varanus dumerili	Dumeril's Monitor
Varanus exanthematicus	Savannah Monitor
Varanus giganteus	Perentee Monitor
Varanus gouldi	Gould's Monitor
Varanus indicus	Pacific Monitor
Varanus komodoensis	Komodo Monitor
Varanus nilocticus	Nile Monitor
Varanus salvadori	Crocodile Monitor
Varanus salvator	Water Monitor
Varanus storri	Storr's Monitor
Varanus varius	Variegated Monitor

[1] Listed as *Macroclemys temminckii* by Hawaii.
[2] Species included among the non-native indigenous herpetofauna of Hawaii.

Restricted Animal List (Part B)

Species included in part B of the Restricted Animal List may be imported and possessed by private individuals, as well as by research institutions, zoos, etc., and these species may be commercially traded. A special possession permit issued by the Hawaii Department of Agriculture is required for these species. Several of the reptiles included in part B of the Restricted Animal List are protected by the U.S. Endangered Species Act and an endangered species permit issued by the U.S. Department of the Interior is required to possess these animals, in addition to any required Hawaiian permit (see U.S. Endangered and Threatened Species). The following amphibians and reptiles are included in part B of Hawaii's Restricted Animal List.

Triturus boscai	Bosca's Newt
Triturus italicus	Italian Newt
Tylototriton verrocosus	Emperor Newt
Dendrobates [1]	Poison Dart Frogs, all species in genus
Hyla vasta	Haitian Giant Treefrog
Rana jerboa [2]	Frog
Rana limnocharis [2]	Rice Frog
Rana pustulosa [2]	Frog

Asterochelys radiata [3]	Radiated Tortoise
Asterochelys yniphora [3]	Angulated Tortoise
Batagur baska	Batagur
Callagur borneoensis	Giant Painted River Turtle
Chelodina longicollis	Australian Snakeneck Turtle
Chelonia mydas	Green Sea Turtle
Chelonidis nigra [4]	Galapagos Tortoise
Chinemys kwangtungensis	Kwangtung Pond Turtle
Chinemys reevsi	Reeves Turtle
Chitra indica	Narrow-headed Softshell
Cuora amboinensis	Malayan Box Turtle
Cuora flavomarginata	Yellow-margined Box Turtle
Cuora galbinifrons	White-fronted Box Turtle
Cuora trifasciata	Three-keeled Box Turtle
Cyclanorbis elegans	Nubian Softshell
Cyclanorbis senegalensis	Senegal Softshell
Cyclemys dentata	Asian Leaf Turtle
Cycloderma aubryi	Aubry's Softshell
Cycloderma frenatum	Bridled Softshell
Geoclemys hamiltoni	Black Pond Turtle
Geoemyda spengleri	Black-bellied Leaf Turtle
Gopherus agassizii	Desert Tortoise
Gopherus flavomarginatus	Bolson Tortoise
Gopherus polyphemus	Gopher Tortoise
Graptemys oculifera	Ringed Sawback
Hardella thurji	Brahminy River Turtle
Heosemys	Asian Pond Turtles, all species in genus except:
	Heosemys grandis [5] Giant Pond Turtle
Hieremys annandalei	Temple Turtle
Indotestudo	Indian Tortoises, all species in genus
Kachuga	Tent Turtles, all species in genus
Kinixys belliana	Bell's Hinged Back Tortoise
Kinixys erosa	Schweigger's Hinged Back Tortoise
Kinixys homeana	Home's Hinged Back Tortoise
Kinosternon	Mud Turtles, all species in genus
Lepidochelys olivacea	Pacific Ridley Sea Turtle
Lissemys punctata	Indian Flapshell Turtle
Malaclemys terrapin	Diamondback Terrapin
Malacochersus tornieri	Pancake Tortoise
Manouria	Brown Tortoises, all species in genus
Mauremys annamensis	Eurasian Pond Turtle
Melanochelys tricarinata	Three-keeled Terrapin
Melanochelys trijuga	Black-bellied Terrapin
Morenia ocellata	Ocellated Peacock Turtle
Morenia petersi	Peter's Peacock Turtle
Notochelys platynota	Flat-back Turtle
Ocadia sinensis	Chinese Striped Turtle
Orlitia borneensis	Borneo River Turtle

Pelochelys bibroni	Giant Softshell
Psammobates geometricus	Geometric Tortoise
Pseudemys alabamensis [6]	Alabama Redbelly Turtle
Pseudemys rubriventris [6]	Plymouth Redbelly Turtle
Pyxidea mouhoti	Indian Thorn Tortoise
Pyxis arachnoides	Spider Tortoise
Rhinoclemmys	Latin American Wood Turtles, all species in genus
Sacalia bealei	Six-eyed Pond Turtle
Siebenrockiella crassicollis	Black Marsh Turtle
Staurotypus salvini	Giant Musk turtle
Staurotypus triporcatus	Giant Musk Turtle
Sternotherus carinatus	Razorback Musk Turtle
Sternotherus depressus	Flattened Musk Turtle
Sternotherus minor minor	Loggerhead Musk Turtle
Sternotherus minor peltifer	Stripeneck Musk Turtle
Terrapene coahuila	Aquatic Box Turtle
Trionyx	Softshell Turtles, all species in genus
Amblyrhynchus cristatus	Galapagos Marine Iguana
Anolis carolinensis	Green Anole
Chamaeleo jacksonii [1]	Jackson's Chameleon
Conolophus subcristatus	Galapagos Land Iguana
Emoia physicae	Five-toed Ground Skink
Lobulia elegans	Elegant Ground Skink
Lobulia morokana	Morokana Ground Skink
Lobulia stanleyana	Stanley's Ground Skink
Phelsuma laticauda [7]	Gold Dust Day Gecko

[1] Species included among the non-native indigenous herpetofauna of Hawaii.
[2] Species not listed in Frank and Ramus (1995).
[3] *Asterochelys* is currently considered a subgenus of *Geochelone*.
[4] *Chelonidis* is currently considered a subgenus of *Geochelone*. Listed as *Chelonidis elephantopus* by Hawaii.
[5] Species included in Restricted Species A list.
[6] Listed in the genus *Chrysemys* by Hawaii.
[7] Species included among the non-native indigenous herpetofauna of Hawaii. Also included in Part A of Restricted Animal List.

Conditionally Approved Animals List

The following amphibian and reptile species may be imported, possessed, and commercially traded through pet shops, etc. in Hawaii. Special Possession Permits are not required.

Ambystoma annulatum	Ringed Salamander
Ambystoma maculatum	Spotted Salamander
Ambystoma mexicanum	Axolotl
Ambystoma opacum	Marbled Salamander
Ambystoma talpoideum	Mole Salamander
Ambystoma tigrinum	Tiger Salamander
Cynops pyrrhogaster	Japanese Fire-bellied Newt
Plethodon cinereus	Redback Salamander
Plethodon dorsalis	Zigzag Salamander

Plethodon dunni	Dunn's Salamander
Plethodon elongatus	Del Norte Salamander
Plethodon glutinosus	Slimy Salamander
Plethodon jordani	Jordan's Salamander
Plethodon vehiculum	Western Redback Salamander
Pseudotriton montanus	Mud Salamander
Pseudotriton ruber	Red Salamander
Salamandra atra	Alpine Salamander
Salamandra salamandra	Fire Salamander
Taricha granulosa	Roughskin Newt
Taricha rivularis	Redbelly Newt
Taricha torosa	California Newt
Triturus alpestris	Alpine Newt
Triturus cristatus	Northern Crested Newt
Triturus helveticus	Palmate Newt
Triturus marmoratus	Marbled Newt
Triturus montandoni	Carpathian Newt
Triturus vittatus	Banded Newt
Triturus vulgaris [1]	Smooth Newt
Hyla andersonii [2]	Pine Barrens Treefrog
Hyla arenicolor	Canyon Treefrog
Hyla avivoca	Bird-voiced Treefrog
Hyla chrysoscelis	Cope's Gray Treefrog
Hyla cinerea	Green Treefrog
Hyla eximia	Mountain Treefrog
Hyla femoralis	Pine Woods Treefrog
Hyla gratiosa	Barking Treefrog
Hyla regilla	Pacific Chorus Frog
Hyla squirella	Squirrel Treefrog
Hyla versicolor	Gray Treefrog
Pseudacris cadaverina [3]	California Chorus Frog
Pseudacris crucifer [3]	Spring Peeper
Rana aurora	Red-legged Frog
Rana boylii [4]	Foothill Yellow-legged Frog
Rana catesbeiana [5]	Bullfrog
Rana clamitans	Green Frog
Rana erythraea	Red-eared Frog
Rana esculenta	Edible Frog
Rana nigromaculata [6]	Black-spotted Frog
Rana pipiens	Leopard Frog
Rana ridibunda	Marsh Frog
Rana rugosa [5]	Wrinkled Frog
Rana septentrionalis	Mink Frog
Rana sylvatica	Wood Frog
Rana temporaria	Eurasian Common Frog
Asterochelys [7]	Tortoises, all species in genus except:
Asterochelys radiata [8]	Radiated Tortoise
Asterochelys yniphora [8]	Angulated Tortoise

HI

Chelonoidis [7]	South American Tortoises, all species in genus except:
	Chelonoidis nigra [9] Galapagos Tortoise
Chersina angulata	Bow-sprit Tortoise
Chinemys megalocephala	Big-headed Pond Turtle
Chrysemys picta	Painted Turtle
Clemmys	Pond Turtles, all species in genus
Cuora yunnanensis	Asian Box Turtle
Deirochelys reticularia	Chicken Turtle
Emydoidea blandingii [10]	Blanding's Turtle
Emys orbicularis	European Pond Turtle
Geochelone [11]	Tortoises, all species in genus
Gopherus berlandieri	Texas Tortoise
Graptemys	Map Turtles, all species in genus except:
	Graptemys oculifera [8] Ringed Sawback
Homopus areolatus	Parrot-beaked Tortoise
Homopus boulengeri	Donner-weer Tortoise
Homopus femoralis	Karoo Tortoise
Homopus signatus	Speckled Tortoise
Mauremys caspica	Caspian Pond Turtle
Mauremys japonica	Japanese Pond Turtle
Mauremys leprosa	Iberian Pond Turtle
Mauremys mutica	Taipei Pond Turtle
Megalochelys [12]	Tortoises, All species in genus
Psammobates oculifera	Serrated Geometric Tortoise
Psammobates tentorius	Knobby Geometric Tortoise
Pseudemys [13]	All species in genus except:
	Pseudemys alabamensis [8] Alabama Redbelly Turtle
	Pseudemys rubriventris [8] Eastern Redbelly Turtle
Pyxis planicauda	Flat-back Spider Tortoise
Sternotherus odoratus [14]	Common Musk Turtle
Terrapene	Box Turtles, all species in genus except:
	Terrapene coahuila [8] Aquatic Box Turtle
Testudo	Eurasian Tortoises, all species in genus
Trachemys [15]	Pond Sliders, all species in genus

[1] Listed as *Triturus vulgaria* by Hawaii.
[2] Listed as *Hyla andersoni* by Hawaii.
[3] Listed in the genus *Hyla* by Hawaii.
[4] Listed as *Rana boylei* by Hawaii.
[5] Included among non-native indigenous herpetofauna of Hawaii.
[6] Listed as *Rana nigromaculatus* by Hawaii.
[7] Currently considered a subgenus of *Geochelone*.
[8] Species included in Restricted Species B list.
[9] Species included in Restricted Species B list. Listed as *Chelonoidis elephantopus* by Hawaii.
[10] Listed as *Emydoidea blandingi* by Hawaii.
[11] Also see *Asterochelys* and *Chelonoidis*.
[12] Currently considered an extinct genus.
[13] Listed in the genus *Chrysemys* by Hawaii.
[14] Listed as *Kinosternon odoratum* by Hawaii.
[15] Not officially included in Hawaii's Conditionally Approved Species list. As currently interpreted by the Hawaii Department of Agriculture, the genus *Chrysemys* also includes all turtles in the genera *Trachemys* and *Pseudemys*.

License and Permit Information

Requirements and applications for any required importation and possession permits may be obtained from the Hawaii Department of Agriculture (address in Appendix I).

CAPTIVE MAINTENANCE REGULATIONS

In addition to the regulations of the previous sections, one additional statute regulates the possession of *Chamaeleo jacksonii*, Jackson's Chameleon, in Hawaii. This regulation is summarized below.

Chamaeleo jacksonii, Jackson's Chameleon may be possessed only on the islands of Hawaii, Maui, and Oahu. The movement of Jackson's Chameleon between islands is prohibited (HRS 158-A).

Captive Maintenance Regulations Review

The following is a brief review of all of Hawaii's restrictions on the captive maintenance of amphibians and reptiles.

a. State and Federal permits are required to possess Endangered and Threatened species.
b. Non-native species occurring in the wild in Hawaii may be possessed without permit, unless otherwise specified.
c. Prohibited species may not be possessed.
d. Permits are required to possess any species included among part A or B of the Restricted Animals List.
e. Permits are not required to possess species included in the Conditionally Approved Animals List.
f. *Chamaeleo jacksonii*, Jackson's Chameleons may only be possessed on the islands of Hawaii, Maui, and Oahu

(b above see Native Wildlife Regulations and Importation and Commercial Trade Regulations)
(c, d, and e see Importation and Commercial Trade Regulations)
(f above see Captive Trade Regulations)

IDAHO

ENDANGERED, THREATENED, AND SPECIAL CONCERN SPECIES

The Idaho Department of Fish and Game utilizes a complex system in which various members of the state's fauna are classified as endangered, threatened, special concern priority, special concern peripheral, special concern, or protected species. Animals in all of these categories receive full legal protection, as specified in chapter 6 of the Rules of the Idaho Fish and Game Commission (reference IDAPA 1301-06-300.02).

The following species of amphibians and reptiles are included in Idaho's current (July 1994) list of fully protected species. Permits are required for all activities involving any of these species.

Species	Common Name	Status
Plethodon idahoensis	Coeur d'Alene Salamander	S.C. Priority
Rana pipiens	Northern Leopard Frog	S.C. Priority
Rana pretiosa	Spotted Frog	S.C. Priority
Clemmys marmorata	Western Pond Turtle	Special Concern
Crotaphytus bicinctores	Mojave Black-Collared Lizard	S.C. Peripheral
Diadophis punctatus	Ringneck Snake	Special Concern
Rhinocheilus lecontei	Longnose Snake	S.C. Peripheral
Sonora semiannulata	Ground Snake	S.C. Peripheral

Protected Species Permit Information

Permits allowing for the collection and/or possession of Idaho's endangered, threatened, and special concern species may be issued to qualified individuals and institutions for legitimate research or educational purposes. Permit requirements and applications may be obtained from the Idaho Department of Fish and Game (address in Appendix I).

NATIVE WILDLIFE REGULATIONS

Restrictions on the collection and possession of amphibians and reptiles wild caught in Idaho are specified in the Rules of the Idaho Game and Fish Commission. The following is a summarized review of Idaho's regulations concerning the non-commercial collection of amphibians and reptiles from the wild.

Native amphibians and reptiles not classified as endangered, threatened, or special concern species, except Bullfrogs, Rana catesbeiana, are considered unprotected wildlife. Unprotected wildlife may be taken in any amount, at any time, and in any manner unless otherwise specified. A valid Idaho hunting or combination hunting and fishing license is required (IDAPA 1301-06-300.03).

* This regulation does not allow for the unlimited possession of any species held alive in captivity (see the two following regulations).

No wildlife except wildlife classified as unprotected or predatory may be taken from the wild and kept alive in captivity (IDAPA 1301-10-100.06).

The possession limit without permit for native amphibians and reptiles held alive in captivity is four of each species unless otherwise specified (IDAPA 1301-10-100.06b).

Frogs

Rana catesbeiana, Bullfrogs are considered game fish by the Idaho Fish and Game Commission and may be taken by hand, bow and arrow, crossbow, spear, or mechanical device excluding firearms. The daily bag and possession limit is 12 specimens. A valid fishing license is required (IDAPA 13-01-06-100.04q and 300.01).

License and Permit Information

Hunting and fishing licenses are available from most bait shops and sporting goods stores. Annual fees for game hunting licenses are $7.50 for residents and $101.50 for non-residents. Non-resident nongame licenses valid from January through August are available for a fee of $16.50. Fishing licenses (for bullfrogs only) cost $16.50 annually for residents and $51.50 annually for non-residents. Ten-, three- and one-day non-resident fishing licenses are also available at a reduced cost. Combination hunting and fishing licenses are available to residents only at an annual fee of $21.50.

IMPORTATION AND COMMERCIAL TRADE REGULATIONS

Native Species

The following regulation concerning the possession and sale of unprotected wildlife is included in the Rules of the Idaho Fish and Game Commission.

No permit shall be required to sell, export, or transport within Idaho any legally taken species of wildlife classified as unprotected (IDAPA 1301-10-100.08).

Exotic Species

The following summarized regulations concerning the importation, possession, and sale of wildlife are included in the Rules of the Idaho Fish and Game Commission.

An import permit is required to import any live wildlife into Idaho (IDAPA 13-01-10-200.04).

Wildlife or wildlife parts legally obtained from outside of Idaho may be possessed and sold unless otherwise specified (IDAPA 1301-10-300.03).

* The sale of amphibians and reptiles obtained from outside of Idaho is only allowed if such sale is legally permitted in the state or country of origin.

License and Permit Information

Information on and applications for importation permits may be obtained from the Idaho Department of Fish and Game (address in Appendix I).

CAPTIVE MAINTENANCE REGULATIONS

In addition to any restrictions included among the previous regulations, the following regulation concerning the caging of venomous reptiles has been incorporated into the Rules of the Idaho Fish and Game Commission.

All venomous reptiles in captivity shall be kept in a cage or in a safety glass enclosure sufficiently strong, and in the case of a cage, of small enough mesh to prevent the animal's escape and with double walls sufficient to prevent penetration of fangs to the outside. All cages and glass enclosures must be locked (IDAPA 13-01-10-200.11f).

Captive Maintenance Regulations Review

The following is a brief review of the restrictions on the possession of amphibians and reptiles included among the previous regulations.

a. Permits are required to possess any amphibian or reptile included in Idaho's lists of endangered, threatened, special concern, or protected species.
b. Possession limit for unprotected native amphibians and reptiles is four of each species unless otherwise specified.
c. *Rana catesbeiana*, Bullfrogs have a possession limit of 12 specimens. A valid fishing license is required.
d. No restrictions on the possession of non-native amphibians and reptiles.

(b and c see Native Wildlife Regulations).

STATE OF IDAHO
Idaho Department of Fish & Game

APPLICATION FOR A SCIENTIFIC COLLECTING PERMIT

Please fill in, sign, and return this form to the Idaho Fish & Game Regional office within your study area (addresses are shown on back side of this page). Refer to the attached restrictions and guidelines. **Allow four to six weeks for processing.**

Name_____ Address_____
SSN# or D.O.B._____   _____
Work Phone #_____   _____
Affiliated with_____

Qualifications and background_____
_____
Purpose: Specimen Collection___, Presence/absence___, Density
Estimate___, Other_____
_____
Species involved_____
_____
Methods & equipment to be used (**METHODS NOT LISTED ARE PROHIBITED**)
_____
_____
Specific waters (see No.3, back page)_____
_____
_____
Disposition of specimens_____
Could this collecting be done during and limited to the regular open season, using conventional gear and within the established bag limits for the species, water, and/or area?_____. If not, it must be limited to a minimum period of time.

Dates_____
Additional information_____
_____
_____

          Signature of applicant_____

APPROVED BY;
_____Regional Fisheries
_____Regional Enforcement
_____/_____Fisheries/Enforcement Bureau

Mandatory Report Form___
scpfor93

Sample Permit Application - Courtesy of the Idaho Department of Fish and Game.

ILLINOIS

ENDANGERED, THREATENED, AND SPECIAL CONCERN SPECIES

Illinois lists various species of the state's flora and fauna as either endangered or threatened and all listed species are protected by the Illinois Endangered Species Protection Act, as specified in chapter 520 of Illinois Revised Statutes (reference: 520 IL RS 10.1 to 10.11). The Illinois Act was enacted in 1973 and was most recently amended in 1986. This law is similar in concept to the Federal Endangered Species Act, and permits are required to possess, take, transport, sell, offer for sale, give or otherwise dispose of any species protected by the Illinois or the U.S. Endangered Species Acts.

The following is the current (October 1993) list of state endangered or threatened amphibians and reptiles, as specified in chapter 17 of the Illinois Administrative Code (reference 17 IL AC 1010). As stated above, permits are required for any and all activities involving these species.

Species	Common Name	Status
Ambystoma platineum [1]	Silvery Salamander	Endangered
Cryptobranchus alleganiensis	Hellbender	Endangered
Desmognathus fuscus	Dusky Salamander	Endangered
Hemidactylium scutatum	Four-toed Salamander	Threatened
Pseudacris streckeri	Illinois Chorus Frog	Threatened
Clemmys guttata	Spotted Turtle	Endangered
Kinosternon flavescens	Illinois Mud Turtle	Endangered
Macrochelys temminckii [2]	Alligator Snapping Turtle	Threatened
Pseudemys concinna	River Cooter	Endangered
Clonophis kirtlandii	Kirtland's Snake	Threatened
Crotalus horridus	Timber Rattlesnake	Threatened
Elaphe emoryi [3]	Great Plains Rat Snake	Threatened
Heterodon nasicus	Western Hognose Snake	Threatened
Masticophis flagellum	Coachwhip Snake	Threatened
Nerodia cyclopion	Green Water Snake	Threatened
Nerodia fasciata	Broad-banded Water Snake	Endangered
Sistrurus catenatus	Eastern Massasauga	Endangered
Thamnophis sauritus	Eastern Ribbon Snake	Endangered

[1] Not listed in Collins (1997).
[2] Listed as *Macroclemys temminckii* by Illinois.
[3] Listed as *Elaphe guttata emoryi* by Illinois. Illinois does differentiate between the Great Plains Rat Snake and the Corn or Red Rat Snake however, and permits are not required to possess, barter, or sell true *Elaphe guttata* in Illinois.

Protected Species Permit Information

Several types of permits authorizing normally prohibited activities involving state protected endangered and threatened species are issued by the Illinois Department of Natural Resources. Scientific permits which are issued to qualified individuals for purposes of legitimate research only. Educational permits are only issued to educational institutions such as schools, zoos, or museums, or to individuals employed or sponsored by such an institution. Zoological permits allow for the public exhibition of state endangered and threatened species and are issued to recognized, qualified institutions. Propagation permits are required to attempt the propagation of any protected species and propagation permits are only issued as an addendum to state scientific or zoological permits. Limited permits allowing for the possession, purchase, and sale of legally acquired specimens of protected species by both individuals and institutions are also issued on occasion. There are currently no fees for any of these permits. A complete list of permit requirements and permit applications may be obtained from the Endangered Species Program Manager, Illinois Department of Natural Resources (address in Appendix I).

NATIVE WILDLIFE REGULATIONS

Illinois is one of a growing number of states which has specific legislation regulating activities involving native amphibians and reptiles. Possession limits, legal capture methods, and a variety of other restrictions are all included in a single Illinois Department of Natural Resources regulation, "The Taking of Reptiles and Amphibians," as specified in chapter 17 of the Illinois Administrative Code (17 IL AC 1-880). In general, all unprotected amphibians and reptiles except turtles and Bullfrogs may be collected and possessed within specified limits without license. A valid fishing license is required to collect Bullfrogs and turtles. Those portions of this legislation restricting the non-commercial collection and possession of native amphibian and reptile species is summarized below.

Amphibians and reptiles may be captured by any device or method which is not designated or intended to bring about the death or serious injury of the animals captured. This shall not restrict the use of legally taken reptiles or amphibians as bait by anglers (17 IL AC 1-880.20e).

* Does not include state threatened or endangered species, Bullfrogs, or turtles (see Frogs and Turtles below).

Any captured reptiles and amphibians which are not to be retained in the possession of the captor shall be immediately released at the site of capture (17 IL AC 1-880.20f).

The daily catch limit for amphibians and reptiles is eight of each species. The possession limit for amphibians and reptiles is 16 of each species (17 IL AC 1-880.30).

Habitat features which are disturbed in the course of a search for reptiles and amphibians shall be returned to as near their original position and condition as possible, e.g. overturned stones and logs shall be restored to their original locations (17 IL AC 1-880.50).

Frogs
Rana catesbeiana, Bullfrogs may be taken by hook and line, gig, spear, bow and arrow, hand, or dip net only. A valid Illinois fishing license is required (17 IL AC 1-880.20a and 880.20c).

Turtles
Turtles may be taken only by hand, hook and line, or dip net. A valid fishing license is required (17 IL AC 1-880.20a and 880.20b).

License and Permit Information
Illinois Sport Fishing Licenses are available at most sporting goods or bait stores at an annual fee of $13.00 for residents and $24.50 for non-residents. Ten day non-resident fishing licenses are also available at a cost of $13.00.

IMPORTATION AND COMMERCIAL TRADE REGULATIONS

Native Species

The following restriction on the sale of native amphibians and reptiles is included in Illinois' Taking of Reptiles and Amphibians regulation.

It is unlawful to take, possess, buy, sell, offer to buy or sell or barter any reptile, amphibian or their eggs or parts taken from the wild in Illinois for commercial purposes unless otherwise authorized by statute (17 IL AC 1-880.10).

* The captive produced offspring of wild caught native amphibians and reptiles may be sold by authority of an Illinois aquaculture license (see License and Permit Information below).

Native and Exotic Species

Illinois considers certain native and non-native reptiles to be dangerous animals and prohibits their possession. This apparently also prohibits their sale (see Captive Maintenance Regulations below).

License and Permit Information

Illinois aquaculture licenses allowing for the sale of captive produced specimens of native amphibians and reptiles are available for an annual fee of $50. Applications for this license may be obtained from the Illinois Department of Natural Resources' Office of Licenses and Permits (address in Appendix I).

CAPTIVE MAINTENANCE REGULATIONS

Native Species

The following portion of Illinois' Taking of Reptiles and Amphibians legislation concerns native species produced in captivity.

Captive born offspring of a legally held reptile or amphibian, not intended for commercial purposes, is exempt from the possession limits of section 880.30 for a period of 90 days 17 IL AC 1-880.40).

Native and Exotic Species

The Illinois Dangerous Animals Act (reference: IL CS 720-585) specifically prohibits the keeping of any poisonous or life-threatening reptile. Although no definition of what constitutes a life-threatening reptile is included in this regulation, Illinois currently considers any adult (over six feet in length) constricting snake and all crocodilians to be life-threatening.

Captive Maintenance Regulations Review

The following is a brief review of the restrictions on the possession of amphibians and reptiles included among Illinois' regulations.
a. Endangered and threatened species may not be possessed except by permit.
b. The possession limit for native amphibians and reptiles is 16 of each species.
c. The keeping of all venomous reptiles is prohibited except by permit
d. The keeping of crocodilians is prohibited except by permit .
e. Any constricting snake over six feet in length may not be possessed without permit.

(b above see Native Wildlife Regulations).
(c, d and e above see Captive Maintenance Regulations).

INDIANA

ENDANGERED, THREATENED, AND SPECIAL CONCERN SPECIES

Rare and vulnerable species of Indiana's indigenous wildlife, as well as all federally listed endangered and threatened species, are legally protected by the Indiana Nongame and Endangered Species Conservation Act, as specified in title 14 of Indiana Statutes Annotated (reference: ISA I.C. 14-2-8-5). Similar in concept to the U.S. Endangered Species Act, this legislation prohibits the collection, possession, transportation, or sale of any listed species without permit. Unlike the federal Endangered Species Act, however, Indian's legislation contains no threatened wildlife classification and all protected animals are simply listed as endangered species by the Indiana Department of Natural Resources.

The following amphibians and reptiles are included in Indiana's current (August 1996) list of endangered species, as specified in the fish and wildlife rules of the Indiana Administrative Code (reference: 310 IAC 3.1-5-4). As stated previously, permits are required for all activities involving any of these species.

Species	Common Name
Aneides aeneus [1]	Green Salamander
Cryptobranchus alleganiensis	Hellbender
Hemidactylium scutatum	Four-toed Salamander
Pseudotriton ruber	Northern Red Salamander
Rana areolata	Crawfish Frog
Clemmys guttata	Spotted Turtle
Emydoidea blandingii [2]	Blanding's Turtle
Kinosternon subrubrum	Eastern Mud Turtle
Macrochelys temminckii [3]	Alligator Snapping Turtle
Pseudemys concinna	Hieroglyphic Turtle
Terrapene carolina	Eastern Box Turtle
Agkistrodon piscivorus	Cottonmouth
Cemophora coccinea	Scarlet Snake
Clonophis kirtlandi	Kirtland's Snake
Crotalus horridus	Timber Rattlesnake
Liochlorophis vernalis [4]	Smooth Green Snake
Nerodia erythrogaster	Copperbelly Watersnake
Sistrurus catenatus	Massasauga
Tantilla coronata	Crowned Snake
Thamnophis butleri	Butler's Garter Snake

[1] Listed as *Aneides aenus* by Indiana.
[2] Listed as *Emydoidea blandingi* by Indiana.
[3] Listed as *Macroclemys temminckii* by Indiana.
[4] Listed as *Opheodrys vernalis* by Indiana.

Protected Species Permit Information

Scientific collectors permits are issued to properly accredited individuals or institutions for legitimate research purposes only. A $10 fee is required to receive a scientific permit. Permits allowing for the possession of legally obtained protected species for educational purposes may also be issued. Permit requirements and applications may be obtained from the Commercial License Clerk of the Division of Fish and Wildlife, Indiana Department of Natural Resources (address in Appendix I).

NATIVE WILDLIFE REGULATIONS

Indiana regulates the collection and possession of native amphibians and reptiles in the fish and wildlife rules of the Indiana Administrative Code (reference: 310 IAC 3.1-5). In this legislation all native amphibians and reptiles, except frogs, turtles, and state listed endangered species, are considered "exempted wildlife" (310 IAC 3.1-5-5). Native amphibian and reptile species designated as exempted wildlife are unprotected and may be taken at anytime without license (310 IAC 3.1-1-5). Frogs and turtles are subject to specified collection methods as well as daily and seasonal limitations and a valid hunting or fishing license is required for their collection. Indiana's regulations restricting the non-commercial collection of native frogs and turtles are summarized below.

Frogs

The season for collecting and possessing frogs is from June 15 through April 30 of the following year. The daily bag limit is 25 frogs. Frogs may be taken by one of the following methods: gig or spear having a head not more than three inches wide with a single row of tines; bow and arrow; club; hand; single pole or hand line with not more than one hook or artificial lure affixed; .22 caliber firearm provided the projectiles discharged are birdshot. The use of artificial light is permitted. A valid fishing or hunting license is required. (310 IAC 3.1-5-3).

* As currently interpreted by the Indiana Department of Natural Resources, this regulation does not prohibited the possession of legally acquired frogs during the closed season.

Turtles

Turtles may be taken at any time of year with no bag limit. Turtles may be taken by the following methods; a trap, or other mechanical device which has no opening below the surface of the water; hand; a gaff, or any method considered sport fishing by Indiana statute. A valid hunting or fishing license is required (310 IAC 3.1-5-2).

*The two preceding regulations do not include any frogs or turtles included in the State's endangered species list.

License and Permit Information

A valid fishing or hunting license is required to take turtles and frogs. Both licenses are available from most bait shops or sporting goods stores. The annual fee for fishing licenses is $8.75 for residents and $15.75 for nonresidents. One, three, and seven day non-resident fishing licenses are also available.

IMPORTATION AND COMMERCIAL TRADE REGULATIONS

Native Species
Although not specifically referring to amphibians or reptiles, the following statute of the Indiana Code restricts the transportation and sale of legally "protected" species of Indiana's native wildlife.

It is unlawful to knowingly or intentionally sell, purchase, barter, or transport or attempt to sell, purchase, barter, or transport, any wild animal, animal nest, or eggs that are protected by law (ISA I.C. 14-22-38-6).

IN

* As currently interpreted by the Indiana Department of Natural Resources, the preceding legislation prohibits the sale, purchase, or transportation of native frog and turtle species wild caught within the state, as well as any amphibian or reptile included in Indiana's list of endangered species. Specimens of native frogs and turtles legally obtained from outside of Indiana may be possessed and possibly sold with legitimate documentation (sales receipts, collecting permits, etc.) recording the legal source of their acquisition. There are currently no restrictions on the importation, possession, or sale of those native amphibians and reptiles designated as exempted wildlife.

Exotic Species

With the exception of the following summarized regulation, the State of Indiana does not currently restrict the importation or sale of any non-native amphibian or reptile species.

No person may bring into the State of Indiana for the purpose of release or selling for release any living fish or wild animal without a permit (ISA I.C. 14-2-7-20).

CAPTIVE MAINTENANCE REGULATIONS

Although not currently affecting the possession of any species of amphibian or reptile, legislation requiring a permit to possess non-native wild animals deemed harmful to native wildlife does exist in Indiana (reference: IC 14-2-7-21).

Captive Maintenance Regulations Review

The following is a review of the current restrictions on the captive maintenance of amphibians and reptiles in Indiana.

a. A permit is required to possess federally listed threatened and endangered species and state listed endangered species.
b. Unless otherwise specified, no restrictions on the possession of unprotected native amphibians and reptiles.
c. A valid hunting or fishing license or documentation of legal source of acquisition is required to possess native frog species.
d. A valid hunting or fishing license or documentation of legal source of acquisition is required to possess native turtle species.
e. No restrictions on the possession of any non-native amphibian and reptile species.

(b above see Native Wildlife Regulations)
(c and d above see Native Wildlife Regulations and Importation and Commercial Trade Regulations).
(e above see Importation and Commercial Trade Regulations).

IOWA

ENDANGERED, THREATENED, AND SPECIAL CONCERN SPECIES

The Iowa Department of Natural Resources lists various species of the state's flora and fauna as endangered, threatened, or as special concern species. Amphibians and reptiles in all three categories are legally protected by the Iowa Nongame and Endangered Species Act, as specified in chapter 481 of the Code of Iowa (reference: IC 481B). This legislation also allows for the protection of species not officially listed as endangered, threatened, or of special concern (see Native Wildlife Regulations).

The following amphibian and reptile species are included in the current (March 1994) listing of endangered, threatened, and special concern species in Iowa, as specified in chapter 77 of the Iowa Administrative Code (reference: IAC 571-77.2). All activities involving any of these species requires a permit.

Species	Common Name	Status
Ambystoma laterale	Blue-spotted Salamander	Endangered
Necturus maculosus	Mudpuppy	Endangered
Notophthalmus viridescens	Central Newt	Threatened
Rana areolata	Crawfish Frog	Endangered
Clemmys insculpta	Wood Turtle	Endangered
Kinosternon flavescens	Yellow Mud Turtle	Endangered
Sternotherus odoratus	Common Musk Turtle	Threatened
Terrapene ornata	Ornate Box Turtle	Threatened
Eumeces obsoletus	Great Plains Skink	Endangered
Ophisaurus attenuatus	Slender Glass Lizard	Endangered
Agkistrodon contortrix	Copperhead	Endangered
Carphophis amoenus	Worm Snake	Threatened
Crotalus viridis	Prairie Rattlesnake	Endangered
Heterodon nasicus	Western Hognose Snake	Endangered
Lampropeltis getula [1]	Speckled Kingsnake	Endangered
Liochlorophis vernalis [2]	Smooth Green Snake	Threatened
Nerodia erythrogaster	Yellowbelly Water Snake	Endangered
Nerodia rhombifer	Diamondback Water Snake	Threatened
Sistrurus catenatus	Massasauga	Endangered
Virginia valeriae	Smooth Earth Snake	Threatened

[1] Listed as *Lampropeltis getulus* by Iowa.
[2] Listed as *Opheodrys vernalis* by Iowa.

Protected Species Permit Information

Portions of chapter 481B of the Iowa Code and chapter 111 of the Iowa Administrative Code (reference: IAC 571-111.1 to 111.9) specifically address the issue of permits allowing for the collection and possession of Iowa's protected species. A variety of permit types, including Scientific Collector's, Educational Project, Wildlife Rehabilitation, and Wildlife Salvage, are available at a $5.00 annual fee. The State of Iowa is very selective about what types of activities will be authorized, however, and each permit request if evaluated on an individual basis. Further information on and applications for any required permits may be obtained from the Iowa Department of Natural Resources (address in Appendix I). Those portions of chapter 481B directly relating to endangered and threatened species permits are included below in their entirety.

The director may permit the taking, possession, purchase, sale, transportation, importation, exportation, or shipment of endangered or threatened species which appear on the state list for scientific, zoological, or educational purposes for propagation in captivity of such fish, plants or wildlife to ensure their survival (IC 481B.7).

A species of fish, plant, or wildlife appearing on any of the lists of endangered species or threatened species which enters the state from another state or from outside the territorial limits of the United States may enter, be transported, possessed, and sold in accordance with rules adopted by the commission (IC 481B.9).

NATIVE WILDLIFE REGULATIONS

Restrictions on the non-commercial possession of native amphibians and reptiles wild caught in Iowa are included among the statutes of the Code of Iowa (reference: IC) and the regulations of the Iowa Administrative Code (reference: IAC). In general, most native species are considered "protected nongame wildlife," and their collection or possession without permit is prohibited unless otherwise specified in the following summarized regulations.

Protected nongame species include wild fish, wild birds, wild bats, wild reptiles, and wild amphibians, or dead bodies, body parts, or products made from the bodies or parts of such animals. Nongame does not include game, fish species which may be legally taken, fur-bearing animals, turtles or frogs. Species which by their abundance or habits are declared a nuisance shall be unprotected (IC 481A.42).

Amphibians
Bait may be taken and possessed for personal use. Bait includes but is not limited to minnows, green sunfish, gizzard shad, frogs, crayfish, salamanders, and mussels. A valid Iowa fishing license is required (IC 481A.145).

Frogs
Frogs, except Bullfrogs, *Rana catesbeiana*, may be taken throughout the year with a daily bag limit of 48 and a possession limit of 96 frogs in total. There is no minimum size limit. Frogs may be used for bait or food purposes. A valid fishing license is required (IAC 81.1).

Rana catesbeiana, Bullfrogs may be taken continuously throughout the year. The daily bag and possession limit is 12 specimens, and there is no minimum size requirement. A valid fishing license is required to take and possess bullfrogs (IAC 81.1).

*The transportation out of state of any frog wild caught in Iowa is prohibited.

Turtles
Legal species of turtles may be taken throughout the state. A valid Iowa resident or non-resident fishing license is required. Non-residents possessing valid Illinois, Nebraska, South Dakota, or Wisconsin fishing licenses may take legal turtle species from those portions of the Big Sioux, Mississippi, and Missouri Rivers forming the boundary between Iowa and each respective state without an Iowa fishing license (IAC 86). Only turtles designated as legal species may be taken, and all other turtle species are protected. Turtles may be taken by hand, turtle hook, turtle trap, or hook and line. The possession limit for legal turtles is 100 pounds for live turtles and 50 pounds for "dressed" turtles (IC 482.11).

The following turtles are designated legal species and may be taken from all areas of the state (IC 482.11):

Apalone spp.	Softshell Turtles, all species
Chelydra serpentina	Common Snapping Turtle
Chrysemys picta	Painted Turtles

Graptemys spp., Map Turtles may be legally taken from the Mississippi River and its connected backwaters only (IC 482.11).

Snakes

The following snakes are designated unprotected nongame wildlife and may be taken without limit throughout the year (IAC 76.1-2):

Crotalus horridus	Timber Rattlesnake
Thamnophis sirtalis	Common Garter Snake

License and Permit Information

Iowa fishing licenses are available from bait shops, sporting goods stores, and other retail outlets at an annual fee of $10.50 for residents and $22.50 for non-residents. Seven-day licenses are also available at a cost of $8.50 for both residents and non-residents. Permits to collect native reptiles included in the list of protected nongame species must be obtained from the Iowa Department of Natural Resources (address in Appendix I).

IMPORTATION AND COMMERCIAL TRADE REGULATIONS

Native Species

The restrictions on the possession of Iowa's native amphibians and reptiles obviously affects the sale of specimens of those species wild caught in the state. What effect these restrictions have on the importation, sale, and possession of specimens of Iowa's protected species legally obtained from outside of the state is unclear at this time. With the exception of unprotected wildlife species, the sale of any native amphibian or reptile wild caught in the state is apparently prohibited unless otherwise specified in the following regulation summary.

Amphibians

Bait, including salamanders and frogs, may be harvested and sold by licensed Iowa bait dealers (IC 481A.144).

Frogs

Frogs legally obtained from outside of Iowa may be imported, possessed, and sold by licensed Iowa bait dealers (IC 481A.145).

Turtles

A commercial fishing license is required to take and possess live or "dressed" turtles for commercial purposes (IC 482.11).

Exotic Species

The State of Iowa does not currently restrict the importation, sale, or possession of non-native amphibian and reptile species.

License and Permit Information

Further information on fees, requirements, and applications for any required licenses or permits of this section may be obtained from the Iowa Department of Natural Resources (address in Appendix I).

CAPTIVE MAINTENANCE REGULATIONS

The following is a brief review of Iowa's restrictions on the possession in captivity of amphibians and reptiles included among the above regulations.

a. Permits are required to possess endangered, threatened, special concern, and protected nongame wildlife species.

b. Salamanders may be possessed; a valid fishing license is required.

c. Frogs, except *Rana catesbeiana*, have a possession limit of 96 frogs in total. A valid fishing license is required.

d. Rana catesbeiana Bullfrogs have a possession limit of 12 specimens. A valid fishing license is required.

e. The following native turtles may be possessed with a possession limit of 100 pounds alive. A fishing license is required.

Apalone spp.	Softshell Turtles, all species
Chelydra serpentina	Common Snapping Turtle
Chrysemys picta	Painted Turtles
Graptemys spp.	Map Turtles

f. The following native snakes are unprotected and may be possessed without permit.

Crotalus horridus	Timber Rattlesnake
Thamnophis sirtalis	Common Garter Snake

g. No restrictions on the possession of non-native amphibian and reptile species.

(a above see Endangered, Threatened and Special Concern Species and Native Wildlife Regulations)
(b, c, d, e and f above see Native Wildlife Regulations)

Timber Rattlesnake, *Crotalus horridus* - One of only two snake species native to Iowa not currently protected by the state's conservation law. Photograph courtesy of James E. Gerholdt.

KANSAS

ENDANGERED, THREATENED, AND SPECIAL CONCERN SPECIES

The Kansas Department of Wildlife and Parks lists various members of the state's fauna as Endangered, Threatened, or as In Need of Conservation species. Amphibians and reptiles in all three categories are legally protected by the Kansas Nongame and Endangered Species Conservation Act of 1975, as specified in the Kansas Statutes Annotated (reference: KSA 1992 Supp. 32-957-963, 32-1009-1012, and 32-1033). While similar in context to the U.S. Endangered Species Act, this legislation pertains only to animal species and contains no provisions for the protection of rare or endangered plants.

The following amphibians and reptiles are included in the current (June 1993) Endangered, Threatened, or In Need of Conservation (N/C) species lists of Kansas. Permits are required for all activities involving any of these species.

Species	Common Name	Status
Eurycea longicauda melanopleura	Dark-sided Salamander	Threatened
Eurycea lucifuga	Cave Salamander	Endangered
Eurycea multiplicata griseogaster	Graybelly Salamander	Endangered
Notophthalmus viridescens louisianensis	Central Newt	Threatened
Typhlotriton spelaeus	Grotto Salamander	Endangered
Bufo debilis debilis [1]	Eastern Green Toad	Threatened
Bufo debilis insidior	Western Green Toad	Threatened
Bufo punctatus	Red-spotted Toad	N/C
Gastrophryne carolinensis	Eastern Narrowmouth Toad	Threatened
Pseudacris crucifer crucifer	Northern Spring Peeper	Threatened
Pseudacris streckeri streckeri [2]	Strecker's Chorus Frog	Threatened
Rana areolata circulosa	Northern Crawfish Frog	Threatened
Rana clamitans melanota	Green Frog	Threatened
Graptemys geographica	Map Turtle	Threatened
Macrochelys temminckii [3]	Alligator Snapping Turtle	N/C
Eumeces laticeps	Broadhead Skink	Threatened
Arizona elegans	Glossy Snake	N/C
Crotalus horridus	Timber Rattlesnake	N/C
Heterodon platirhinos	Eastern Hognose Snake	N/C
Heterodon nasicus	Western Hognose Snake	N/C
Hypsiglena torquata jani	Texas Night Snake	Threatened
Leptotyphlops dulcis dissectus	New Mexico Blind Snake	Threatened
Rhinocheilus lecontei tessellatus	Texas Longnose Snake	Threatened
Storeria occipitomaculata occipitomaculata	Northern Redbelly Snake	Threatened
Thamnophis marcianus marcianus	Checkered Garter Snake	Threatened
Virginia striatula	Rough Earth Snake	N/C
Virginia valeriae elegans	Western Earth Snake	Threatened

[1] According to the range map in Conant and Collins (1991) this subspecies does not occur in Kansas.
[2] No subspecies recognized in Collins (1997).
[3] Listed as *Macroclemys temminckii* by Kansas.

Protected Species Permit Information

The Kansas Department of Wildlife and Parks issues scientific, educational, and exhibition permits for species protected by the Nongame and Endangered Species Conservation Act. Each type of permit allows for a specific activity involving state protected species. There is a $10.50 permit application fee. For a list of permit conditions and any required permit applications, contact the Kansas Department of Wildlife and Parks (address in Appendix I).

NATIVE WILDLIFE REGULATIONS

Kansas Department of Wildlife and Parks regulations concerning the collection and possession of wild caught native amphibians and reptiles are specified in chapter 115 of the Kansas Administrative Regulations (reference: KAR 115). Those portions of this legislation regulating the non-commercial collection and possession of amphibians and reptiles wild caught within the state are summarized below.

Native amphibians and reptiles may be legally taken for non-commercial purposes throughout the year. There is a possession limit of five of each species. A valid hunting license is required. Amphibians and reptiles may be legally taken by the following methods (KAR 115-20-2):

1. Firearms, except fully automatic weapons
2. Bow and arrow
3. Pellet and BB gun
4. Crossbow
5. Falconry
6. Projectiles hand thrown or propelled by slingshot
7. Trap
8. Deadfall
9. Snare or noose
10. Net or seine
11. Glue board
12. Hand
13. Dogs
14. Poison, poisonous gas or smoke, provided the toxicant is registered and labeled for that use and that all permit requirements for the use of poison, poisonous gas or smoke have been met.

* Does not include endangered, threatened, or in need of conservation species.

Frogs

Rana catesbeiana, Bullfrogs may be taken from July 1 through October 31. The daily bag limit is eight and the possession limit is 24 on or after the third day. The use of artificial lights and boats is permitted while taking bullfrogs. A valid fishing license is required. Frogs may be taken by the following methods: hand, hand dip net, hook and line, gig, and bow and barbed head arrow with line attached to bow (KAR 115-7-5).

Turtles

Chelydra serpentina, Common Snapping Turtles and *Apalone* spp., Softshell Turtles may be taken throughout the year. The daily bag limit is eight and the possession limit is 24 (single species or in combination). Turtles may be taken by the following methods: hand, hook and line, set line, hand dip net, seine, turtle trap, and gig. A valid fishing license is required to take Snappers and Softshells (KAR 115-7-5).

License and Permit Information

Kansas hunting and fishing licenses may be purchased from most bait or sporting goods stores. The annual hunting license fee is $15.00 for residents and $65.00 for non-residents. Annual fishing: licenses cost resident $15.00 and non-resident $35.00.

IMPORTATION AND COMMERCIAL TRADE REGULATIONS

Native Species

Restrictions on the sale of indigenous amphibians and reptiles, including both specimens wild caught within the state and specimens legally acquired outside of Kansas, are included among the wildlife legislation of the Kansas Administrative Regulations (reference: KAR 115) and in chapter 32 of Kansas Statutes Annotated (reference: KSA 32). The following is a summarization of these statutes and regulations.

It is unlawful to take any wildlife in Kansas for sale, exchange or other commercial purposes, except as otherwise permitted by law (KSA 32-1002).

A game breeder permit is required to raise and sell any amphibian and reptile species indigenous to Kansas (KAR 115-12-3).

Amphibians

The following native amphibians may be commercially harvested for sale as bait (115-17-2):

Ambystoma tigrinum	Tiger Salamander
Acris crepitans blanchardi	Blanchard's Cricket Frog
Bufo americanus	American Toad
Bufo cognatus	Great Plains Toad
Bufo woodhousii	Woodhouse's Toad
Pseudacris clarkii	Spotted Chorus Frog
Rana blairi	Plains Leopard Frog
Spea bombifrons [1]	Plains Spadefoot Toad

[1] Listed as *Scaphiopus bombifrons* by Kansas.

Only amphibian species native to or naturalized in Kansas may be sold as live bait. A commercial fish bait permit is required to harvest or sell amphibians as bait (KAR 115-17-2 and 115-17-3).

Commercial Rattlesnake Hunting Regulations

A significant portion of the amphibian and reptile legislation of Kansas specifically restricts the timing, duration, and location of "Annual Commercial Rattlesnake Harvesting Events" (i.e. rattlesnake roundups). This legislation also regulates the collection, possession, and sale of harvested rattlesnakes and establishes event permit requirements and fees. In its entirety, the Rattlesnake Roundup legislation is over 13 pages in length and the following is only a very brief review of these regulations. Complete copies of this legislation may be obtained from the Kansas Department of Wildlife and Parks (address in Appendix I).

Crotalus viridis viridis, Prairie Rattlesnake is the only species which may be commercially harvested. All rattlesnakes over 18 inches in length not otherwise disposed of and all rattlesnakes under 18 inches in length must be released alive upon completion of any harvesting event.

A permit from the Department of Wildlife and Parks is required to hold a commercial rattlesnake harvest event. The events may be held from April 1 to June 15 and may not exceed 30 days in length. The open area for the commercial collection of rattlesnakes is the portion of Kansas west of U.S. Highway 283, with the exception of Morton County.

All individuals participating in the actual collection of rattlesnakes during a harvest event must have a Commercial Prairie Rattlesnake Harvest permit. With a valid Kansas hunting license a permit costs $5, without a hunting license the fee is $20. This permit only allows for the collection of rattlesnakes during licensed harvesting events. Provided they are not purchased for resale, a permit holder may sell prairie rattlesnakes or their parts during a licensed commercial event only. Finished rattlesnake products may be sold without limit in time or purpose. The daily bag limit is 10 rattlesnakes per day. The possession limit is 20 rattlesnakes or rattlesnake parts. Snakes may be taken by the following methods: hand, noose, hook, tong, or fork.

A Commercial Prairie Rattlesnake Dealer permit is required to purchase rattlesnakes for resale. Any person may purchase prairie rattlesnakes, prairie rattlesnake parts, or finished rattlesnake products (KAR 115-17-16 to 115-17-20).

Exotic Species

The following regulation concerning the sale and possession of non-native amphibians and reptiles is included among the wildlife legislation of the Kansas Administrative Regulations.

Amphibian and reptile species which are not native or indigenous to Kansas may be imported, possessed, sold, offered for sale, or purchased provided it was legally obtained from outside of the State (KAR 115-20-3).

License and Permit Information

Information and applications for all of the required commercial permits and licenses of this section may be obtained from the Kansas Department of Wildlife and Parks (address in Appendix I).

CAPTIVE MAINTENANCE REGULATIONS

In addition to the restrictions on the captive maintenance of both native and exotic species of amphibians and reptiles included among the preceding regulations, the following summarized regulation is applicable to the captive maintenance of these animals.

Exotic wildlife shall be confined or controlled at all times and shall not be released in Kansas (KAR 115-20-3c).

Captive Maintenance Regulations Review

The following is a brief review of Kansas' restrictions on the captive possession of amphibians and reptiles.

a. A permit is required to possess endangered, threatened, or in need of conservation species.

b. Possession of unprotected indigenous amphibians and reptiles is limited to five of each species without a game breeders permit unless otherwise specified.

KS

c. *Rana catesbeiana*, Bullfrogs have a possession limit of 24 specimens. A fishing license is required.

d. The following native turtle species have a possession limit of 24 specimens in aggregate (all species combined). A valid fishing license is required:

Chelydra serpentina	Common Snapping Turtle
Apalone spp.	Softshell Turtles, all species indigenous to Kansas

e. Game breeders permits are required to breed or sale all amphibians and reptiles indigenous to Kansas.

f. All exotic amphibian and reptile species may be possessed without limit.

(b above see Native Wildlife Regulations and Importation and Commercial Trade Regulations).
(c and d above see Native Wildlife Regulations).
(e and f above see Importation and Commercial Trade Regulations).

Illegal Herpetological Collecting Equipment - With the exception of fully automatic firearms, virtually anything can be used to collect amphibians and reptiles within the State of Kansas. Photograph courtesy of Terry Scheiber.

KENTUCKY

ENDANGERED, THREATENED, AND SPECIAL CONCERN SPECIES

Although Kentucky has endangered species legislation, as specified in chapter 150 of the state's Revised Statutes (reference: KRS 150.183), there is currently no official list of state threatened or endangered wildlife. Because of this lack of an official state list, only those species included in the U.S. Endangered and Threatened Species list are legally protected by Kentucky's endangered species legislation at this time. All other published listings of endangered and threatened species native to Kentucky are purely "suggested" lists.

The Copperbelly Water Snake, *Nerodia erythrogaster neglecta*, is the only reptile species native to Kentucky included in the current (January 1997) list of federally protected endangered and threatened species. The population of this species occurring within Kentucky, however, is not currently protected by the U.S. Endangered Species Act (see U.S. Endangered and Threatened Species).

Protected Species Permit Information

Although not currently required for any native amphibian or reptile species, authorization from the Kentucky Department of Fish and Wildlife Department is necessary to conduct any activity involving a federally listed endangered or threatened species. Before such authorization is granted to any individual, that individual must be named an "Agent of the State." Further information on this "Agent of the State" requirement may be obtained from the Kentucky Department of Fish and Wildlife Resources (address in Appendix I).

NATIVE WILDLIFE REGULATIONS

Restrictions on the non-commercial collection and possession of native amphibians and reptiles wild caught in the state are specified in the Kentucky Revised Statutes (reference: KRS) or in Kentucky Administrative Regulations (reference: KAR}. In general, Kentucky's wildlife is classified as unprotected or protected, with "protected wildlife" being defined as any species for which an open or closed season for taking has been designated (reference: KRS 150.010.20). The following is a summarization of Kentucky's restrictions on the non-commercial collection and possession of native amphibians and reptiles.

No wildlife may be taken by the use of fire, smoke, gas, explosives, or any mechanical, electric, or hand operated sonic recording device. The molestation or destruction of the den, hole, or nest of any wildlife is prohibited (KRS 150.365).

Unprotected wildlife may be taken without license throughout the year except during the firearm deer season. All native species of snakes and lizards are classified as unprotected wildlife (301 KAR 3:030.2).

Salamanders

Salamanders may be collected from the public waters of the State for personal use as live bait. There is a possession limit of 100 specimens. A valid fishing license is required (301 KAR 1:130).

Frogs

Frogs and tadpoles, except Bullfrogs, *Rana catesbeiana*, may be collected from the public waters of the state for personal use as bait. The possession limit is 100 frogs and 100 tadpoles. A valid fishing license is required (301 KAR 1:130).

Rana catesbeiana, Bullfrogs may be taken from noon on the third Friday in May through October 31st. The daily bag limit is 15 and the possession limit is 30 frogs. A fishing license is required to take frogs by pole and line. A hunting license is required to take frogs by firearm or archery equipment. Either license allows frogs to be taken by hand or gig (301 KAR 1:082).

Artificial lighting may be used to take frogs (KRS 150.360.3).

Turtles

Turtles may be taken throughout the year without limit. Turtles may be taken by hand or hooked line while wading, only in those waters open for gigging, grabbing, snagging, or tickling and noodling. Turtles may be taken by gig or by legal turtle trap. Legal turtle traps include barrel and floating log devices. Turtle traps must be inspected at least once every 24 hours while in use. A valid fishing license is required. A hunting license is required to take turtles by the use of bow and arrow or firearm (301 KAR 1:058).

* The Kentucky Department of Fish and Wildlife Resources interprets this regulation as prohibiting the collection of Box Turtles, genus *Terrapene*.

License and Permit Information

Kentucky hunting and fishing licenses are available from numerous retail outlets including most bait and sporting goods stores. Annual hunting license fees are $12.50 for residents and $95.00 for non-residents. Annual fees for fishing licenses are $12.50 for residents and $30.00 for non-residents. Limited short term non-resident hunting and fishing licenses are also available at a reduced cost. In addition to the above licenses, the Kentucky Department of Fish and Wildlife Resources issues two types of permits which authorize the collection and possession of native species for various purposes including; biological surveys, educational research projects, and nuisance wildlife control. Of these two permits, a Scientific Collecting permit is required for activities which involve monetary profit (i.e. paid biological surveys, environmental consultations, etc.), while Educational Collecting permits allow for activities of a purely non-profit nature. There is a $10.00 fee for an Educational Collecting permit and a $200.00 fee for a Scientific Collecting permit. Permit applications and requirements may be obtained from the Kentucky Department of Fish and Wildlife Resources (address in Appendix I).

IMPORTATION AND COMMERCIAL TRADE REGULATIONS

Native Species

Several portions of Kentucky's wildlife laws regulate the commercial taking and sale of native amphibians and reptiles including specimens wild caught in the state. The following is a summary of these restrictions.

Unless otherwise specified, it is unlawful to buy, attempt to buy, sell, barter, exchange, or trade, or have in possession with intent to buy, sell, exchange, or trade any species of protected wildlife whether wild caught in the state or lawfully obtained outside Kentucky (KRS 150.180.1).

* Protected wildlife is any species for which an open or closed season for taking has been designated (see Native Wildlife Regulations).

Amphibians

A Live Fish and Bait Dealer's License is required to sell salamanders and frogs including their larvae for use as bait (KRS 150.485).

Commercial Propagation permits are required to propagate salamanders and frogs for commercial purposes (KAR 1:115).

* The Kentucky Department of Fish and Wildlife Resources interpret these regulations to include all native and non-native species including specimens harvested from the wild within the State or legally obtained outside of Kentucky.

Turtles

A Commercial Fishing License is required to sell turtles harvested from the wild in Kentucky (301 KAR 1:058).

Native and Exotic Species

The following summarized regulation applies to the importation, possession, and sale of both native and non-native species.

The possession, propagation, exhibition, sale, or purchase for commercial purposes of any wildlife without a Commercial Pet and Propagation permit is prohibited. Transportation permits are required to import, transport, or receive shipments of live wildlife. All wildlife must be legally obtained from permitted sources only (301 KAR 2:081.4-1).

* The complete text of regulation 301 KAR 2:081 contains a list of animals which are excluded from the definition of "wildlife" (reference: 301 KAR 2:081.1). Reptiles are specifically included in this list, and are presumably exempt from any permit requirements. Amphibians are not included in the exempt animal list, however, and permits are required for their importation and sale.

License and Permit Information

Live Fish and Bait Dealer's license fees are $30.00 for residents and $60.00 for non-residents annually. Commercial Fishing licenses including 10 commercial gear tags have an annual fee of $100.00 for residents and $500.00 for non-residents. Additional commercial gear tags are available in blocks of 10 at a cost of $10.00 for residents and $75.00 for non-residents. Commercial Wildlife Pet and Propagation permits cost $200.00 annually. Wildlife Transportation permits are subject to a $25.00 fee. Further information on and applications for any required licenses and permits of this section may be obtained from the Kentucky Department of Fish and Wildlife Resources (address in Appendix I).

CAPTIVE MAINTENANCE REGULATIONS

In addition to any restrictions on the possession of amphibians and reptiles included among the regulations of the preceding sections, the following summarized portions of regulation 301 KAR 2:081 applies to the non-commercial possession of wildlife.

A Non-commercial Pet and Propagation permit is required to possess, purchase, or propagate wildlife for non-commercial purposes. Transportation permits are required to import, transport, or receive any live wildlife. Specimens may be legally collected from the wild or obtained from permitted sources (301 KAR 2:081.4).

* Reptiles are specifically excluded from the definition of "wildlife" in regulation 301 KAR 2:081, and are presumably exempt from permit requirements. Permits are required, however, to possess and/or propagate amphibians.

License and Permit Information

The fee for a Non-commercial Pet and Propagation permit is $75.00 annually. There is a $25.00 fee for a Transportation permit. Requirements and applications for these permits may be obtained from the Kentucky Department of Fish and Wildlife Resources (address in Appendix I).

Captive Maintenance Regulations Review

The following is a brief review of Kentucky's restrictions on the captive possession of amphibians and reptiles included among the regulations of the previous sections.

a. Fishing licenses or Pet and Propagation permits may be required to possess native species of salamanders, frogs, and their larvae. Possession limit 100 specimens of each category, unless otherwise specified.

b. *Rana catesbeiana*, Bullfrog possession limit is 30 specimens. In addition to the required fishing license, a Non-commercial Pet and Propagation permit is required to possess Bullfrogs during the closed season.

c. Fishing licenses may be required to possess native turtle species.

d. Non-commercial Pet and Propagation permits are required to possess non-native amphibians.

e. No restrictions on the possession of any non-native reptile species.

(a and b above see Native Wildlife Regulations and Captive Maintenance Regulations).
(c above see Native Wildlife Regulations).
(d and e above see Captive Maintenance Regulations).

TICKLING & NOODLING

LOUISIANA

ENDANGERED, THREATENED, AND SPECIAL CONCERN SPECIES

The Louisiana Natural Heritage Program maintains a listing of special concern species, in which rarer members of the state's fauna are assigned to one of 10 status categories. The inclusion of a species among the categories of the special concern list does not grant that species any legal protection, however. Although Louisiana has state endangered species legislation as specified in title 56 of the Louisiana Statutes Annotated Revised Statutes (reference: LSA R.S. 56:1901-1907), this legislation currently only protects those native species which are included in the federal endangered and threatened species list. These species are fully protected by the U.S. Endangered Species Act, as well as by the State of Louisiana.

The following reptile species native to Louisiana are included in the current (January 1997) U.S. Endangered and Threatened Species list. In addition to any permits required by the State of Louisiana, a federal permit is required for all activities involving any of these species.

Species	Common Name	Status
Alligator mississippiensis [1]	American Alligator	S/A
Caretta caretta	Loggerhead Sea Turtle	Threatened
Chelonia mydas	Green Sea Turtle	Threatened
Dermochelys coriacea	Leatherback Sea Turtle	Endangered
Eretmochelys imbricata	Hawksbill Sea Turtle	Endangered
Gopherus polyphemus	Gopher Tortoise	Threatened
Graptemys oculifera	Ringed Sawback	Threatened
Lepidochelys kempii	Atlantic Ridley Sea Turtle	Endangered

[1] Listed as threatened due to similar appearance for law enforcement purposes only. Biologically, American Alligators are neither threatened nor endangered, and various activities, including limited hunting, are regularly authorized by permit by the State of Louisiana, in conjunction with the U.S. Department of the Interior.

Protected Species Permit Information

Permits issued by the U.S. Department of the Interior are required for all activities involving any of Louisiana's listed species (see U.S. Endangered and Threatened Species). All federal permits must be obtained before any state permits will be issued. Requirements and applications for state protected species permits may be obtained from the Louisiana Department of Wildlife and Fisheries (address in Appendix I).

NATIVE WILDLIFE REGULATIONS

Louisiana is one of an elite group of states that have specific amphibian and reptile legislation which regulates both the recreational and commercial collection and possession of native species wild caught in the state. Among the unique features of Louisiana's legislation is a Reptile and Amphibian Research Fund financed by revenue generated by the sale of special licenses and, best of all, an advisory board known as the Reptile and Amphibian Task Force. The task force is specifically organized to address the concerns of a broad spectrum of special interest groups and includes representatives from the academic, conservation, hobbyist, and commercial trade communities, as well as professional herpetologists. In addition to the general amphibian and reptile legislation, specific American Alligator regulations are also included among the wildlife laws of Louisiana. As with the amphibian and reptile regulations, Louisiana's American Alligator legislation provides for an Alligator Resource

Fund financed through the proceeds of annual license fees. The following is a summary of the restrictions on the non-commercial collection and possession of wild caught amphibians and reptiles included among the wildlife laws in title 56 of the Louisiana Statutes Annotated Revised Statues (reference: LSA R.S. 56) and title 76 of the Louisiana Administrative Code (reference: LAC 76).

A valid fishing license is required to collect amphibians and reptiles for non-commercial purposes (LSA R.S. 56:632.3).

* Except as otherwise noted, there are no size or possession limits for native amphibians and reptiles.

The use of gasoline, chemicals, or other volatile substances to flush reptiles and amphibians from natural hiding places, nests, or dens is prohibited. The destruction of natural habitats is prohibited. Any logs, rocks, or other objects turned over or moved must be replaced in their original position upon completion of any inspection. Any trap or other device designed to capture amphibians and reptiles, which remains in the field, must bear a tag with the name, address and license number of the collector. All such devices must be checked every 24 hours or rendered inoperable when not in use (LSA R.S. 56:632.6).

Salamanders
The following salamander species are deemed to be especially sensitive to over collection due to low population levels or limited ranges in Louisiana. These species may not be collected from the wild at any time without permit (LAC 76 XV 101J):

Ambystoma tigrinum	Tiger Salamander
Plethodon serratus	Southern Redback Salamander
Plethodon websteri	Webster's Salamander
Pseudotriton montanus	Mud Salamander
Pseudotriton ruber	Red Salamander

*Permits allowing the collection of these species will only be issued for legitimate scientific purposes.

Frogs
The use of gigs, spears, mechanical frog catchers, and artificial lights while taking frogs is permitted. Firearms may not be possessed while hunting frogs at night (LSA R.S. 56:634A).

The following frog species may not be taken during the months of April and May (LSA R.S. 56:634B):

Rana catesbeiana	Bullfrog
Rana grylio	Pig Frog [1]

Listed as Lagoon Frog or Grunter by the State of Louisiana.

There is a minimum length requirement of five inches for Bullfrogs, *Rana catesbeiana*, and three inches for Pig Frogs, *Rana grylio*. Length is measured from the muzzle tip to the posterior end of the body (LSA R.S. 56:634C).

Alligators
Louisiana has specific American Alligator legislation consisting of a complete statutory text (reference: LSA R.S. 56:251 to 280) 10 pages in length with an additional 12 pages of associated regulations (reference: LAC 76 V 701). This extensive legislation regulates all aspects of both the non-commercial and commercial harvest and possession of the species in the state and includes importation, exportation, farming, and nuisance control provisions. The following is a brief summary of the non-commercial portions of these regulations. The complete text of Louisiana's alligator legislation may be obtained from the Louisiana Department of Wildlife and Fisheries (address in Appendix I).

Alligator Hunting licenses and individual alligator hide tags are required to harvest *Alligator mississippiensis* in Louisiana during the designated open season. The daily and seasonal bag limit is equal to the number of valid hide tags possessed. Non-residents may not harvest more than three alligators per season. The possession of any untagged alligators or alligator hides is prohibited. There are no minimum size requirements for alligators harvested from the wild during the open season. Alligators may be legally taken by hook and line of at least 300 pound test, long bow and barbed arrow attached with at least 300 pound test line, and firearm. There is a severance tax of $00.25 per alligator hide taken in Louisiana (LAC 76 V 701).

* The exact opening date and duration of the wild alligator harvest season varies on an annual basis, as designated by the Louisiana Department of Wildlife and Fisheries. The open season generally extends from mid September through early to mid October.

Alligators may not be taken between the hours of sunset and sunrise (LSA R.S. 56:259D).

Live alligators may only be taken and/or possessed under the authority of an alligator farmer license, non-game quadruped exhibitor license, or by special permit for exhibition, educational, or scientific purposes (LAC 76 V 701).

Egg collection permits and a non-game quadruped breeders license or designated agent collection permit are required to remove and/or possess alligator eggs (LAC 76 V 701).

White or albino specimens of the American Alligator may not be taken from the wild. Landowners and licensed alligator farmers may take white alligators from the wild in order to protect the specimen provided the Louisiana Department of Wildlife and Fisheries is notified of all such actions (LSA R.S. 56:280).

Turtles

Turtle traps may be used to capture turtles. All such devices must be clearly marked with the words "TURTLE TRAP" and must be placed in such a manner to allow for continuous breathing opportunities for captured specimens. All fish and/or other non-target species, except watersnakes and salamanders (e.g. Amphiumas) must be released within 24 hours of capture (LAC 76 XV 101G).

Macrochelys temminckii, Alligator Snapping Turtles have a recreational take limit of four specimens. There is no minimum size requirement (LAC 76 XV 101G).

* Listed as *Macroclemys temminckii* by Louisiana.

Malaclemys terrapin, Diamondback Terrapins may not be taken by traps of any kind. Diamondback Terrapins taken between April 15 and June 15 shall be immediately returned to the water alive (LSA R.S. 56:635).

The taking of the eggs of any species of turtle, except the Red-eared Slider, *Trachemys scripta*, is prohibited (LSA R.S. 56:635).

License and Permit Information

Louisiana freshwater fishing licenses are available from most bait shops and sporting goods stores at an annual fee of $5.50 for residents and $31 for non-residents. Non-resident seven-day licenses at a cost of $15.50 and three-day licenses at a cost of $12.50 are also available. Scientific Collector's permits will be issued free of charge for legitimate herpetological research purposes. Alligator Hunter licenses have an annual fee of $25 for residents and $150 for non-residents. There is no charge for individual alligator hide tags. Applications for Scientific Collector's permits, Alligator Hunter's license, and individual alligator tags and labels may be obtained from the Louisiana Department of Wildlife and Fisheries (address in Appendix I).

IMPORTATION AND COMMERCIAL TRADE REGULATIONS

Native Species

Restrictions on the collection, possession, propagation, exportation, and importation for commercial purposes of native amphibians and reptiles, including alligators, are specified in Louisiana's fish and wildlife laws. In addition to the legislation of the Louisiana Department of Wildlife and Fisheries, the Louisiana Department of Agriculture and Forestry regulates the commercial propagation and trade of native turtle species, as specified in title 3 of the Louisiana Statutes Annotated (reference: LSA R.S. 3.2358). The following is a summarization of Louisiana's commercial trade restrictions.

Reptile and amphibian collector's licenses are required to collect native amphibians and reptiles from the wild for commercial purposes (LSA R.S. 56:632.4).

* Does not include state listed endangered and threatened species, the prohibited salamander species of LAC 76 XV
  101J (see Native Wildlife Regulations), or American Alligators.

A Reptile and Amphibian Wholesale/Retail Dealer's license is required to import, export, transport, purchase, acquire, or sell any native amphibian or reptile for resale purposes. The sale of captive produced native species requires a Reptile and Amphibian Collector's license (LSA R.S. 56:632.5).

Frogs

Rana catesbeiana, Bullfrogs and *Rana grylio*, Pig Frogs under the legal size limits (see Native Wildlife Regulations) may be taken and sold from privately owned waters for stocking purposes. Permits are required (LAC R.S. 56:634C).

Alligators

The following is a brief summary of the portions of Louisiana's legislation regulating the commercial harvest, propagation, and transportation of American Alligators in the state.

Alligator Hunter licenses are required to harvest *Alligator mississippiensis* for commercial purposes. Alligators or alligator skins may not be purchased or sold without a Fur Buyer's license. The tanning or exportation of alligators and alligator skins for commercial purposes requires a Fur Dealer's license (LAC 76 V 701).

Unprocessed alligator parts may not be purchased or sold without an alligator parts dealer's license. Alligator parts retailer licenses are required to purchase and sell finished alligator products other than hides. Hide tags or labels are required on all unfinished alligator products (LAC 76 V 701).

Live alligators or alligator eggs may be exported from Louisiana under special authorization of the Department of Wildlife and Fisheries with the concurrence of the U.S. Fish and Wildlife Service for scientific purposes only (LAC 76 V 701).

Live alligators or alligator eggs may not be imported into Louisiana without permit (LAC 76 V 701).

Non-game quadruped exhibitors licenses are required to possess live alligators or alligator eggs for exhibition purposes (LAC 76 V 701).

LA

Alligator Farming

Non-game quadruped breeder's licenses are required to raise, possess, propagate, exhibit, or sell alligator eggs, live alligators, or alligator parts. Alligator eggs or live alligators may only be sold following the issuance of a Transfer Authorization permit. Alligator hide tags are required for all hides harvested from farm raised alligators. Alligator eggs may be harvested from the wild by licensed non-game quadruped breeders from May 15 through September 1. Egg collection permits are required. All alligator farmers harvesting eggs must hatch at least 70% of harvested eggs and maintain an 85% hatchling survival rate or egg collecting permits will be revoked. A percentage of the hatchlings from wild harvested eggs is required to be returned to the wild within two years at the original point of harvest. All released offspring shall be at least 36 inches in length, and at least 50% of the released individuals must be females (LAC 76 V 701).

Turtles

Turtles may be taken commercially with legal commercial fishing gear or by other legal methods (see Native Wildlife Regulations). A reptile and amphibian collector's license is required. The possession of finfish while engaged in commercial turtle collection activities is prohibited (LAC 76 XV 101G).

Macrochelys temminckii, Alligator Snapping Turtles have a commercial take minimum size requirement of 15 inches straight line carapace length. There is no limit on the number of specimens which may be taken (LAC 76 XV 101G-2).

* Listed as *Macroclemys temminckii* by Louisiana.

Malaclemys terrapin, Diamondback Terrapins may not be exported between April 15 through June 15 (LSA R.S. 56:635B).

Turtle Farming

Restrictions on the commercial propagation and sale of turtles are included among the Department of Agriculture and Forestry legislation in title 3 of the Louisiana Statutes Annotated Revised Statutes (reference: LSA R.S. 3) and in title 7 of the Louisiana Administrative Code (reference: LAC 7). The purpose of this legislation is to minimize the introduction and spread of salmonella or other infectious diseases within the state, while at the same time promoting the economic benefits of commercial aquaculture in Louisiana. As the actual text of the turtle farming legislation is several pages in length, the following is only a brief summary of Louisiana's restrictions on the commercial propagation of turtles. Copies of the complete text of Louisiana's turtle farming legislation may be obtained from the Louisiana Department of Agriculture and Forestry (address in Appendix I).

Pet turtles or pet turtle eggs may not be bred, hatched, propagated, raised, grown, received, shipped, transported, exported, or sold without a Pet Turtle Farmer's license. All turtle eggs must be sanitized by methods authorized by the Louisiana Department of Agriculture and Forestry. Turtles or turtle eggs may not be shipped or transported from a licensed pet turtle farm without a certificate of inspection or health certificate. Turtles or turtle eggs may not be shipped into Louisiana without permit. Accurate records documenting the source, identity, medical treatment, health, inspection, and disposal of all turtles or turtle eggs must be maintained at all times (LSA R.S. 3:2358).

Lizards

Anolis carolinensis, Green Anoles less than 1-3/4 inches in snout vent length or less than five inches in total length with the tail intact may not be purchased or sold (LAC 76 XV 101H).

Exotic Species

With the exception of the following regulation included among the turtle farming legislation of the Department of Agriculture and Forestry, the State of Louisiana does not prohibit the importation, possession, or sale of any non-native amphibian or reptile.

The importation of any species of turtle or turtle egg from any other state or foreign country without permit is prohibited (LSA R.S. 3:2358.13-8).

* It is unclear what affect, if any, this regulation has on the personal possession of non-native turtle species in Louisiana.

License and Permit Information

Reptile and Amphibian Collector's licenses are available for an annual fee of $25 for residents and $200 for non-residents. Wholesale/Retail Dealer's licenses cost $105 for residents and $405 for non-residents annually. Proceeds from the sale of these two licenses are allocated to the Reptile and Amphibian Research Fund. Alligator Hunting licenses have an annual fee of $25 for residents and $150 for non-residents. Fur Buyer's licenses cost $25 for residents and $100 for non-residents annually. A fee of $150 plus a $500 deposit is required to obtain a resident Fur Dealer's license, and non-resident Fur Dealer's licenses cost $300 with a $1,000 deposit required. Alligator Parts Dealer's licenses cost $50 at the wholesale level and $5 at the retail level. The fee for a Non-game Quadruped Exhibitor's license is $10 and for a Non-game Quadruped Breeder's license is $25 annually. Complete requirements and applications for these licenses may be obtained from the Louisiana Department of Fisheries and Wildlife (address in Appendix I). Requirements and applications for Pet Turtle Farmer's licenses may be obtained from the Louisiana Department of Agriculture and Forestry (address in Appendix I). Pet Turtle Farmer's licenses cost $250 annually.

CAPTIVE MAINTENANCE REGULATIONS

Restrictions on the possession of amphibians and reptiles in captivity are included among the regulations of the previous sections. The following is a brief review of these restrictions.

a. Endangered and threatened species may not be possessed without permit.
b. Valid fishing license may be required to possess native amphibian and reptile species.
c. *Alligator mississippiensis*, American Alligators may not be possessed without non-game quadruped exhibitor's or breeder's licenses, or special scientific or educational permits.
d. *Macrochelys temminckii*, Alligator Snapping Turtles have a possession limit of four specimens.
e. With the exception of non-native turtle species which may require permits to possess, there are no restrictions on the possession of non-native amphibians and reptiles.

(b and d above see Native Wildlife Regulations).
(c and e above see Importation and Commercial Trade Regulations).

MAINE

ENDANGERED, THREATENED, AND SPECIAL CONCERN SPECIES

The Maine Department of Inland Fisheries and Wildlife classifies various species of the state's flora and fauna into one of six categories: Endangered, Threatened, Special Concern, Indeterminate Status, Watch, and Extirpated. Only those species officially designated as endangered or threatened, however, are legally protected by Maine's Endangered Species Act as specified in title 12 of the Maine Revised Statutes Annotated (reference: MRSA 12-7751 to 7758).

The following amphibian and reptile species are included in the current (January 1995) list of endangered and threatened wildlife in Maine. Permits issued by the Maine Department of Inland Fisheries and Wildlife are required for all activities involving these species. In addition, permits issued by the U.S. Department of the Interior are required for any of the following species included in the federal list of threatened and endangered wildlife (see U.S. Endangered and Threatened Species).

Species	Common Name	Status
Caretta caretta	Loggerhead Sea Turtle	Threatened
Clemmys guttata	Spotted Turtle	Threatened
Dermochelys coriacea	Leatherback Sea Turtle	Endangered
Emydoidea blandingii	Blanding's Turtle	Endangered
Lepidochelys kempii	Atlantic Ridley Sea Turtle	Endangered
Terrapene carolina	Eastern Box Turtle	Endangered
Coluber constrictor	Black Racer	Endangered

* The Maine Department of Inland Fisheries and Wildlife is currently in the process of revising the state's endangered and threatened species list. When this revision will be completed is uncertain at this time.

Protected Species Permit Information

Scientific collection permits allowing for the collection and/or possession of Maine's endangered and threatened species may be issued to qualified individuals and institutions for educational, scientific, propagation, rehabilitation or exhibition purposes. There is no fee for scientific collection permits. Complete permit requirements and permit applications may be obtained from the Maine Department of Inland Fisheries and Wildlife (address in Appendix I).

NATIVE WILDLIFE REGULATIONS

Specific restrictions on the collection and possession of native wildlife species harvested from the wild in the state are included among the laws of the Maine Revised Statutes Annotated and among the regulations of Maine Inland Fisheries and Wildlife Rules (reference: MIFWR). In general, amphibians and reptiles are not included among the various statutes and regulations, and the collection without permit of Maine's native species (except endangered and threatened species) for non-commercial or recreational purposes is not currently prohibited. Permits may be required for scientific or research collecting activities, however, and specific legislation restricting the commercial harvest of several native species is included among the wildlife laws of Maine (see Importation and Commercial Trade Regulations).

License and Permit Information

Scientific Collection permits may be required to collect and possess native amphibian and reptile species wild caught in the state for scientific, educational, or exhibition purposes. Further information and permit applications may be obtained from the Maine Department of Inland Fisheries and Wildlife (address in Appendix I).

ME

IMPORTATION AND COMMERCIAL TRADE REGULATIONS

Native Species

Restrictions regulating the commercial trade of native species wild caught in the state are included among the legislation of the Maine Revised Statutes Annotated (reference: MRSA) and the Inland Fisheries and Wildlife Rules (reference: MIFWR). The following is a summarization of these restrictions.

The collection and possession of snakes and turtles from the wild for export, sale, or other commercial purposes is prohibited, except as specified for Common Snapping Turtles, *Chelydra serpentina* (MRSA 12-7471).

Turtles

Chelydra serpentina, Common Snapping Turtles may be taken for commercial purposes in any manner except by use of explosives, drugs, poisons, lime, or any other deleterious substances. A Commercial Snapping Turtle permit is required (MIFWR 4.15).

Native and Exotic Species

Restrictions on the importation, sale, and possession of both non-native amphibians and reptiles, and specimens of Maine's native species legally acquired outside of the state, are specified in the Wildlife Importation Regulations included among the state's Inland Fisheries and Wildlife Rules (reference: MIFWR 7.60). While this regulation generally prohibits the importation of any wildlife into the State of Maine without a specific Wildlife Importation and Possession Permit, certain species are classified as "Unrestricted Wildlife and these species may be imported, possessed, purchased, and sold without permit. Wildlife Importation and Possession Permits are required to import or possess any species not specifically included in the list of unrestricted wildlife species. This regulation, including the list of unrestricted amphibian and reptile species, is summarized below

No species of wildlife may be imported into the State of Maine without a wildlife importation permit, unless otherwise specified. All imported wildlife must be legally acquired and lawfully possessed. An evaluation of the permit applicant's qualifications and of any possible detrimental effects to native wildlife, domestic livestock and poultry, captive wild or exotic wildlife, or the health and safety of the public will be made prior to the issuance of an importation permit (MIFWR 7.60).

Restricted snake species or their offspring held under the authority of an Importation and Possession permit may not be sold, exchanged, bartered, or disposed of within the State of Maine without the prior authorization of such transfer by the Maine Department of Inland Fisheries and Wildlife (MIFWR 7.60).

Unrestricted Wildlife Species List

The following amphibians and reptiles are included in the current (January 1997) list of designated unrestricted species and may be imported, possessed, and sold without a Wildlife Importation and Possession Permit. All other species, including those listed as exceptions in the following list, are considered restricted wildlife and may only be imported and/or possessed under the authorization of a Wildlife Importation and Possession Permit.

Ceratophrys spp.	Horned Frogs (Captive Bred Only)
Hyla cinerea	Green Treefrog
Litoria caerulea [1]	White's Treefrog (Captive Bred Only)
Trachemys scripta elegans [2]	Red-eared Slider (4 inches minimum diameter)

ME

Agama agama	Common Agama
Amevia amevia	Giant Amevia
Anolis spp.	New World Anoles
Basiliscus spp.	Basilisks
Callisaurus spp. [3]	Zebra-tailed Lizard
Callopistes spp.	Dwarf Tegu
Calotes spp.	Mountain Horned Agama
Cnemidophorus spp.	Whiptail Lizards
Coleonyx spp.	Banded Geckos
Cordylus spp.	Girdled-tailed Lizard
Corythophanes cristatus	Helmeted Iguana
Crotaphytus spp.	Collared Lizard
Ctenosaura spp. [4]	Spiny-tailed Iguana
Dipsosaurus dorsalis [5]	Desert Iguana
Eublepharis spp.	Leopard Gecko
Eumeces inexpectatus	Southeastern Five-lined Skink [6]
Gambelia spp. [7]	Leopard Lizard
Gekko gecko [8]	Tokay Gecko
Gerrhonotus spp.	Alligator Lizard
Gerrhosaurus spp.	Plated Lizard
Hemidactylus spp. [9]	Mediterranean Gecko
Holbrookia spp.	Greater Earless Lizard
Iguana iguana	Green Iguana
Leiocephalus spp.	Curly-tailed Lizards
Liolaemus spp.	South American Swifts

Exceptions: *Liolaemus altissimus* [10]   Tree Lizard

Ophisaurus spp.	Glass Lizard
Phelsuma spp.	Day Geckos
Phymaturus spp.	Chilean Chuckwalla
Physignathus spp.	Water Dragon
Platysaurus spp.	Rock Lizard
Pogona vitticeps	Bearded Dragon
Pseudocordylus spp.	False Club-tailed Lizard
Sceloporus spp.	Spiny Lizards
Tiliqua spp.	Blue-tongued Skinks (Captive Bred Only)
Tupinambis spp.	Tegu (Captive Bred Only)
Urosaurus spp.	Tree Lizards
Uta spp.	Side-blotched Lizard
Xantusia spp.	Night Lizards

Antaresia childreni [11]	Children's Python
Arizona spp.	Glossy Snakes
Boa constrictor constrictor	Boa Constrictor
Boaedon spp. [12]	House Snakes
Drymarchon corais corais [13]	Central American Indigo (Captive Bred Only)
Elaphe spp.	Rat Snakes

Exceptions: *Elaphe obsoleta obsoleta*   Black Rat Snake
                 Elaphe spp.   Old World Rat Snakes

Epicrates cenchria [14]	Rainbow Boa	
Eryx colubrinus loveridgei	Kenyan Sand Boa (Captive Bred Only)	
Eryx conicus	Rough-scaled Sand Boa (Captive Bred Only)	
Lampropeltis spp.	Kingsnakes and Milk Snakes	
Exceptions:	*Lampropeltis triangulum elapsoides*	Scarlet Kingsnake
	Lampropeltis triangulum syspila	Red Milk Snake
	Lampropeltis triangulum triangulum	Eastern Milk Snake
	Lampropeltis zonata zonata	St. Helena Mountain Kingsnake
Lichanura trivirgata [15]	Rosy Boa	
Nerodia spp.	Water Snakes	
Exceptions:	*Nerodia clarkii taeniata*	Atlantic Salt Marsh Snake
	Nerodia paucimaculata	Concho Water Snake
	Nerodia sipedon	Northern Water Snake
Pituophis spp. [16]	Gopher and Pine Snakes	
Python regius	Ball Python	
Xenopeltis unicolor	Sunbeam Snake	

[1] Included in the genus *Pelodryas* by Frank and Ramus (1995).
[2] Listed as *Chrysemys scripta elegans* by Maine.
[3] Listed as *Calisaurus* by Maine.
[4] Listed as *Ctenosaurus* spp. by Maine.
[5] Listed as *Dipsosaurus dorales* by Maine.
[6] Listed as Southwestern Five-lined Skink by Maine.
[7] Listed as *Crotaphytus* spp. by Maine.
[8] Listed as *Gecko gecko* by Maine.
[9] Listed as *Hemidaclybus* spp. by Maine.
[10] Species not listed in Frank and Ramus (1995).
[11] Listed as *Liasis childreni* by Maine.
[12] Genus not listed in Frank and Ramus (1995).
[13] Listed as *Drymarchon* spp. by Maine.
[14] Listed as *Epicrates cenchin* spp. by Maine.
[15] Listed as *Lichanur trivirgata* and Rosey Boa by Maine.
[16] Listed as *Pituophis melanoleucu* sub spp. by Maine.

Turtles

In addition to the above Wildlife importation and possession permit requirements, the following summarized portion of Maine's Revised Statutes regulates the sale of turtles within the state.

It is unlawful to sell, display, raffle, give away, or offer for sale to the public any live turtles under eight weeks of age in lots of less than six (MRSA 7-3972).

License and Permit Information

All Wildlife Importation and Possession permit applications for restricted species are appraised on an individual basis. Possible environmental and/or public safety hazards, as well as the permit applicant's qualifications, are fully evaluated prior to the issuance of restricted wildlife permits. There is a one-time, non-refundable permit application fee of $25, and Wildlife Importation and Possession Permits are valid indefinitely. Multiple species may be included in a single permit request. As stated previously, permits are not required to import, possess, or sell unrestricted species. Commercial Snapping Turtle permits basically function as a method of monitoring the annual take of the species, and there is currently no fee for snapping turtle permits. Further information on and applications for any of the required permits of this section may be obtained from the Maine Department of Inland Fisheries and Wildlife (address in Appendix I).

CAPTIVE MAINTENANCE REGULATIONS

In addition to restrictions on the possession of both native and non-native amphibians and reptiles included among the regulations of the previous sections, the following summarized captive maintenance restriction is included among the importation and possession permit requirements for restricted species.

Cages must be designed to keep the animal in complete and continuous captivity, restrict entry of unauthorized persons, and minimize any potential danger to the public or licensee (MIFWR 7.60).

Captive Maintenance Regulations Review

The following is a brief review of Maine's restrictions on the captive possession of amphibians and reptiles.

a. Permits required to possess endangered and threatened species.
b. Permits required to possess imported amphibians and reptiles not designated as unrestricted species.
c. Permits required to possess venomous reptiles.

(b and c above see Importation and Commercial Trade Regulations).

Eastern Box Turtle, *Terrapene carolina carolina* - This popular "pet" turtle is currently listed as an endangered species by the State of Maine. Photograph by J.P. Levell.

MARYLAND

ENDANGERED, THREATENED, AND SPECIAL CONCERN SPECIES

Maryland's rare, threatened, and endangered species are legally protected by the Maryland Nongame and Endangered Species Conservation Act, as specified in chapter 127 of the Annotated Code of Maryland (reference: ACM 127 -2). Enacted in 1975, this legislation allows for the protection of species not officially designated as threatened or endangered.

The following amphibian and reptile species are included on Maryland's current (December 1993) legally protected list, as specified in the legislation Reptile and Amphibian Possession and Permits (reference: COMAR 08.03.11.03C). State permits are required for all activities involving these species. In addition, permits issued by the U.S. Department of the Interior are required for any species included in the federal endangered species list (see U.S. Endangered and Threatened Species).

Species	Common Name
Ambystoma jeffersonianum	Jefferson's Salamander
Ambystoma tigrinum	Eastern Tiger Salamander
Aneides aeneus	Green Salamander
Cryptobranchus alleganiensis	Hellbender
Necturus maculosus	Mudpuppy
Plethodon wehrlei	Wehrle's Salamander
Siren lacertina	Greater Siren
Gastrophryne carolinensis	Eastern Narrow-mouthed Toad
Hyla gratiosa	Barking Treefrog
Pseudacris brachyphona	Mountain Chorus Frog
Rana virgatipes	Carpenter Frog
Apalone spinifera	Spiny Softshell Turtle
Caretta caretta	Loggerhead Sea Turtle
Chelonia mydas	Green Sea Turtle
Dermochelys coriacea	Leatherback Sea Turtle
Eretmochelys imbricata	Hawksbill Sea Turtle
Graptemys geographica	Map Turtle
Lepidochelys kempii	Atlantic Ridley Sea Turtle
Eumeces anthracinus	Northern Coal Skink
Cemophora coccinea	Scarlet Snake
Crotalus horridus	Timber Rattlesnake
Farancia erytrogramma	Rainbow Snake
Virginia pulchra [1]	Mountain Earth Snake

[1] Listed as *Virginia valeriae pulchra* by Maryland.

Protected Species Permit Information

Permits allowing for the collection and possession of State protected amphibians and reptiles for scientific or educational purposes may be issued on occasion. Permit requirements and applications may be obtained from the Maryland Department of Natural Resources (address in Appendix I).

MD

NATIVE WILDLIFE REGULATIONS

In addition to protecting the amphibians and reptiles listed above under Endangered, Threatened and Special Concern Species, Maryland has several restrictions on the collection and possession of amphibians and reptiles native to the state. Most of these regulations are included in the Department of Natural Resources legislation, Reptile and Amphibian Possession and Permits (reference: COMAR 08.03.11). Diamondback Terrapins and Snapping Turtles are considered commercial fish in the State of Maryland, and additional restrictions on the collection and possession of these species are specified in the regulations of the Maryland Tidewater Administration (reference: COMAR 08.02.0~.01-.02). The following is a summarization of these restrictions.

A person without permit may not possess more than four of each individual reptile or salamander, live or dead. These specimens may have been: 1. Collected from the wild, 2. Captively produced, or 3. Legally obtained from outside Maryland (COMAR 8.03.11.04A).

*Special regulations apply to several turtle species native to Maryland (see Turtles below).

Unlawful Methods for Taking from the Wild

Reptiles or amphibians may not be taken by: lethal methods, the use of a hook and line, trot line, bow and arrow, spear, gig or gig iron, or any other device capable of piercing any part of the reptile or amphibian; use of traps, pit falls, snares, seines, or nets other than dip net; or use of chemicals, including gasoline (COMAR 08.03.11.09A).

A person may not destroy or alter dens, burrows, basking sites, or refugia while in the act of taking (COMAR 08.03.11.09B).

Conditions for Release

Captively produced specimens may not be released into the wild. (COMAR 08.03.11.10A)

With written authorization from the Department of Natural Resources, native species taken from the wild may be released, if it was not held in captivity with any other reptile or amphibian and it was not held in captivity for more than 30 days (COMAR 08.03.11.10B).

Release of an individual reptile or amphibian shall occur at or near the point of capture (COMAR 08.03.11.10C).

Frogs

A person without permit may not possess more than four adults and 25 eggs or tadpoles of each individual frog or toad, live or dead. These specimens may have been: 1. Obtained from the wild, 2. Captively produced, or 3. Legally obtained outside of Maryland (COMAR 08.03.11.04B).

An educational facility without a permit may possess an unlimited number of individual frogs and toads provided they are obtained from a permittee or legally from outside Maryland (COMAR 08.03.11.04D).

A person without a permit, but who possesses a fishing license valid in Maryland, or a person entitled to fish without a license, may possess not more than 25 individual amphibians in total, for use as bait (COMAR 08.03.11.04E).

MD

Turtles

A person without a permit may possess only one of each individual turtle, live or dead, listed below. Of these four species, only one specimen of Eastern Box Turtle may be wild caught. Bog, Wood, and Spotted Turtles may not be taken from the wild. A certificate of origin, bill of sale, or other documentation proving captive origin is required for these three species. Turtles must have a carapace length of four inches (COMAR 08.03.11.03B and .04C):

Clemmys muhlenbergii	Bog Turtle
Clemmys insculpta	Wood Turtle
Clemmys guttata	Spotted Turtle
Terrapene carolina carolina	Eastern Box Turtle

Chelydra serpentina, Snapping Turtles may not be collected by use of hook and line, trot line, bow and arrow, spear or gig, or any device capable of piercing any part of a turtle (COMAR 08.02.06.01).

Malaclemys terrapin, Diamondback Terrapins less than 6 inches in plastron length may not be collected from the wild or possessed in Maryland. Terrapins may be legally taken from May 1 through July 31 (COMAR 08.02.06.02).

* Size limit does not apply to Diamondback Terrapins maintained in captivity. The possession limit without permit for captive specimens is three.

License and Permit Information

The Reptile and Amphibian Possession and Permits legislation of Maryland specifically includes provisions providing for the acquisition of special captive reptile and amphibian permits at a fee of $25.00. A brief review of the portion of this regulation concerning the taking and possession of native amphibians and reptiles is included below. An application for this permit may be obtained from the Wildlife Division of the Maryland Department of Natural Resources (address in Appendix I).

A Captive Reptile and Amphibian Permit allows for the possession of an unlimited number of any native reptile or amphibian, provided that the number of specimens obtained from the wild does not exceed the following limits (COMAR 08.03.11.05A):

1. No more than one Eastern Box Turtle (see Native Wildlife Regulations - Turtles).
2. No more than 4 adult and 25 eggs or tadpoles of each individual frog or toad.
3. No more than four of each individual reptile or salamander.

* Does not include any species requiring an Endangered Species or a Scientific Collecting permit.

IMPORTATION AND COMMERCIAL TRADE

Maryland has some restrictions on the importation and sale of both native and non-native amphibians and reptiles. These regulations are specified in the Code of Maryland Regulations (reference: COMAR) and in article 27, section 70D of the Annotated Code of Maryland (reference: ACM). The following is a brief summary of these regulations.

Native Species

A Captive Reptile and Amphibian Permit allows the permittee to sell, offer for sale, trade, or barter individuals of each species and subspecies of native reptiles or amphibians provided they are; captively produced , or legally obtained outside Maryland (COMAR 08.03.11.07).

*Does not include any species requiring an Endangered Species, Scientific Collecting, or Aquaculture permit.

MD

An Aquaculture permit is required to purchase, sell, possess, capture, produce, breed, transport, and process fish in the State of Maryland. The term fish includes any native or non-native amphibian or reptile including any parts, eggs, or larvae, which spend the majority of their life cycle in water (COMAR 08.02.14.01-.12).

* As currently interpreted by the Maryland Department of Natural Resources aquaculture permits are required to propagate and sell aquatic or semi-aquatic turtle and amphibian species.

Exotic Species

Live reptiles specifically included in the following family groups may not be imported, offered for sale, traded, bartered, or exchanged in Maryland for use as a household pet. These species may be imported and sold or traded to a zoo, park, museum, educational institution, or to a person holding valid state or federal permits for educational, medical, scientific, or exhibition purposes (ACM 27-70D):

Crocodilia	Alligators and Crocodiles

Crotalidae [1]	Pit Vipers		
Elapidae	Cobras, Mambas, Coral Snakes, etc.	Hydrophidae	Sea Snakes
Viperidae	Vipers		

[1] As currently interpreted by Maryland Department of Natural Resources Copperheads, *Agkistrodon contortrix*, legally collected and possessed within Maryland may be possessed without permit (see Native Wildlife Regulations).

License and Permit Information

A list of requirements and applications for Aquaculture Permits may be obtained from the Maryland Tidewater Administration of the Department of Natural Resources. Applications for the other permits are available from the Maryland Department of Natural Resources' Wildlife Division (addresses in Appendix I).

CAPTIVE MAINTENANCE REGULATIONS

Portions of Maryland's Reptile and Amphibian Possession and Permits legislation specifically regulates the captive maintenance and/or propagation of amphibians and reptiles native to Maryland. These regulations include the following.

A Captive Reptile and Amphibian Permit allows for the captive propagation of any native species, except for prohibited turtle species (see Native Wildlife Regulations) which may not be bred and State protected species (COMAR 08.03.11.05A - 4 and 08.03.11.06B).

A person without a permit may possess an unlimited number of albino, or other color mutations, resulting from captive breeding. The burden of proving the mutant is a legitimate color mutant lies with the owner. Permits are required to sell, trade, barter, or exchange albinos and other color mutations (COMAR 08.03.11.04F).

* Does not include prohibited turtle species (see Native Wildlife Regulations).

Possession of a hybrid applies to the possession limit for each species or subspecies in it's lineage (COMAR 08.03.11.04G).

* The three preceding regulations do not include any species requiring an Endangered Species or a Scientific Collecting Permit.

Any person possessing specimens under the authority of a Captive Reptile and Amphibian permit is required to maintain and submit accurate, current, and complete records on forms provided by the Department of Natural Resources (COMAR 08.03.11.11).

MD

At any reasonable hour the records and facilities of any person in possession of a Captive Reptile and Amphibian permit are subject to inspection by the Department of Natural Resources (COMAR 08.03.11.12).

Sanitary Housing Requirements (COMAR 08.03.11.08)

A. Reptiles and amphibians held in captivity shall be housed under conditions which are humane, safe, and healthy.

B. Housing conditions shall meet all the following requirements:

    1) Enclosures shall be designed to:

        a) Provide appropriate lighting, temperatures, humidity, and clean water to meet the physical requirements of the reptile or amphibian,

        b) Keep the reptile or amphibian in complete and continuous captivity,

        c) Restrict the entry of unauthorized persons or predatory animals.

        d) Provide sufficient fresh food and clean water to fulfill the reptile or amphibian's dietary requirements and present the food and water in a manner compatible with the captive's particular eating habits, and

        e) Minimize any potential danger to humans;

    2) Enclosures shall be maintained in a sanitary condition and good repair;

    3) Equipment shall be available for proper storage and disposal of waste material to control vermin, insects, and obnoxious odors;

    4) Effective measures shall be provided to prevent and control infection and infestation of disease, parasites, or vermin;

    5) Adequate shelter shall be provided for the comfort of the animal and, when necessary, for the isolation of diseased reptiles or amphibians; and

    6) Reptiles and amphibians that are housed together shall be in compatible groups without overcrowding.

* The preceding regulation has been included in it's entirety. This has been done not only for the sake of clarity, but also because this legislation serves as an excellent example of the minimum standards by which captive amphibians and reptiles should be maintained everywhere.

Captive Maintenance Regulations Review

The following is a brief review of Maryland's regulations on the possession of captive amphibians and reptiles.

a. Species listed as protected may not be possessed without permit.

b. Only one of each of the following species may be possessed without permit. Only the Eastern Box Turtle (one specimen) may be collected from the wild in Maryland.

Clemmys guttata	Spotted Turtle
Clemmys insculpta	Wood Turtle
Clemmys muhlenbergii	Bog Turtle
Terrapene carolina	Box Turtle

c. The possession without permit of native species of frogs and toads not included in a or b above is limited to four adults and 25 eggs or tadpoles of each species.

d. The possession without permit of native salamanders and reptiles not included in a or b above is limited to four of each species.

e. A Captive Reptile and Amphibian Permit allows for the possession of a unlimited number of specimens of the species of c and d above. Only 4 specimens may be wild caught within the State of Maryland.

f. The breeding of turtles is prohibited except by authority of an Aquaculture permit.

g. Crocodilians and venomous snakes (except for Copperheads, *Agkistrodon contortrix*, legally obtained in Maryland) apparently may not be possessed without permit.

(b through d above see Native Wildlife Regulations).
(f and g above see Importation and Commercial trade Regulations).

MASSACHUSETTS

ENDANGERED, THREATENED, AND SPECIAL CONCERN SPECIES

The Massachusetts Division of Fisheries and Wildlife lists numerous species and subspecies of the state's flora and fauna as Endangered, Threatened, or Species of Special Concern. Species in all three categories, as well as all federally listed endangered and threatened species, are fully protected by the Massachusetts Endangered Species Act, as specified in chapter 131A of Massachusetts General Laws Annotated (reference: M.G.L. 131A:1-6).

The following amphibians and reptiles are included in the current list (November 1995) of legally protected species as specified in the Code of Massachusetts Regulations (reference: 321 CMR 10.60). A state educational or scientific collecting permit is required for all activities involving these species. In addition, a federal permit is required for some species included in this list (see U.S. Endangered and Threatened Species).

Species	Common Name	Status
Ambystoma jeffersonianum [1]	Jefferson's Salamander	Special Concern
Ambystoma laterale [1]	Blue-spotted Salamander	Special Concern
Ambystoma opacum	Marbled Salamander	Threatened
Gyrinophilus porphyriticus	Spring Salamander	Special Concern
Hemidactylium scutatum	Four-toed Salamander	Special Concern
Scaphiopus holbrookii	Eastern Spadefoot Toad	Threatened
Caretta caretta	Loggerhead Sea Turtle	Threatened
Chelonia mydas	Green Sea Turtle	Threatened
Clemmys guttata	Spotted Turtle	Special Concern
Clemmys insculpta	Wood Turtle	Special Concern
Clemmys muhlenbergii	Bog Turtle	Endangered
Dermochelys coriacea	Leatherback Sea Turtle	Endangered
Emydoidea blandingii	Blanding's Turtle	Threatened
Eretmochelys imbricata	Hawksbill Sea Turtle	Endangered
Lepidochelys kempii [2]	Atlantic Ridley Sea Turtle	Endangered
Malaclemys terrapin	Diamondback Terrapin	Threatened
Pseudemys rubriventris	Eastern Redbelly Turtle	Endangered
Terrapene carolina	Eastern Box Turtle	Special Concern
Agkistrodon contortrix	Copperhead	Endangered
Carphophis amoenus	Worm Snake	Threatened
Crotalus horridus	Timber Rattlesnake	Endangered
Elaphe obsoleta [3]	Black Rat Snake	Endangered

[1] Includes all native triploid or polyploid forms within the *Ambystoma jeffersonianum/laterale* complex.
[2] Listed as *Lepidochelys kempi* by Massachusetts.
[3] Legally obtained albinistic and leucistic specimens of *Elaphe obsoleta* are exempt from permit requirements.

Protected Species Permit Information

Scientific collecting permits are issued for purposes of legitimate scientific research or for the salvage of usable dead specimens. There is a permit application fee of $1.00. Educational permits allowing for the possession of legally obtained endangered or threatened wildlife may also be issued on occasion. Applications and requirements for permits may be obtained from the Massachusetts Division of Fisheries and Wildlife (address in Appendix I).

MA

NATIVE WILDLIFE REGULATIONS

Restrictions on the non-commercial collection and possession of native species of amphibians and reptiles wild caught in the state are specified in the Code of Massachusetts Regulations (reference: 321 CMR 3.05). In addition to the species protected by the Massachusetts Endangered Species Act, the state also prohibits the collection and possession of Spotted Salamanders and Leopard Frogs without permit. These regulations are summarized below.

Reptiles and amphibians, except bullfrogs, green frogs, and snapping turtles may be hunted, fished, trapped, or taken throughout the year. Possession limit of two of each species. No reptile or amphibian may be taken by firearm or bow and arrow on any Sunday. (321 CMR 3.05-1).

It is unlawful to take any amphibian or reptile by means of poison, explosives, seines, gill nets or fyke nets (321 CMR 3.05-5).

The hunting, fishing, trapping, or collection of the following two species, in any developmental stage, without an educational or scientific permit is prohibited (321 CMR 3.05.3):

Ambystoma maculatum	Spotted Salamander
Rana pipiens	Northern Leopard Frog

* Although not specifically prohibited by regulation, the Massachusetts Division of Fisheries and Wildlife considers the possession of the above species illegal.

Frogs

Frogs of the family Ranidae, except *Rana pipiens* (Leopard Frogs) may be taken for use as bait by licensed fishermen, provided they are not sold. Frogs must have a snout-vent length less than 2-1/2 inches. Possession limited to 10 per day (321 CMR 3.05-6).

The following frogs may be taken from July 16 to September 30. Not more than 12 frogs of either species can be taken, or more than 24 in possession. Frogs must have a snout vent length of at least three inches. A license is not required (321 CMR 3.05-2):

Rana catesbeiana	Bullfrog
Rana clamitans melanota	Green Frogs

* Does not include the eggs of either species.

Turtles

Chelydra serpentina, Snapping Turtles may be taken throughout the year with no daily or seasonal bag limit. A license is not required (321 CMR 3.05-2).

License and Permit Information

Although apparently only required to take frogs for bait purposes, Massachusetts fishing licenses cost $27.50 for residents and $37.50 for non-residents. Non-resident seven day fishing licenses are also available at a reduced fee. (See Endangered, Threatened, and Special Concern Species for scientific collecting permit information).

MA

IMPORTATION AND COMMERCIAL TRADE REGULATIONS

Native Species

The following restriction on the sale of amphibians and reptiles native to the state is included among the wildlife legislation of the Code of Massachusetts Regulations (reference: 321 CMR 3.05).

Native reptiles and amphibians taken from the wild in Massachusetts may not be sold, except by permit (321 CMR 3.05-4).

* Except for Snapping Turtles, *Chelydra serpentina*, the Massachusetts Division of Fisheries and Wildlife does not issue any permits allowing for the sale of native amphibians and reptiles.

Exotic Species

Restrictions on the importation, sale, and possession of both native and non-native amphibians and reptiles are included in the Exotic Wildlife legislation of the Code of Massachusetts Regulations (reference: 321 CMR 9.00). This legislation specifies exactly which animal species may or may not be imported, sold, or possessed without permit within the State of Massachusetts. For example, all species currently included in the U.S. endangered and threatened species list, the I.U.C.N. Red Data Book, or the Massachusetts list of endangered, threatened, and special concern species may not be imported, sold, or possessed without permit. Permits are also required to import, sell, or possess all venomous snake species, the Gila Monster and Beaded Lizards (family Helodermatidae), all Monitors (family Varanidae), and all Old World Chameleons (family Chamaeleonidae). In addition to the general prohibitions outlined above, Massachusetts' Exotic Wildlife regulation also includes an extensive listing of species requiring permits or for which permit requirements have been waived (reference: 321 CMR 9.01). The amphibian and reptile portion of this list, in somewhat modified and hopefully more user friendly form, is provided below. Common names, mainly derived from Frank and Ramus (1995), have been included in all instances where such information is absent from the original government document. Annotations in the form of footnotes are provided where necessary as well.

Permit Exempt/Permit Required Species List

Except when specified otherwise, the following amphibian and reptile families, genera, and species may be imported without permit. Please note, permits are required to possess any family, genus, or species not specifically included in the following list.

Amphibians   All species exempt

Turtles   All species exempt

Except (permit required):

Geochelone chilensis	Chaco Tortoise
Gopherus spp.	Gopher Tortoises
Malacochersus tornieri	Pancake Tortoise

Lizards

Agamidae - Agamids   Only the following species are exempt:

Amphibolorus spp.	Australian Dragons
Calotes spp.	Varied Agamas
Hydrosaurus spp.	Sailfin Lizards
Pogona spp.	Bearded Dragons
Physignathus spp.	Water Dragons

Anguidae - Lateral-fold Lizards   Only the following species are exempt:

Anguis spp.	Slowworm
Gerrhonotus spp.	Alligator Lizards
Ophisaurus spp.	Glass Lizards

Cordylidae - Girdle-tailed Lizards   Only the following species are exempt:

Corydylus spp.	Girdle-tailed Lizards
Gerrhosaurus spp.	Plated Lizards
Platysaurus spp.	Rock Lizards
Pseudocordylus spp.	False Club-tailed Lizard
Zonosaurus spp.	Girdled Lizards

Gekkonidae - Geckos   All species exempt

Except (permit required):

Coleonyx reticulatus	Big Bend Banded Gecko

Iguanidae - Iguanids   Only the following species are exempt:

Anolis spp.	Anoles
Basiliscus spp.	Basilisks
Calisaurus spp.	Zebra-tailed Lizards
Crotaphytus spp.	Collared and Leopard Lizards
Ctenosaurus spp.	Spiny-tailed Iguana
Ctenotus spp. [1]	New World Chameleons ?
Iguana iguana	Green Iguana
Liolaemus spp.	Tree Iguanas
Sceloporus spp.	Spiny Lizards
Uranoscodon spp.	Mophead Iguanas
Urosaurus spp.	Tree and Bush Lizards

Lacertidae - Lacertids   Only the following species are exempt:

Acanthodactylus spp.	Fringe-fingered Lizards
Gallotia spp.	Gallot's Lizards
Lacerta spp.	Eurasian Lacertas
Podacris spp.	Wall Lizards
Psammodromus spp.	Sand Lizards

Scincidae - Skinks   All species exempt

Except: (permit required):

Acontias spp.	Dart Skinks
Neoseps spp.	Florida Sand Skink
Tribolonotus spp.	Solomon Island Ground Skink

Teiidae - Teiids All species exempt

Except (permit required):

Bachia spp.	Earless Teiid
Dicordon spp.	Desert Tegus
Echinosaura spp.	Rough Teiids
Gymnophtalumus spp.	Spectacled Teiids
Neusticurus spp.	Brown Water Teiids
Ophiognomon spp.	Snake Teiids
Scolecosaurus spp.	Worm Teiids

Xantusidae - Night Lizards   All species exempt

Except (permit required):

Xantusia virgilis utahensis	Utah Night Lizard

MA

Snakes

Anomalepididae - Blind Snakes All species exempt

Boidae - Pythons and Boas All species exempt

      Except (permit required):

Chondropython spp.	Green Tree Python
Corallus canina	Emerald Tree Boa
Eunectes spp.	Anacondas
Python reticulatus	Reticulated Python
Python sebae	African Rock Python

Colubridae - Colubrids   Only the following species are exempt:

Arizona spp.	Glossy Snakes
Bogertophis spp. [2]	Trans Pecos and Baja Rat Snakes
Drymarchon corais erebennus	Texas Indigo Snake
Elaphe spp. [3]	Asian and North American Rat Snakes
Heterodon nasicus	Western Hognose Snake
Lampropeltis spp.	Kingsnakes and Milk Snakes
Lamprophis spp. [4]	House Snakes
Natrix spp.	Old World Water Snakes
Neordia spp.	New World Water Snakes
Opheodrys spp.	Green Snakes
Pituophis spp.	Gopher and Pine Snakes
Psammophis spp.	Sand Snakes
Pseudaspis spp.	Mole Snakes
Pseustes spp.	Puffing Snakes
Ptyas spp.	Indian Rat Snakes
Sonora spp.	Ground Snakes
Spalerosophis spp.	Diadem Snakes
Spilotes spp.	Tropical Rat Snakes
Storeria spp.	Brown and Redbelly Snakes
Thamnophis spp.	Garter and Ribbon Snakes
Zaocys spp.	Keeled Rat Snakes

Leptotyphlopidae - Thread Snakes All species exempt

Typhopidae - Worm Snakes All species exempt

Uropeltidae - Shield-tailed Snakes All species exempt

Xenopeltidae - Sunbeam Snakes All species exempt

[1] Despite the inclusion of the genus *Ctenotus* among the family Iguanidae by the State of Massachusetts, these animals are actually Australian Skinks, family Scincidae.

[2] Listed as *Bogetophis* by Massachusetts.

[3] Includes albinistic and leucistic specimens of *Elaphe obsoleta*, the Black or Eastern Rat Snake. All other specimens of *Elaphe obsoleta* require permits.

[4] Listed as *Boaedon* (*Lamprophis*) spp. by Massachusetts.

License and Permit Information

Class 4 Propagator's Licenses permitting the possession, propagation, purchase, and sale of specified amphibians and reptiles, as well as Class 7 Possessor's Licenses allowing only the captive maintenance of non-exempt amphibian and reptile species are available from the Massachusetts Division of Fisheries and Wildlife. Issuance of either license is dependent upon a wide variety of minimum requirements and other conditions including inspection of holding facilities, as specified in the extensive Artificial Propagation of Birds, Mammals, Reptiles, and Amphibians legislation of the Code of Massachusetts Regulations (reference: 321 CMR 2:12). All license applications are evaluated on an individual case by case basis, and the Massachusetts Division of Fisheries and Wildlife currently has very high standards which all applicants must meet before any license will be approved. Licenses will definitely not be issued to any individual the department perceives as a "crackpot" wanting a Komodo Dragon to impress friends and neighbors. Licenses are issued on occasion, however, to qualified individuals and institutions. A complete list of license requirements and license applications may be obtained from the Massachusetts Division of Fisheries and Wildlife (address in Appendix I).

CAPTIVE MAINTENANCE REGULATIONS

Restrictions on the captive maintenance of both native and non-native species of amphibians and reptiles are included in many of the previous regulations. The following is a brief review of these restrictions.

a. Endangered, threatened, and special concern species may only be possessed by permit.
b. *Ambystoma maculatum*, Spotted Salamanders may only be possessed by permit.
c. *Rana pipiens*, Leopard Frogs may only be possessed by permit.
d. Possession of native amphibians and reptiles not included in the above regulations limited to two of each species unless otherwise authorized by permit.
e. Albinistic and leucistic specimens of the Black Rat Snake, *Elaphe obsoleta*, may be possessed without permit.
f. Permits are required for any animal not included in the list of exempt species.
g. Venomous reptiles (all species) may not be possessed without permit.
h. Crocodilians (all species) may not be possessed without permit.
i. All Old World Chameleons (Chamaeleonidae) and all Monitors Lizards (Varanidae) may not be possessed without permit.

(b, c and d above see Native Wildlife Regulations)
(e, f, g, h and i above see Importation and Commercial Trade Regulations).

MA

MICHIGAN

ENDANGERED, THREATENED, AND SPECIAL CONCERN SPECIES

The Michigan Department of Natural Resources lists various members of the state's flora and fauna as endangered, threatened, or as species of special concern. Amphibians and reptiles listed as endangered or threatened are legally protected by the endangered species legislation of Michigan's Natural Resources and Environmental Protection Act (Public Act 451), as specified in the Michigan Compiled Laws Annotated (reference: MI CL 324.36501). Species of special concern are protected by the Michigan Sport Fishing legislation of Public Act 451, and the collection and possession of these species without permit is likewise prohibited (reference: MI CL 324.48701 to 324.48740).

The following amphibians and reptiles are included in the current (December 1991) list of legally protected species in Michigan. State permits are required for all activities involving any of these amphibian and reptile species.

Species	Common Name	Status
Ambystoma opacum	Marbled Salamander	Threatened
Ambystoma texanum	Smallmouth Salamander	Endangered
Acris crepitans blanchardi	Blanchard's Cricket Frog	Special Concern
Clemmys guttata	Spotted Turtle	Special Concern
Clemmys insculpta	Wood Turtle	Special Concern
Emydoidea blandingii	Blanding's Turtle	Special Concern
Terrapene carolina carolina	Eastern Box Turtle	Special Concern
Clonophis kirtlandii	Kirtland's Snake	Endangered
Elaphe obsoleta obsoleta	Black Rat Snake	Special Concern
Elaphe gloydi [1]	Eastern Fox Snake	Threatened
Nerodia erythrogaster neglecta	Copperbelly Water Snake	Endangered
Sistrurus catenatus catenatus	Eastern Massasauga	Special Concern

[1] Listed as *Elaphe vulpina gloydi* by Michigan.

* The Michigan Department of Natural Resources is currently revising the State's endangered and threatened species list. This revision is expected to be adopted sometime late in 1997 and interested parties are advised to seek supplemental information at that time.

Protected Species Permit Information

Permits allowing for the collection and/or possession of Michigan's protected species may be issued to qualified individuals and institutions for legitimate research purposes or for other special purposes. Requirements and applications for protected species permits may be obtained from the Michigan Department of Natural Resources (address in Appendix I).

NATIVE WILDLIFE REGULATIONS

Restrictions on the collection and possession of amphibians and reptiles wild caught in the state are specified in the Michigan Department of Natural Resources Director's Order entitled, "Regulations on the Take of Reptiles and Amphibians" (reference: DFI-166). The statutory authority for these regulations is included among the sport fishing laws of Michigan (reference: MI CL 324.48701 to 324.48740). The following is a summarization of Michigan's restrictions on the non-commercial collection and possession of wild caught native amphibians and reptiles.

MI

It is unlawful to kill, take, trap, or possess, any amphibian or reptile or their eggs from the wild unless otherwise specified.

It is illegal to possess or transport in the field dressed or processed reptiles or amphibians that cannot be measured or identified.

Salamanders

Salamanders may be taken from the last day of Saturday in May to November 15. Legal methods for taking salamanders are hand, hand net, hook and line, or trap unless otherwise prohibited. The daily bag and possession limit for salamanders is ten specimens in any combination with all other amphibians.

* Does not include any endangered, threatened or special concern species.

Frogs

A valid sport fishing license is required to take frogs. The open season for frogs is from the last Saturday in May to November 15. Frogs may be taken by hand, hand net, hook and line, trap, and spear. The use of artificial light while spearing frogs is prohibited. The daily bag and possession limit is ten, in any combination with all other amphibians.

* Does not include any endangered, threatened or special concern species.

Reptiles

With the exception of Snapping Turtles, *Chelydra serpentina*, and Softshell Turtles, *Apalone* spp., reptiles may be taken at any time. Reptiles may be legally taken by hand, hand net, hook and line, trap, or seine 12 x 4 feet overall or less. The daily bag limit for reptiles is three and the possession limit is six of all species combined. A valid sport fishing license is required.

* Does not include any endangered, threatened or special concern species.

Turtles

A valid fishing license is required to collect turtles. Turtle traps shall be constructed of mesh at least one inch wide at the narrowest measurement and shall be set in a manner to allow turtles to surface and breathe. There is a three-trap limit.

The following turtles may be taken from June 23 to September 30 in Michigan's Lower Peninsula Region III, from July 1 to September 30 in Michigan's Lower Peninsula Region II, and from July 15 to September 30 in Michigan's Upper Peninsula Region I:

Apalone spp.	Softshell Turtles
Chelydra serpentina	Common Snapping Turtle

Chelydra serpentina, Common Snapping Turtles have a minimum size limit of 12 inches in carapace length. The daily bag limit is three and the possession limit is six.

* Other turtles not protected as endangered, threatened, or species of special concern may be legally taken throughout the year. Daily bag and possession limits are as specified for reptiles in general.

License and Permit Information

Michigan fishing licenses are available from bait shops, sporting goods stores, and other retail outlets. Annual fees for fishing licenses are $9.85 for residents and $20.35 for non-residents. One day licenses at cost of $5.35 for both residents and non-residents are also available.

MI

IMPORTATION AND COMMERCIAL TRADE REGULATIONS

Native Species

The following summarized restrictions on the sale of native amphibians and reptiles are included in Michigan's Regulations on the Take of Reptiles and Amphibians (Director's Order DFI-166).

It is unlawful to kill, trap, possess, buy, sell, barter, or attempt to take, trap, possess, or barter any reptile or amphibian or their eggs taken from the wild in Michigan, unless otherwise specified.

A Commercial Reptile and Amphibian license is required to take and sell wild caught amphibians and reptiles in Michigan.

Only the following species may be taken from the wild in Michigan for commercial purposes:

> *Rana clamitans*   Green Frog (daily bag limit 25, possession limit 50)
> *Chelydra serpentina*,   Common Snapping Turtle (daily bag limit 10, possession limit 50)

* What affect, if any, these regulations have on the importation and sale of specimens of native amphibians and reptiles legally obtained from outside of Michigan is unknown at the time of this writing.

Exotic Species

With the exception of the following regulation which applies to both native and non-native turtles, the State of Michigan does not currently restrict the importation and sale of non-native amphibians and reptiles.

A health advisory sheet prepared by the Michigan Department of Agriculture shall be provided by the seller to all purchasers of viable turtle eggs or live turtles less than four inches in carapace length (MI CL 287.311-.314).

License and Permit Information

Commercial Reptile and Amphibian license applications and requirements may be obtained from the Michigan Department of Natural Resources (address in Appendix I). Information on the health advisory sheets needed to sell turtle eggs or live turtles less than four inches in length may be obtained from the Michigan Department of Agriculture (address in Appendix I).

CAPTIVE MAINTENANCE REGULATIONS

The following is a review of the restrictions on the captive maintenance of amphibians and reptiles in Michigan.

a. Endangered, threatened, and species of special concern may not be possessed without permit.
b. The possession limit without permit for native salamanders wild caught in Michigan is 10 specimens in combination with all other amphibian species.
c. The possession limit without permit for native frogs wild caught in Michigan is 10 specimens in combination with all other amphibian species.
d. Unless otherwise specified, the possession limit without permit of reptiles wild caught in Michigan is six specimens in any combination.
e. *Chelydra serpentina*, Snapping Turtles wild caught in Michigan have a daily bag limit of three and a possession limit without permit of six specimens and a minimum size limit of 12 inches in carapace length.
f. No restrictions on the possession of non-native amphibian and reptile species.

(b through e above see Native Wildlife Regulations).

MI

MINNESOTA

ENDANGERED, THREATENED, AND SPECIAL CONCERN SPECIES

The Minnesota Department of Natural Resources classifies various members of the state's fauna and flora as endangered, threatened, or as species of special concern . Only those species officially designated as threatened or endangered, however, are legally protected by Minnesota's Endangered Species Statute as specified in section 84.0895 of the Minnesota Statutes Annotated (reference: MNSA 84.0895).

The following amphibian and reptile species are included in Minnesota's current (July 1996) list of endangered and threatened wildlife, as specified in Minnesota Rules chapter 6134 (reference: MNR 6134). Permits issued by the Minnesota Department of Natural Resources are required for all activities involving any listed species.

Species	Common Name	Status
Acris crepitans	Northern Cricket Frog	Endangered
Clemmys insculpta	Wood Turtle	Threatened
Emydoidea blandingii	Blanding's Turtle	Threatened
Crotalus horridus	Timber Rattlesnake	Threatened
Sistrurus catenatus	Massasauga	Endangered

Protected Species Permit Information

Permits authorizing the collection and/or possession of Minnesota's threatened and endangered species may be issued for scientific, educational, or rehabilitation purposes. Permits allowing for the possession of specimens legally obtained outside of Minnesota may also be issued on occasion. A complete list of permit requirements, as specified in Minnesota Rules (Reference: MNR 6212.1800-.2300), and permit applications may be obtained from the Minnesota Department of Natural Resources (address in Appendix I).

NATIVE WILDLIFE REGULATIONS

With the exception of state threatened and endangered species, Minnesota has relatively few restrictions on the collection and possession of amphibians and reptiles wild caught within the state. These few restrictions are specified in the Fish and Wildlife legislation of the Minnesota Statutes Annotated (reference: MNSA) or in Minnesota Rules (reference: MNR). In general, all of Minnesota's native amphibians and reptiles, except for those species regulated by the following summarized legislation, are unprotected and may be collected and possessed without license.

Frogs

Frogs may be taken from May 16 to March 31. Frogs may not be taken or possessed for purposes other than bait without a special frog license to take and possess frogs. Only frogs measuring six inches or more from the tip of the nose to the tip of the hind toes when the legs are fully extended may be taken or possessed for bait purposes. Bait frogs may be taken and possessed in unlimited numbers. A valid fishing license is required to take frogs for bait purposes (MNSA 97C.601).

Frogs may not be taken by the use of cloth screens or similar devices (MNSA 97C.601.3).

Frogs may only be taken between sunrise and sunset (MNR 6256.0100).

Only *Rana pipiens* and *Rana catesbeiana* (Leopard Frogs and Bullfrogs) more than six inches long may be taken or possessed for purposes other than bait (MNR 6256.0200).

* Although the above regulations appear to prohibit the collection and possession without license of all frogs except *Rana pipiens* and *Rana catesbeiana* for non-bait purposes, it was not the intention of the Minnesota Department of Natural Resources to restrict the collection and possession of other frog species for personal use. In reality, the intention of these regulations is to restrict the collection of native frogs for use in the food industry, biological supply companies, and scientific research facilities. The Department of Natural Resource does not currently enforce these rules regarding the maintenance of frogs in captivity. Unfortunately, much confusion regarding these regulations exists due to the incomplete nature of the actual text of the statues involved.

Turtles

Turtles may be taken throughout the year by any method except explosives, drugs, poisons, lime, and other harmful substances, turtle hooks or traps, or nets other than anglers landing nets. A valid fishing license is required (MNSA 97C.605).

* Does not include endangered and threatened species.

Chelydra serpentina, Snapping Turtles have a possession limit of three specimens without a special turtle seller's license. Minimum size requirement is 10 inches in width measured over the curvature at the midpoint of the carapace (MNSA 97C.611).

License and Permit Information

Minnesota fishing licenses are available from numerous retail outlets including most bait and sporting goods stores. Annual fishing license fees are $13.00 for residents and $27.50 for non-residents. Non-resident seven-day and three-day fishing license are available at a reduced cost. One-day fishing licenses are also available for a fee of $7.50 for both residents and non-residents. (See Importation and Commercial Trade Regulations for information on the special frog and turtle seller's license.)

IMPORTATION AND COMMERCIAL TRADE REGULATIONS

Native Species

Restrictions on the collection, importation, and possession of native amphibians and reptiles are included among the game and fish laws of the Minnesota Statutes Annotated. The following is a summary of these regulations.

Bait frogs six inches in length and over may be possessed, transported, bought, or sold in unlimited numbers during the open season (MNSA 97C.601.5).

Frogs may not be taken, possessed, transported, purchased, or sold for purposes other than bait without a license to take, possess, transport, purchase, or sell frogs (MNSA 97C.601.2).

Live frogs may not be imported for purposes other than bait except by permit (MNR 6256.0300).

A record book must be maintained recording the number or weight of each frog species acquired by taking or purchase and each frog sold for purposes other than bait. These records are to include the name and address of each purchaser and/or seller, and the date of each transaction (MNR 6256.0400).

* As is the case with other portions of Minnesota's frog regulations, this legislation is intended to regulate the collection, importation, possession, and/or sale of frogs for use in the food industry, research facilities, and biological specimen supply companies. It is not the intention of the Minnesota Department of Natural Resources to restrict the possession of any native or non-native frog species for personal pet or hobby purposes.

Turtles

A turtle seller's license is required to take, possess, transport, purchase, or sell turtles commercially. Turtles may be taken commercially by turtle traps, turtle hooks, and commercial fishing gear. Records of the number, pounds, and species of turtles taken and of all commercial transactions must be maintained (MNSA 6256.0500).

Exotic Species

With the exception of those portions of the previous regulations which may be interpreted otherwise, the State of Minnesota does not currently restrict the importation, possession, or sale of any non-native amphibian or reptile species.

License and Permit Information

Licenses to take and sell frogs for purposes other than bait cost $10 annually and are available to Minnesota residents only. Licenses to transport, possess, and purchase frogs for purposes other than bait are available at an annual fee of $70 for residents and $200 for non-residents. The fee for the turtle seller's license is $55 annually. License requirements and applications may be obtained from the Minnesota Department of Natural Resources (address in Appendix I).

CAPTIVE MAINTENANCE REGULATIONS

Minnesota's few restrictions on the possession in captivity of amphibians and reptiles are included among the regulations of the preceding sections. The following is a brief review of these restrictions.

a. Endangered and threatened species may not be possessed without permit.
b. A valid fishing or frog license may be required to possess native frogs.
c. A fishing license is required to possess native turtles.
d. *Chelydra serpentina*, Snapping turtles have a possession limit of three specimens without a turtle seller's license.
e. No restrictions on the possession of non-native amphibians and reptiles.

Rare Turtle Crossing - One of several Minnesota roadway signs specifically identifying areas where the state threatened Blanding's Turtle, *Emydoidea blandingii*, are frequently encountered crossing roads. Photograph courtesy of James E. Gerholdt.

MISSISSIPPI

ENDANGERED, THREATENED, AND SPECIAL CONCERN SPECIES

The Mississippi Department of Wildlife, Fisheries and Parks classifies various members of the state's fauna as Endangered or In Need of Management species. Species classified as endangered receive the full legal protection of the Mississippi Nongame and Endangered Species Act, as specified in title 49 of the Mississippi Code Annotated (reference: MS CA 49-5-101 to 119). As with the endangered species legislation of most states, this law automatically protects all species included in the federal list of threatened and endangered wildlife.

The following amphibians and reptiles are included in the current (March 1994) list of endangered wildlife species of Mississippi or in the current (January 1997) list of federally endangered and threatened species, as specified in Mississippi Public Notice No. 3357 (reference: MS PN 3357). Permits issued by the Mississippi Department of Wildlife, Fisheries and Parks are required for all activities involving any of these species. In addition to any required state permits, federal permits are required for activities involving any of the following species included in the U.S. Department of the Interior's endangered species list (see U.S. Endangered and Threatened Species).

Species	Common Name
Aneides aeneus	Green Salamander
Eurycea lucifuga	Cave Salamander
Gyrinophilus porphyriticus	Spring Salamander
Rana capito sevosa	Dusky Gopher Frog
Caretta caretta	Loggerhead Sea Turtle
Chelonia mydas	Green Sea Turtle
Dermochelys coriacea	Leatherback Sea Turtle
Eretmochelys imbricata	Hawksbill Sea Turtle
Gopherus polyphemus	Gopher Tortoise
Graptemys flavimaculata	Yellow-blotched Map Turtle
Graptemys nigrinoda	Black-knobbed Map Turtle
Graptemys oculifera	Ringed Map Turtle
Lepidochelys kempii [1]	Atlantic Ridley Sea Turtle
Pseudemys sp. [2]	Mississippi Redbelly Turtle
Drymarchon couperi [3]	Eastern Indigo Snake
Farancia erytrogramma	Rainbow Snake
Heterodon simus	Southern Hognose Snake
Pituophis melanoleucus lodingi	Black Pine Snake

[1] Listed as *Lepidochelys kempi* by Louisiana.
[2] Not listed in Collins (1997). The Mississippi Department of Wildlife, Fisheries and Parks currently recognizes the State's indigenous Redbelly Turtle population as a yet to be described species.
[3] Listed as *Drymarchon corais couperi* by Mississippi.

Protected Species Permit Information

Endangered species permits authorizing the collection and/or possession of species included in Mississippi's list of endangered wildlife may be issued for scientific, zoological, educational, propagation, or other special purposes. Complete permit requirements and permit applications may be obtained from the Mississippi Department of Wildlife, Fisheries and Parks (address in Appendix I).

NATIVE WILDLIFE REGULATIONS

Mississippi has several restrictions on the non-commercial collection and possession of native amphibians and reptiles wild caught in the state. These restrictions are included among the statutes of the Mississippi Code Annotated (reference: MS CA) or are specified in Public Notices (reference: MS PN) which are published in various periodicals throughout the state. The following is a summarization of the restrictions on the recreational collection of amphibians and reptiles wild caught in Mississippi.

Amphibians and reptiles designated as nongame species in need of management may be collected throughout the year. Nongame amphibians have a possession limit of four of each species or subspecies not to exceed 40 specimens in total (all species combined). The possession limit for nongame reptiles is four of each species or subspecies not to exceed 20 specimens in total (all species combined). A valid hunting license is required. All amphibians and reptiles native to Mississippi, except Bullfrogs, *Rana catesbeiana*, Green Frogs, *Rana clamitans*, Pig Frogs, *Rana grylio*, Alligators, *Alligator mississippiensis*, Common Snapping Turtles, *Chelydra serpentina*, and state listed endangered species are classified as nongame species in need of management (MS PN 3201.001-I and 3201.001-II).

* The possession limits of the previous regulation may be exceeded under the authorization of a captive propagation permit (see Importation and Commercial Trade Regulations) or a scientific collecting permit.

Frogs
The following frogs are classified as game species and may be taken from April 1 to October 1. The daily bag limit is 25 with a possession limit of 50 frogs in total (all species combined). A valid hunting or fishing license is required (MS PN 3297):

Rana catesbeiana	Bullfrog
Rana clamitans	Green Frog
Rana grylio	Pig Frog

Alligators
It is unlawful to intentionally feed or entice with feed any wild American Alligator, *Alligator mississippiensis*, except as authorized (MS PN 2884-I).

Alligator mississippiensis, American Alligators, parts, or eggs may not be taken or possessed, and alligator nests may not be disturbed except as authorized by permit from the Mississippi Department of Wildlife, Fisheries and Parks (MS PN 2884-III).

Nuisance alligators may be taken and possessed by designated alligator control agents or trappers only. Only those alligators specifically designated by permit may be taken. Nuisance alligators may only be possessed alive for 24 hours except as authorized by the Department of Wildlife, Fisheries and Parks. Alligators may not be taken by use of firearm unless authorized by the department. Nuisance alligator tags at a cost of $25 per tag must be immediately attached to any alligator killed by a licensed alligator agent or trapper (MS PN 2884-IV).

* The complete text of the nuisance alligator control portion of Mississippi's alligator regulation is approximately three pages in length, and includes numerous restrictions and requirements. Further information on this regulation may be obtained from the Mississippi Department of Wildlife, Fisheries and Parks (address in Appendix I).

Turtles
Chelydra serpentina, Common Snapping Turtles are not included in the list of amphibians and reptiles designated as nongame species in need of management, and specific restrictions on the recreational collection and possession of this species are not included among the regulations of the Mississippi Department of Wildlife, Fisheries and Parks. Common Snappers may apparently be taken without restriction throughout the year for non-commercial purposes. A valid hunting or fishing license may be required.

MS

License and Permit Information

Mississippi hunting and fishing licenses may be purchased from numerous retail outlets or from the Mississippi Department of Wildlife, Fisheries and Parks (address in Appendix I). Residents may purchase a combination all game hunting and fishing license for a $17 annual fee. Non-resident all game hunting licenses cost $225 annually. Five-day all game hunting licenses are also available to non-residents for a $105 fee. Non-resident freshwater fishing license (valid for Bullfrogs, Green Frogs, and Pig Frogs only) fees are $25 annually or $6 for three days. An agent fee of $1 for residents and $3 for non-residents may be added to all license costs.

IMPORTATION AND COMMERCIAL TRADE REGULATIONS

Native Species

Restrictions on the collection, propagation, and importation of native amphibians and reptiles for commercial purposes are specified in various public notices of the Mississippi Department of Wildlife, Fisheries and Parks or in the statutes of the Mississippi Code Annotated. The following is a summary of these restrictions.

Nongame amphibians and reptiles taken from the wild in Mississippi may not be purchased, sold, offered for sale, bartered, or exported for sale (MS PN 3201.001-II[4]).

Amphibians and reptiles designated as species in need of management may be propagated in captivity for commercial purposes within the State of Mississippi under the authorization of a captive propagation permit. Only those species specified in each individual permit may be propagated. A valid commercial fishing license is also required. Up to eight specimens of any species or subspecies of nongame reptile and sixteen specimens of any species or subspecies of nongame amphibian wild caught in Mississippi may be possessed. Specimens in excess of the previous possession limits must be legally obtained from outside of Mississippi or have been propagated in captivity. Proper documentation is required. Captive produced offspring of nongame amphibians and reptiles in need of management may be sold. Proper documentation is required (MS PN 3201.001-III through 3201.001-VI).

A fur buyers license is required to purchase captive produced nongame amphibians and reptiles in need of management for resale purposes (MS PN 3201.001-VI).

Nongame amphibians and reptiles in need of management lawfully acquired outside of Mississippi may be imported and exported only under the authorization of a nongame importer's permit (MS PN 3201.001-VII).

* The complete list of permit requirements to commercially propagate, sell, and import nongame amphibians and reptiles in need of management is approximately five pages in length. The complete text of these regulations may be obtained from the Mississippi Department of Wildlife, Fisheries and Parks (address in Appendix I).

Frogs

The sale of Bullfrogs, *Rana catesbeiana*, Green Frogs, *Rana clamitans*, and Pig Frogs, *Rana grylio*, is apparently prohibited by the following summarized statute.

It is unlawful to buy, sell, or barter game animals or their parts including specimens lawfully acquired outside Mississippi (MS CA 49-7-51).

Alligators

Alligator mississippiensis, American Alligators, eggs, or parts lawfully obtained outside of Mississippi may only be imported by permit (MS PN 2884-III).

* Does not include lawfully acquired cured and mounted trophies or articles manufactured from alligator skins or parts.

American Alligators, eggs, parts, and meat may be possessed, propagated, imported, exported, and sold under the authorization of an alligator rancher's permit. Alligators and alligator eggs may not be obtained from the wild population native to Mississippi. Ranch raised alligators under four feet in length may not be harvested. Tags are required for all harvested hides, parts or meat. All sales of living alligators are subject to prior approval of the Department of Wildlife, Fisheries and Parks (MS PN 2884-V and 2884-VI).

Nuisance alligator control agents may sell tagged hides, feet, viscera, and skeletal parts as authorized by the Department of Wildlife, Fisheries and Parks (MS PN 2884-IV and 2884-VI).

* The complete text of Mississippi's alligator legislation is nine pages in length and contains numerous other restrictions and requirements. Copies of the complete regulation may be obtained from the Mississippi Department of Wildlife, Fisheries and Parks (address in Appendix I).

Turtles

Chelydra serpentina, Common Snapping Turtles may be harvested from the wild for commercial purposes throughout the year. There is no size or possession limit. A commercial license is required (MS CA 49-7-47).

Exotic Species

The State of Mississippi does not currently regulate the importation, sale, or possession on any non-native amphibian or reptile species.

License and Permit Information

Commercial fishing licenses have annual fees of $25 for residents and $200 for non-residents. Fur buyer's license fees are $50 for residents and $200 for non-residents. Captive propagation permits are issued free of charge. Nongame wildlife importation permits cost $500 annually. Alligator rancher's licenses are available for a $50 annual fee and individual alligator tags and/or transportation permits cost $1 each. Requirements and applications for all the licenses and permits of this section may be obtained from the Mississippi Department of Wildlife, Fisheries and Parks (address in Appendix I).

CAPTIVE MAINTENANCE REGULATIONS

In addition to the restrictions on the captive possession of amphibians and reptiles included among the regulations of the preceding sections, the following restriction regulates the possession of venomous snakes.

Containers or cages holding venomous snakes shall be prominently labeled in a conspicuous place with the word "DANGER" along with the common name of the species (MS PN 3201.001-11[5]).

Captive Maintenance Regulations Review

The following is a brief review of Mississippi's restrictions on the captive maintenance of amphibians and reptiles.

a. Endangered species may not be possessed without permit.
b. *Alligator mississippiensis*, American Alligators may not be possessed without permit.
c. The following native frog species have a possession limit of 50 specimens in total (all species combined). A valid hunting or fishing license is required.

Rana catesbeiana	Bullfrog
Rana clamitans	Green Frog
Rana grylio	Pig Frog

d. The possession limit for all other native amphibians is four of each species or subspecies up to a total of 40 specimens of all species combined. A valid hunting license is required. These possession limits may be exceeded under the authorization of a captive propagation permit only.

e. *Chelydra serpentina*, Common Snapping Turtles may be possessed without limit. A valid hunting or fishing license may be required.

f. All other native reptiles have a possession limit of four of each species or subspecies up to a total of 20 specimens of all species combined. A valid hunting license is required. These possession limits may be exceeded under the authorization of a captive propagation permit only.

g. Cages housing venomous snakes must be conspicuously labeled with the species common name and the word "Danger."

h. No restrictions on the possession of non-native amphibian and reptile species.

(c and e above see Native Wildlife Regulations).
(b, d and f above see Native Wildlife Regulations and Importation and Commercial Trade Regulations).
(g above see Captive Maintenance Regulations).
(h above see Importation and Commercial Trade Regulations).

$5,000 Fine - Shoreline signs warning of the dangers and/or consequences of feeding or molesting Alligators are common throughout the southeastern United States. Photograph by J.P. Levell.

MISSOURI

ENDANGERED, THREATENED, AND SPECIAL CONCERN SPECIES

The Missouri Department of Conservation utilizes a system in which certain species of the state's flora and fauna are classified into one of six status categories: Endangered, Rare, Status Undetermined, Watch List, Extirpated, or Extinct. Species designated as endangered or extirpated are legally protected by the state's endangered species legislation, as specified in chapter 252 of the Annotated Revised Statutes of Missouri (reference: RSMO 252.240). As with the endangered species legislation of most states, Missouri's law contains provisions for the protection of species included in the federal list of endangered and threatened wildlife.

The following reptiles are included in Missouri's current (September 1995) list of endangered or extirpated plant and animal species. Permits issued by the Missouri Department of Conservation are required for all activities involving any of these species.

Species	Common Name	Status
Deirochelys reticularia miaria	Western Chicken Turtle	Endangered
Emydoidea blandingii	Blanding's Turtle	Endangered
Kinosternon flavescens flavescens	Yellow Mud Turtle	Endangered
Kinosternon flavescens spooneri	Illinois Mud Turtle	Endangered
Elaphe vulpina vulpina [1]	Western Fox Snake	Endangered
Liochlorophis vernalis [2]	Smooth Green Snake	Extirpated
Nerodia cyclopion cyclopion [1]	Mississippi Green Water Snake	Extirpated
Sistrurus catenatus catenatus	Eastern Massasauga	Endangered
Sistrurus catenatus tergeminus	Western Massasauga	Endangered

[1] No subspecies recognized in Collins (1997).
[2] Listed as *Opheodrys vernalis* by Missouri.

Protected Species Permit Information

Scientific collector's permits allowing for the limited collecting and/or possession of Missouri's endangered species are issued to qualified individuals and institutions for legitimate research, exhibition, or educational purposes only. Permits allowing for the possession of specimens of state endangered species legally obtained from outside of Missouri may also be issued. Further information and permit applications may be obtained from the Missouri Department of Conservation (address in Appendix I).

NATIVE WILDLIFE REGULATIONS

Restrictions on the collection and possession of native amphibians and reptiles wild caught in the state are specified in the Wildlife Code of Missouri (reference: WCMO). In general, the Wildlife Code of Missouri is a permissive code which means that only those activities that are specifically listed are permitted. For example, there are no provisions in Missouri's code allowing for the collection of nongame amphibian and reptile species within the state by non-residents, and all such collecting activities are prohibited without permit. The following is a review of those portions of Missouri's Wildlife Code regulating the recreational take of amphibians and reptiles within the state. As stated previously, any activity not specifically included among the following provisions is prohibited.

With the exception of those native amphibians and reptiles designated as game or bait species (see below) and state endangered species, Missouri residents may collect and possess five specimens of native amphibian and reptile species for personal use without permit, unless otherwise specified. The purchase or sale of these specimens is prohibited (WCMO 3CSR10-9.110).

Salamanders

Ambystoma tigrinum, Tiger Salamander larvae may be harvested throughout the year for personal use as live bait. The daily bag limit is 150 specimens in total (all bait species combined). Legal methods for harvesting larval salamanders are: minnow trap with throat openings 1-1/2 inches or less, seine of 1/2 mesh 20 feet long by 4 feet wide or less, dip net, throw net, hook and line, or hand. A valid fishing permit is required (WCMO 3CSR10-6.310, 3CSR10-6.330, and 3CSR10-11.805).

Cryptobranchus alleganiensis, Hellbenders may not be collected or possessed without permit (WCMO 3CSR10-9.110).

Frogs

Frogs may be taken for personal use as live bait throughout the year. The daily possession limit is 150 total specimens (all bait species combined). A valid fishing permit is required. Bait may be taken by minnow trap with a throat opening of 1-1/2 inches or less; dip net, throw net, hook and line, seine 20 feet long by 4 feet deep and 1/2 mesh or less, or hand (WCMO 3CSR10-6.310, 3CSR10-6.330, and 3CSR10-11.805).

* Bullfrogs, *Rana catesbeiana*, Green Frogs, *Rana clamitans*, and Wood Frogs, *Rana sylvatica*, may not be harvested as bait and are not included in the previous regulation.

The following frogs may be taken, possessed, and transported from sunset June 30 to October 31. The daily bag limit is eight frogs and the possession limit is 16 frogs in aggregate. A valid fishing or hunting permit is required. With a fishing permit frogs may be legally taken by hand, hand net, gig, longbow, or hook and line. The taking of frogs by .22 caliber rimfire rifle or pistol, pellet gun, or crossbow requires a hunting permit. The use of artificial lighting while taking frogs is permitted (WCMO 3CSR10-6.335 and 3CSR10-7.445):

Rana catesbeiana	Bullfrog
Rana clamitans	Green Frog

Turtles

The shooting of turtles by firearm is prohibited (WCMO 3CSR10-6.328).

Chelydra serpentina, Common Snapping Turtles may be taken throughout the year. The daily bag limit is five turtles with a total possession limit 10 specimens. Turtles may be taken by snagging, snaring, grabbing, longbow, crossbow, and hook and line. A valid fishing permit is required (WCMO 3CSR10-6.328).

Apalone sp., Softshell Turtles may be legally taken from July 1 to December 31. The daily bag limit is five turtles with a total possession limit of 10 specimens. Softshells may be taken by snagging, snaring, grabbing, longbow, crossbow, and hook and line. A valid fishing permit is required (WCMO 3CSR10-6.32B).

License and Permit Information

Missouri fishing permits are available from most sporting goods and bait stores for an annual fee of $8 for residents and $25 for non-residents. Short term non-resident fishing licenses of 14 days at a cost of $15 and three days at a cost of $8 are also available. Small game hunting permit fees are $8 for residents and $50 for non-residents annually. Five-day non-resident small game hunting permits are available for a $25 fee. The collection of Missouri's nongame amphibian and reptile species by non-residents requires a scientific collector's permit. In general, scientific permits are issued to qualified individuals and/or institutions for legitimate research purposes only. Scientific collector's permit requirements and applications may be obtained from the Missouri Department of Conservation (address in Appendix I).

IMPORTATION AND COMMERCIAL TRADE REGULATIONS

Regulations governing the importation, possession, and sale of both native and non-native amphibians and reptiles are included among the rules of the Wildlife Code of Missouri. In general, the sale of any amphibian or reptile harvested from the wild in Missouri is prohibited with the exception of those animals designated as commercial fish species (see below). The following is a review of the commercial trade restrictions included in the Wildlife Code of Missouri.

Native and Exotic Species

Except as authorized by regulation, the transportation, importation, possession, purchase, sale, trade, or liberation of any wildlife including eggs within Missouri is prohibited. (WCMO 3CSR10-4.110).

* Includes both native and non-native species.

Specimens of native amphibians and nonvenomous reptiles legally obtained from outside Missouri may be imported, purchased, sold, or given away under the authorization of Class I Wildlife Breeders Permit (WCMO 3CSR10-9.230 and 3CSR10-9.353).

Legally obtained non-native amphibian and reptile species may be bought, sold, possessed, transported, and exhibited without permit (WCMO 3CSR10-9.110).

* Does not include venomous species.

Venomous reptiles, including native species legally acquired from outside Missouri, may be imported, purchased, sold, or given away under the authorization of a Class II Wildlife Breeders Permit. Venomous reptiles must be transported in strong, escape-proof, locked, and prominently labeled containers (WCMO 3CSR10-9.220, 3CSR10-9.351, and 3CSR10-9.353).

* Legitimate circuses, zoos, and research facilities are exempt from the above wildlife breeder's permit requirements.

Salamanders

Legally obtained salamanders may be purchased, sold, transported, or propagated without permit. Proper documentation is required (WCMO 3CSR10-9.110[3]).

* Includes both native and non-native species.

Turtles

The following native turtle species may be commercially harvested from the wild in Missouri by legal commercial fishing methods. A commercial fishing permit is required (WCMO 3CSR10-10.720 and 3CSR10-11.805[7]):

Chelydra serpentina	Common Snapping Turtle
Apalone mutica	Smooth Softshell
Apalone spinifera	Spiny Softshell

License and Permit Information

Annual fees for Class I and Class II wildlife breeder's permits are $50 and $150 respectively. Various permit conditions, requirements, and guidelines apply. Commercial fishing permits are available at an annual cost of $25 for residents and $200 for non-residents. Various commercial gear tag fees are also applicable. Requirements and permit applications for these three permits may be obtained from the Missouri Department of Conservation (address in Appendix I).

CAPTIVE MAINTENANCE REGULATIONS

In addition to the possession restrictions included among the regulations of the previous sections, Missouri regulates the possession of potentially dangerous reptiles with the following summarized statute.

No person may keep any deadly, dangerous, or poisonous reptile in any place other than a properly maintained zoological park, circus, scientific or educational institution, research laboratory, veterinary hospital, or animal refuge, unless the animals are registered with the local law enforcement agency in the county in which the animal is kept (RSMO 578.023).

* What effect, if any, the preceding legislation has on the captive possession of large constricting snakes is uncertain at this time.

Captive Maintenance Regulation Review

The following is a brief review of Missouri's restrictions on the captive possession of native and exotic amphibians and reptiles.

a. State endangered and extirpated species may not be possessed without permit.

b. *Cryptobranchus alleganiensis*, Hellbenders may not be possessed without permit.

c. Unless otherwise specified, the possession limit without permit for native amphibians and reptiles is five specimens of each species.

d. *Ambystoma tigrinum*, Tiger Salamander larvae have a possession limit of 150 specimens in aggregate with all other bait species. A valid fishing license is required.

e. Unless otherwise specified, native frogs have a possession limit of 150 specimens in aggregate with all other bait species. A valid fishing license is required.

f. *Rana catesbeiana*, Bullfrogs and *Rana clamitans*, Green Frogs have a possession limit of 16 total specimens of both species combined. A valid fishing or hunting license is required.

g. *Rana sylvatica*, Wood Frogs have a possession limit of five specimens.

h. *Chelydra serpentina*, Common Snapping Turtles have a possession limit of 10 specimens. A valid fishing license is required.

i. *Apalone* sp., Softshell Turtles have a possession limit of 10 specimens of all native species combined. A valid fishing license is required.

j. Dangerous reptiles, including venomous species, must be registered with local law enforcement agencies.

k. No restrictions on the possession of non-native amphibians and non-venomous reptiles.

(b through i above see Native Wildlife Regulations)
(j above see Captive Maintenance Regulations)
(k above see Importation and Commercial Trade Regulations)

MONTANA

ENDANGERED, THREATENED, AND SPECIAL CONCERN SPECIES

Endangered and threatened species of wildlife in the State of Montana are legally protected by the Montana Nongame and Endangered Species Conservation Act of the Montana Codes Annotated (reference: MCA 87-5-101-112). This legislation has provisions for the protection of nongame species deemed "in need of management," as well as any endangered and threatened species.

There are no native amphibians or reptiles included in Montana's current (March 1994) Endangered, Threatened, or In Need of Management species lists or in the current (January 1997) U.S. Endangered and Threatened Species list.

Protected Species Permit Information

Although not required for any native amphibian or reptile, scientific collecting permit applications may be obtained from the Law Enforcement Division of the Montana Department of Fish, Wildlife, and Parks (address in Appendix I).

NATIVE WILDLIFE REGULATIONS

Montana currently does not have any regulations on the collection or possession of native amphibians and reptiles wild caught in the state. All native amphibians and reptiles are considered nongame species with no closed seasons or bag limits. Licenses are not required.

IMPORTATION AND COMMERCIAL TRADE

With the exception of the following summarized restriction concerning the introduction of wildlife into the natural environment, the State of Montana does not restrict the importation or sale of any native or non-native amphibian or reptile species. However, although not currently applicable to any amphibians or reptiles, legislation does exist in Montana which would allow the state to prohibit the importation, sale, and possession of any species deemed detrimental to public safety or Montana's native flora and fauna (reference: MCA 87-5-712).

The importation for introduction or the transplantation or introduction of any wildlife is prohibited except as otherwise authorized (MCA 87-5-711).

CAPTIVE MAINTENANCE REGULATIONS

The State of Montana does not currently regulate the possession of any native or non-native amphibians or reptiles. However, the possession of any federally protected endangered or threatened species would require a permit issued by the U.S. Department of the Interior (see U.S. Endangered and Threatened Species).

* The Legislature of the State of Montana is currently considering revising the State's wildlife importation and possession rules and regulations. When this revision will be completed is uncertain at this time.

NEBRASKA

ENDANGERED, THREATENED, AND SPECIAL CONCERN SPECIES

The Nebraska Game and Parks Commission classifies rarer members of the state's flora and fauna as Endangered, Threatened, or as species in Need of Conservation. Species in all three categories are legally protected by the Nebraska Nongame and Endangered Species Conservation Act and may not be collected or possessed without permit, as specified in chapter 37 of the Revised Statutes of Nebraska (reference: NE R.S. 37-430 to 439). As with the endangered species legislation of most states, Nebraska's law contains provisions for the protection of any species included in the federal list of threatened and endangered wildlife.

The following species is the only amphibian or reptile included in the current (May 1994) list of endangered, threatened, or in need of conservation (N/C) species in Nebraska. State permits are required for all activities involving this species.

Species	Common Name	Status
Phrynosoma douglassii	Short-horned Lizard	N/C

Protected Species Permit Information

Scientific collecting permits authorizing the collection and possession of Nebraska's protected species may be issued for research, educational, or exhibition purposes. Scientific permits allowing for the possession of specimens of protected species legally acquired from outside of Nebraska may also be issued. Permit requirements and applications may be obtained from the Nebraska Game and Parks Commission (address in Appendix I).

NATIVE WILDLIFE REGULATIONS

The State of Nebraska has relatively few restrictions on the collection and possession of amphibians and reptiles wild caught in the state for recreational (non-commercial) purposes. These restrictions are included among the wildlife legislation of the Revised Statutes of Nebraska (reference: NE R.S.) and in the regulations of the Game and Parks Commission in title 163, chapter 2 of the Nebraska Administrative Code (reference: NE A.C.). In general, most of Nebraska's native amphibians and reptiles are considered nongame species and may be collected without restriction. As game species, various restrictions apply to *Ambystoma tigrinum*, Tiger Salamanders, *Rana catesbeiana*, Bullfrogs, and *Chelydra serpentina*, Snapping Turtles. The following is a summary of those portions of Nebraska's wildlife legislation regulating the non-commercial collection of amphibians and reptiles within the state.

It is unlawful for any non-resident to take or possess any amphibian or turtle wild caught in Nebraska without a non-resident small game hunting permit (NE R.S. 37-507.01).

Salamanders

Ambystoma tigrinum, Tiger Salamanders may be taken throughout the year with a daily bag and possession limit of 100 specimens. A valid fishing permit is required (NE R.S. 37-213 and NE A.C. 2-006.03M).

Frogs

Rana catesbeiana, Bullfrogs may be taken from August 15 through October 31, with a daily bag limit of eight and a possession limit of 16 specimens. There is a minimum snout to vent length requirement of 4-1/2 inches. Frogs may be taken by hand, hand net, and hook and line. The use of artificial light is permitted. A valid fishing permit is required (NE R.S. 37-226 and A.C. 2-006.030).

Turtles

Chelydra serpentina, Common Snapping Turtles may be taken throughout the year with a daily bag limit of 10 and a possession limit of 20 specimens. Snappers may be taken by hand, hand net, hook and line, bow and arrow, or gaff hook. A valid fishing permit is required (NE R.S. 37-213 and NE A.C. 2-006.03P).

* Non-residents apparently require both fishing and small game hunting permits to collect Tiger Salamanders, Bullfrogs, and Snapping Turtles.

License and Permit Information

Nebraska fishing and hunting licenses are available from numerous retail outlets including most bait shops and sporting goods stores. Fishing permits have an annual fee of $11.50 for residents and $25.00 for non-residents. Three-day non-resident fishing permits are also available for a $7.50 fee. Non-resident small game hunting permits cost $40.00.

IMPORTATION AND COMMERCIAL TRADE REGULATIONS

Native Species

Specific restrictions on the commercial exploitation of native amphibians and reptiles wild caught in the state are included among the regulations of the Game and Parks Commission in Nebraska's Administrative Code. The following is a summary of these regulations.

The following amphibian and reptile species may be harvested from the wild for commercial or exportation purposes without restriction (NE A.C. 2-002.08):

Crotalus viridis	Prairie Rattlesnake
Pituophis catenifer	Bullsnake
Thamnophis radix	Plains Garter Snake
Thamnophis sirtalis	Red-sided Garter Snake

The following amphibian and reptile species may be harvested from the wild for commercial or exportation purposes by permit only (NE A.C. 2-002.10):

Acris crepitans	Northern Cricket Frog
Bufo cognatus	Great Plains Toad
Bufo woodhousii	Woodhouse's Toad
Hyla chrysoscelis	Cope's Gray Treefrog
Pseudacris triseriata	Western Chorus Frog
Rana blairi	Plains Leopard Frog
Rana pipiens	Northern Leopard Frog
Spea bombifrons	Plains Spadefoot Toad
Apalone mutica	Smooth Softshell Turtle
Apalone spinifera	Spiny Softshell Turtle
Chrysemys picta	Painted Turtle
Terrapene ornata	Ornate Box Turtle
Cnemidophorus sexlineatus	Six-lined Racerunner
Eumeces multivirgatus	Many-lined Skink
Eumeces septentrionalis	Prairie Skink
Holbrookia maculata	Lesser Earless Lizard
Sceloporus undulatus	Northern Prairie Lizard

Coluber constrictor	Blue Racer
Diadophis punctatus	Ringneck Snake
Elaphe obsoleta	Black Ratsnake
Elaphe vulpina	Fox Snake
Heterodon nasicus	Western Hognose Snake
Heterodon platirhinos	Eastern Hognose Snake
Lampropeltis triangulum	Milk Snake
Nerodia sipedon	Northern Water Snake
Storeria dekayi	Brown Snake
Thamnophis elegans	Wandering Garter Snake
Tropidoclonion lineatum	Lined Snake

Ambystoma tigrinum, Tiger Salamanders harvested from the wild in Nebraska may be commercially exploited under the authority of a resident or non-resident bait vendor's permit (NE R.S. 37-503).

Rana catesbeiana, Bullfrogs harvested from the wild in Nebraska may not be purchased, sold, or bartered (NE R.S. 37-505).

The following frogs harvested from the wild in Nebraska may be commercially exploited under the authority of a resident or non-resident bait vendor's permit (NE R.S. 37-503):

Rana pipiens	Northern Leopard Frog
Rana blairi	Plains Leopard Frog

* The sale of Leopard Frogs wild caught in the State of Nebraska by non-residents is prohibited (see Native and Exotic Species below).

Chelydra serpentina, Common Snapping Turtles taken from the wild in Nebraska may be commercially exploited within the bag and possession limits specified (see Native Wildlife Regulations). Special permits are not required (NE Legislative Bill 830).

* All other native amphibian and reptile species wild caught in Nebraska may not be exported or commercially exploited.

Native and Exotic Species

Portions of the wildlife legislation of Nebraska's Revised Statutes regulate the importation, possession, and/or sale of both non-native species and specimens of native amphibians and reptiles legally obtained from outside the state. This legislation is summarized below.

The importation into the state or the release into the wild of any live amphibian or reptile is prohibited (NE R.S. 37-536).

Amphibian and reptile importation restrictions shall not apply to the buying, selling, bartering, importing, exporting, or otherwise disposing of any wildlife produced at any municipal, state, or federal museum, zoo, park, refuge, or wildlife area, or to the importation of any amphibian or reptile intended for exhibition, aquarium, or other totally contained purposes (NE R.S. 37-537).

* As currently interpreted by the Nebraska Game and Parks Commission the two previous regulations, in combination, do not prohibit the importation, possession, and/or sale of any legally obtained amphibian or reptile for exhibition, pet, or captive propagation purposes.

Non-residents require a non-resident bait vendor's permit to sell frogs in Nebraska. All frogs sold by non-residents must be lawfully acquired from outside the state or from a licensed fish hatchery (NE R.S. 37-505).

License and Permit Information

Commercial collection permits required for the commercial harvest of the species specified in regulation NE A.C. 002-2.10 are issued free of charge, and currently function as a monitoring system only. Bait vendor's permits are available for an annual fee of $25 for residents and $150 for non-residents. The cost of a non-resident bait vendor's license is about $50 to $65 annually. Permit and license requirements and applications may be obtained from the Nebraska Game and Parks Commission (address in Appendix I).

CAPTIVE MAINTENANCE REGULATIONS

The following is a brief review of the restrictions on the captive possession within the state of amphibians and reptiles included among the regulations of the preceding sections.

a. *Phrynosoma douglassii*, Short-horned Lizards may not be possessed without permit.

b. *Ambystoma tigrinum*, Tiger Salamanders have a possession limit of 100 specimens. A valid fishing permit may be required.

c. *Rana catesbeiana*, Bullfrogs have a possession limit of 16 specimens. A valid fishing license may be required.

d. *Chelydra serpentina*, Common Snapping Turtles have a possession limit of 20 specimens. A valid fishing license may be required.

e. All other native amphibian and reptile species may be possessed without restriction.

f. No restrictions on the possession of non-native amphibian and reptile species.

(b, c, d and e above, see Native Wildlife Regulations)

Hatchling Amelanistic Corn Snakes, *Elaphe guttata* - Contrary to what some wildlife organizations would have you believe, captive propagation can and does have a positive impact on the conservation of some amphibians and reptiles. For example, species like the Corn Snake are now captive produced in such large quantities that a wide variety of "designer" color phases are readily available at extremely low prices and there is little profit to be made from commercially harvesting specimens from the wild. With the exception of species protected by state conservation law, captive bred amphibians and reptiles of all types may be possessed in Nebraska without permit. Photograph courtesy of William B. Love.

NEVADA

ENDANGERED, THREATENED, AND SPECIAL CONCERN SPECIES

Native amphibians and reptiles in the State of Nevada are classified into one of three categories of wildlife: game species, unprotected species, or protected species. Wildlife designated as protected species may be further categorized as sensitive, threatened, or endangered. All species included in the list of protected wildlife may not be collected or possessed without a permit, as specified in the regulations of the Nevada Administrative Code (reference: NAC 503.093).

The following native reptile species are included in the current (May 1994) list of legally protected wildlife in the State of Nevada. Authorization is required for all activities involving these species.

Species	Common Name	Status
Gopherus agassizii	Desert Tortoise	Threatened
Heloderma suspectum	Gila Monster	Protected

Protected Species Permit Information

Scientific collection permits allowing for the collection and possession of protected species wild caught in Nevada are issued strictly for legitimate research or educational purposes only. Permits allowing for the possession of legally acquired specimens of Nevada's protected species are also available. There is a fee of $5 for each of these permits, and permit applications and requirements may be obtained from the Nevada Division of Wildlife (address in Appendix I).

NATIVE WILDLIFE REGULATIONS

Restrictions on the non-commercial collection and possession of unprotected wild caught native amphibians and reptiles classified as unprotected or game species are specified in the regulations of the Nevada Administrative Code (reference: NAC) and in the Revised Statutes of Nevada (reference: NRS). The following is a summarization of these statutes and regulations.

Unprotected amphibians are all species of amphibians which are not classified as game or protected amphibians (NRS 503.075-1).

All species of reptiles which are not classified as protected, sensitive, threatened or endangered are unprotected (NRS 503.080-3).

There is no open season on those species of wild animal, wild bird, fish, reptile or amphibian classified as protected (NRS 503.090-1).

There is no closed season on those species of wild animals or wild birds classified as unprotected (NRS 503.090-2).

* As currently interpreted by the Nevada Division of Wildlife, the preceding regulations DO NOT allow for the recreational or non-commercial collection and/or possession of unprotected amphibians and reptiles wild caught within the state by virtue of the fact that the words "amphibian" and "reptile" are not specifically included in regulation 503.090-2 above. The State of Nevada currently has no provisions allowing for the collection of unprotected native amphibians and reptiles for personal use, and the Nevada Division of Wildlife considers the possession of any species indigenous to Nevada, whether wild caught in the state or legally obtained from outside of Nevada, to be prohibited without a license (see the two following regulations). The commercial harvest of unprotected species is allowed under the authorization of a Commercial Permit (see Importation and Commercial Trade Regulations).

Live wildlife may not be possessed without license unless otherwise specified (NRS 504.295-1a).

Live wildlife may not be captured in Nevada to stock a commercial or non-commercial wildlife facility unless otherwise specified (NRS 504.295-1b).

Frogs

Rana catesbeiana, Bullfrogs are classified as game amphibians (NAC 503.070). The open season for bullfrogs is year round, and frogs may be taken at any time of day or night. The possession and daily bag limit is 15 specimens. Bullfrogs may be taken by hand, hook and line, gig, spear, or bow and arrow. The use of firearms and airguns is prohibited. A valid fishing license is required to collect bullfrogs.

License and Permit Information

Non-commercial possession of wildlife licenses allowing for the possession of legally obtained specimens of unprotected native amphibians and reptiles are available at a cost of $5.00, and applications may be obtained from the Nevada Division of Wildlife (address in Appendix I). Fishing licenses (required to collect and possess Bullfrogs) are available from most bait shops and sporting goods stores at an annual fee of $20.00 for residents and $50.00 for non-residents. One-day limited fishing licenses are also available for both residents and non-residents at a cost of $6.00 and $11.00 respectively..

IMPORTATION AND COMMERCIAL TRADE REGULATIONS

Native Species

Restrictions on the importation, sale, and possession indigenous amphibians and reptiles are included among the rules and regulations of both the Revised Statutes of Nevada and the Nevada Administrative Code. The following is a summarization of these regulations.

It is unlawful to sell, barter, trade, or purchase, or attempt to sell, barter, trade, or purchase any species of wildlife, or parts thereof, unless otherwise specified (NRS 501.379).

A commercial wildlife permit is required to harvest unprotected wildlife for commercial purposes in the State of Nevada (NRS 503.095).

* Commercial permits are only issued to residents of Nevada. In addition, indigenous species harvested from the wild in Nevada for commercial purposes may apparently only be sold outside of the state (see Native Wildlife Regulations).

Importation permits are required to import or transport wildlife in Nevada unless otherwise specified (NAC 503.130).

A Commercial Possession of Live Wildlife license is required to sell or possess for commercial purposes legally acquired specimens of indigenous amphibians and reptiles. Wildlife is considered legally acquired if it is obtained from a licensed breeder or dealer of that species or is lawfully collected in another state or country. Importation permits are also required. Indigenous species may only be sold to individuals and institutions authorized by permit to possess the species in question (NAC 504.450 – 504.470).

A non-commercial possession of live wildlife license is required to purchase and possess any indigenous amphibian or reptile in Nevada for non-commercial purposes (NAC 504.450 – 504.470).

Albino specimens of indigenous reptiles are exempt from importation and possession permit requirements (NAC 503.130).

Exotic Species

Restrictions on the importation and possession of non-native amphibian and reptile species are specified in the Nevada Administrative Code. In general, non-native species are classified as either prohibited wildlife, which may only be imported or possessed by permit, or as exempt wildlife, which are free of any permit requirements. The following is a review of the amphibians and reptiles included in both categories.

Prohibited Wildlife

The following amphibian and reptile families, genera, and/or species may not be imported into or possessed in the State of Nevada except by permit (NAC 503.110):

Bufo horribilus	Giant Toad	
Bufo marinus	Marine Toad	
Bufo paracnemis	Giant Toad	
Xenopus spp.	African Clawed Frogs	All species in genus
Chelydridae	Snapping Turtles	All species in family
Alligatoridae	Alligators and Caimans	All species
Crocodylidae	Crocodiles All species	
Gavilidae	Gharials All species	
Atractaspidae	Burrowing Asps All species	
Dispholidus typus	Boomslang	
Elapidae	Elapids All species in family except those in the subfamily: Hydrophiinae Sea Snakes	
Rhabdophis	Keelbacks All species in genus	
Thelotornis	Bird Snakes All species in genus	
Viperidae	Vipers and Pit Vipers All species in family except those species indigenous to Nevada.	

Exempt (Non-Regulated) Wildlife

Importation and possession permits are not required for the amphibians or reptiles listed below, except where otherwise noted. Permits are required for any species not included in the following list (NAC 503.140):

Non-indigenous species of amphibians, except for *Rana catesbeiana*, Bullfrogs and those species included in the prohibited wildlife list as specified in NAC 503.110 (see list above).

Albino forms of indigenous reptile species.

Nonvenomous, non-indigenous reptiles, except for those species included in the prohibited wildlife list as specified in NAC 503.110.

License and Permit Information

Commercial wildlife permits which authorize the harvest of unprotected indigenous wildlife are available at a cost of $100 annually. Non-commercial possession of live wildlife licenses (required to possess any species indigenous to Nevada) have an annual fee of $5, and there is a $100 annual fee for a commercial possession of live wildlife license. Applications and requirements for these licenses, permits, and for any required importation permits may be obtained from the Nevada Division of Wildlife (address in Appendix I).

CAPTIVE MAINTENANCE REGULATIONS

In addition to any restrictions on the possession of amphibians and reptiles contained among the regulations of the previous sections, the following licensing requirements regarding the captive maintenance of live wildlife for public display are included in the wildlife laws of Nevada.

A commercial possession of live wildlife license is required to exhibit wildlife, except as otherwise specified (NAC 504.468).

Specimens of live wildlife held under the authority of a scientific collection permit may be displayed in public without a commercial license provided the exhibit is for strictly scientific or educational purposes and no fee is charged to view the wildlife (NAC 504.484).

Individuals licensed by the U.S. Department of the Interior to exhibit live wildlife are exempt from state licensing requirements for a period of 90 days (NAC 504.486).

License and Permit Information

As stated previously, a license to possess live wildlife is required for all species included in the list of prohibited wildlife and all indigenous species except albino specimens. Non-commercial possession of live wildlife licenses will not be issued for any of the amphibians or reptiles included among the species in the prohibited wildlife list, and permits to possess prohibited wildlife species are issued to legitimate zoos, scientific institutions, or educational facilities only. Further information on any required permits of this section may be obtained from the Nevada Division of Wildlife (address in Appendix I).

Captive Maintenance Regulations Review

The following is a brief review of Nevada's restrictions on the possession of live amphibians and reptiles included among the previous regulations.

a. Permits are required to possess all species designated as protected.
b. Possession licenses are required to possess any amphibian or reptile species indigenous to Nevada, except for albino specimens and *Rana catesbeiana*, Bullfrogs .
c. *Rana catesbeiana*, Bullfrogs wild caught in the state have a possession limit of 15 specimens. A valid fishing license is required.
d. Unless otherwise specified, permits are not required to possess nonvenomous, non-indigenous amphibian and reptile species.
e. Permits are required to possess non-indigenous amphibian species designated as prohibited wildlife including Giant Toads, African Clawed Frogs, and imported specimens of Rana catesbeiana.
f. Licenses are required to possess any non-indigenous reptile species designated as prohibited wildlife including all crocodilians, venomous reptiles, and Snapping Turtles.

(b and c above see Native Wildlife Regulations).
(d, e and f above see Importation and Commercial Trade Regulations).

NEW HAMPSHIRE

ENDANGERED, THREATENED, AND SPECIAL CONCERN SPECIES

Rarer members of New Hampshire's fauna are listed as endangered, threatened, or as species of special concern. Only species officially designated as endangered or threatened, however, receive the full legal protection of the state's Endangered Species Conservation Act as specified in title XVIII, chapter 212 of New Hampshire Revised Statutes Annotated (reference: NHRSA XVIII 212-A.). As is the case with numerous states, the New Hampshire Endangered Species Conservation Act contains no recovery plan or critical habitat provisions and the state's legislation can do little more than prohibit the collection, possession, and trade without permit of any listed endangered or threatened species. In addition to the state's endangered species legislation, the New Hampshire Nongame Species Management Act (reference: NHRSA XVIII 212-B) authorizes the New Hampshire Fish and Game Department to regulate the taking, possession, and handling of indigenous nongame wildlife. Currently four native reptiles, all turtles, have been designated as fully "controlled" and their collection, possession, and sale without permit is also completely prohibited, as specified in the wildlife legislation of the New Hampshire Code of Administrative Rules (reference: NMCAR Fis 804.07, 8o4.29, 810.01, and 1407.1). As this closely approximates the protective status of state threatened and endangered species, these four controlled turtles have been included in the following list of New Hampshire's fully protected amphibians and reptiles. In an attempt at further clarification, those portions of New Hampshire's nongame legislation pertinent to state controlled species have been summarized within the context of the respective sections below.

The following reptile species are included in the current (June 1994) endangered and threatened species list in New Hampshire, or are included in the state's current (February 1996) list of fully controlled wildlife. As stated previously, permits are required for all collection, possession, and trade activities involving these species.

<u>Species</u>	<u>Common Name</u>	<u>Status</u>
Clemmys guttata	Spotted Turtle	Controlled
Clemmys insculpta	Wood Turtle	Controlled
Emydoidea blandingii	Blanding's Turtle	Controlled
Terrapene carolina carolina	Eastern Box Turtle	Controlled
Crotalus horridus	Timber Rattlesnake	Endangered

Protected Species Permit Information

Scientific permits allowing for the collection and the limited possession of Crotalus horridus will be issued to qualified individuals and institutions for legitimate research, conservation, or exhibition purposes only. There is no charge for a scientific permit. Collection and possession permits for state fully controlled species are subject to similar requirements and conditions, although individuals will generally be issued possession permit for specimens legally obtained before January 1, 1996 (NMCAR 804.07c). Further information on permit conditions and requirements, as well as permit applications, may be obtained from the New Hampshire Fish and Game Department (address in Appendix I).

NATIVE WILDLIFE REGULATIONS

With the exception of state listed endangered, threatened, or controlled species, the State of New Hampshire does not currently regulate the possession of any amphibian or non-venomous reptile, including specimens of native species wild caught within the state. All other native amphibians and reptiles are considered "non-controlled" wildlife, and permits are not required to collect or possess these species recreationally. Those portions of New Hampshire's wildlife legislation regulating the non-commercial collection and possession of native amphibians and reptiles are summarized below.

Permits are not required to possess amphibians and reptiles designated as uncontrolled (NMCAR Fis 804.03)

The possession of controlled wildlife without permit is prohibited (NHCAR Fis 804.29).

Turtles

The collection and possession of the following turtles, including eggs or parts, without permit is prohibited (NHCAR Fis 1401):

Clemmys guttata	Spotted Turtle
Clemmys insculpta	Wood Turtle
Emydoidea blandingii	Blanding's Turtle
Terrapene carolina carolina	Eastern Box Turtle

License and Permit Information

(see Protected Species Permit Information Above)

IMPORTATION AND COMMERCIAL TRADE REGULATIONS

Native and Exotic Species

Restrictions on the importation of wildlife are specified in the New Hampshire Code of Administrative Rules. These regulations are summarized below and apply to both native and non-native amphibian and reptile species.

A permit is not required to import wildlife designated as non-controlled (NHCAR Fis 803.03).

Controlled Species

No wildlife designated as controlled may be imported into or possessed within New Hampshire without permit (NHCAR Fis 803.05 and 803.06). The following reptiles are included in New Hampshire's list of controlled wildlife species (NHCAR Fis 807.29b):

Venomous Reptiles	All Species
Clemmys guttata	Spotted Turtle
Clemmys insculpta	Wood Turtle
Emydoidea blandingii	Blanding's Turtle
Terrapene carolina carolina	Eastern Box Turtle

Turtles

The sale of the following turtle species is prohibited (NHCAR Fis 810.01):

Clemmys guttata	Spotted Turtle
Clemmys insculpta	Wood Turtle
Emydoidea blandingii	Blanding's Turtle
Terrapene carolina carolina	Eastern Box Turtle

* There are apparently no restrictions on the sale of any other amphibians or non-venomous reptiles in New Hampshire at this time.

License and Permit Information

Importation and possession permits for controlled wildlife species, including all venomous reptiles, are generally issued to qualified institutions and individuals for legitimate research and exhibition purposes only (see Protected Species Permit Information for exceptions). Permit applications and requirements may be obtained from the New Hampshire Fish and Game Department (address in Appendix I).

CAPTIVE MAINTENANCE REGULATIONS

In addition to the restrictions on the possession of both native and non-native amphibians and reptiles included among the legislation of the preceding sections, the following summarized regulation is applicable to the captive maintenance of these animals.

The release into the natural environment of New Hampshire of all indigenous amphibians and reptiles imported into the state and all exotic amphibian and reptile species is prohibited (NHCAR Fis 805.02).

Captive Maintenance Regulations Review

a. Endangered, threatened, and controlled species may not be possessed without permit.
b. Permits are required to possess any venomous reptile species.
c. No restrictions on the possession of other native and non-native amphibians and non-venomous reptiles.

(a above see Endangered, Threatened, and Special Concern Species and Native Wildlife Regulations)
(b above see Importation and Commercial Trade Regulations)
(c above see Native Wildlife Regulations and Importation and Commercial Trade regulations).

Watch for Snakes - Signs designed to alert people to the presence of snakes are starting to become much more prevalent across the United States. Photograph courtesy of Barney Oldfield.

NEW JERSEY

ENDANGERED, THREATENED, AND SPECIAL CONCERN SPECIES

The New Jersey Division of Fish, Game and Wildlife utilizes a relatively complex system in which virtually every indigenous vertebrate found in the state is classified as either endangered, non-game, or game species. Non-game species are further categorized into one of a multitude of different status designations including threatened, unusual, declining, stable, increasing, introduced, and extirpated. All officially designated endangered species receive the full legal protection of the New Jersey Endangered and Nongame Species Conservation Act and their collection or possession for any purpose without permit is prohibited, as specified in title 23 of the New Jersey Statutes Annotated (reference: NJSA 23:2A-1 to 2A-13). As is the case with the endangered species law of many states, New Jersey's legislation does contains provisions to legally protect any species included in the federal list of threatened and endangered wildlife and the state's endangered species permit requirements are among the most stringent in the nation. In addition to state and federally listed endangered species, New Jersey also prohibits the collection and possession of all indigenous non-game wildlife species wild caught within the state. While less restrictive than state endangered species permit requirements, permits are never-the-less required for any activity involving wild caught non-game species, as specified in the Endangered, Nongame and Exotic Wildlife legislation of the New Jersey Administrative Code (reference: NJAC 7:25-4.1 to 7:25.17). As currently interpreted by the New Jersey Division of Fish, Game and Wildlife, all specimens of the vast majority of both native and introduced non-game species are subject to non-game wildlife permit requirements, including specimens legally obtained from outside New Jersey.

The following amphibians and reptiles are included in New Jersey's current (June 1996) lists of endangered and fully protected non-game species, as specified in the Endangered, Nongame and Exotic Wildlife legislation of the New Jersey Administrative Code (reference: NJAC 7:25-4.10, 7:25-4.17, and 7:25-4.4). With the exception of those non-game species officially designated as threatened by the State of New Jersey, all fully protected indigenous non-game species are simply classified as protected in the list below. As stated previously, permits issued by the New Jersey Division of Fish, Game and Wildlife are required for any activity involving all specimens of the following species, including animals lawfully acquired from outside the state. In addition, U.S. Department of Interior permits are required for any of the following species included in the U.S. Department of the Interior's list of federally protected endangered and threatened wildlife (see U.S. Endangered and Threatened Species).

Species	Common Name	Status
Ambystoma jeffersonianum	Jefferson's Salamander	Protected
Ambystoma laterale	Blue-spotted Salamander	Endangered
Ambystoma maculatum	Spotted Salamander	Protected
Ambystoma opacum	Marbled Salamander	Protected
Ambystoma platineum [1]	Silvery Salamander	Protected
Ambystoma tigrinum tigrinum [2]	Eastern Tiger Salamander	Endangered
Ambystoma tremblayi [1]	Tremblay's Salamander	Endangered
Eurycea bislineata bislineata [2]	Northern Two-lined Salamander	Protected
Eurycea longicauda longicauda	Longtail Salamander	Threatened
Gyrinophilus porphyriticus porphyriticus	Northern Spring Salamander	Protected
Hemidactylium scutatum	Four-toed Salamander	Protected
Plethodon cinereus cinereus [2]	Redback Salamander	Protected
Plethodon glutinosus glutinosus [2]	Slimy Salamander	Protected
Pseudotriton montanus montanus	Eastern Mud Salamander	Threatened
Pseudotriton ruber ruber	Northern Mud Salamander	Protected

Acris crepitans crepitans	Northern Cricket Frog	Protected
Hyla andersonii [3]	Pine Barrens Treefrog	Endangered
Hyla chrysoscelis	Cope's Gray Treefrog	Endangered
Hyla gratiosa	Barking Treefrog	Protected
Hyla versicolor	Gray Treefrog	Protected
Pseudacris crucifer crucifer [4]	Northern Spring Peeper	Protected
Pseudacris feriarum [5]	Upland Chorus Frog	Protected
Pseudacris kalmi [6]	New Jersey Chorus Frog	Protected
Rana palustris	Pickerel Frog	Protected
Rana sylvatica	Wood Frog	Protected
Rana sphenocephala [7]	Southern Leopard Frog	Protected
Rana virgatipes [8]	Carpenter Frog	Protected
Scaphiopus holbrookii holbrookii [2]	Eastern Spadefoot Toad	Protected
Apalone spinifera [9]	Spiny Softshell Turtle	Protected
Caretta caretta	Loggerhead Sea Turtle	Endangered
Chelonia mydas	Green Sea Turtle	Threatened
Clemmys guttata	Spotted Turtle	Protected
Clemmys insculpta	Wood Turtle	Threatened
Clemmys muhlenbergii [10]	Bog Turtle	Endangered
Chrysemys picta marginata	Midland Painted Turtle	Protected
Dermochelys coriacea	Leatherback Sea Turtle	Endangered
Eretmochelys imbricata	Hawksbill Sea Turtle	Endangered
Graptemys geographica	Common Map Turtle	Protected
Kinosternon subrubrum subrubrum	Eastern Mud Turtle	Protected
Lepidochelys kempii [11]	Atlantic Ridley Sea Turtle	Endangered
Pseudemys rubriventris	Redbelly Turtle	Protected
Sternotherus odoratus [12]	Common Musk Turtle	Protected
Terrapene carolina carolina	Eastern Box Turtle	Protected
Trachemys scripta elegans [13]	Red-eared Slider	Protected
Eumeces fasciatus	Five-lined Skink	Protected
Scincella lateralis	Ground Skink	Protected
Agkistrodon contortrix mokasen	Northern Copperhead	Protected
Carphophis amoenus amoenus	Eastern Worm Snake	Protected
Cemophora coccinea copei	Northern Scarlet Snake	Protected
Coluber constrictor constrictor	Northern Black Racer	Protected
Crotalus horridus	Timber Rattlesnake	Endangered
Diadophis punctatus edwardsii [14]	Northern Ringneck Snake	Protected
Diadophis punctatus punctatus	Southern Ringneck Snake	Protected
Elaphe guttata guttata [15]	Corn Snake	Endangered
Elaphe obsoleta obsoleta [16]	Black Rat Snake	Protected
Heterodon platirhinos [17]	Eastern Hognose Snake	Protected
Lampropeltis getula getula [18]	Eastern Kingsnake	Protected
Lampropeltis triangulum triangulum	Eastern Milk Snake	Protected
Liochlorophis vernalis vernalis [19]	Eastern Smooth Green Snake	Protected
Nerodia sipedon sipedon	Northern Water Snake	Protected
Opheodrys aestivus	Rough Green Snake	Protected
Pituophis melanoleucus melanoleucus	Northern Pine Snake	Threatened
Regina septemvittata	Queen Snake	Protected
Storeria dekayi dekayi	Northern Brown Snake	Protected
Storeria occipitomaculata occipitomaculata	Northern Redbelly Snake	Protected
Virginia valeriae valeriae	Eastern Earth Snake	Protected

[1] Not listed in Collins (1997).
[2] No subspecies recognized in Collins (1997).
[3] Listed as *Hyla andersoni* by New Jersey.
[4] Listed in the genus *Hyla* by New Jersey.
[5] Listed as *Pseudacris triseriata feriarum* by New Jersey.
[6] Listed as *Pseudacris triseriata kalmi* by New Jersey.
[7] Listed as *Rana spenocephala* by New Jersey.
[8] Listed as *Rana varigatipes* by New Jersey.
[9] Listed as *Trionyx spiniferus* by New Jersey. Species included among the non-native indigenous herpetofauna of New Jersey.
[10] Listed as *Clemmys muhlenbergi* by New Jersey.
[11] Listed as *Lepidochelys kempi* by New Jersey.
[12] Listed as *Kinosternon odoratum* by New Jersey.
[13] Listed in the genus *Chrysemys* by New Jersey. Species included among the non-native indigenous herpetofauna of New Jersey.
[14] Listed as *Diadophis punctatus edwardsi* by New Jersey.
[15] No subspecies recognized in Collins (1997). As currently interpreted by the New Jersey Division of Fish, Game and Wildlife albino specimens of this species are exempt from endangered and non-game species permit requirements.
[16] As currently interpreted by the New Jersey Division of Fish, Game and Wildlife albino specimens of this species are exempt from endangered and non-game species permit requirements.
[17] Listed as *Heterodon platyrhinos* by New Jersey.
[18] Listed as *Lampropeltis getulus getulus* by New Jersey.
[19] Listed as *Opheodrys vernalis vernalis* by New Jersey. No subspecies recognized in Collins (1997).

Protected Species Permit Information

Endangered species permits allowing for the collection and possession of New Jersey's endangered species may be issued for scientific, zoological, educational, or propagation purposes. In general, these permits are issued to qualified individuals and institutions for legitimate research, conservation, or exhibition purposes only, and all applicants must meet New Jersey's demanding criteria before any activities involving endangered species will be authorized. The fee for an endangered species permit is $7 annually. A wide variety of different permit types, including individual hobby, scientific collecting, scientific holding, zoological holding, animal exhibitor, and wildlife rehabilitation permits, are available for activities involving New Jersey's threatened and other listed non-game species. In general, issuance criteria for these non-game wildlife permits are much less stringent than state endangered species permit requirements. Annual fees for non-game wildlife permit range in price from $10.00 for individual hobby permits to over $100.00 for certain categories of zoological holding and commercial permits. Further information on permit requirements and fees, and required permit applications may be obtained from the Division of Fish, Game and Wildlife of the New Jersey Department of Environmental Protection and Energy (address in Appendix I).

NATIVE WILDLIFE REGULATIONS

Restrictions on the collection and possession of both native and introduced indigenous amphibians and reptiles wild caught within the state are included among the fish and wildlife legislation of New Jersey Statutes Annotated (reference: NJSA) and the New Jersey Administrative Code (reference: NJAC). With the exception of the designated game species covered in the following summarized regulations, all of New Jersey's indigenous amphibian and reptile species are classified as non-game wildlife and their collection from the natural environment of the state and their subsequent possession without permit is prohibited. Specimens of a few of New Jersey's indigenous non-game species legally obtained from outside the state may be possessed without permit, however (see Importation and Commercial trade Regulations. Those portions of New Jersey's fish and wildlife legislation regulating the non-commercial collection and possession of indigenous amphibians and reptiles wild caught within the state are summarized below.

The possession of any non-game or exotic amphibian and reptile without permit is prohibited unless otherwise specified (NJAC 7:25-4.2).

NJ

Frogs

The open season for frogs is from July 1 through April 15. Frogs may be taken by hand, dip nets 24 inches in diameter or less, hooks, spears, or traps. The daily bag limit is 15 frogs in total. A valid fishing license is required. Special permits may be issued to take frogs in excess of the above possession limits. Only the following frogs are species that may be legally taken (NJAC 7:25-6.22):

Rana catesbeiana	Bullfrog
Rana clamitans	Green Frog

Turtles

Chelydra serpentina, Common Snapping Turtles may be taken from June 16 through April 30. Snapping Turtles may be taken by hand, spear, hook, dip nets less than 24 inches in diameter, or trap. The daily bag limit is three specimens. A valid fishing license is required. Special permits may be issued authorizing the taking of snappers in excess of the above possession limits (NJAC 7:25-6.22).

Malaclemys terrapin, [1] Diamondback Terrapins may only be taken and possessed from November 1 through March 31. The use of traps, pots, fykes, seines, weirs, or nets of any description to take terrapins is prohibited. There is a five-inch plastron length minimum size requirement. Terrapin eggs may not be taken or destroyed at any time (NJAC 7:25-21.1 to 7:25-21.3).

[1] Listed as *Malaclemys palustris* by New Jersey.

* Licenses are apparently not required to collect Diamondback Terrapins.

License and Permit Information

Scientific collecting permits are required to collect all native and introduced indigenous amphibians and reptiles in New Jersey except for Bullfrogs, Green Frogs, Snapping Turtles, and Diamondback Terrapins which are the species with a designated open season. Generally, scientific collecting permits will only be issued to qualified individuals and institutions for legitimate research, educational, or conservation purposes. There is a $22 annual fee for scientific collecting permits. Applications and requirements may be obtained from the New Jersey Division of Fish, Game and Wildlife (address in Appendix I). Fishing licenses are available from most bait shops and sporting goods stores at an annual fee of $16.50 for residents and $25.25 for non-residents. Non-resident seven-day fishing licenses at a cost of $16.50 are also available.

IMPORTATION AND COMMERCIAL TRADE REGULATIONS

Native and Exotic Species

Restrictions on the importation, possession, and sale of both native and non-native amphibians and reptiles are specified in the Endangered, Nongame and Exotic Wildlife regulations of the New Jersey Administrative Code (reference: NJAC), as well as among the fish and wildlife legislation of New Jersey Statutes Annotated (reference: NJSA). As with most aspects of the state's wild animal legislation, New Jersey's importation and commercial trade regulations are extremely restrictive and only a very few specifically exempted amphibian and reptile species may be possessed within the state without permit. While the possession and sale of most indigenous species is prohibited without permit, a few amphibians and reptiles native to New Jersey are included in the state's permit exempt species list, and specimens of these "exempted species" legally obtained from outside the state may be imported, possessed, and, presumably, sold without permit. Additional listings of "potentially dangerous species" and other "permit required species" are also included in the non-game wildlife regulations of the State of New Jersey. The following is a summary of New Jersey's restrictions on the importation, possession, and sale of amphibians and reptiles.

The possession, transportation, exportation, or sale of any non-game species is prohibited except as otherwise specified (NJSA 23:2A-6).

The possession of any non-game or exotic species of amphibian or reptile without permit is prohibited except as otherwise specified (NJAC 7:25-4.2a).

Potentially Dangerous Species

Potentially dangerous species include animals capable of inflicting serious or fatal injuries, have the potential to become agricultural pests, or are a possible menace to the public health or indigenous wildlife of New Jersey. The following reptile families are included in the list of potentially dangerous species and may not be possessed within the state without permit (NJAC 7:25-4.8):

Alligatoridae	Alligators and Caimans
Crocodylidae	Crocodiles
Gavialidae	Gharials
Helodermatidae	Gila Monsters and Beaded Lizards
Crotalidae	Pit Vipers
Elapidae	Cobras, Coral Snakes, etc.
Viperidae	Vipers

Permit Required Species

The following reptile families, genera, and species may not be possessed in New Jersey without permit (NJAC 7:25-4.3):

Amevia spp.	Amevias	
Cordylus cataphractus	Armadillo Lizard	
Crotaphytus collaris	Collared Lizard	
Gekkonidae	Geckos All species except:	
	Gekko gecko	Tokay Gecko
Gerrhonotus spp. [1]	Alligator Lizards	
Sauromalus obesus	Chuckwalla	
Scincidae	Skinks	
Varanus spp.	Monitors	
Boidae	Boas All species except:	
	Boa constrictor	Boa Constrictor
Coluber spp.	Racers	
Diadophis punctatus	Ringneck Snake	
Elaphe spp.	Rat Snakes	
Lampropeltis spp.	Kingsnakes	
Opheodrys spp.	Green Snakes	
Pythonidae [2]	Pythons	

[1] Listed as *Gerrhonitus* spp. by New Jersey.
[2] Not usually recognized as a valid family designation.

Exempted Species

The following amphibians and reptiles may be possessed in New Jersey without permit. Permits are required to possess any non-game or exotic amphibian or reptile not specifically included in the following list of permit exempt species (NJAC 7:25-4-4 and 7:25-4.5):

Desmognathus fuscus [1]	Dusky Salamander
Notophthalmus viridescens [1]	Red-spotted Newts
Bufo americanus [2]	American Toad
Bufo woodhousii fowleri [1]	Fowler's Toad
Rana catesbeiana [3]	Bullfrog
Rana clamitans [3]	Green Frog
Rana pipiens	Leopard Frog
Chelydra serpentina [3]	Common Snapping Turtle
Chrysemys picta picta [1]	Eastern Painted Turtle
Anolis carolinensis	American Anole
Gekko gecko	Tokay Gecko
Iguana iguana	Green Iguana
Sceloporus occidentalis	Western Fence Lizard
Sceloporus undulatus	Fence Lizard
Boa constrictor [4]	Boa constrictor
Thamnophis spp.	Garter and Ribbon Snakes All species except:
	Thamnophis sirtalis tetrataenia [5] San Francisco Garter Snake

[1] Species included among the indigenous non-game herpetofauna of New Jersey. As currently interpreted by the New Jersey Division of Fish, Game & Wildlife the permit exemption for this species only applies to specimens lawfully obtained from outside the state.

[2] Listed as *Bufo woodhousei americana* by New Jersey. Species included among the indigenous non-game herpetofauna of New Jersey. As currently interpreted by the New Jersey Division of Fish, Game & Wildlife the permit exemption for this species only applies to specimens lawfully obtained from outside the state.

[3] Species currently listed as a game species by the State of New Jersey. As currently interpreted by the New Jersey Division of Fish, Game & Wildlife specimens lawfully harvested within the state or legally obtained from outside New Jersey may be possessed without permit.

[4] Listed as *Constrictor constrictor* by New Jersey.

[5] Subspecies not listed in Collins (1997).

Turtles

The following summarized restriction regarding the sale of turtles is included among the Department of Health regulations of the New Jersey Administrative Code.

No live turtles shall be offered for sale, sold, or in any way distributed in New Jersey, except when demonstrated to the satisfaction of the State Department of Health to be free from *Salmonella* contamination. This requirement may be waived at the discretion of the Health Department for turtles used for research, zoological, or food purposes (NJAC 8:23-4.1).

License and Permit Information

Permits to possess animals on the potentially dangerous species list in New Jersey will generally only be issued to qualified individuals sponsored by a legitimate research, scientific, zoological, or similar accredited institution. Adequate holding facilities and clearly demonstrated handling and care experience are also required. Permits authorizing the possession of potentially dangerous species as a household pet will not be issued. New Jersey has established several categories of possession permits for other restricted species, some of which allow for various commercial activities including the sale of amphibians and reptiles. Pet shop permits are issued to individuals and institutions engaged in the importation, exportation, and sale at the retail level. An animal dealer permit is required to import, export, or sell specimens at the wholesale level. Annual inspection and application fees for each of these permits are $100.00 annually. Zoological permits allow qualified public and private institutions to import, export, exhibit, and sell amphibians and reptiles. Zoological permit inspection and application fees for institutions with 10 animals or less are $60.00 annually, while institutions with more than 10 specimens pay $110.00 in annual permit application and inspection fees. Other New Jersey wildlife possession permits, including animal exhibitor and animal theatrical agency permits, also contain provisions allowing for the sale of specimens. A complete list of permit types, requirements, and permit applications may be obtained from the New Jersey Department of Fish, Game and Wildlife (address in Appendix I).

CAPTIVE MAINTENANCE REGULATIONS

In addition to the New Jersey's restrictions on the captive possession of amphibians and reptiles included among the legislation of the preceding sections, the following summarized regulation is also applicable to the maintenance of these animals in captivity.

The liberation of any non-game or exotic species of amphibian or reptile within the State of New Jersey without permit is prohibited (NJAC 7:25-4.2b).

License and Permit Information

Among New Jersey's various permit categories, two specifically allow for the non-commercial possession of amphibians and reptiles. Individual hobby permits, at an annual fee of $10, allow for the possession for pet purposes of species requiring permits. There is no annual inspection fee for individual hobby permits. Scientific holding permits, which also cost $10 annually, authorize the holding of species requiring permits for scientific, educational, or captive propagation purposes. The inspection fee for scientific holding permits is $25 annually. Permit applications and requirements may be obtained from the New Jersey Department of Environmental Protection and Energy's Division of Fish and Game (address in Appendix I).

Captive Maintenance Regulation Review

The following is a brief review of New Jersey's restrictions on the captive possession of amphibians and reptiles.

a. Permits are required to possess endangered species.
b. Permits are required to possess all native amphibian and reptile species unless otherwise specified.
c. Native amphibians and reptiles designated as game species may be possessed without permit. A valid fishing license may be required.
d. Native non-game amphibians and reptiles included in the exempted species list legally obtained from outside New Jersey may be possessed without permit.
e. Permits are required to possess any non-native amphibian or reptile not specifically included in the list of permit exempt species.
f. Potentially dangerous species list may not be possessed without permit.

(b above see Endangered, Threatened, and Special Concern Species and Native Wildlife Regulations).
(c above see Native Wildlife Regulations).
(d. e, and f above see Importation and Commercial Trade Regulations).

New Jersey Nongame Species Check-off Logo - New Jersey's Endangered and Nongame Species Tax Check-off Program emblem is one of only a few "official" state logos to feature an amphibian or reptile. Logo courtesy of the New Jersey Division of Fish, Game, and Wildlife.

American Toad, *Bufo americanus* -The American Toad is one of the few amphibian or reptile species native to New Jersey which may be possessed within the state without permit. All captive specimens must be legally obtained from outside of New Jersey. Photograph by J.P. Levell.

NEW MEXICO

ENDANGERED, THREATENED, AND SPECIAL CONCERN SPECIES

New Mexico now utilizes a relatively standard system in which the rarer members of the state's fauna are classified as either threatened or endangered species. All animals included in one of these two categories are fully protected by the New Mexico Wildlife Conservation Act, as specified in chapter 17 of New Mexico Statutes Annotated (reference: NMSA 17-2-37-46). A complete listing of New Mexico's threatened and endangered animal species is provided in title 19, chapter 33 of the New Mexico Administrative Code (reference: NMAC 19 - 33 -1).

The following amphibian and reptile species are included in New Mexico's current (January 1997) list of endangered and threatened species. State permits are required for all activities involving any of these species.

Species	Common Name	Status
Aneides hardii	Sacramento Mountain Salamander	Threatened
Plethodon neomexicanus	Jemez Mountains Salamander	Threatened
Bufo alvarius	Colorado River Toad	Threatened
Bufo boreas	Western Toad	Endangered
Gastrophryne olivacea	Great Plains Narrowmouth Toad	Endangered
Pseudacris clarkii [1]	Spotted Chorus Frog	Endangered
Rana yavapaiensis	Lowland Leopard Frog	Endangered
Pseudemys gorzugi	Western River Cooter	Threatened
Cnemidophorus burti	Giant Spotted Whiptail	Threatened
Cnemidophorus dixoni	Gray-checkered Whiptail	Endangered
Eumeces callicephalus	Mountain Skink	Threatened
Heloderma suspectum	Gila Monster	Endangered
Sceloporus arenicolous	Dunes Sagebrush Lizard	Threatened
Sceloporus scalaris [2]	Bunch Grass Lizard	Threatened
Crotalus lepidus lepidus	Mottled Rock Rattlesnake	Threatened
Crotalus willardi obscurus	New Mexico Ridgenose Rattlesnake	Endangered
Nerodia erythrogaster	Plainbelly Water Snake	Endangered
Senticolis triaspis	Green Rat Snake	Threatened
Thamnophis eques	Mexican Garter Snake	Endangered
Thamnophis proximus	Western Ribbon Snake	Threatened
Thamnophis rufipunctatus	Narrowhead Garter Snake	Threatened

[1] *Pseudacris clarkii*, the Spotted Chorus Frog is no longer considered a component of New Mexico's native herpetofauna as its reputed occurrence in the State is now believed to be based upon a single erroneous record and the species will most likely be deleted from the next revision of the State's endangered and threatened species list.
[2] Species not listed in Collins (1997).

Protected Species Permit Information

Permits authorizing the collection and possession of state endangered species may be issued for scientific, zoological, educational, or captive propagation purposes. Permit requirements and applications may be obtained from the New Mexico Department of Game and Fish (address in Appendix I).

NATIVE WILDLIFE REGULATIONS

Restrictions on the non-commercial collection and possession of amphibians and reptiles wild caught in New Mexico are included among the regulations of the New Mexico Game and Fish Commission (reference NM GFCR), the New Mexico Administrative Code (reference: NMAC), or New Mexico's Statutes Annotated (reference: NMSA). The following is a summarization of the few restrictions on the collection of native amphibians and reptiles in New Mexico.

Unless otherwise specified, native amphibian and reptile species may be collected and possessed without limit. No license is required for residents of New Mexico. Non-residents are required to have a hunting license or a scientific collecting permit to collect amphibians and reptiles in New Mexico (NM GFCR 705).

* Does not include state endangered or threatened species.

Frogs

Rana catesbeiana, Bullfrogs may not be captured or killed without a valid fishing license (NMSA 17-2-16).

Lizards

Phrynosoma spp., Horned Lizards (all native species) are listed as protected wildlife and may not be taken from the wild in New Mexico without a special permit from the New Mexico Department of Game and Fish (NM GFCR 705.1G).

* Apparently does not prohibit the possession of legally obtained Horned Lizards.

License and Permit Information

Hunting licenses are required for all non-residents collecting amphibians and reptiles in New Mexico. Non-resident hunting licenses are available from many retail outlets at a cost of $53. Fishing licenses for Bullfrogs may be obtained from most bait and sporting goods stores for an annual fee of $14 for residents and $30 for non-residents. Five and one day non-resident fishing licenses are also available at a reduced cost. Scientific collection permits are required to collect Horned Lizards in New Mexico. Requirements and applications for scientific collection permits may be obtained from the New Mexico Department of Game and Fish (address in Appendix I).

IMPORTATION AND COMMERCIAL TRADE REGULATIONS

Native Species

With the exception of the following summarized regulations, New Mexico does not currently restrict the importation or sale of any native amphibians or reptiles.

Protected species may not be imported into New Mexico without an importation permit issued from the New Mexico Department of Game and Fish (NMAC 19-31.1-11).

* Includes endangered and threatened species and all native Horned Lizards, *Phrynosoma* spp.

Frogs

Rana catesbeiana, Bullfrogs taken from public waters or the banks of public waters in New Mexico may not be sold or bartered at any time (NMSA 17-2-16).

Lizards

Phrynosoma spp., Horned Lizards may not be sold within or shipped from the State of New Mexico (NMSA 17-2-15).

* Does not prohibit the owners of Horned Lizards from carrying them across the state line.

Exotic Species

With the exception of the following summarized regulations, the State of New Mexico does not specifically prohibit the importation or sale of any non-native species of amphibians and reptiles.

Live animals may not be imported into New Mexico without an importation permit (NMSA 17-2-32).

The release of any amphibian or reptile, intentionally or otherwise, into the natural environment of New Mexico without a permit is prohibited (MNAC 19-31.1 -13).

* Apparently applies to both native and non-native species.

License and Permit Information

Permit conditions and stipulations vary according to the requirements of each individual permit application. More information on the required permits of this section may be obtained from the New Mexico Department of Game and Fish (address in Appendix I).

CAPTIVE MAINTENANCE REGULATIONS

Restrictions on the possession of both exotic and native amphibian and reptile species by residents of New Mexico are included among the regulations of the previous sections. The following is a brief review of New Mexico's restrictions on the captive maintenance of amphibians and reptiles.

a. Permits are required to possess state endangered and threatened species.
b. Native species may be possessed without limit or permit unless otherwise specified.
c. *Rana catesbeiana*: a fishing license is required to possess Bullfrogs
d. *Phrynosoma* spp. Horned Lizards native to New Mexico require possession permits.
e. No restriction on the possession of non-native amphibians and reptiles.

(b and c above see Native Wildlife Regulations)
(d above see Native Wildlife Regulations and Importation and Commercial Trade Regulations)
(e above see Importation and Commercial Trade Regulations)

NM

Respect Rattlesnakes - A particularly enlightened snake sign from New Mexico's Pecos National Monument. Hopefully, similar signs and other programs designed to protect rattlesnakes will become much more common place throughout the United States in the very near future. Photograph courtesy of Barney Oldfield.

NEW YORK

ENDANGERED, THREATENED, AND SPECIAL CONCERN SPECIES

The New York State Department of Environmental Conservation categorizes various species of the state's fauna as endangered, threatened, or as species of special concern. Only those species designated as endangered or threatened are officially protected by New York's endangered species legislation, as specified in the Environmental Conservation Law (reference: NY ECL 11-0535 and 0536) contained in Chapter 43-B, Article 11 of the Consolidated Laws of New York Annotated. Although species designated as special concern are not protected by the state's endangered species legislation, both the Wood Turtle, *Clemmys insculpta*, and the Box Turtle, *Terrapene carolina*, are fully protected by other portions of New York's Environmental Conservation Law (see Native Wildlife Regulations and Importation and Commercial Trade Regulations), and the collection or possession of these two species without permit is also prohibited.

The following amphibians and reptiles are included in the current (1987) list of threatened and endangered species of New York or are otherwise fully protected by state wildlife law. State permits are required for all activities involving any of these species. In addition, permits issued by the U.S. Department of the Interior are required for any of the following species included in the federal endangered species list (see U.S. Endangered and Threatened Species).

Species	Common Name	Status
Ambystoma tigrinum	Tiger Salamander	Endangered
Acris crepitans	Northern Cricket Frog	Threatened
Caretta caretta	Loggerhead Sea Turtle	Threatened
Chelonia mydas	Green Sea Turtle	Threatened
Clemmys insculpta	Wood Turtle	Protected
Clemmys muhlenbergii	Bog Turtle	Endangered
Dermochelys coriacea	Leatherback Sea Turtle	Endangered
Emydoidea blandingii	Blanding's Turtle	Threatened
Eretmochelys imbricata	Hawksbill Sea Turtle	Endangered
Kinosternon subrubrum	Eastern Mud Turtle	Threatened
Lepidochelys kempii	Atlantic Ridley Sea Turtle	Endangered
Terrapene carolina	Eastern Box Turtle	Protected
Crotalus horridus	Timber Rattlesnake	Threatened
Sistrurus catenatus	Massasauga	Endangered

* As currently interpreted by the New York State Department of Environmental Conservation, the inclusion of a species in the preceding list applies to all specimens regardless of their place of origin including subspecies not native to New York. The New York State Department of Environmental Conservation is currently in the process of revising the state list of threatened and endangered species. When this revision will be complete is uncertain at this time.

Protected Species Permit Information

Scientific collection licenses authorizing the collection and/or possession of New York's endangered and threatened species are issued for legitimate propagation, scientific, or exhibition purposes only. Each license application is evaluated on an individual basis, and the New York State Department of Environmental Conservation is very selective about what types of activities will be authorized. At the discretion of the New York Department of Environmental Conservation, a $10 license fee may or may not be assessed. A $200 bond may also be required. Qualified individuals and institutions may obtain further information and permit applications from the Special Licenses Unit of the New York State Department of Environmental Conservation (address in Appendix I).

NY

NATIVE WILDLIFE REGULATIONS

All wildlife species in the State of New York are classified into one of two categories: protected and unprotected. Protected amphibians and reptiles include endangered and threatened species, species designated small game, and one species, *Malaclemys terrapin*, protected by Environmental Conservation Law 11-0311. This particular law (reference: NY ECL 11-0311) allows the Department of Environmental Conservation to grant protection to any species on the basis of a filed petition signed by 10 or more citizens. Restrictions on the taking and possession of Malaclemys terrapin are specified in Title 6 of the New York Code of Rules and Regulations (reference: 6 NY CRR). Unprotected species may be taken at any time. It is uncertain if a license is required to collect unprotected amphibian and reptile species. Unprotected species may be possessed without permit, however. The following is a summary of the various restrictions on the non-commercial collection and possession of wild caught native amphibians and reptiles included in the Environmental Conservation Law and Code of Rules and Regulations of New York.

Frogs

Rana spp., The open season for frogs is from June 16 through September 30, between sunrise and sunset. Frogs may be taken in unlimited numbers by hand, spear, club, hook, or longbow. A valid fishing or small game hunting license is required. A small game hunting license also allows frogs to be taken by firearm (NY ECL 11-0905-2.1).

* Frogs of the genus *Rana* are classified as small game in New York (NY ECL 11-0103.2c).

The use of any device which prevents frogs from having free access to and egress from water is prohibited (ECL 11-0505.4).

Turtles

The following turtles are classified as small game species in New York (NY ECL 11-0103.2c). There is no open season for these species, however, and their collection or possession without permit is prohibited (NY ECL 11-0905):

Clemmys insculpta [1]	Wood Turtle
Clemmys muhlenbergii [2]	Bog Turtle
Terrapene spp. [3]	Box Turtles, all species

[1] Listed as a species of Special Concern by New York.
[2] Also listed as an Endangered Species in New York.
[3] Includes both native and non-native species and subspecies.

Malaclemys terrapin, Diamondback Terrapins have been granted protection under the authority of ECL 11-0311 as a result of a petition filed in 1990 by the New York Turtle and Tortoise Society. Terrapins may only be taken from August 1 to May 4, and there is a straight line carapace length limit of from four to seven inches. A special Diamondback Terrapin license is required to collect terrapins from the wild (6 NY CRR 3.1-2).

License and Permit Information

Scientific collector's licenses are required to collect and/or possess New York's protected species, including those species designated as small game for which there is no open season. In general, these licenses will only be issued for legitimate propagation, research, educational, or exhibition purposes, and it is the policy of the New York Department of Environmental Conservation to not issue licenses to keep protected species as pets. As with the license to collect and/or possess endangered and threatened species, a fee and bond may be required at the discretion of the Department of Environmental Conservation. Further information on and applications for these licenses may be obtained from the Special Licenses Unit of the New York State Department of Environmental Conservation (address in Appendix I). Special Diamondback Terrapin licenses cost $10 annually. Applications for Diamondback Terrapin licenses may be

NY

obtained from the NY DEC office at the State University of New York (address in Appendix I). Small game hunting licenses and fishing licenses are available from most sporting goods stores, bait shops, and many other retail outlets. Annual small game hunting license fees are $13 for residents and $50 for non-residents. Fishing licenses cost $14 for residents and $35 for non-residents. Five day non-resident licenses are also available for a $20.00 fee.

IMPORTATION AND COMMERCIAL TRADE REGULATIONS

Portions of New York's Code of Rules and Regulations and Environmental Conservation Law regulate the importation, possession, and sale of amphibians and reptiles. In general, these restrictions apply to native species, whether wild caught in the state or legally obtained from outside of New York. In many cases, however, these regulations also restrict the importation, possession, and sale of non-native species as well. In addition to the restrictions included among the state's wildlife laws, portions of New York's State Sanitation Code (reference: NY SSC) and Agriculture and Markets Law (reference: NY AML) also regulate the importation, possession, and/or sale of amphibians and reptiles. The following is a summarization of these rules and regulations.

Native and Exotic Species
The liberation of any species within the State of New York without permit is prohibited (NY ECL 11-0507).

The importation, exportation, transportion, or possession of all venomous reptiles without permit or license is prohibited (NY ECL 11-0511).

* The two previous regulations apply to both native and non-native species.

Frogs
Frogs lawfully taken outside the state may be imported and transported during the open season. During the closed season, legally obtained frogs may be imported, transported, possessed, bought, and sold without license provided a record of all transactions is kept (NY ECL 11-1705).

* Applies to both native and non-native species.

Turtles
Protected species, including small game species for which there is no open season (Bog, Wood, and Box Turtles) may not be imported, possessed, or sold without permit (NY ECL 11-0515.2).

* Applies to all specimens regardless of place of origin, including species and subspecies of the genus *Terrapene* not native to the State of New York.

Malaclemys terrapin, Diamondback Terrapins may only be sold from August 1 to May 4. Only specimens with a straight line carapace length of four to seven inches may be sold (6 NY CRR 3.1).

Live turtles under four inches in carapace length may not be imported, sold, or given away. Signs warning of the possible transmission of salmonella or other diseases to humans from turtles must be prominently displayed anywhere live turtles are sold or may be handled (NY SSC 10-2.58).

The New York State Department of Agriculture prohibits any live animals, including amphibians and reptiles, within retail food stores (NY AML 211-7.30).

* The preceding turtle regulations apply to both native species, including specimens lawfully obtained from outside of New York, and to non-native species.

License and Permit Information

Further information and applications for any required licenses or permits of this section may be obtained from the New York State Department of Environmental Conservation Special Licenses Unit (address in Appendix I). Diamondback Terrapin license information and applications are obtained from NY DEC office at the State University of New York (address in Appendix I).

CAPTIVE MAINTENANCE REGULATIONS

Restrictions on the possession of amphibians and reptiles are included among the regulations of the preceding sections. The following is a brief review of New York's restrictions on the captive maintenance of amphibians and reptiles.

a. Permits required to possess any specimens of endangered and threatened species, including subspecies not native to the state.

b. Permits required to possess all specimens of the following small game species, including specimens legally obtained from outside New York:

Clemmys insculpta	Wood Turtle
Terrapene spp.	Box Turtle, all species and subspecies

c. Venomous reptiles may not be possessed without permit.

d. No restrictions on the possession of other legally obtained non-native amphibian and reptile species.

(b above see Native Wildlife Regulations)
(c and d above see Importation and Commercial Trade Regulations)

Eastern Massasauga, *Sistrurus catenatus* - One of two species of rattlesnakes to be granted the full legal protection of New York's conservation law. Photograph courtesy of James E. Gerholdt.

NORTH CAROLINA

ENDANGERED, THREATENED, AND SPECIAL CONCERN SPECIES

The North Carolina Wildlife Resources Commission lists several of the state's native amphibians and reptiles as endangered, threatened, or as special concern species. Animals in all three categories are fully protected by the North Carolina Nongame and Endangered Species Conservation Act, as specified in North Carolina's General Statutes (reference: NC G.S. 113-331-337).

The following amphibian and reptile species are currently (March 1994) legally protected in North Carolina. Permits issued by the North Carolina Wildlife Resources Commission are required for all activities involving any of these species. Some of North Carolina's listed species are also protected by the U.S. Endangered Species Act, and a permit issued by the U.S. Department of the Interior is required for activities involving these species (see U.S. Endangered and Threatened Species).

Species	Common Name	Status
Ambystoma talpoideum	Mole Salamander	Special Concern
Ambystoma tigrinum tigrinum [1]	Eastern Tiger Salamander	Threatened
Aneides aeneus	Green Salamander	Endangered
Cryptobranchus alleganiensis	Hellbender	Special Concern
Eurycea junaluska	Junaluska Salamander	Special Concern
Eurycea longicauda	Long-tailed Salamander	Special Concern
Eurycea quadridigitata [2]	Dwarf Salamander	Special Concern
Hemidactylium scutatum	Four-toed Salamander	Special Concern
Necturus lewisi	Neuse River Waterdog	Special Concern
Necturus maculosus	Mudpuppy	Special Concern
Plethodon dorsalis	Zigzag Salamander	Special Concern
Plethodon longicrus [3]	Crevice Salamander	Special Concern
Plethodon wehrlei	Wehrle's Salamander	Threatened
Plethodon welleri	Weller's Salamander	Special Concern
Pseudacris brachyphona	Mountain Chorus Frog	Special Concern
Rana capito capito [4]	Carolina Gopher Frog	Special Concern
Rana heckscheri	River Frog	Special Concern
Alligator mississippiensis [5]	American Alligator	Threatened
Apalone spinifera spinifera	Eastern Spiny Softshell	Special Concern
Caretta caretta	Loggerhead Sea Turtle	Threatened
Chelonia mydas	Green Sea Turtle	Threatened
Clemmys muhlenbergii	Bog Turtle	Threatened
Dermochelys coriacea	Leatherback Sea Turtle	Endangered
Eretmochelys imbricata	Hawksbill Sea Turtle	Endangered
Lepidochelys kempii	Atlantic Ridley Sea Turtle	Endangered
Malaclemys terrapin	Diamondback Terrapin	Special Concern
Sternotherus minor peltifer	Stripeneck Musk Turtle	Special Concern
Ophisaurus mimicus	Mimic Glass Lizard	Special Concern

NC

Lampropeltis getula sticticeps [6]	Outer Banks Kingsnake	Special Concern
Liochlorophis vernalis [7]	Smooth Green Snake	Special Concern
Nerodia sipedon williamengelsi	Carolina Salt Marsh Snake	Special Concern
Pituophis melanoleucus melanoleucus	Northern Pine Snake	Special Concern

[1] No subspecies recognized in Collins (1997).
[2] Silver morph only.
[3] Not listed in Collins (1997).
[4] Listed as *Rana areolata capito* and Carolina Crawfish Frog by North Carolina.
[5] Does not apply to processed Alligator meat or products legally obtained outside of North Carolina (NC AC T15A: 101.0002e).
[6] Listed as *Lampropeltis getulus sticticeps* by North Carolina. Subspecies not listed in Collins (1997).
[7] Listed as *Opheodrys vernalis* by North Carolina.

Protected Species Permit Information

Permits allowing for the taking and possession of North Carolina's legally protected species may be issued to qualified institutions and individuals for research, propagation, or restoration purposes. For permit requirements and applications, contact the North Carolina Wildlife Resources Commission (address in Appendix I).

NATIVE WILDLIFE REGULATIONS

The following restrictions on the non-commercial collection and possession of native species of amphibians and reptiles wild caught in the state are included in North Carolina's Administrative Code (reference: 15A NCAC 10B .0119).

The following species may not be collected from the wild without a special permit issued by the North Carolina Wildlife Resources Commission:

Clemmys guttata	Spotted Turtle
Crotalus adamanteus	Eastern Diamondback Rattlesnake
Micrurus fulvius	Eastern Coral Snake
Sistrurus miliarius miliarius	Carolina Pygmy Rattlesnake

* As currently interpreted by the North Carolina Wildlife Resources Commission, this regulation prohibits the possession without permit of all specimens of these species, including those legally obtained from outside of North Carolina.

A wildlife collection license is required to possess more than five reptiles or more than 25 amphibians. The possession limits are for total specimens of all species combined.

*Applies only to those species not protected by North Carolina's non-game and endangered species legislation.

Permit And License Information

Permits to collect the four restricted species of regulation 15A NCAC 10B .01119 are issued for legitimate research purposes only. Wildlife collection licenses are issued to recognized educational and scientific institutions, but may also be issued to qualified individuals provided that the proposed activities will not be detrimental to the conservation of the species involved or the ecosystem in general. License and permit requirements and applications may be obtained from the North Carolina Wildlife Resources Commission (address in Appendix I).

NC

IMPORTATION AND COMMERCIAL TRADE REGULATIONS

Native Species

With the exception of the restricted species and possession limits specified in regulation 15A NCAC 10B .0119 (see Native Wildlife Regulations), North Carolina apparently does not restrict the sale of native amphibians and reptiles.

Exotic Species

The following restriction regulating the importation, sale, and possession of African Clawed Frogs is included among wildlife legislation of the North Carolina Administrative Code.

Xenopus sp., African Clawed Frogs may not be transported, purchased, possessed or released into the public or private waters of North Carolina without permit (NCAC 10B .0123).

License and Permit Information

Permits authorizing the possession of frogs of the genus *Xenopus* may be issued to legitimate scientific or educational institutions. Permit requirements and applications may be obtained from the North Carolina Wildlife Resources Commission (address in Appendix I).

CAPTIVE MAINTENANCE REGULATIONS

The following is a review of the restrictions on the possession of captive amphibians and reptiles in North Carolina.

a. Permits are required for any species listed as endangered, threatened, or special concern.
b. Permits may be required to possess the following native species not listed as endangered, threatened, or special concern:

Clemmys guttata	Spotted Turtle
Crotalus adamanteus	Eastern Diamondback Rattlesnake
Micrurus fulvius	Eastern Coral Snake
Sistrurus miliarius miliarius	Carolina Pygmy Rattlesnake

c. A wildlife collectors license is required to possess more than five total reptiles of all native species combined.
d. A wildlife collectors license is required to possess more than 25 total amphibians of all native species combined.
e. *Xenopus sp.*, African Clawed Frogs may not be possessed without a permit.
f. The possession of non-native amphibians and reptiles is not restricted.

(b, c and d above see Native Wildlife Regulations)
(e and f above see Importation and Commercial Trade Regulations)

NC

NORTH DAKOTA

ENDANGERED, THREATENED, AND SPECIAL CONCERN SPECIES

Of the 50 states, North Dakota is one of the few that does not have individual state endangered and threatened species legislation. Although all federally listed species of North Dakota's native flora and fauna are fully protected by the U.S. Endangered Species Act, none of the amphibian or reptile species indigenous to the state are included in the current (January 1997) U.S. Department of the Interior list of endangered and threatened wildlife.

Protected Species Permit Information
State or federal endangered species permits are not required for any amphibian or reptile species native to North Dakota.

NATIVE WILDLIFE REGULATIONS

Restrictions on the collection and possession of amphibians and reptiles wild caught in the state for non-commercial purposes are included among the wildlife legislation in title 20 of the North Dakota Century Code (reference: NDCC 20) and in title 30 of the North Dakota Administrative Code (reference: NDAC 30). In addition, North Dakota's governor may by proclamation establish open seasons and bag limits for the taking of wildlife species in the state, as specified in title 20 of the North Dakota Century Code (reference: NDCC 20.1-08-01 to 05). The following is a summarization of North Dakota's restrictions on the recreational collection from the wild of native amphibians and reptiles.

Non-residents may not hunt, catch, or kill any unprotected bird or animal without a non-resident non-game hunting license or a non-resident furbearer and non-game hunting license (NDCC 20.1-03-07.1).

* With the exception of frogs and Common Snapping Turtles, all of North Dakota's native amphibians and reptiles are considered unprotected species. North Dakota residents may collect unprotected species without permit.

Frogs
Frogs may be taken by legal fishing methods throughout the year, except during specifically closed seasons in designated waters of the state. The daily bag and possession limit is 24 frogs. A valid fishing license is required. A non-commercial frog license is required to take and possess more than 24 frogs for non-commercial purposes (NDCC 20.1-03-04.1).

Turtles
Chelydra serpentina, Common Snapping Turtles may be taken by hook and line throughout the year, except during specifically closed seasons in designated waters of the state. There is a season limit of two specimens (Governor's Proclamation).

License and Permit Information
Non-resident non-game hunting licenses are available for a fee of $15 annually. Non-resident furbearer and non-game hunting combination licenses cost $25 annually. The annual fees for fishing licenses are $9 for residents and $25 for non-residents. Seven-day and three-day non-resident fishing licenses are also available at a cost of $15 and $10 respectively. Non-commercial frog licenses are available to North Dakota residents only at an annual fee of $3. License requirements and applications may be obtained from the North Dakota Game and Fish Department (address in Appendix I).

IMPORTATION AND COMMERCIAL TRADE REGULATIONS

Native Species

There are very few restrictions among the wildlife laws of North Dakota's Century Code and Administrative Code on the importation, possession, and/or sale of native amphibians and reptiles, including specimens wild caught in the state. The following is a summary of these restrictions.

Frogs

A bait dealer's license is required to take, purchase, sell, or ship frogs within the state for angling purposes (NDCC 20.1-03-04.1).

Frogs may not be taken for sale for human consumption or scientific purposes without a commercial frog license. Commercial frog licenses are required to purchase, job, take on consignment, or ship frogs. Frogs may not be taken from private property without the written permission of the landowner (NDCC 20.1-06-17).

Frogs may be taken by hand held contrivances only. The use of traps, seines, dug trenches, and bait is prohibited (NDAC 30-03-04-03).

Reports recording the number, manner of take, collection location, and disposition of all frogs taken under the authority of a Commercial Frog License must be submitted to the North Dakota Game and Fish Department annually (NDAC 30-03-04-03).

Turtles

Turtles may not be taken commercially without permit (NDCC 20.1-06-16).

* North Dakota does not currently issue permits authorizing the commercial collection of turtles from the waters of the state.

Exotic Species

With the exception of possible restrictions included among the commercial frog regulations, North Dakota does not currently regulate the importation, sale, or possession of any non-native amphibian or reptile species.

License and Permit Information

Wholesale commercial bait dealer's licenses have an annual cost of $30 for residents and $200 for non-residents. Retail commercial bait dealer's licenses are available to North Dakota residents only for an annual fee of $15. Commercial frog licenses are available for an annual fee of $50 for residents and $200 for non-residents. Complete requirements and applications may be obtained from the North Dakota Game and Fish Department (address in Appendix I).

CAPTIVE MAINTENANCE REGULATIONS

The following is a brief review of the few possession restrictions included among the regulations of the previous sections.

a. Native frogs have a possession limit of 24 specimens without a frog license. A valid fishing license may be required.
b. *Chelydra serpentina*, Common Snapping Turtles have a possession limit of two specimens without permit. A valid fishing license may be required.
c. No restrictions on the possession of non-native amphibian and reptile species.

OHIO

ENDANGERED, THREATENED, AND SPECIAL CONCERN SPECIES

The Ohio Department of Natural Resources lists various species of the state's fauna as endangered, threatened, special interest, extirpated, or extinct. The four latter categories are purely for administrative purposes, and only those species officially designated as endangered are legally protected by the state's endangered species legislation, as specified in the Revised Code of Ohio (reference: OHRC 1531.25).

The following amphibians and reptiles are included in the current (May 1994) endangered species list of the State of Ohio. A permit is required for all activities involving any of these species.

Species	Common Name
Ambystoma laterale	Blue-Spotted Salamander
Aneides aeneus	Green Salamander
Cryptobranchus alleganiensis	Hellbender
Eurycea lucifuga	Cave Salamander
Scaphiopus holbrookii [1]	Eastern Spadefoot Toad
Crotalus horridus	Timber Rattlesnake
Nerodia erythrogaster neglecta	Copperbelly Water Snake
Thamnophis radix radix [2]	Eastern Plains Garter Snake

[1] Listed as *Scaphiopus holbrooki* by Ohio.
[2] No subspecies recognized in Collins (1997).

Protected Species Permit Information

Endangered Wild Animal permits allowing for the collection and possession of Ohio's endangered species are issued to qualified individuals and institutions for scientific, zoological, and educational purposes and for propagation in captivity to preserve the species. Permits allowing for the possession and propagation of specimens of Ohio's endangered species legally obtained from outside the state are also available. Applications for these permits may be obtained from the Division of Wildlife of the Ohio Department of Natural Resources (address in Appendix I).

NATIVE WILDLIFE REGULATIONS

Restrictions on the collection and possession of native species of amphibians and reptiles wild caught in Ohio are specified in the Revised Code of Ohio (reference: OHRC) or in the Ohio Administrative Code (reference: OHAC). The following is a summarization of these regulations.

All native species of lizards, snakes, salamanders, and toads may be taken, possessed, bought, sold, or transported unless otherwise specified. A license is not required. (OHAC 1501:31-19-01D).

Frogs

The open season for frogs is from 6 p.m. June 15 through April 30 except at Pymatuning Lake. Frogs may not be taken by shooting except by longbow and arrow. The daily bag and possession limit is 10 frogs. A valid fishing license is required, and frogs may not be taken from state owned or controlled areas posted "no fishing" or from state fish farms (OHAC 1501:31-13-05).

It is illegal to take frogs from Pymatuning Lake from July 1 through October 31. The daily possession limit is 15 frogs or tadpoles. The use of artificial light is prohibited. A valid fishing license is required (OHAC 1501:31-13-07).

The frog season in Magee Marsh (Ottawa and Lucas counties) closes on September 15. Frogs may be taken in Magee Marsh by angling only. Frogs may not be taken from those portions of Magee Marsh designated as a state game refuge (OHAC 1501:31-13-07M).

* The above regulations do not apply to any anurans of the family Bufonidae (Toads).

Turtles

A valid fishing license is required to collect turtles in Ohio. Turtles may not be taken by steel or spring trap or by shooting except with longbow and arrow. Turtle traps may not have a mesh size of less than four inches unless equipped with a six-inch escape ring. Turtles may be legally taken in unlimited numbers throughout the year except at Pymatuning Lake, Magee Marsh, state owned or controlled areas posted "no fishing," and state fish farms. With the exception of those species listed below, turtles may not be taken from state owned or controlled areas (OHAC 1501:31-13-05):

Apalone spp.	Softshell Turtles, all species
Chelydra serpentina	Common Snapping Turtle
Chrysemys picta marginata	Midland Painted Turtle

* As currently interpreted by the Ohio Department of Natural Resources, a fishing license is only required to capture turtles and no license is required to possess native turtle species.

Turtles may not be taken from Pymatuning Lake from July 1 through October 31. The daily bag limit is 10 turtles, except for Snapping Turtles, *Chelydra serpentina*, which may be taken in unlimited numbers (OHAC 1501:31-13-07).

Turtles may be taken from Magee Marsh (Ottawa and Lucas counties) from March 1 through September 15 only. Turtles may not be taken from those portions of Magee Marsh designated as a state game refuge (OHAC 1501:31-13-07M).

License and Permit Information

Ohio fishing licenses are available from most bait shops and sporting goods stores. The annual fishing license fees are $15 for residents and $24 for non-residents. Three-day non-resident licenses are also available for a $12 fee.

IMPORTATION AND COMMERCIAL TRADE REGULATIONS

Native Species

Ohio has relatively few restrictions on the sale of native amphibians and reptiles. The following summarized regulations are included in the wildlife laws of the Ohio Administrative code.

Lizards, snakes, and amphibians except frogs may be taken, possessed, bought, sold, and transported unless otherwise specified (OHAC 1501:31-19-01D).

Frogs

Frogs wild caught in Ohio may not be bought or sold at any time except from privately owned or leased ponds or lakes with an appropriate permit. Specimens of native frog species legally obtained from outside of Ohio may be bought and sold if accompanied by a bill of lading (OHAC 1501:31-13-05E).

Turtles

Legally acquired turtles may be bought and sold (OHAC 1501:31-13-05G).

* The three preceding regulations do not include species designated as endangered in Ohio.

Exotic Species

The State of Ohio does not currently restrict the importation and sale of legally acquired non-native amphibian and reptile species.

License and Permit Information

Information and applications for the permit to sell frogs from privately owned ponds and lakes may be obtained from the Division of Wildlife of the Ohio Department of Natural Resources (address in Appendix I).

CAPTIVE MAINTENANCE REGULATIONS

Ohio has very few restrictions on the possession of both native and non-native amphibians and reptiles. The following is a brief review of these restrictions.

a. Permits are required to possess any native species listed as endangered in Ohio.
b. No restrictions on the possession of native species of lizards, snakes, salamanders, and toads.
c. A fishing license is required to possess native frog species wild caught in Ohio during the open season.
d. No restrictions on the possession of non-native amphibian and reptile species.

(b and c above see Native Wildlife Regulations).

Dead on Road (D.O.R.) - Although often overlooked by most state and federal wildlife agencies, mortality while crossing roadways is one of the major amphibian and reptile conservation issues in the United States today. Photograph courtesy of William B. Love.

OKLAHOMA

ENDANGERED, THREATENED, AND SPECIAL CONCERN SPECIES

Endangered and threatened species in Oklahoma are protected by various regulations of the state's Wildlife Conservation Code found in Title 29 of the Oklahoma Statutes (reference: OS 29 5-412, 5-412.1, 7-502, and 7-503). These regulations prohibit the hunting, capture, sale, or possession without permit of all species designated as threatened or endangered by the Oklahoma Department of Wildlife Conservation.

The following species is the only amphibian or reptile included in Oklahoma's current (May 1994) list of endangered and threatened wildlife. Permits are required for all activities involving this species.

Species	Common Name	Status
Alligator mississippiensis	American Alligator	Threatened

Protected Species Permit Information
A scientific collectors permit or a special letter of permission from the Director of the Oklahoma Department of Conservation is required for any activity involving all state and federally listed endangered and threatened species. There is a fee of $5 for scientific collectors permits. Further information on permit procedures may be obtained from the Oklahoma Department of Wildlife Conservation (address in Appendix I).

NATIVE WILDLIFE REGULATIONS
Specific restrictions on the non-commercial collection and possession of native amphibians and reptiles wild caught in the state are specified in the Oklahoma Administrative Code (reference: OAC). The following is a summarization of these regulations.

A valid hunting license is required to collect any land dwelling amphibian or reptile (OAC 800:25-7-7.1A).

A valid fishing license is required to collect any water dwelling amphibian or reptile (OAC 800:25-7-7.1B).

A non-commercial wildlife breeders license is required to collect or possess any native species for hobby (non-commercial) purposes (OAC 800:25-7-7.6).

It is unlawful to introduce, deposit, place, or drain any deleterious, noxious, toxic, or petroleum-based substance into or around any underground dens or rock crevices for the purpose of taking amphibians or reptiles (OAC 800:25-7-7.4).

Amphibians
Unless otherwise specified, amphibians may be taken throughout the year with a daily bag and possession limit of four of each species (OAC 800:25-7-9.1C).

Frogs
Frogs of the genera *Pseudacris* and *Rana* (except *Rana areolata* and *Rana catesbeiana*) have an unlimited bag limit (OAC 800:25-7-9.1A).

Rana catesbeiana, Bullfrogs have a bag limit of 15 specimens (OAC 800:25-7-9.1A).

Bufo woodhousii, Woodhouse's Toad have an unlimited bag limit (OAC 800:25-7-9.1A).

* *Rana areolata*, Crawfish Frog bag and possession limit is four specimens.

OK

Salamanders

Aquatic salamanders of the genera *Necturus* and *Ambystoma* (except *Ambystoma talpoideum*) have an unlimited bag and possession limit (OAC 800:25-7-9.1B).

The following salamanders have a statewide closed season and may not be taken at any time except under the authorization of a scientific collectors permit (OAC 800:25-7-9.2):

Ambystoma talpoideum	Mole Salamander
Eurycea lucifuga	Cave Salamander
Eurycea tynerensis	Oklahoma Salamander
Hemidactylium scutatum	Four-toed Salamander
Plethodon albagula [1]	Western Slimy Salamander
Plethodon dorsalis angusticlavius [2]	Ozark Zigzag Salamander
Plethodon kiamichi [1]	Kiamichi Slimy Salamander
Plethodon ouachitae	Rich Mountain Salamander
Plethodon sequoyah [1]	Sequoayah Slimy Salamander
Typhlotriton spelaeus	Grotto Salamander

1 Listed as *Plethodon* sp. by Oklahoma
2 No subspecies recognized in Collins (1997).

Reptiles

Unless otherwise specified, reptiles may be taken throughout the year with a daily bag and possession limit of six of each species (OAC 800:25-7-8.5).

Turtles

There is a statewide closed season on the following turtles, and these species may not be taken without a scientific collectors permit at any time (OAC 800:25-7-8.6):

Deirochelys reticularia	Chicken Turtle
Graptemys geographica	Map Turtle
Macrochelys temminckii [1]	Alligator Snapping Turtle

[1] Listed as *Macroclemys temminckii* by Oklahoma.

Lizards

The following lizards have a statewide closed season and may not be taken at any time without a scientific collectors permit (OAC 800:25-7-8.6):

Cnemidophorus tesselatus	Checkered Whiptail
Holbrookia maculata	Lesser Earless Lizard
Phrynosoma cornutum	Texas Horned Lizard
Phrynosoma modestum	Roundtail Horned Lizard
Uta stansburiana	Desert Side-blotched Lizard

Snakes

The following snakes may be taken in unlimited numbers from March 1 through June 30 (OAC 800:25-7-8.1-5):

Crotalus atrox	Western Diamondback Rattlesnake
Crotalus horridus	Timber Rattlesnake
Crotalus viridis	Prairie Rattlesnake
Sistrurus catenatus	Massasauga

There is a statewide closed season on the following snakes, and these species may not be taken at any time without a scientific collectors permit (OAC 800:25-7-8.6):

Regina rigida sinicola	Gulf Crawfish Snake
Thamnophis elegans vagrans	Wandering Garter Snake

License and Permit Information

Hunting and fishing licenses are available from most sporting goods and bait stores. Annual hunting license fees are $10.25 for residents and $74.50 for non-residents. Five-day nonresident hunting licenses at a cost of $25.00 are also available. Annual fishing license fees are $10.25 for residents and $23.50 for nonresidents. Ten-day and three-day nonresident fishing licenses are available at a reduced cost. The fee for a non-commercial wildlife breeders license is $5.00. Scientific collectors permits, which are required to collect all species designated as having a statewide closed season, also have a $5.00 fee. Applications for both the non-commercial wildlife breeders license and scientific collectors permit may be obtained from the Oklahoma Department of Wildlife Conservation (address in Appendix I).

IMPORTATION AND COMMERCIAL TRADE REGULATIONS

Native Species

Restrictions on the importation, exportation, sale, and other commercial activities involving native amphibians and reptiles are included among the rules and regulations of both the Oklahoma Administrative Code (reference: OAC) and the Oklahoma Statutes (reference: OS). The following is a summary of these regulations.

Except as otherwise provided for by law, no person may buy, barter, trade, sell or offer, or expose for sale any wildlife protected by law (OS 29 7-503A). Persons licensed to propagate or sell wildlife and persons who have documentation of legally purchased wildlife for resale are exempt from this provision (OS 29 7-503B).

It is unlawful to engage in any commercial activities involving any indigenous species or subspecies collected from the wild in Oklahoma unless otherwise specified (OAC 800:25-7-7.1).

Persons wishing to raise, breed, collect for hobby or commercial purposes, or otherwise possess any lawfully obtained reptiles or amphibians must first obtain the appropriate commercial wildlife breeders license, non-commercial wildlife breeders license, aquatic culture license, or commercial fishing license (OAC 800:25-7-7.6).

An import/export permit is required to ship or transport wildlife into or out of the State of Oklahoma (OAC 800:25-23-2).

Aquatic Salamanders of the genera *Necturus* and *Ambystoma* (except *Ambystoma talpoideum*) may be harvested from the wild for sale as bait; a commercial minnow dealers license is required (OAC 800:25-7-72D).

Legal aquatic turtles may be harvested from the wild and sold under the authorization of a commercial fishing turtle harvest license (OAC 800:25-7-7.2C).

Rattlesnakes harvested from the wild may be sold during the open season to licensed commercial or non-commercial wildlife breeders only. A commercial wildlife breeders license is required to purchase rattlesnakes for resale. A valid hunting license is required to harvest rattlesnakes (OAC 800:25-7-7.3).

Exotic Species

The following portion of the Oklahoma Administrative Code's importation regulations specifically pertains to non-native amphibian and reptile species. For the sake of clarity, this regulation is included in its entirety below.

Except as otherwise provided, monotypic species and subspecies of reptiles and amphibians not indigenous to Oklahoma are exempt from import and export requirements and commercial and non-commercial wildlife breeder's license, except those which are biologically capable of establishing self-sustaining populations in the wild in Oklahoma and which may be potentially injurious or detrimental to Oklahoma's wildlife, agriculture, or public safety in accordance with existing USDI or APHIS regulations (OAC 800:25-25-3C).

Prohibited Species

All venomous reptiles belonging to the following families or genera are not exempt from any permit requirements (OAC 800:25-25-3C):

Helodermatidae	Gila Monsters and Beaded Lizards
Elapidae	Cobras, Coral Snakes, etc.
Hydrophiidae	Sea Snakes
Viperidae	Vipers
Crotalidae	Rattlesnakes, Copperheads, etc.
Dispholidus	Boomslangs

License and Permit Information

Commercial wildlife breeders licenses are required to propagate and sell native amphibian and reptile species. The fee for a commercial wildlife breeders license is $48 annually. Import/export permits cost $5 and are a requirement to import or export any native amphibian and reptile species. Commercial minnow dealers licenses and commercial fishing licenses cost about $100 annually. Applications for these licenses and permits may be obtained from the Oklahoma Department of Wildlife Conservation (address in Appendix I).

CAPTIVE MAINTENANCE REGULATIONS

In addition to the restrictions on the possession of amphibians and reptiles included among the regulations of the previous sections, several portions of Oklahoma's wildlife legislation specifically relate to the captive maintenance of these animals. The following is a summary of these regulations.

Except as otherwise provided, the possession of any wildlife or parts thereof during the closed season for that particular wildlife species is prohibited (OS 29 7-502A 2). Persons possessing legally obtained wildlife as pets are exempt from this provision (OS 29 7-502B 4).

The applicable commercial or non-commercial wildlife breeders license shall be obtained if any wildlife is being propagated (OS 29 7-502C).

Persons licensed to propagate reptiles and amphibians shall keep detailed breeding and hatching records (OAC 800:25-7-7.7).

Progeny of lawfully held reptiles may, for six months from date of birth, be held in captivity in excess of stated possession limits. Before or upon reaching six months of age, such progeny must be disposed of according to the requirements of the license held, or as directed by the Oklahoma Department of Wildlife Conservation. Progeny may be retained for brood stock if replacing parent stock disposed of in the above manner so as not to exceed the possession limit (OAC 800:25-7-7.8).

* A scientific collectors permit is required to hold amphibians and reptiles in excess of prescribed possession limits.

Venomous Reptile Caging Requirements

Any venomous reptile shall be kept in a solid enclosure that is structurally sound so that it restricts access and contains the animal. Any ventilation ports shall be constructed of a double layer of fine mesh screen or similar suitable material firmly secured to the cage, and any transparent sides shall be of a thickness of not less than 1/4 inch glass or plexiglass. Additionally, each cage door shall be key locked or secured with a similar type mechanical lock (OAC 800:25-27-2E).

Captive Maintenance Regulations Review

The following is a brief review of Oklahoma's restrictions on the possession of live amphibians and reptiles.

a. *Alligator mississippiensis*, Alligators may not be possessed without proper authorization.
b. Permits are required to possess any native amphibian and reptile species.
c. Unless otherwise specified, the possession limit for native amphibians is four of each species.
d. *Ambystoma* sp. Aquatic larvae of all species except *Ambystoma talpoideum* may be possessed in unlimited numbers.
e. The following amphibians may be possessed in unlimited numbers:

Necturus sp.	Mudpuppies
Bufo woodhousii	Woodhouse's Toad
Pseudacris sp.	Chorus Frogs
Rana sp.	Ranid Frogs, all species except *Rana areolata* and *Rana catesbeiana*.

f. *Rana catesbeiana*, Bullfrogs have a possession limit of 15 specimens.
g. Unless otherwise specified, the possession limit for native reptiles is six of each species.
h. The following snakes may be possessed in unlimited numbers:

Crotalus atrox	Western Diamondback Rattlesnake
Crotalus horridus	Timber Rattlesnake
Crotalus viridis	Prairie Rattlesnake
Sistrurus catenatus	Massasauga

i. Permits are required to possess non-native venomous reptiles.
j. No restrictions on non-native amphibians and non-venomous reptile species.

(b through h above see Native Wildlife Regulations).
(i and j above see Importation and Commercial Trade Regulations).

Okeene Rattlesnake Round-up - While usually a source of civic pride, annual organized rattlesnake hunts or "round-ups" are in no way compatible with any concept of sound wildlife management or conservation. At the same time, these events are among the most inhumane, unethical, and dangerous uses of wildlife tolerated anywhere making it difficult to comprehend why they are not more strictly regulated. Photograph courtesy of Barney Oldfield.

OREGON

ENDANGERED, THREATENED, AND SPECIAL CONCERN SPECIES

The Oregon Department of Fish and Wildlife classifies various members of the state's native fauna as endangered or threatened species. Species in both categories are fully protected by the state's Threatened or Endangered Wildlife Species legislation, as specified in title 41, chapter 496 of the Oregon Revised Statutes Annotated (reference: OR RSA 41-496.172 to 496.192). As with the endangered species legislation of most states, Oregon's law contains provisions for the protection of species included in the U.S. Department of Interior's list of endangered and threatened wildlife. Currently four federally protected marine turtles are included in the official list of threatened and endangered species in Oregon. In addition to the species included in the state list of endangered and threatened wildlife, most of Oregon's native amphibians and reptiles are classified as "protected nongame wildlife species" and the collection and/or possession of these species without permit is also prohibited, as specified in the fish and wildlife regulations of Oregon Administrative Rules (reference: OAR 635-044-0000 to 0235).

The following species of amphibians and reptiles are included in Oregon's current (December 1995) threatened and endangered species list or in the current (December 1996) list of protected nongame wildlife. Permits issued by the Oregon Department of Fish and Wildlife are required for all activities involving any of these species. In addition to any required state permits, federal endangered species permits are also required for the four marine turtles included in the following list.

Species	Common Name	Status
Ambystoma mavortium melanostictum [1]	Blotched Tiger Salamander	Protected
Aneides ferreus	Clouded Salamander	Protected
Aneides flavipunctatus	Black Salamander	Protected
Batrachoseps attenuatus	California Slender Salamander	Protected
Batrachoseps wrightorum [2]	Oregon Slender Salamander	Protected
Dicamptodon copei	Cope's Giant Salamander	Protected
Plethodon elongatus	Del Norte Salamander	Protected
Plethodon larselli	Larch Mountain Salamander	Protected
Plethodon stormi	Siskiyou Mountain Salamander	Protected
Rhyacotriton cascadae	Cascade Seep Salamander	Protected
Rhyacotriton kezeri	Columbia Seep Salamander	Protected
Rhyacotriton variegatus	Southern Seep Salamander	Protected
Ascaphus truei	Tailed Frog	Protected
Bufo boreas	Western Toad	Protected
Bufo woodhousii [3]	Woodhouse's Toad	Protected
Rana aurora	Red-legged Frog	Protected
Rana boylii	Foothill Yellow-legged Frog	Protected
Rana cascadae	Cascades Frog	Protected
Rana pipiens	Northern Leopard Frog	Protected
Rana pretiosa	Spotted Frog	Protected
Caretta caretta	Loggerhead Sea Turtle	Threatened
Chelonia mydas	Green Sea Turtle	Endangered
Chrysemys picta bellii [4]	Western Painted Turtle	Protected
Clemmys marmorata	Western Pond Turtle	Protected
Dermochelys coriacea	Leatherback Sea Turtle	Endangered
Lepidochelys olivacea	Pacific Ridley Sea Turtle	Threatened

Crotaphytus bicinctores [5]	Mojave Black-collared Lizard	Protected
Gambelia wislizenii	Longnosed Leopard Lizard	Protected
Phrynosoma douglassii [6]	Short-horned Lizard	Protected
Phrynosoma platyrhinos	Desert Horned Lizard	Protected
Contia tenuis	Sharptail Snake	Protected
Lampropeltis getula [7]	Common Kingsnake	Protected
Lampropeltis zonata	California Mountain Kingsnake	Protected
Sonora semiannulata	Western Ground Snake	Protected

[1] Listed as *Ambystoma tigrinum melanostictum* by Oregon.
[2] Listed as *Batrachoseps wrighti* by Oregon.
[3] Listed as *Bufo woodhousei* by Oregon.
[4] Listed as *Chrysemys picta* by Oregon.
[5] Listed as *Crotaphytus insularis bicinctores* by Oregon.
[6] Listed as *Phrynosoma douglasi* by Oregon.
[7] Listed as *Lampropeltis getulus* by Oregon.

Protected Species Permit Information

Scientific taking permits authorizing the collection and/or possession of protected nongame wildlife species are issued to qualified individuals and institutions for legitimate educational, exhibition, or research purposes only. There is an $11 annual application fee for scientific taking permits. Scientific taking permits are not valid for the taking of endangered and threatened species, and specific endangered species permits are required to collect or possess any species included in Oregon's list of threatened and endangered wildlife. Further information, permit restrictions and requirements, and permit applications may be obtained from the Oregon Department of Fish and Wildlife (address in Appendix I).

NATIVE WILDLIFE REGULATIONS

Restrictions on the non-commercial collection and possession of amphibians and reptiles wild caught in the state are included among the wildlife legislation of the Oregon Revised Statutes Annotated (reference: OR RSA) and in the Department of Fish and Wildlife Regulations of the Oregon Administrative Rules (reference: OAR). The following is a summary of these restrictions.

Nongame amphibians and reptiles not included in the list of "Protected Nongame Wildlife" as specified in OAR 635-44-0130 (see Endangered, Threatened, and Special Concern Species above) are considered unprotected. Unprotected nongame species may be taken and possessed without restriction. Permits are not required (OAR 635-44-0020).

* All amphibian and reptile species occurring in Oregon, except Bullfrogs, *Rana catesbeiana*, (see below) are included in the state's definition of nongame wildlife.

Frogs

Rana catesbeiana, Bullfrogs are classified as game fish by the State of Oregon (OR RSA 41-496.009). Bullfrogs may be taken at any time throughout the year. There is no daily bag or possession limit and no minimum size requirement. Bullfrogs may be legally taken by hand, hook and line, bow and arrow, gig, spear, spear gun, or dip net. A valid fishing license is required (OAR 635-11-145).

* Bullfrogs are not native to the State of Oregon.

License and Permit Information

Oregon fishing licenses are available from numerous retail outlets including most bait shops and sporting goods stores. Annual fishing license fees are $14.25 for residents and $34.25 for non-residents. Seven-day and one-day non-resident fishing licenses are also available at a cost of $26.75 and $4.50 respectively.

IMPORTATION AND COMMERCIAL TRADE REGULATIONS

Native and Exotic Species

Restrictions on the importation, possession, and sale of both native and non-native amphibians and reptiles are included among the statutes and regulations of the Oregon Department of Agriculture (reference: OR RSA 48), as well as among the wildlife legislation of the Oregon Department of Fish and Wildlife (OR RSA 41 and OAR 635). In general, the sale of all native amphibians and reptiles is prohibited, including specimens legally obtained from outside the state. In addition to regulating commercial activities involving native species, the Oregon Fish and Game Commission has established lists of non-native animals which may or may not be imported into the state without permit. Oregon Department of Agriculture rules require importation permits and veterinary health certification for all shipments of live animals entering the state, including those species exempt from Oregon Department of Fish and Wildlife permit requirements. The following is a summarization of Oregon's restrictions on the commercial trade of both native and non-native amphibian and reptile species.

The purchase, sale, or exchange of any wildlife is prohibited except as otherwise provided (OR RSA 41-498.022).

Salamanders

Ambystoma tigrinum, Tiger Salamanders all subspecies, except *Ambystoma tigrinum melanostictum*, Blotched Tiger Salamander, may be propagated for commercial purposes and sold. A wildlife propagation license is required (OAR 635-44-060).

* *Ambystoma tigrinum* and *Ambystoma melanostictum* are recognized as separate species in Collins (1997).

Prohibited Species

Live wildlife designated as prohibited species may not be imported, possessed, sold, purchased, exchanged, or transported in Oregon without permit. The following amphibian and reptile families, genera, and species are included in Oregon's current (December 1996) list of prohibited wildlife species (OAR 635-056-0050):

Xenopus	African Clawed Frogs, all species and hybrids
Apalone	North American Softshell Turtles, all species and hybrids
Chelydridae	Snapping Turtles, all species and hybrids
Chinemys	Chinese Pond Turtles, all species and hybrids
Chrysemys	Painted Turtles, all non-native species
Clemmys	Pond Turtles, all non-native species
Deirochelys	Chicken Turtles, all species and hybrids
Graptemys	Map Turtles, all species and hybrids
Kinosternon	Mud Turtles, all species and hybrids
Pseudemys	Pond Sliders, all species and hybrids
Trachemys	Pond Sliders, all species and hybrids
Trionyx	African Softshell Turtles, all species and hybrids
Bioga irregularis	Brown Tree Snake

OR

Noncontrolled Species

Live wildlife designated as noncontrolled species may be imported, possessed, sold, purchased, exchanged, or transported in Oregon without permit except as otherwise specified. The following amphibian and reptile families, genera, and species are included in Oregon's current (December 1996) list of noncontrolled wildlife species. Oregon Department of Fish and Wildlife permits are required for any species listed as an exception in the following list unless otherwise specified (OAR 635-056-0060):

Dendrobatidae	Poison Arrow Frogs, all species
Chamaeleo antimena [1]	White-lined Chameleon
Chamaeleo balteatus	Rainforest Chameleon [2]
Chamaeleo bitaeniatus	Two-lined Chameleon [3]
Chamaeleo brevicornis	Short-horned Chameleon [4]
Chamaeleo calyptratus	Veiled Chameleon
Chamaeleo campani	Madagascar Forest Chameleon [5]
Chamaeleo chamaeleon	Common Chameleon [6]
Chamaeleo dilepis [7]	Flapneck Chameleon
Chamaeleo fischeri	Fischer's Chameleon
Chamaeleo globifer	Flat-casqued Chameleon [8]
Chamaeleo gracilis	Graceful Chameleon
Chamaeleo helioti [9]	Smallmouth Chameleon
Chamaeleo jacksonii [10]	Jackson's Chameleon
Chamaeleo johnstoni	Johnston's Chameleon
Chamaeleo lateralis	Jeweled Chameleon [11]
Chamaeleo melleri	Meller's Chameleon
Chamaeleo minor	Southcentral Chameleon [12]
Chamaeleo montium	Cameroon Sailfin Chameleon [13]
Chamaeleo oshaughnessyi	O'Shaughnessy's Chameleon
Chamaeleo oustaleti	Oustalet's Chameleon
Chamaeleo oweni	Owen's Chameleon
Chamaeleo pardalis	Panther Chameleon [14]
Chamaeleo parsonii	Parson's Chameleon
Chamaeleo phillibornii [9]	Flapjack Chameleon
Chamaeleo quadricornis	Four-horned Chameleon
Chamaeleo senegalensis	Senegal Chameleon
Chamaeleo verrucosus	Warty Chameleon [15]
Gekkonidae	Geckos, all non-native species
Helodermatidae	Gila Monster and Beaded Lizard, all species
Iguanidae	Iguanid Lizards, all non-native species except:

	Crotaphytus spp. [16]	Collared Lizards
	Gambelia spp.	Leopard Lizards
	Phrynosoma spp.	Horned Lizards
	Uta spp.	Side-blotched Lizards

Scincidae	Skinks, all non-native species except:	
	Eumeces spp.	Eyelid Skinks
Varanidae	Monitor Lizards, all species except:	
	Varanus griseus	Desert Monitor

Boidae	Boas and Pythons, all non-native species
Elaphe spp. [17]	Rat Snakes, all non-native species
Lampropeltis spp. [17]	Milk Snakes and Kingsnakes, all non-native species except:
	Lampropeltis getula Common Kingsnake
	Lampropeltis zonata California Mountain Kingsnake
Lampropeltis getula [18]	Common Kingsnake
Lampropeltis zonata [18]	California Mountain Kingsnake [18]
Naja haje	Egyptian Cobra
Naja melanoleuca	Forest Cobra [19]
Naja naja	Indian Cobra
Naja nivea	Cape Cobra
Ophiophagus hannah	King Cobra
Pituophis spp. [17]	Pine, Gopher, and Bull Snakes, all non-native species
Pituophis catenifer [20]	Gopher Snake

[1] Listed as *Chamaeleo antimenas* and Antimenas Chameleon by Oregon.
[2] Listed as Rhinosaurus Chameleon by Oregon.
[3] Listed as Short-horned Chameleon by Oregon.
[4] Listed as Elephant-eared Chameleon by Oregon.
[5] Listed as Madagascar Dwarf Chameleon by Oregon.
[6] Listed as Egyptian Desert Chameleon by Oregon.
[7] Listed as *Chamaeleo delepis* and Stripe Dwarf Chameleon by Oregon.
[8] Listed as Globifer Chameleon by Oregon.
[9] Not listed in Frank and Ramus (1995).
[10] Listed as *Chamaeleo jacksoni* by Oregon.
[11] Listed as Carpet Chameleon by Oregon
[12] Listed as Serrated Chameleon by Oregon.
[13] Listed as Mountain Chameleon by Oregon.
[14] Listed as Leopard Chameleon by Oregon.
[15] Listed as Verrucosus Desert Chameleon by Oregon.
[16] Listed as *Crotophytus* by Oregon.
[17] No genus specified by Oregon.
[18] Specimens that are morphologically distinct from native species (subspecies?) only.
[19] Listed as Black and White Cobra by Oregon.
[20] Listed as *Pituophis melanoleucus* by Oregon.

Specimens of the following snakes which are morphologically similar to native species (subspecies?) may be possessed, transported, purchased, sold, or exchanged if lawfully acquired and bred in captivity. These species may not be collected from the natural environment of Oregon (OAR 635-056-0080):

Lampropeltis getula	Common Kingsnake
Lampropeltis zonata	California Mountain Kingsnake
Pituophis catenifer [1]	Gopher Snake

[1] Listed as *Pituophis melanoleucus* by Oregon.

The importation, purchase, sale, or exchange of any species which is not listed or classified is prohibited without permit (OAR 635-056-0130).

* The effective date of the preceding regulation is January 1, 1998.

Importation permits issued by the Department of Agriculture are required to import any wildlife into the State of Oregon. Veterinary certificates of health inspection are also required (OR RSA 48-596.341).

* The Oregon Department of Agriculture's importation permit and health certification requirements apply to all wildlife shipments, including those species exempt from Oregon Department of Fish and Wildlife permit requirements.

License and Permit Information

Permits authorizing the importation and possession of amphibians and reptiles designated as prohibited species will be issued to properly qualified and accredited individuals and institutions only. Permit requirements for animals not classified as prohibited and included in the designated list of noncontrolled species are determined on an individual species by species basis, and this permit type is issued solely at the discretion of the Oregon Department of Fish and Wildlife. Applications and further information on these permits, as well as on the wildlife propagation license required to propagate and sell Tiger Salamanders may be obtained from the Oregon Department of Fish and Wildlife (address in Appendix I). Veterinary certificates of health inspection must be obtained within the state or country from which individual animal shipments originate and should be included with any importation permit request. Animal importation permits are issued free of charge on the basis of individual health certificates. Importation permits may be obtained from the Oregon Department of Agriculture (address in Appendix I).

CAPTIVE MAINTENANCE REGULATIONS

In addition to any restrictions on the captive possession of amphibians and reptiles included among the regulations of the preceding sections, the following summarized Oregon Department of Fish and Wildlife statutes and regulations are also applicable to the captive maintenance of these animals.

The release of any domestically raised or imported wildlife into the natural environment of Oregon without permit is prohibited (OR RSA 41-498.052).

Any wildlife held in captivity, whether a permit is required or not, must be treated in a humane manner. Facilities for the care of captive wildlife must be maintained in a sanitary manner, large enough to provide room for exercise and sturdy enough to prevent escape and protect the public. Food and water must be provided in sufficient quantity and quality to maintain the wildlife in a healthy condition (OAR 635-44-0035).

Rehabilitation holding permits are required to maintain amphibians and reptiles in captivity for rehabilitation purposes (OAR 635-44-200 to 635-44-0235).

License and Permit Information

Rehabilitation holding permits are issued to qualified individuals for legitimate rehabilitation purposes only. Further information on permit requirements and permit applications may be obtained from the Oregon Department of Fish and Wildlife (address in Appendix I).

Captive Maintenance Regulations Review

The following is a brief review of Oregon's restrictions on the captive maintenance of amphibians and reptiles.

a. Endangered, threatened, and protected nongame species may only be possessed by permit.

b. Native amphibians and reptiles designated as unprotected nongame species may be possessed without restriction.

c. *Rana catesbeiana*, Bullfrogs may be possessed in unlimited numbers. A valid fishing license is required.

d. Permits are required to possess any non-native amphibian or reptile designated as a prohibited or controlled species.

e. No restrictions on the non-commercial captive possession of non-native amphibian and reptile species.

(b and c above see Native Wildlife Regulations).
(d and e above see Importation and Commercial Trade Regulations).

OREGON | **OREGON DEPARTMENT OF FISH & WILDLIFE**
Fish & Wildlife | **PO Box 59, 2501 SW First Ave.**
| **Portland, Oregon 97207**

For Office Use Only
Permit #
Date
Payment
Annual Report

SCIENTIFIC TAKING PERMIT APPLICATION
FOR BIRDS, MAMMALS, AMPHIBIANS AND REPTILES

☐ **FIRST-TIME APPLICATION**   ☐ **RENEWAL**
(Enclose previous year's permit)

Name _____

Mailing Address _____

Previous year's permit number _____

_____

Federal Permit No. if applicable _____

City, State, Zip _____

Agency Affiliation or Occupation _____   Phone (daytime) _____

I WISH TO: ☐ COLLECT
       ☐ LIVE-TRAP, MARK, AND RELEASE
       ☐ SALVAGE (EDUCATIONAL USE ONLY)

Number	Species/Common Name	Specific Location (County)	Method

If you are a teacher, do you intend to use the permit for students collecting on supervised field trips?
☐ Yes   ☐ No   (Students collecting on their own must possess personal permits.)

Please use a separate page to summarize your research project or otherwise substantiate your need to collect. Please be specific, usually a project proposal will suffice. In addition, if you are a student, give the name, address and phone number of your sponsoring professor and the degree you are working on.

_____   _____
Applicant Signature   Date

Please send this form and a check for $11.00 to ODFW at the above address

Permit Stipulations on Back

Sample Permit Application - Courtesy of the Oregon Department of Fish and Wildlife.

PENNSYLVANIA

ENDANGERED, THREATENED, AND SPECIAL CONCERN SPECIES

The Pennsylvania Fish and Boat Commission is responsible for the management of the state's native amphibians and reptiles. This agency lists various species of Pennsylvania's herpetofauna as Endangered, Threatened, or as Candidate species. Only those species designated as threatened or endangered however, are officially protected by the Pennsylvania Endangered Species Act, as specified in the Pennsylvania Consolidated Statutes Annotated (reference: PA CSA. 2305-175-30). The Fish and Boat Commission encourages the release of any wild caught candidate species. Candidate species are subject to season, size, bag, and possession limits (see Native Wildlife Regulations).

The following amphibians and reptiles are the species currently (January 1994) listed as threatened or endangered in the State of Pennsylvania. Any activity involving these species requires a permit.

Species	Common Name	Status
Aneides aeneus	Green Salamander	Threatened
Pseudotriton montanus montanus	Eastern Mud Salamander	Endangered
Pseudacris kalmi [1]	New Jersey Chorus Frog	Endangered
Rana sphenocephala [2]	Southern Leopard Frog	Endangered
Clemmys muhlenbergii	Bog Turtle	Endangered
Pseudemys rubriventris	Red-bellied Turtle	Threatened
Clonophis kirtlandii	Kirtland's Snake	Endangered
Opheodrys aestivus	Rough Green Snake	Threatened
Sistrurus catenatus	Massasauga	Endangered

[1] Listed as *Pseudacris feriarum kalmi* by Pennsylvania.
[2] Listed as *Rana utricularius* and Coastal Plain Leopard Frog by Pennsylvania.

Protected Species Permit Information

Scientific collector's permits allowing for the collection and possession of state endangered and threatened species are issued by the Pennsylvania Fish and Boat Commission. Three different categories of permits are available, each issued for a specific collection classification. Type I permits are issued for legitimate scientific research purposes or for educational purposes which are not being conducted for monetary gain. There is a $10 fee for a Type I permit. Type II permits are issued to federal or state government employees engaged in research activities and are issued free. Type III permits are issued to qualified individuals conducting research for monetary gain via private consulting companies, etc. There is a $50 fee for Type III permits. Applicants for all three permit types must have a valid Pennsylvania fishing license. The complete list of permit requirements and a permit application may be obtained from the Pennsylvania Fish and Boat Commission (address in Appendix I).

NATIVE WILDLIFE REGULATIONS

Restrictions on the collection and possession of native amphibian and reptile species for noncommercial purposes are specified in chapter 77 of Pennsylvania's Fishing and Boating Regulations (reference: PA FBR 77.1-.8). The following is a summary of these regulations.

No reptile or amphibian may be taken through the use of chemicals, smoke, explosives, winches, jacks, or other device or material that may damage or destroy the den or the immediate surroundings thereof (PA FBR 77.3a).

It is unlawful to damage or disrupt the nest or eggs of a reptile or to gather, take or possess the eggs of a reptile in the natural environment of Pennsylvania (PA FBR 77.3c).

An organized reptile and amphibian hunt may not be conducted without first obtaining a permit for such an event from the Pennsylvania Fish and Boat Commission (PA FBR 77.2c). Sacking contests and the free-handling of venomous reptiles is prohibited (PA FBR 77.2g). With the exception of Timber Rattlesnakes, the possession limit of each species taken during an organized hunt shall not exceed the daily limit of the species hunted times the number of people engaged in the hunt. The possession limit for Timber Rattlesnakes taken during an organized hunt is two times the number of people engaged in the hunt (PA FBR 77.6b).

When season or annual limits apply, such limits have been reached once a reptile or amphibian, dead or alive, has not been immediately released and is in the possession of a person (PA FBR 77.6d).

Unless otherwise specified, the daily bag and possession limit for native amphibians and reptiles is two of each species (PA FBR 77.6e).

* Does not include Threatened or Endangered species.

Frogs
It is unlawful to catch, take, or kill frogs with the use of light at night (PA FBR 77.5).

The following frogs may be taken from July 1 to October 31 with a daily bag limit of 15 and a possession limit of 30 total specimens of both species combined (PA FBR 77.6e):

| *Rana catesbeiana* | Bullfrog |
| *Rana clamitans* | Green Frog |

Tadpoles may be taken throughout the year. The possession and daily bag limit is 15 total specimens of all species combined (PA FBR 77.6d).

* Does not include State Threatened and Endangered species.

Turtles
Chelydra serpentina, Snapping Turtles may be taken from July 1 to October 31 with a daily bag limit of 15 and a possession limit of 30 specimens (PA FBR 77.6e).

Emydoidea blandingii, [1] Blanding's Turtles may not be taken at any time (PA FBR 77.6e).

Lizards
Eumeces laticeps, [1] Broad-headed Skinks may not be taken at any time (PA FBR 77.6e).

Snakes
Crotalus horridus, [1] Timber Rattlesnake may be taken from the second Saturday in June to July 31. The possession and daily bag limit is one rattlesnake (PA FBR 77.6e). A rattlesnake hunter's permit is required to collect, kill, or possess a timber rattlesnake (PA FBR 77.2b).

[1] Candidate for State Endangered and Threatened species list.

Zoos, other scientific or educational institutions, taxidermists, wildlife rehabilitators, licensed pest control agents, or other individuals may exceed specified possession limits for scientific, educational, research, or other purposes with the written permission of the Executive Director or designee of the Pennsylvania Fish and Boat Commission (PA FBR 77.6b)

License and Permit Information

As Pennsylvania's definition of fish includes all amphibians and reptiles, the collection of any native species is subject to all state fishing regulations, and a valid fishing license is required. Fishing licenses are available from most bait shops and sporting goods stores at annual fees of $12.50 for residents and $25.00 for nonresidents. Organized reptile and amphibian hunt permits must be applied for between January 1 and March 1 of the year in which the event is to be held. There is a $25.00 fee for organized hunt permits. Rattlesnake hunter's permits are a requirement for anyone hunting rattlesnakes, whether hunting individually or as a participant in an organized hunting event. There is a $5.00 fee for individual rattlesnake hunter's permits. Applications for both permits may be obtained by writing the Herpetology and Endangered Species Coordinator of the Fish and Boat Commission (address in Appendix I).

IMPORTATION AND COMMERCIAL TRADE REGULATIONS

Native Species

The following summarized restrictions on the collection, importation and/or sale of native amphibians and reptiles both wild caught in Pennsylvania or legally obtained from outside of the State are included in PA FBR 77.

With the exception of the Common Snapping Turtle, *Chelydra serpentina*, it is unlawful to take, catch, kill or possess an amphibian or reptile, whether dead or alive, in whole or in parts including eggs or any lifestage, in Pennsylvania for the purpose of selling or offering for sale (PA FBR 77.3b).

With the exception of the Common Snapping Turtle, *Chelydra serpentina*, it is unlawful to sell, purchase, barter or trade any native amphibian or reptile species, whether dead or alive, in whole or in parts including eggs or any lifestage, that was wild caught in the State of Pennsylvania (PA FBR 77.3c).

In prosecutions for violations of the previous two regulations, it shall be a refutable presumption that any species which is native to Pennsylvania was taken from within the State (PA FBR 77.3d).

Crotalus horridus, Timber Rattlesnakes may not be imported into Pennsylvania for use in prohibited activities at organized hunting events (PA FBR 77.8).

Exotic Species

The following summarized portion of PA FBR 77 is the only restriction on the importation of non-native species into Pennsylvania.

It is illegal to introduce any non-native species of reptile or amphibian into the natural environment of the State of Pennsylvania. Anyone who imports non-native species into Pennsylvania shall institute appropriate safeguards to prevent their introduction into the environment (PA FBR 77.7).

CAPTIVE MAINTENANCE REGULATIONS

The State of Pennsylvania does not prohibit the possession of any non-native species of amphibian or reptile. The following is a review of the restrictions on the possession of amphibians and reptiles in Pennsylvania.

a. Endangered and threatened species may not be possessed except by permit.

b. Possession of native species wild caught in Pennsylvania is limited to two of each species, unless otherwise specified.

c. *Rana catesbeiana*, Bullfrogs and *Rana clamitans*, Green Frogs have a possession limit of 30 specimens in total (all species combined).

d. *Chelydra serpentina*, Common Snapping Turtles have a possession limit of 30 specimens.

e. *Crotalus horridus*, Timber Rattlesnakes have a possession limit of one specimen.

f. Specimens of native species in excess of the prescribed possession limits may not be wild caught in Pennsylvania and must be legally obtained. The burden of proof lies with the owner.

g. No restrictions on the possession of non-native species.

(a, b, c, d, and e above see Native Wildlife Regulations).
(f above see Native Wildlife Regulations and Importation and Commercial Trade Regulations).
(g above see Importation and Commercial Trade Regulations).

Turtle Xing - Turtles, unlike snakes and other amphibians and reptiles, evoke little fear or revulsion in the minds of most people. That average citizens are often greatly concerned with the well-being of these animals is clearly evident in this "home-made" sign. Photograph courtesy of Barney Oldfield.

RHODE ISLAND

ENDANGERED, THREATENED, AND SPECIAL CONCERN SPECIES

The Rhode Island Department of Environmental Management classifies various rare or unusual species of the state's flora and fauna into one of four categories, endangered, threatened, concern, and historical. Only those animals or plants officially classified as a state endangered species, however, are legally protected by the Rhode Island State Endangered Species Act, as specified in title 20 of the General Laws of Rhode Island (reference: RI GL 20-37-1-5). Currently, only one reptile and no amphibians are included in the state's endangered species list. As is the case with most states, Rhode Island's endangered species legislation automatically protects any native species included in the U.S. Endangered and Threatened Species list, and five federally protected marine turtles do occasionally occur in the coastal waters of the state. In addition, Rhode Island also prohibits the collection and possession without permit of five additional native reptile species, as specified in the nongame legislation of the General Laws of Rhode Island (reference: RI GL 20-1-12-13). This restriction applies to all specimens regardless of their place of origin.

The following native reptiles are included in Rhode Islands current list (1995) of endangered, threatened and protected species or in the federal list of threatened and endangered wildlife. Permits issued by the Rhode Island Department of Environmental Management are required for all activities involving these species. As always, permits issued by the U.S. Department of the Interior are also required for any federally protected species in the following list (see U.S. Endangered and Threatened Species).

Species	Common Name	Status
Caretta caretta	Loggerhead Sea Turtle	Federal Threatened
Chelonia mydas	Green Sea Turtle	Federal Threatened
Clemmys guttata	Spotted Turtle	Protected
Clemmys insculpta	Wood Turtle	Protected
Clemmys muhlenbergii	Bog Turtle	Protected
Dermochelys coriacea	Leatherback Sea Turtle	Federal Endangered
Eretmochelys imbricata	Hawksbill Sea Turtle	Federal Endangered
Lepidochelys kempii	Atlantic Ridley Sea Turtle	Federal Endangered
Malaclemys terrapin	Diamondback Terrapin	Endangered
Terrapene carolina	Eastern Box Turtle	Protected
Crotalus horridus	Timber Rattlesnake	Protected

Protected Species Permit Information

Scientific collection permits will be issued to qualified individuals and/or institutions for legitimate research purposes only. No permits will be issued if commercial considerations are involved in any way, and possession permits are generally not issued. Applications for scientific collection permits may be obtained from the Rhode Island Department of Environmental Management (address in Appendix I).

NATIVE WILDLIFE REGULATIONS

With the exception of state threatened and endangered species, Rhode Island does not restrict the non-commercial collection and possession of wild caught native amphibians and reptiles. There are no collection restrictions or possession limits for unprotected species of native amphibians and reptiles specified among the General Laws of Rhode Island (reference: RI GL 20-1-12-13).

License and Permit Information

Licenses are not currently required to collect and possess unprotected amphibians and reptiles recreationally.

IMPORTATION AND COMMERCIAL TRADE REGULATIONS

Native Species

Restrictions on the commercial collection and sale of native amphibian and reptile species wild caught in the state are included among Rhode Island's fish and wildlife laws. In general, the commercial harvest of all species except Snapping Turtles is prohibited as specified in the following summarized regulations (reference: RI GL 20-1-12-13). With the exception of any species requiring an importation permit (see Exotic Species below), Rhode Island does not currently restrict the sale of native amphibians and reptiles legally obtained from outside the state.

The removal from the wild, for commercial purposes, of any reptile or amphibian is prohibited except by special permit.

* With the exception of Snapping Turtles, *Chelydra serpentina*, Rhode Island does not issue permits allowing for the sale of native species wild caught in the state (see Turtle Regulations below).

Turtles

Chelydra serpentina, Snapping Turtles may be harvested for sale, a permit is required. Snapping Turtles may be legally taken by one of the following methods; traps, snagging, snaring, grabbing, jugging, bow and arrow, while legally fishing.

* Does not include any of the listed protected species (see Endangered, Threatened, and Special Concern Species).

Exotic Species

The Rhode Island Division of Agriculture, as well as the Department of Environmental Management, regulates the importation, possession, and sale of non-native amphibian and reptile species. In general, this legislation (RI GL 4-18-1 to 13) restricts the importation without permit of specified animal species. The portions of this regulation restricting the importation of reptiles are summarized below.

Restricted Species List

Except as otherwise provided, the following reptiles may not be imported into, received, or possessed in Rhode Island without a permit:

Chamaeleonidae	Old World Chameleons
Helodermatidae	Beaded Lizards and Gila Monsters
Crotalidae	Pit Vipers
Boiginae [1]	Boigine Vipers [1]
Dispholidus typus	Boomslang
Elapidae	Cobras, Coral Snakes, etc.
Eunectes sp.	Anacondas
Hydrophiidae	Sea Snakes
Leptotyphlopidae	Thread Snakes
Lycodontinae	Mole Vipers
Python reticulatus	Reticulated Pythons
Thelotornis kirtlandi	African Twig Snake
Viperidae	Vipers

[1] Rear-fanged, venomous colubrid snakes of the genus *Boiga* such as; Mangrove Snake, Brown Tree Snake, etc. Not currently recognized as a valid family or sub-family.

Turtles

A final health department regulation restricts the sale of both native and non-native species of turtles as follows:

All turtles sold in Rhode Island must be certified by the seller as being free from salmonellosis (reference: RI GL 4-4-27).

License and Permit Information

Permits authorizing the importation and possession of specified restricted species may be issued to qualified individuals and institutions. Issuance of permits is dependent upon a variety of Rhode Island Division of Agriculture permit conditions, including quarantine, veterinary examination, facility inspection, and safe caging requirements. Further information and permit applications may be obtained from the Rhode Island Division of Agriculture (address in Appendix I).

CAPTIVE MAINTENANCE REGULATIONS

The following is a brief review of the restrictions on the possession of amphibians and reptiles included in the above regulations.

a. Protected species may not be possessed without a permit.
b. Unprotected native species may be possessed without limit.
c. Species prohibited from importation may not be possessed without permit.

(b above see Native Wildlife Regulations).
(c above see Importation and Commercial Trade Regulations)

SOUTH CAROLINA

ENDANGERED, THREATENED, AND SPECIAL CONCERN SPECIES

The South Carolina Department of Natural Resources classifies various members of the state's fauna as Endangered or Threatened, and species in both categories are fully protected by the South Carolina Nongame and Endangered Species Conservation Act, as specified in title 50, chapter 15 of the Code of Laws of South Carolina (reference: SC CL 50-15-10 through 50-15-90). As with the endangered species legislation of most states, South Carolina's endangered species law automatically protects all species appearing on the U.S. list of federally protected endangered and threatened wildlife.

The following amphibian and reptile species are included in South Carolina's current (July 1994) list of endangered and threatened wildlife. Permits issued by the South Carolina Department of Natural Resources are required for all activities involving any of these species. In addition, permits issued by the U.S. Department of the Interior are required for any of the following species included in the federal list of endangered and threatened wildlife (see U.S. Endangered and Threatened Species).

Species	Common Name	Status
Ambystoma cingulatum	Flatwoods Salamander	Endangered
Plethodon websteri [1]	Webster's Salamander	Endangered
Pseudobranchus striatus	Dwarf Siren	Threatened
Hyla andersonii	Pine Barrens Treefrog	Threatened
Alligator mississippiensis [2]	American Alligator	Threatened S/A
Caretta caretta	Loggerhead Sea Turtle	Threatened
Chelonia mydas	Green Sea Turtle	Endangered
Clemmys muhlenbergii	Bog Turtle	Threatened
Dermochelys coriacea	Leatherback Sea Turtle	Endangered
Eretmochelys imbricata	Hawksbill Sea Turtle	Endangered
Gopherus polyphemus	Gopher Tortoise	Endangered
Lepidochelys kempii	Atlantic Ridley Sea Turtle	Endangered
Eumeces anthracinus	Coal Skink	Threatened
Drymarchon couperi [3]	Eastern Indigo Snake	Endangered

[1] Some confusion exists concerning the legal status of *Plethodon websteri* in South Carolina, as the species is omitted from at least one official list of state threatened and endangered wildlife. In that list (reference: SC CL R 123-150.1), the Zig Zag Salamander, *Plethodon dorsalis* is included instead. According to the range map in Conant and Collins (1991), however, *Plethodon dorsalis* does not occur in South Carolina, and the actual species protected is apparently *Plethodon websteri.*

[2] *Alligator mississippiensis* is listed as threatened due to similarity of appearance by the U.S. Department of the Interior mainly to help facilitate the effective legal protection of the American Crocodile, *Crocodylus acutus,* and other endangered and threatened crocodilian species. Biologically, American Alligators are neither endangered or threatened in the wild and the species is protected by South Carolina for management and law enforcement purposes only. The limited harvest of wild caught American Alligators is allowed in South Carolina by license or permit (see Native Wildlife Regulations).

[3] Listed as *Drymarchon corais couperi* by South Carolina.

Protected Species Permit Information

Scientific collection permits authorizing the collection and/or possession of South Carolina's endangered and threatened species may be issued to qualified individuals or institutions for legitimate research or propagation purposes only. Both federal and state permits are required for all species included in the U.S. Department of the Interior's list of endangered and threatened wildlife, and all federal permit requirements must be met before state permits will be issued. Permits authorizing the possession of specimens of South Carolina's endangered and threatened species legally obtained outside of the state may also be issued on occasion. There is a $10 initial application or permit renewal fee. Requirements and applications for scientific collection permits may be obtained from the South Carolina Department of Natural Resources (address in Appendix I).

NATIVE WILDLIFE REGULATIONS

South Carolina has relatively few restrictions on the non-commercial or recreational collection and possession of native amphibians and reptiles wild caught in the state. Included among the wildlife statutes and regulations of South Carolina's Code of Laws, these restrictions are summarized below.

A scientific collection permit is required to collect all nongame species including amphibians and reptiles (SC CL R 123-150.3).

Scientific collection permits are required to collect protected wildlife for scientific or propagation purposes. No permit shall be required for the collecting or taking of unprotected wildlife (SC CL 50-11-2190).

* Due to the contradictory wording of the previous two regulations, it is unclear whether or not a permit is actually required to collect and possess those native amphibian and reptile species not included in South Carolina's list of endangered and threatened wildlife. As currently interpreted by the South Carolina Department of Natural Resources, permits are only required for collections made for scientific or captive propagation purposes.

Alligators

Alligator mississippiensis, American Alligators originating from populations native to South Carolina may not be taken or possessed except as otherwise authorized by regulation (SC CL R 123-151.2).

Alligator mississippiensis, American Alligators may be taken and possessed by designated agents of the Alligator Control Management Program. Control agents may only harvest specific alligators in the manner authorized by South Carolina Department of Natural Resources permit. Hide tags must be affixed to any alligator killed by control agents. Alligators harvested by control agents may only be skinned at designated sites and all hides procured during the course of alligator control activities must be delivered to the South Carolina Department of Natural Resources. The meat of harvested alligators may be consumed by designated control agents and their immediate families and may only be otherwise transferred as specified by regulation. Alligators may only be possessed alive for 24 hours unless otherwise specified (SC CL R 123-151).

Land owners or lessees of 100 acres or more of contiguous alligator habitat may harvest alligators from such properties within specified quotas established by the South Carolina Department of Natural Resources. Alligator hide tags, alligator trappers licenses, and valid South Carolina hunting licenses are required. All harvested alligators must measure at least 4 feet in length and all captured alligators must be immediately killed and tagged. Hide tags must be attached within six inches of the tail tip. Alligator harvest reports are required for all alligators taken and all hides must be validated at designated validation sites. Tag validation fees also apply (SC CL R 123-151).

The feeding or enticing with food of any non-captive American Alligator, *Alligator mississippiensis*, is prohibited. Alligator control agents may use bait or enticement if authorized while attempting to capture alligators for relocation (SC CL 50-11-750).

Turtles

Malaclemys terrapin, Diamondback Terrapins may not be taken, purchased, or possessed between the first day of April and July 15, except for those specimens left over from the open season. A report recording number and location of all leftover terrapins must be submitted to the South Carolina Department of Natural Resources by April 10. Only terrapins measuring five inches or more in plastron length may be taken or possessed (SC CL 50-17-910 to 50-17-950).

Cheloniidae and Dermochelidae, Sea Turtle species not included in South Carolina's endangered and threatened wildlife list are considered threatened species. The collection, possession, trade, transportation, exportation, or sale of sea turtles without permit is prohibited. Sea turtles captured incidentally during legal fishing activities which appear vigorous must be returned to the water immediately in a manner to prevent injury to released turtles. Turtles which appear weak or dead will be turned on their back and held until they have regained their strength or appear to be definitely dead. Apparently dead turtles must be held on deck for a minimum of 30 minutes and appropriate revival attempts must be performed (SC CL R 123-150.1).

A Turtle Excluder Device (TED) must be used in trawl nets in state waters under the same conditions required under federal regulations. The South Carolina Department of Natural Resources must follow federal enforcement guidelines when enforcing any state turtle excluder device regulations (SC CL 50-17-685).

License and Permit Information

Scientific collection permits are available from the South Carolina Department of Natural Resources (address in Appendix I) for a $10 fee. Alligator trappers licenses (required to harvest alligators from designated private lands) have an annual fee of $150 for residents and $300 for non-residents. Assistant alligator trappers licenses allowing for the taking of alligators while accompanied by a licensed alligator trapper are also available at a cost of $100 for residents and $250 for non-residents. In addition, there is a $55 dollar application fee to receive alligator harvest tags for hunting designated private lands. Hide tag validation fees are $20 for alligators between 4 to 6 feet in length, $35 for hides 6 to 8 feet in length, $45 for hides 8 to 10 feet in length, and $65 for any alligator 10 feet long or longer. Unused alligator hide tags must be returned to the South Carolina Department of Natural Resources or a $250 fee per tag will be assessed. Further information on and applications for alligator trappers licenses, alligator hide tags, and the Private Lands Alligator Management Program, as well as designated control agent tag and permit information, may be obtained from the South Carolina Department of Natural Resources' Alligator Management Program Office at the Dennis Wildlife Center (address in Appendix I). Hunting licenses (also required to harvest alligators from private lands) are available from most bait or sporting goods stores at an annual cost of $12 for residents and $75 for non-residents. Limited 10 day and 3 day non-resident hunting licenses are also available at a cost of $50 and $25 respectively.

IMPORTATION AND COMMERCIAL TRADE REGULATIONS

Native Species

With the exception of the following summarized restrictions concerning American Alligators and Diamondback Terrapins, South Carolina does not currently regulate the commercial exploitation of any native amphibian or reptile species.

Alligators

Alligator mississippiensis, American Alligator hides procured by designated control agents during the course of alligator management activities will be sold by the South Carolina Department of Natural Resources under appropriate conditions, and the net proceeds of such sales will be distributed to the control agent as specified by contract. Alligator meat and other by-products (i.e. skulls, teeth, claws, etc.) may be sold by control agents. Marketing permits issued by the South Carolina Department of Natural Resources are required. Alligator meat must be packaged in sealed cardboard boxes of 5 pounds or less and must be processed in accordance with all federal, state, and local sanitation requirements (SC CL R 123-151).

American Alligator hides, meat, and other products lawfully acquired during the course of authorized private lands alligator management activities may be possessed, sold or exported. Proper alligator tag validation is required. Sales of such alligator hides, meat, or products within South Carolina must comply with all applicable state marking permit requirements and sales conditions (SC CL R 123-151).

Alligator mississippiensis, American Alligator meat, hides, and products lawfully obtained from outside South Carolina may be sold. A permit issued by the South Carolina Department of Natural Resources is required and all applicable sales conditions apply (SC CL R 123-151).

Turtles
Malaclemys terrapin, Diamondback Terrapins under five inches in plastron length may not be possessed, purchased, or sold (SC CL 50-17-920).

Native and Exotic Species
The following summarized regulations apply to both native and non-native species.

Importation permits are not required to import amphibians and reptiles for sale in the pet trade (SC CL 50-16-60).

Crocodilian products sold in South Carolina must be labeled as to species of origin, i.e., American Alligator, Caiman, or Crocodile (SC CL R 123-151.6B).

License and Permit Information
Permits authorizing the sale of legally acquired alligator products are available at a cost of $35 and may be obtained from the South Carolina Department of Natural Resources Alligator Program Supervisor at the Dennis Wildlife Center (address in Appendix I).

CAPTIVE MAINTENANCE REGULATIONS

The following is a brief review of the restrictions on the captive possession of amphibians and reptiles included among the regulations of the preceding sections.

a. Endangered and threatened species may not be possessed without permit.
b. Scientific collection permits may be required to possess native amphibians and reptiles wild caught in the state.
c. *Malaclemys terrapin*, Diamondback Terrapins have a minimum size restriction of five inches in plastron length.
d. No restrictions on the possession of non-native amphibian and reptile species.

(b and c above see Native Wildlife Regulations).
(d above see Importation and Commercial Trade Regulations).

SC

SOUTH DAKOTA

ENDANGERED, THREATENED, AND SPECIAL CONCERN SPECIES

The South Dakota Department of Game, Fish, and Parks lists various species of the state's flora and fauna as endangered or threatened. All species listed as either threatened or endangered are legally protected by the state's endangered species legislation as specified in chapter 34A of South Dakota's Codified Laws (reference: SD C.L. 34A-8-1-12).

At this time there are no threatened or endangered amphibians included on South Dakota's list of protected species. The following reptile species are currently (May 1996) listed as threatened or endangered in South Dakota, however, and permits are required for all activities involving these species.

Species	Common Name	Status
Emydoidea blandingii	Blanding's Turtle	Endangered
Graptemys pseudogeographica	False Map Turtle	Threatened
Heterodon platirhinos	Eastern Hognose Snake	Threatened
Tropidoclonion lineatum	Lined Snake	Endangered

Protected Species Permit Information

Scientific collector's permits are issued to qualified individuals and institutions for purposes of legitimate research. There is no fee for a scientific collector's permit. The possession of specimens of state threatened or endangered species legally obtained outside of South Dakota may also be allowed by permit. Permit applications and information on permit requirements may be obtained from the South Dakota Department of Game, Fish, and Parks (address in Appendix I).

NATIVE WILDLIFE REGULATIONS

All native amphibians and reptiles, with the exception of Bullfrogs and turtles, are considered to be bait or biological specimens by the State of South Dakota. Restrictions on the collection and possession of all species, including turtles and Bullfrogs, are specified in chapter 41 of the State Regulations of South Dakota (reference: SDR 41). The following is a review of these regulations.

Licensed fishermen may take bait, including snakes, lizards, salamanders, and frogs, except Bullfrogs, for non-commercial purposes. The possession limit is 12 dozen of any combination of species. Bait may be taken by the following methods (SDR 41-09-04):
1. seines (30 feet long, 6 feet deep, 3/8 inch mesh or less)
2. lift net (4 feet by 4 feet square, 3/8 inch mesh or less)
3. cast net (24 feet in diameter, 3/8 inch mesh or less)
4. trap (diameter 12 inches, 3 feet long, 1 inch openings)
5. dip net (30 inches in diameter, 3/8 inch mesh or less)

Frogs

Rana catesbieana, Bullfrogs may be taken from May 1 through October 15. The daily bag limit is 15, the possession limit is 30. The use of firearms is prohibited. A valid fishing license is required (SDR 41-07-09).

Turtles

Turtles may be taken from January 1 through December 31. The limit on all species of turtles, except State listed threatened or endangered species, is two daily with a possession limit of four for each species. A valid fishing license is required (SDR 41-07-10).

Turtles may be legally taken by: hook and line, seines (legal bait size), gaff hooks, or spear.

License and Permit Information

Fishing licenses can be obtained from most sporting goods stores and bait shops. Annual license fees are $14 for residents and $49 for nonresidents. One day and five day licenses are also available at a reduced cost.

IMPORTATION AND COMMERCIAL TRADE REGULATIONS

Restrictions on the sale of native amphibians and reptiles are included among the regulations of SDR 41. The following is a summarization of these regulations.

Native Species

The following native amphibians and reptiles may be collected and sold under authority of either a commercial bait dealer's license or a biological specimen dealer's license only. Possession limit is 12 dozen of each species. (SDR 41-09-04-02):

Ambystoma tigrinum	Tiger Salamander
Bufo americanus	American Toad
Bufo cognatus	Great Plains Toad
Bufo hemiophrys	Canadian Toad
Bufo woodhousii	Woodhouse's Toad
Pseudacris triseriata	Western Chorus Frog
Rana pipiens	Northern Leopard Frog
Spea bombifrons	Plains Spadefoot Toad
Chrysemys picta	Painted Turtle
Eumeces fasciatus	Five-lined Skink
Eumeces septentrionalis septentrionalis [1]	Northern Prairie Skink
Coluber constrictor flaviventris	Eastern Yellowbelly Racer
Crotalus viridis	Prairie Rattlesnake
Heterodon nasicus nasicus	Plains Hognose Snake
Lampropeltis triangulum multistriata	Pale Milk Snake
Pituophis catenifer	Bullsnake
Thamnophis radix haydenii [1]	Western Plains Garter Snake
Thamnophis sirtalis parietalis	Red-sided Garter Snake

[1] No subspecies recognized in Collins (1997).

Chelydra serpentina, Snapping Turtles taken in South Dakota may not be purchased, sold, bartered, or exported for purposes other than personal consumption (SDR 41-07-10).

Exotic Species

The State of South Dakota does not currently regulate the importation or sale of any non-native amphibian and reptile species.

License and Permit Information

Requirements and applications for both the commercial bait dealer's license and the biological specimens dealer's license may be obtained from the License Office of the South Dakota Department of Game, Fish, and Parks (address in Appendix I).

CAPTIVE MAINTENANCE REGULATIONS

Any restrictions on the captive maintenance of amphibians and reptiles are included in the above regulations. The following is a brief review of these regulations.

a. State and federally listed endangered and threatened species may only be possessed by permit.
b. Unless otherwise specified, the possession limit for unprotected native amphibians and reptiles is 12 dozen.
c. *Rana catesbeiana*, Bullfrog possession limit is 30 frogs.
d. Native turtles have a possession limit of four specimens of each species.
e. Fishing license is required to possess unprotected native amphibians and reptiles.
f. No restrictions on the possession of non-native species.

(b, c, d, and e above see Native Wildlife Regulations)

1994 FREE SCIENTIFIC COLLECTOR'S PERMIT
State of South Dakota
Department of Game, Fish, and Parks

To Whom It May Concern
Permit Authorizes:

License Number_____This

NAME

ADDRESS

CITY   STATE   ZIP

Collecting for (Institution or Association):

NAME

ADDRESS

CITY   STATE   ZIP

To take, possess, transport, collect, or study for scientific purposes the following wild animals or plants in such manner and under such conditions set forth below:

COMMON NAME & SPECIES	NUMBER	VICINITY OF COLLECTION
1.		
2.		
3.		
4.		
5.		

** MONITORED SPECIES, PLEASE LIST SPECIFIC COLLECTION LOCATION(S).

DISPOSITION OF SPECIMENS AND/OR SPECIAL CONDITIONS:

NOTICE: Collecting that may be authorized under this permit does not relieve the permit holder from compliance with any Federal law or regulation. ***** The taking of any federal and/or state threatened or endangered species will ONLY be authorized under special exemption of this permit. Please inform this office (605-773-4191) if you incidently take any of these species, so that changes can be made. ***** The permit holder MUST notify the local Conservation Officer prior to engaging in any collections. The enclosed collection report forms must be submitted to the Department of Game, Fish, and Parks, 523 East Capital, Pierre, SD 57501-3182 no later than January 31, following the year this permit is issued. This permit is granted under the provisions of SDCL 41-6-32 and expires on the 31st day of December for the year issued.

Dated at Pierre, South Dakota this_____day of_____, 19____

By_____
South Dakota Department of Game, Fish, and Parks

Sample Permit - Courtesy of the South Dakota Department of Game, Fish and Parks.

TENNESSEE

ENDANGERED, THREATENED, AND SPECIAL CONCERN SPECIES

The Tennessee Wildlife Resources Agency lists various members of the state's fauna as either endangered, threatened, or in need of management species. All of Tennessee's in need of management, threatened, and endangered amphibians and reptiles are legally protected by the Tennessee Nongame and Endangered or Threatened Wildlife Species Conservation Act of 1974, as specified in chapter 8 of the Tennessee Code Annotated (reference: TCA 70-8-101-112). This legislation also provides for the protection of all native nongame species, and the collection without a scientific collection permit of any native amphibian or reptile not designated a fish or game species is technically prohibited (see Native Wildlife Regulations).

The following amphibians and reptiles are included in Tennessee's current (September 1994) Endangered, Threatened, or In Need of Management (N/M) species lists. A permit is required for all activities involving any of these species.

Species	Common Name	Status
Ambystoma talpoideum	Mole Salamander	N/M
Cryptobranchus alleganiensis alleganiensis	Hellbender	N/M
Desmognathus aeneus	Seepage Salamander	N/M
Desmognathus quadramaculatus	Black Belly Salamander	N/M
Desmognathus welteri	Black Mountain Salamander	N/M
Desmognathus wrighti	Pygmy Salamander	N/M
Eurycea junaluska	Junaluska Salamander	N/M
Gyrinophilus palleucus	Tennessee Cave Salamander	Threatened
Hemidactylium scutatum	Four-toed Salamander	N/M
Plethodon wehrlei	Wehrle's Salamander	N/M
Plethodon welleri	Weller's Salamander	N/M
Hyla gratiosa	Barking Treefrog	N/M
Clemmys muhlenbergii	Bog Turtle	Threatened
Macrochelys temminckii [1]	Alligator Snapping Turtle	N/M
Anolis carolinensis	Green Anole	N/M
Eumeces anthracinus	Coal Skink	N/M
Ophisaurus attenuatus longicaudus	Eastern Slender Glass Lizard	N/M
Nerodia cyclopion	Green Water Snake	N/M
Pituophis melanoleucus melanoleucus	Northern Pine Snake	Threatened
Sistrurus miliarius streckeri	Western Pygmy Rattlesnake	Threatened

[1] Listed as *Macroclemys temminckii* by Tennessee.

Protected Species Permit Information

Scientific collection permits allowing for the collection and possession of Tennessee's protected species are issued for legitimate research purposes. Because of concerns regarding the possible over-exploitation of many of Tennessee's rarer amphibians and reptiles, even by legitimate scientific researchers, all permit requests are evaluated on an individual basis and permits are awarded solely on the merits of the proposed research activities. There is no fee for a scientific collection permit. Permits allowing for the possession of specimens of state protected species legally acquired outside of Tennessee are issued for educational, exhibition, or propagation purposes. Applications and requirements for both these permits may be obtained from the Tennessee Wildlife Resources Agency (address in Appendix I).

NATIVE WILDLIFE REGULATIONS

Restrictions on the collection and possession of native amphibians and reptiles wild caught in Tennessee are included in the Tennessee Nongame and Endangered Species Act or in the regulations of the Tennessee Wildlife Resources Commission (reference: TN WRCR). As stated previously, the collection and possession of the majority of amphibian and reptile species native to Tennessee is prohibited except by permit. The following is a summary of Tennessee's regulations on the non-commercial collection and possession of amphibians and reptiles wild caught in the state.

It is unlawful to take, attempt to take, possess, transport, export, process, sell, offer for sale, or ship nongame wildlife except as otherwise specified (TCA 70-8-104C).

No wildlife may be taken from the wild in Tennessee except as provided for by statute, proclamation, and/or rule (TN WRCR 1660-1-18).

Salamanders
All salamander species, except those listed as endangered, threatened, or in need of management, may be collected and possessed for personal use bait purposes. A valid fishing license is required (TN WRCR 1660-1-17-.01A).

Turtles
The following turtle species may be legally taken throughout the state year round. The daily bag limit is 20 turtles, with a minimum size limit of 9 inches in carapace length. Turtles may be taken by all legal sport fishing methods except archery or speargun. A valid fishing license is required (Proc. 93-26):

Chelydra serpentina	Common Snapping Turtle
Apalone mutica mutica	Midland Smooth Softshell Turtle
Apalone spinifera spinifera	Eastern Spiny Softshell Turtle

Up to 3 turtle hoop traps may also be used in Benton, Carroll, Chester, Crockett, Decatur, Dyer, Fayette, Gibson, Hardeman, Hardin, Haywood, Henderson, Henry, Houston, Humphreys, Lake, Lauderdale, McNairy, Madison, Obion, Perry, Shelby, Stewart, Tipton, and Weakley Counties.

All sizes and species of turtles, except Box Turtles, Terrapene spp., and endangered, threatened, or in need of management species may be taken without limit in Lake and Obion Counties.

License and Permit Information
A valid fishing license is required to collect or possess any native wild caught turtle or salamander species in Tennessee. Fishing licenses are available from sporting goods and bait dealers at annual fees of $19 for residents and $26 for non-residents. Ten-day and three-day non-resident licenses are also available at a reduced cost. Scientific collection permits are required to collect all other amphibians and reptiles in Tennessee. Applications and requirements for scientific collection permits may be obtained from the Tennessee Wildlife Resources Agency (address in Appendix I).

IMPORTATION AND COMMERCIAL TRADE REGULATIONS

Native Species
Restrictions on the sale of native amphibians and reptiles are included among the rules and regulations of the Tennessee Wildlife Resources Agency. With few exceptions, the sale of native amphibians and reptiles wild caught in Tennessee is prohibited. The following is a summarization of the regulations restricting the sale of both wild caught and imported native species.

It is unlawful to possess, transport, import, export, buy, sell, barter, propagate, or transfer any wildlife, whether indigenous to Tennessee or not, except as otherwise specified (TCA 70-4-401).

Specimens of native amphibians and reptiles legally obtained from outside of Tennessee may be imported and sold under the authority of a propagation permit and an importation permit. Both permits are required (TCA 70-4-410 and 411).

* Does not include any venomous snake species.

The following amphibians and reptiles are the only species which may be harvested for commercial purposes in Tennessee.

Salamanders

Desmognathus fuscus, Dusky Salamanders may be harvested and sold for bait purposes under authority of a fish dealer's license (TN WRCR 1660-1-17-.01B).

Turtles

Legal turtle species (see Native Wildlife Regulations) may be commercially harvested and sold without limit under the authority of a commercial fishing license (Proc. 92-22 IIC).

Native and Exotic Species

Tennessee restricts the importation, possession, and sale of animals deemed inherently dangerous to humans. Species in this category obtained after June 25, 1991 may not be possessed except by licensed commercial propagators, zoos, or other legitimate research or educational facilities (TCA 70-4-403). The following groups of amphibians and reptiles are considered inherently dangerous by the State of Tennessee:

Crocodilians:	All species, except Caimans
Venomous Snakes:	All species, including those native to Tennessee
Amphibians:	All poisonous species

* As currently interpreted by the Tennessee Wildlife Resources Agency permits are not required to import or possess Caimans, *Caiman* spp. in Tennessee.

Non-native amphibians and reptiles not included among the species listed as inherently dangerous may be imported, possessed, and sold without a propagation permit. Importation permits are not required (TCA 70-4-411).

License and Permit Information

Propagation permits required for the sale of native species are available at an annual fee of $100. Importation permits cost $10 per shipment or $100 annually. Commercial propagation permits required for the importation of inherently dangerous wildlife are issued to qualified individuals and institutions for a $1,000 annual fee. Applications and requirements for these and other required permits are available from the Tennessee Wildlife Resources Agency (address in Appendix I).

CAPTIVE MAINTENANCE REGULATIONS

In addition to the restrictions on the possession of native species of amphibians and reptiles of the preceding regulations, Tennessee also requires legitimate documentation (i.e. sales receipts, out-of-state collection permits, etc.) of legal source of acquisition for any native amphibians and reptiles maintained in captivity. Non-native species, except those included in the list of Inherently Dangerous Wildlife (see Importation and Commercial Trade Regulations above), may be possessed without permit or other documentation. Other portions of Tennessee's live wildlife regulations address specific caging and transportation requirements for species included in the list of inherently dangerous wildlife. The complete text of these regulations and applications for any required permits may be obtained from the Tennessee Wildlife Resources Agency (address in Appendix I).

Captive Maintenance Regulations Review

The following is a review of the restrictions on the captive maintenance of amphibians and reptiles in Tennessee.

a. Endangered, threatened, and in need of management species may not be possessed without a scientific collection permit.

b. Legitimate documentation (i.e. sales receipt, etc.) of legal source of acquisition is required to possess native amphibians and reptiles unless otherwise specified. Does not include any poisonous species (see e below).

c. Crocodilians may be possessed under the authorization of a Class I Commercial Propagation and/or Exhibitor permit only, unless otherwise specified (see d below).

d. *Caiman* spp., Caimans may be possessed without permit or documentation.

e. Poisonous snakes including native species may be possessed under the authorization of a Class I Commercial Propagation and/or Exhibitor permit only.

(b above see Native Wildlife Regulations)
(c, d, and e above see Importation and Commercial Trade Regulations.)

TENNESSEE WILDLIFE RESOURCES AGENCY

ELLINGTON AGRICULTURAL CENTER
P. O. BOX 40747
NASHVILLE, TENNESSEE 37204

```
                      SCIENTIFIC COLLECTION PERMIT
                             October 1, 1993


         Scientific Study Permit No.:          Expires:
         ================================================================
         Pursuant to authority of T.C.A. 70-2-213:

            Name:                    Organization:
            Address:                 City, State, Zip:
            County:                  Telephone:

         is granted permission to take, capture, possess, and transport, for
         purely scientific purposes, the following species and numbers of
         wild animals:



               Location(s)                      Date(s)



         Summary of Need:


         Collection Method(s):

         Subject to the following restrictions:

              Submit annual report of collections at or before permit
              expiration. Whenever possible, the appropriate TWRA Regional
              Office should be notified within one week prior of collection
              from the wild, as follows:

              Jackson:     1-800-372-3928;    Nashville: 1-800-255-8972
              Crossville: 1-800-262-6704;     Talbott:   1-800-332-0900




         ================================================================


              Executive Director            Date: October 1, 1993
              Tennessee Wildlife Resources Ag.

         RMH:bh01066/sciperm/93PerFrm.wp    cc: TWRA Regional Office(s)
                         The State of Tennessee
                      AN EQUAL OPPORTUNITY EMPLOYER
```

Sample Permit - Courtesy of the Tennessee Wildlife Resources Agency.

TEXAS

ENDANGERED, THREATENED, AND SPECIAL CONCERN SPECIES

The Texas Parks and Wildlife Commission classifies various species of the state's fauna as threatened or endangered. Species in both categories are legally protected by the endangered and threatened species legislation included among the Texas Parks and Wildlife regulations of the Texas Administrative Code (reference: TAC 65.171 to 65.181).

The following amphibians and reptiles are included in the current (January 1997) list of threatened and endangered species of Texas. Permits issued by the Texas Parks and Wildlife Department are required for all activities involving these species. In addition, federal endangered and threatened species permits are required for several animals included in the following list (see U.S. Endangered and Threatened Species).

Species	Common Name	Status
Eurycea latitans [1]	Cascade Caverns Salamander	Threatened
Eurycea nana	San Marcos Salamander	Threatened
Eurycea tridentifera	Comal Blind Salamander	Threatened
Notophthalmus meridionalis	Black-Spotted Newt	Threatened
Siren sp. [2]	South Texas Siren (large form)	Threatened
Typhlomolge rathbuni [3]	Texas Blind Salamander	Endangered
Typhlomolge robusta [3]	Blanco Blind Salamander	Threatened
Bufo houstonensis	Houston Toad	Endangered
Hypopachus variolosus	Sheep Frog	Threatened
Leptodactylus labialis	White-Lipped Frog	Threatened
Rhinophrynus dorsalis	Mexican Burrowing Toad	Threatened
Smilisca baudinii	Mexican Treefrog	Threatened
Caretta caretta	Loggerhead Sea Turtle	Threatened
Chelonia mydas	Green Sea Turtle	Threatened
Dermochelys coriacea	Leatherback Sea Turtle	Endangered
Eretmochelys imbricata	Hawksbill Sea Turtle	Endangered
Gopherus berlandieri	Texas Tortoise	Threatened
Kinosternon hirtipes murrayi [4]	Chihuahuan Mud Turtle	Threatened
Lepidochelys kempii	Atlantic Ridley Sea Turtle	Endangered
Macrochelys temminckii [5]	Alligator Snapping Turtle	Threatened
Coleonyx reticulatus	Reticulated Gecko	Threatened
Crotaphytus reticulatus	Reticulated Collared Lizard	Threatened
Phrynosoma cornutum	Texas Horned Lizard	Threatened
Phrynosoma douglassii hernandesi [6]	Mountain Short-Horned Lizard	Threatened
Cemophora coccinea	Scarlet Snake	Threatened
Coniophanes imperialis	Black-Striped Snake	Threatened
Crotalus horridus	Timber Rattlesnake	Threatened
Drymarchon corais	Indigo Snake	Threatened
Drymobius margaritiferus	Speckled Racer	Threatened
Leptodeira septentrionalis	Cat-Eyed Snake	Threatened

TX

Liochlorophis vernalis	Smooth Green Snake	Threatened
Nerodia harteri	Brazos Water Snake	Threatened
Nerodia paucimaculata	Concho Water Snake	Threatened
Pituophis ruthveni [7]	Louisiana Pine Snake	Threatened
Tantilla cucullata [8]	Big Bend Blackhead Snake	Threatened
Trimorphodon biscutatus vilkinsonii [9]	Texas Lyre Snake	Threatened

[1] Not listed in Collins (1997).
[2] Currently recognized as an undescribed species by the Texas Parks and Wildlife Department. Not listed in Collins (1997).
[3] Listed in the genus *Eurycea* by Texas.
[4] Listed as *Kinosternon hirtipes* by Texas.
[5] Listed as *Macroclemys temminckii* by Texas.
[6] Listed as *Phrynosoma douglassii* by Texas.
[7] Listed as *Pituophis melanoleucus ruthveni* by Texas.
[8] Listed as *Tantilla rubra* by Texas.
[9] Listed as *Trimorphodon biscutatus* by Texas.

Protected Species Permit Information

A variety of permits authorizing the collection and/or possession of endangered and threatened species are available from the Texas Parks and Wildlife Department. These include Scientific Research, Zoological Collection, Transportation, and Educational Display permits, all of which are subject to an assortment of requirements, conditions, and fees as specified in the Texas Administrative Code (reference: TAC 57.271 to 57.284). In general, permits authorizing the collection or possession of state protected wildlife will be issued to recognized or accredited institutions or qualified individuals for legitimate research or educational display purposes only. A complete list of permit conditions and fees, as well as required permit applications, may be obtained from the Texas Parks and Wildlife Department (address in Appendix I).

NATIVE WILDLIFE REGULATIONS

Restrictions on the non-commercial collection and possession of native amphibians and reptiles are specified in the Texas Parks and Wildlife Code and department regulations. In general, all native amphibians and reptiles except threatened and endangered species and American Alligators are considered non-game species in Texas. An appropriate hunting license is required to take both non-game species and American Alligators. The following is a summary of these regulations.

A valid hunting, special hunting, or combination hunting and fishing license is required to hunt any bird or animal in Texas (TAC 42.002-42.012).

* Special license requirements apply to American Alligators (see Alligators below).

The hunting of any wild bird or animal from a motor vehicle on a public road is prohibited (TAC 62.003).

* Texas Parks and Wildlife Department game wardens consider stopping a vehicle alongside a public road and walking the roadway to collect specimens to be a legal activity, provided a firearm is not discharged. Shining a light from a vehicle or driving in an abnormal, unlawful, or erratic manner, including frequent stops and starts, excessively slow speeds, driving in the wrong lane, or turning crosswise in the roadway is considered to constitute hunting from a vehicle and may also violate traffic codes.

TX

Alligators

Regulations restricting the collection, possession, propagation, transportation, and sale of the American Alligator, *Alligator mississippiensis*, are included in the Texas Parks and Wildlife Department legislation of the Texas Administrative Code (reference: TAC 65.351 to 65.363). The following is a brief summarization of the departmental regulations governing the recreational collection and possession of alligators and alligator eggs harvested from the wild in Texas.

Alligator mississippiensis, Live American Alligators or alligator eggs may only be possessed by licensed alligator farmers (TAC 65.353).

Alligator hunter's licenses and alligator nest stamp permits are required to harvest alligator eggs. Alligator eggs may only be collected by hand (TAC 65.353 and 65.357).

The open season for harvesting alligators from the wild is September 10th through September 30th. The daily and annual bag limit is equal to the number of valid Alligator hide tags possessed (TAC 65.354).

An alligator hunter's license and individual alligator hide tags are required to take alligators from the wild in Texas. All persons in the hunting party must be properly licensed and at least one unused alligator hide tag must be in the possession of the hunting party. All alligators removed from a taking device must be immediately killed and tagged. Alligator hide tags must be permanently locked around a medial scute in the last six inches of tail immediately upon the possession of an alligator by a licensed hunter (TAC 65.353).

Alligators may be taken from one-half hour before sunrise to sunset; there is no minimum size restriction. Legal methods for taking alligators are baited hook and line (line set), harpoon or gig, legal archery equipment and barbed arrow, and hand held snare with integral locking mechanism. All attached lines must be of at least 300 pound test. Line sets are limited to no more than 3 per unused alligator hide tag. Firearms, axes, or hatchets may only be used to kill alligators caught on legal taking devices (TAC 65.355).

Alligator eggs may only be harvested during periods specified in egg collection authorization forms (TAC 65.357).

Nuisance alligators may be taken by designated nuisance control hunters only by methods specified by the Texas Parks and Wildlife Department at the time of authorization of take. Alligators approved for removal may be taken by designated control hunters at anytime (TAC 65.359).

An alligator hide tag report must be completed and submitted within 24 hours of take (TAC 65.360).

* Applies to recreational, commercial, and nuisance control hunters.

License and Permit Information

Hunting licenses are available from numerous retail outlets including ranger stations, bait shops, and sporting goods stores. Annual general hunting license fees are $19 for residents and $250 for non-residents. Special hunting licenses which allow the taking of nongame species are available at annual fees of $6 for residents and $100 for non-residents. Non-resident five-day special licenses at a cost of $35 are also available. Alligator hunter's license fees are $35 for residents and $300 for non-residents. Individual alligator hide tags for wild caught animals cost $10 each and alligator nest stamps have a fee of $50 each. In addition to any required licenses, all license holders over 17 years of age must have valid identification (i.e., drivers license, state I.D. card, etc.) in their possession at all times. Further information on these licenses and the complete text of the alligator hunting regulations may be obtained from the Texas Parks and Wildlife Department (address in Appendix I).

IMPORTATION AND COMMERCIAL TRADE REGULATIONS

Native Species

With the exception of state threatened and endangered species, and the following summarized regulations concerning alligators, Texas does not currently restrict the sale of native amphibian and reptile species.

Legally obtained alligators or alligator parts or products may be imported under the authority of an alligator import permit; proper documentation is required. Alligators taken in another state under a sport hunting license may be imported without permit. Alligators may be purchased by licensed alligator buyers or farmers. Alligator import permit holders may only purchase alligators from sources outside Texas. Licensed alligator hunters and farmers may sell specimens that they have legally harvested to licensed alligator buyers. Alligator farmers may sell live alligators only to other alligator farmers or licensed alligator buyers. Alligator eggs may only be sold to and purchased by licensed alligator farmers. Legally obtained and properly documented processed alligator products may be purchased and sold to anyone. Nuisance alligator hunters may sell harvested alligators as specified above. Legally tagged and documented alligators and alligator parts may be exported by all categories of license and permit holders (TAC 65.353 to 65.358).

Living Alligators originating in Texas may not be exported outside the United States without the specific authorization of the Texas Parks and Wildlife Department (TAC 65.358[b]).

Requirements for alligator farms include adequate barriers to prevent escape or entry by alligators; a reliable source of clean, fresh water; provision for protection from cold (denning space or temperature controlled environment); pooled water of sufficient depth to allow complete submersion of alligators; and dry ground sufficient to permit alligators complete exit from the water. Licensed alligator farmers must maintain complete daily records of all alligator stock and nesting activities and submit annual reports to the Texas Parks and Wildlife Department (TAC 65.561).

Exotic Species

Texas does not currently restrict the importation, sale, or possession of non-native amphibian and reptile species.

License and Permit Information

Alligator buyer's license annual fees are $200 for residents and $650 for non-residents. The fee for an alligator farmer's permit is $200 annually, with a $4 fee for individual captive propagated alligator hide tags. Alligator import permits cost $25. Applications and requirements for these licenses and permits may be obtained from the Texas Parks and Wildlife Department (address in Appendix I).

CAPTIVE MAINTENANCE REGULATIONS

Texas has very few restrictions on the possession of both native and non-native amphibians and reptiles in captivity. The following is a review of these restrictions.

a. Endangered and threatened species may not be possessed without permit.
b. *Alligator mississippiensis*, American Alligators may not be possessed without permit.
c. No restrictions on the possession of other native amphibian and reptile species.
d. No restrictions on the possession of non-native amphibian and reptile species.

(b and c above see Native Wildlife Regulations).

Snake Sign - Well known author, photographer, and colleague Jim Gerholdt scanning the horizon for snake sign in Zapata Co., Texas. Photograph courtesy of Barney Oldfield.

UTAH

ENDANGERED, THREATENED, AND SPECIAL CONCERN SPECIES

Unlike the majority of U.S. states, Utah does not have individual state endangered species legislation. Instead, the Utah Department of Natural Resources utilizes a complex system in which all wildlife is classified in one of three species categories: prohibited, controlled, or uncontrolled. The determination of the wildlife category classification of each individual species is based upon a consideration of the potential disease, ecological, environmental, and human health or safety consequences of various activities involving the species in question, and the level of protection differs for each of the three wildlife designations. In general, all native species designated as prohibited or controlled wildlife may not be collected or possessed without a "Certificate of Registration," as specified in the Administrative Rules of Utah (reference: ARU R657-3-1 to 48). To complicate matters, however, numerous species normally designated as uncontrolled wildlife are considered controlled wildlife if specified possession limits are exceeded (see Native Wildlife Regulations). As a further complication, these same three designations of wildlife are also utilized to regulate the importation of both native and non-native species as well (see Importation and Commercial Trade Regulations).

The following amphibians and reptiles are included in the current (April 1995) list of native species for which collection and possession "Certificates of Registration" are always required. In addition, permits issued by the U.S. Department of the Interior are also required for any of the following species included in the federal list of threatened and endangered wildlife (see U.S. Endangered and Threatened Species).

Species	Common Name	Status
Bufo boreas boreas	Boreal Toad	Prohibited
Bufo microscaphus microscaphus [1]	Arizona Toad	Controlled
Hyla regilla [2]	Pacific Chorus Frog	Controlled
Rana onca	Relict Leopard Frog	Prohibited
Rana pipiens	Northern Leopard Frog	Controlled
Rana pretiosa	Spotted Frog	Prohibited
Rana yavapaensis	Lowland Leopard Frog	Prohibited
Gopherus agassizii	Desert Tortoise	Prohibited
Callisaurus draconoides rhodostictus	Mojave Zebra-tailed Lizard	Controlled
Coleonyx variegatus utahensis	Utah Banded Gecko	Controlled
Dipsosaurus dorsalis dorsalis	Desert Iguana	Prohibited
Heloderma suspectum cinctum	Banded Gila Monster	Prohibited
Sauromalus obesus multiforaminatus	Glen Canyon Chuckwalla	Prohibited
Sauromalus obesus obesus	Western Chuckwalla	Prohibited
Xantusia vigilis utahensis	Utah Night Lizard	Controlled
Xantusia vigilis vigilis	Desert Night Lizard	Controlled
Arizona occidentalis eburnata [3]	Desert Glossy Snake	Prohibited
Crotalus cerastes cerastes	Sidewinder	Prohibited
Crotalus mitchellii	Speckled Rattlesnake	Prohibited
Crotalus scutulatus	Mojave Rattlesnake	Prohibited
Crotalus viridis [4]	Western Rattlesnake	Controlled
Elaphe emoryi [5]	Great Plains Rat Snake	Controlled
Lampropeltis getula californiae [6]	California Kingsnake	Controlled

UT

Lampropeltis pyromelana infralabialis [7]	Utah Mountain Kingsnake	Prohibited
Lampropeltis triangulum taylori	Utah Milk Snake	Prohibited
Leptotyphlops humilis utahensis	Utah Blind Snake	Prohibited
Trimorphodon biscutatus lambda	Sonoran Lyre Snake	Prohibited

[1] No subspecies recognized in Collins (1997).
[2] Listed as *Pseudacris regilla* by Utah.
[3] Listed as *Arizona elegans eburnata* by Utah.
[4] *Crotalus viridis* may be killed without permit for purposes of human safety only (ARU R 657-3-8.2a).
[5] Listed as *Elaphe guttata emoryi* by Utah.
[6] Black and white banded form only.
[7] Subspecies not listed in Collins (1997).

Protected Species Permit Information

As with other aspects of Utah's wildlife legislation, the issuance of a Certificate of Registration is dependent upon a variety of factors including specific activities and the individual wildlife category designation of the species in question. In general, Certificates of Registration authorizing the collection and possession of native amphibians and reptiles classified as Prohibited Wildlife Species will be issued to qualified individuals or institutions for legitimate scientific, educational, rehabilitation, or public exhibition purposes only. Certificates of Registration allowing for the collection and possession of native amphibians and reptiles designated as controlled species may be issued for both scientific research purposes and for the non-commercial personal use of private individuals. Approval or denial of all Certificate of Registration requests is determined on an individual case-by-case basis. Annual fees for both scientific research and personal use collection and possession Certificates of Registration are $10 for residents and $25 for non-residents. Possession only Certificates of Registration are also available for an annual fee of $5 for both residents and non-residents. Permit fees for individual Certificates of Registration for scientific or educational purposes may be waived at the discretion of the Utah Department of Natural Resources. There is no fee for Certificates of Registration for rehabilitation purposes. Applications for Certificates of Registration may be obtained from the Wildlife Registration Office of the Utah Department of Natural Resources (address in Appendix I).

NATIVE WILDLIFE REGULATIONS

Restrictions on the non-commercial collection, killing, and/or possession of designated uncontrolled amphibian and reptile species wild caught in the state are specified in the wildlife legislation of Utah's Administrative Rules (ARU R657-3-1 to R657-3-48). Generally, all native or naturalized amphibians and reptiles not included in Utah's list of prohibited and controlled wildlife are considered uncontrolled species, and Certificates of Registration are not required to collect and possess those species within specified possession limits. These restrictions and possession limits are summarized below.

Amphibians

Unless otherwise specified, three specimens of each uncontrolled amphibian species may be collected, killed, or possessed within a calendar year without a Certificate of Registration. Certificates of Registration are required to exceed the specified possession limit, and includes any progeny produced in captivity (ARU R657-3-20.3).

Salamanders

Ambystoma tigrinum nebulosum, Arizona Tiger Salamander are uncontrolled amphibian species and may be collected and possessed in unlimited numbers. A Certificate of Registration is not required (ARU R657-3-20.4a).

* No subspecies recognized in Collins (1997).

UT

Frogs

The following frogs are uncontrolled amphibian species and may be collected and possessed (dead only) in unlimited numbers. Certificates of Registration are not required. These species may not be transported alive from waters where captured and the live possession of these species without a Certificate of Registration is prohibited (ARU R657-3-20.4a and 20.4b):

Rana catesbeiana	Bullfrog
Rana clamitans	Green Frog

* Although wild populations exist in Utah, neither Bullfrogs or Green Frogs are native to the state.

Reptiles

It is unlawful to disturb the den of any reptile or to kill, capture, or harass any reptile within 100 yards of a reptile den without a Certificate of Registration (ARU R657-3-8-1a).

The indiscriminate killing of all reptiles is prohibited (ARU R657-3-8-1b).

Three specimens of each species of uncontrolled reptile may be collected, killed, or possessed within a calendar year without a Certificate of Registration, unless otherwise specified. Certificates of Registration are required to exceed the specified possession limit, and includes any progeny produced in captivity (ARU R657-3-25.3).

The following uncontrolled reptile species may be collected and possessed in unlimited numbers. A Certificate of Registration is not required (ARU R657-3-25.4):

Uta stansburiana	Side-blotched Lizard
Thamnophis elegans	Western Terrestrial Garter Snake

Turtles

The following turtles are uncontrolled reptile species and may be collected and possessed in unlimited numbers (dead only) without Certificates of Registration. These species may not be transported alive from waters where captured and the live possession of these species without a Certificate of Registration is prohibited (ARU R657-3-25.3 and 25.5):

Apalone spinifera emoryi	Texas Spiny Softshell Turtle
Chelydra serpentina	Common Snapping Turtle

* Softshells and Common Snapping Turtles are not considered native wildlife by the State of Utah.

License and Permit Information

(See Endangered, Threatened, and Special Concern Species)

IMPORTATION AND COMMERCIAL TRADE REGULATIONS

Native Species

Restrictions on the collection, sale and possession of native amphibians and reptiles are included among the general wildlife legislation of Utah's Administrative Rules (reference: ARU). In general, the sale of any native or naturalized amphibian and reptile species wild caught within Utah, is prohibited as specified in the following summarized regulation.

UT

The commercial collection or possession of live wildlife, or dead wildlife, or parts thereof is prohibited (ARU R657-18-1).

* As currently interpreted by the Utah Department of Natural Resources, the preceding regulation applies to all prohibited, controlled, and uncontrolled native amphibian and reptile species, including specimens legally obtained outside of Utah.

Native and Exotic Species

Restrictions on the importation and subsequent possession of both native species legally obtained outside of Utah and non-native amphibians and reptiles are included among the regulations of the State Department of Natural Resources. As with other portions of Utah's wildlife legislation, species to be imported are classified as prohibited, controlled, or uncontrolled wildlife on the basis of possible disease, ecological, environmental, and human health or safety considerations. Utah's importation and subsequent possession restrictions are summarized below.

The release of any live animal into the natural environment of Utah without a Certificate of Registration is prohibited (ARU R657-3-10).

In addition to the preceding regulations of the Utah Department of Natural Resources, the State Department of Agriculture restricts the importation of all wildlife with the following summarized regulation.

A Certificate of Veterinary Inspection or Health Certificate and an Entry Permit are required to import, transport, or possess any live zoological animal in Utah (ARU R58-1).

Prohibited Amphibian and Reptile Species

Species designated as prohibited wildlife and their eggs may not be imported into Utah without a Certificate of Registration. Certificates of Registration authorizing the importation, possession, and/or commercial trade of any prohibited wildlife species will only be issued to qualified individuals or institutions for legitimate scientific, educational, or public exhibition purposes. The following amphibian and reptile families, genera, and species are designated as prohibited wildlife in Utah (ARU R657-3-31 and 36).

Bufo marinus	Marine Toad
Rana catesbeiana	Bullfrog
Rana clamitans	Green Frog
Rana pretiosa	Spotted Frog
Xenopus spp.	Clawed Frogs, all species
Alligatoridae	Alligators and Caimans, all species
Crocodylidae	Crocodiles, all species
Gavialis gangeticus	Gharial
Apalone spinifera emoryi	Texas Softshell Turtle
Chelydra serpentina	Common Snapping Turtle
Gopherus agassizii	Desert Tortoise
Helodermatidae	Gila Monster and Beaded Lizard, all species

UT

Arizona occidentalis eburnata [1]	Desert Glossy Snake
Atractaspidae spp.	Burrowing Asps, all species
Dispholidus typus	Boomslang
Elapidae [2]	Cobras, Mambas, etc., all species
Hydrophiidae [2]	Sea Snakes, all species
Lampropeltis pyromelana infralabialis [3]	Utah Mountain Kingsnake
Lampropeltis triangulum taylori	Utah Milk Snake
Rhabdophis spp.	Keelbacks, all species
Saladora hexalepis mojavensis	Mojave Patch-nosed Snake
Thelotornis spp.	Bird Snakes, all species
Trimorphodon biscutatus lambda	Sonoran Lyre Snake
Viperidae	Vipers and Pit Vipers, all species

[1] Listed as *Arizona elegans eburnata* by Utah.
[2] Listed as Proteroglyphus (fixed front fanged) snakes by Utah.
[3] Subspecies not listed in Collins (1997).

Controlled Amphibians

The following amphibian species are designated as controlled wildlife and the importation, subsequent possession, and commercial trade of any specimens of these species within the State of Utah requires a Certificate of Registration (ARU R657-3-6B.4b):

Bufo boreas	Western Toad
Bufo microscaphus microscaphus [1]	Arizona Toad
Hyla regilla [2]	Pacific Treefrog
Rana onca	Relict Leopard Frog
Rana pipiens	Northern Leopard Frog
Rana yavapaensis	Lowland Leopard Frog

[1] No subspecies recognized in Collins (1997).
[2] Listed as *Pseudacris regilla* by Utah.

Uncontrolled Amphibians

Amphibians not listed as prohibited or controlled wildlife are considered uncontrolled species and may be imported, possessed, and sold in Utah without Certificates of Registration (ARU R657-3-6B.4c).

* As currently interpreted by the Utah Department of Natural Resources, Certificates of Registration are required to possess four or more specimens of uncontrolled native species, including specimens legally obtained from outside of Utah.

Controlled Reptiles

The following reptile species are designated as controlled wildlife and the importation, subsequent possession, and commercial trade of any specimens of these species within the State of Utah requires a Certificate of Registration (ARU R657-3-36-1):

Gopherus agassizii [1]	Desert Tortoise
Callisaurus draconoides rhodostictus	Zebra-tailed Lizard
Coleonyx variegatus utahensis	Utah Banded Gecko
Dipsosaurus dorsalis dorsalis	Desert Iguana
Sauromalus obesus	Chuckwalla
Xantusia vigilis utahensis	Utah Night Lizard
Xantusia vigilis vigilis	Desert Night Lizard

Elaphe emoryi [2]	Great Plains Rat Snake
Lampropeltis getula californiae [3]	California Kingsnake
Leptotyphlops humilis utahensis	Utah Blind Snake

[1] Also included in Utah's list of prohibited species.
[2] Listed as *Elaphe guttata emoryi* by Utah. Controlled status applies to the *intermontanus* morph only.
[3] Black and white banded morph only.

Uncontrolled Reptiles

Reptiles not listed as prohibited or controlled wildlife are considered uncontrolled species and may be imported and possessed in Utah without Certificate of Registration (ARU R657-3-36-2).

* As currently interpreted by the Utah Department of Natural Resources, Certificates of Registration are required to possess four or more specimens of uncontrolled native species including specimens legally obtained outside of Utah.

Turtles

In addition to any species regulated by the preceding legislation, the following summarized regulation restricts the commercial trade of all turtle species.

The commercialization of any turtle less than four inches in carapace length is prohibited (ARU R657-3-28.4).

License and Permit Information

Fees for importation and possession Certificates of Registration are $10 annually for both scientific and personal use purposes. Possession only Certificates of Registration cost $5 annually, again for both scientific and personal use purposes. Certificates of Registration for species designated as prohibited wildlife will be issued to qualified individuals and institutions for legitimate scientific, educational, or exhibition purposes only. Permit fees may be waived for research or educational activities at the discretion of the Utah Department of Natural Resources. Utah's wildlife importation legislation also contains provisions for the issuance of Certificates of Registration for commercial purposes. Commercial permit fees are determined on the basis of gross annual sales and are currently $25 for annual sales of $5,000 or less and $100 for over $5,000 in annual sales. Commercial purposes Certificates of Registration are not required to import, possess, and sell uncontrolled amphibians and reptiles in Utah. Certificates of Veterinary Inspection are obtained within the state or country from which imported animal shipments originate. Information on Entry permit requirements may be obtained from the Utah Department of Agriculture. (address in Appendix I).

CAPTIVE MAINTENANCE REGULATIONS

Restrictions on the captive possession of both native and non-native amphibians and reptiles are included among the regulations of the preceding sections. The following is a brief review of these restrictions.

a. Certificates of Registration are required to possess any native species designated as prohibited wildlife. Certificates of Registration for prohibited species are issued for legitimate scientific purposes only.
b. Certificates of Registration are required to possess all native species designated as controlled wildlife.
c. The following uncontrolled amphibians may not be possessed alive without a Certificate of Registration:

Rana catesbeiana	Bullfrog
Rana clamitans	Green Frog

d. The following uncontrolled reptiles may not be possessed alive without a Certificate of Registration:

Apalone spinifera emoryi	Texas Spiny Softshell Turtle
Chelydra serpentina	Common Snapping Turtle

UT

e. *Ambystoma tigrinum nebulosum*, Arizona Tiger Salamander may be possessed in unlimited numbers. A Certificate of Registration is not required.

f. The following uncontrolled reptile species may be possessed in unlimited numbers. A Certificate of Registration is not required:

Uta stansburiana	Six-blotched Lizard
Thamnophis elegans	Western Terrestrial Garter Snake

g. All other uncontrolled native amphibians and reptiles have a possession limit of 3 specimens without a Certificate of Registration.

h. Non-native amphibians and reptiles designated as prohibited species may not be possessed without a Certificate of Registration. Certificates of Registration for prohibited species will be issued for legitimate scientific purposes only.

i. Certificates of Registration are required to possess any imported species designated as controlled wildlife.

j. No restrictions on the possession of uncontrolled non-native amphibian and reptile species.

(a above see Endangered, Threatened, and Special Concern Species).

(b above see Endangered, Threatened, and Special Concern Species, Native Wildlife Regulations, and Importation and Commercial Trade Regulations).

(c and d above see Native Wildlife Regulations and Importation and Commercial Trade Regulations).

(e, f, and g above see Native Wildlife Regulations).

(h, i, and j, above see Importation and Commercial Trade Regulations).

Gila Monster, *Heloderma suspectum* - One of only two species of venomous lizards, Gila Monsters are never-the-less highly prized by lizard enthusiasts and the species is legally protected in every U.S. state in which it naturally occurs. While now captive bred with some regularity, Gila Monsters and their venomous relative the Beaded Lizard, *Heloderma horridum*, still command high prices in the reptile marketplace. Photograph courtesy of James E. Gerholdt.

UT

VERMONT

ENDANGERED, THREATENED, AND SPECIAL CONCERN SPECIES

The Vermont Fish and Wildlife Department classifies selected species of the state's flora and fauna as Endangered or Threatened. Species in both categories are fully protected by Vermont's Endangered Species Act, as specified in title 10, chapter 123 of the Vermont Statutes Annotated (reference: VSA 10-123-5401 to 5408). As with the endangered species legislation of most states, Vermont's law automatically protects all species included in the federal list of threatened and endangered wildlife.

The following amphibians and reptiles are included in Vermont's current (December 1994) list of endangered and threatened species. Permits are required for all activities involving any listed species.

Species	Common Name	Status
Pseudacris triseriata	Western Chorus Frog	Endangered
Apalone spinifera	Spiny Softshell Turtle	Threatened
Clemmys guttata	Spotted Turtle	Threatened
Eumeces fasciatus	Five-lined Skink	Endangered
Crotalus horridus	Timber Rattlesnake	Endangered

Protected Species Permit Information

Endangered species permits authorizing the collection and/or possession of Vermont's endangered and threatened species may be issued for scientific, propagation, zoological, education, economic hardship, or other special purposes. Permits allowing for the possession of specimens of state listed endangered or threatened species lawfully obtained from outside of Vermont may also be issued. There is no fee for endangered species permits. Applications for permit requirements may be obtained from the Vermont Fish and Wildlife Department (address in Appendix I).

NATIVE WILDLIFE REGULATIONS

The State of Vermont does not currently classify any native amphibian or reptile as a game species, and species specific collection and possession regulations are not included among the wildlife legislation of the Vermont Statutes Annotated. Amphibians and reptiles are included in the state's official definitions of wildlife and wild animal, however, and various nongame wildlife regulations are applicable to native species wild caught in the state. As is evident in the following summarized regulations, Vermont's existing statutes are somewhat vague and contradictory, and the actual current legal status of the recreational collection and possession of wild caught native amphibians and reptiles is uncertain at this time. In an attempt to clarify the situation, Vermont is in the process of revising the state's wildlife code. At this time, it is not known when this revision will be complete.

Wild animals, other than protected birds, game, or furbearing animals, may be taken at any time, by any lawful means. A valid hunting license is required (VSA 10 App. 1.1).

Scientific collection permits may be issued to properly accredited individuals or institutions authorizing the collection and possession of birds, their nests or eggs, or fish or wild animals for public scientific or educational purposes. Permits may be also issued to collect and possess wildlife for art or photographic purposes (VSA 10-4152).

* As currently interpreted by the Vermont Fish and Wildlife Department, scientific collection permits are required to collect and possess native amphibians and reptiles.

License and Permit Information

Scientific collection permits are currently issued to qualified individuals and institutions for legitimate educational, research, art, or photographic purposes only. There is no fee for scientific collection permits. Permit applications and requirements may be obtained from the Vermont Fish and Wildlife Department (address in Appendix I). Small game hunting licenses are available from most bait and sporting goods stores for an annual fee of $12 for residents and $35 for non-residents. Non-resident limited five-day small game hunting licenses at a cost of $20 are also available.

IMPORTATION AND COMMERCIAL TRADE REGULATIONS

Native and Exotic Species

As with other aspects of Vermont's wildlife law, the exact legal status of the importation and commercial trade of both native and exotic species of amphibians and reptiles is unclear at this time. To complicate the issue further, the Department of Agriculture, as well as the Fish and Wildlife Department, has regulatory authority on the importation and exportation of animals within the state. There are currently no statutes specifically regulating the sale of native amphibians and reptiles included among the Fish and Wildlife legislation in title 10 of the Vermont Statutes Annotated. Likewise, specific commercial trade restrictions for both native and non-native amphibians and reptiles are not specified in the Department of Agriculture statutes in title 6 of the Vermont Statutes Annotated. Both agencies regulate the importation of animals into the state, however, with the following summarized restrictions.

The importation of any live wild bird or animal without permit is prohibited (VSA 10-4709).

Importation permits are required to import any species of domestic animal. Certificates of veterinary inspection are also required (VSA 6-1471).

* Non-native amphibians and reptiles are included in the Vermont Department of Agriculture's official definition of domestic animal.

Exportation of any animal from the State of Vermont must comply with the import rules of the receiving state or country (VSA 6-1471).

License and Permit Information

Importation permits are issued free of charge and multiple species may be imported under the authorization of an individual permit. Certificates of veterinary inspection must be obtained from sources within the state or country from which imported animals are to be shipped. Permit applications and further information may be obtained from the Vermont Fish and Wildlife Department and the Vermont Department of Agriculture (addresses in Appendix I).

CAPTIVE MAINTENANCE REGULATIONS

In addition to any restrictions included among the regulations of the preceding sections, the following summarized provisions of Vermont's wildlife laws are applicable to the captive possession of amphibians and reptiles.

Captive propagation licenses are required to propagate wild animals in captivity. Licensed wildlife breeders may sell and transport wild animals at all times (VSA 10-5207 and 5208).

License and Permit Information

Captive propagation licenses are available for a first time application fee of $50 and $10 annual renewal fees. Applications and requirements may be obtained from the Vermont Fish and Wildlife Department (address in Appendix I).

Captive Maintenance Regulations Review

The following is a brief review of Vermont's restrictions on captive possession of native and exotic amphibians and reptiles.

a. Endangered species permits are required to possess any species included in Vermont's list of endangered and threatened wildlife.

b. Scientific collection permits may be required to possess native amphibians and reptiles.

c. Importation permits may be required to possess non-native amphibian and reptile species.

d. Captive propagation permits may be required to breed amphibians and reptiles in captivity.

(b above see Native Wildlife Regulations).
(c above see Importation and Commercial Trade Regulations).
(d above see Captive Maintenance Regulations).

APPLICATION FOR AN IMPORTATION PERMIT

PROVISIONS

1. If a dealer, one application may list different kinds (Species) of fishes, amphibians, reptiles, birds and mammals on the form provided. A permit must be amended when permittee adds a new species after the initial permit is issued.

2. A dealer must renew his importation permit each year on the anniversary date of first issuance even though his initial importation permit has been amended as required above.

C. If mixed lots of tropical aquarium fishes, birds, etc., it will be necessary to list on a separate sheet by common or scientific name, and attached to the forms provided.

D. Return completed forms and attachments to the Vermont Fish and Wildlife Dept., Agency of Natural Resources, 103 South Main Street, 10 South, Waterbury, VT 05676. Attn: Law Enforcement Division

Information required from applicant:

1. Name of Applicant: _____

   Home Address of Applicant: _____
                                   (Street)

   _____ _____ _____ _____
    (Town)   (County)   (State)   (Zip)

   Day Time Phone: _____   Date: _____

   Business address of Applicant if one of the following categories: (Check One)

   Pet Shop ____   Bait Dealer ____   Commercial Hatchery ____

   Retail Store ____   Other ____ (Explain) __   _____

   _____ _____

   _____
   (Street)

   _____ _____ _____ _____
    (Town)   (County)   (State)   (Zip)

   Business Phone: _____

2. Species to be imported: Please fill out attached form(s)

Sample Permit Application - Courtesy of the Vermont Fish and Wildlife Department.

VIRGINIA

ENDANGERED, THREATENED, AND SPECIAL CONCERN SPECIES

The Virginia Department of Game and Inland Fisheries lists various species of the state's flora and fauna as either endangered, threatened, or as species of special concern. Species listed as special concern, however, receive no official protection from Virginia's endangered and threatened species legislation. In addition to protecting all state listed endangered and threatened species, the Virginia Endangered Species Act automatically protects all native populations of federally listed endangered and threatened species, as specified in article 6, chapter 5, title 29.1 of the Code of Virginia (reference: VC 29.1-5-6).

The following species are the amphibians and reptiles included in Virginia's current (May 1992) list of endangered and threatened species, as specified in the Virginia Administrative Code (reference: VAC 15-20-130) or in the current (August 1996) list of federally protected species. Permits issued by the Virginia Department of Game and Inland Fisheries are required for all activities involving any of these species. In addition, permits issued by the U.S. Department of the Interior are required for any of the following species included in the federal list of threatened and endangered wildlife (see U.S. Endangered and Threatened Species).

Species	Common Name	Status
Ambystoma mabeei	Mabee's Salamander	Threatened
Ambystoma tigrinum	Tiger Salamander	Endangered
Plethodon shenandoah	Shenandoah Salamander	Endangered
Hyla gratiosa	Barking Treefrog	Threatened
Caretta caretta caretta	Loggerhead Sea Turtle	Threatened
Chelonia mydas mydas	Green Sea Turtle	Threatened
Clemmys insculpta	Wood Turtle	Threatened
Clemmys muhlenbergii	Bog Turtle	Endangered
Deirochelys reticularia reticularia	Eastern Chicken Turtle	Endangered
Dermochelys coriacea coriacea [1]	Leatherback Sea Turtle	Endangered
Eretmochelys imbricata	Hawksbill Sea Turtle	Endangered
Lepidochelys kempii	Atlantic Ridley Sea Turtle	Endangered
Ophisaurus ventralis	Eastern Glass Lizard	Threatened
Crotalus horridus atricaudatus [1]	Canebrake Rattlesnake	Endangered

[1] No subspecies recognized in Collins (1997).

Protected Species Permit Information

Permits allowing for the collection and possession of state endangered and threatened species for legitimate research purposes are issued to qualified individuals and institutions. Salvage permits allowing for the recovery of usable dead specimens are also available. Permits allowing for the possession of legally obtained specimens of protected amphibians and reptiles for exhibition or educational purposes may be issued on occasion. Applications and requirements for these permits may be obtained from the Virginia Department of Game and Inland Fisheries (address in Appendix I).

NATIVE WILDLIFE REGULATIONS

Restrictions on the non-commercial collection and possession of native amphibians and reptiles are specified in the wildlife regulations of the Virginia Administrative Code (reference: VAC). The following is a summary of these regulations.

Except as otherwise specified, native amphibians and reptiles may be collected and possessed for personal use only. There is a possession limit of five of each species (VAC 15-360-10A).

* Does not include threatened or endangered species.

Salamanders

Salamanders may be collected for use as fish bait. The possession limit for bait salamanders is 50 individuals in total (all bait species combined). A valid freshwater fishing license is required (VAC 15-360-10A-3).

Salamanders may not be taken in Grayson Highlands State Park or from those portions of the Jefferson National Forest in Grayson, Smyth, and Washington Counties bounded on the east by State Route 16, on the north by State Route 603, and on the south and west by U.S. Route 58 (VAC 15-360-10D).

Frogs

Rana catesbeiana, Bullfrogs may be collected except in areas designated as stocked trout waters. The daily possession limit is 15 frogs. A valid freshwater fishing license is required. Bullfrogs may be taken by: hand, hook and line, seines (4 feet deep by 10 feet long or less), umbrella net (5 feet by 5 feet square or less), minnow traps (openings 1 inch or less), cast nets (6 feet in radius or less), 20 inch dip nets (handle length 8 feet or less), gigging, and bow and arrow. Bullfrogs may also be taken by .22 caliber rimfire firearm from private waters only (VAC 15-360-10A and 10B).

Turtles

Chelydra serpentina, Common Snapping Turtles may be taken except from designated stocked trout waters. The daily possession limit is 15 turtles. A valid freshwater fishing license is required. Turtles may be legally taken by: hand, hook and line, seine (4 feet deep by 10 feet long or less), nets (see size restrictions under frogs above), trot line, jugline, or set pole. The use of live bait other than worms is prohibited (VAC 15-360-10).

License and Permit Information

Fishing licenses may be obtained from most bait or sporting goods dealers. Annual fees are $12.50 for residents and $30.50 for non-residents. Licenses limited to five consecutive days are also available.

IMPORTATION AND COMMERCIAL TRADE REGULATIONS

Restrictions on the importation, possession, and sale of both native and non-native amphibians and reptiles are included among the wildlife regulations of the Virginia Administrative Code. In general, the sale of all native amphibians and reptiles (including specimens lawfully acquired outside the state) within Virginia is prohibited, although commercial activities involving some native species are allowed through various permits. Permits are also required to possess a variety of non-native amphibian and reptile species. The following is a summarization of Virginia's restrictions on the importation, sale, and possession of native and exotic amphibians and reptiles.

Native Species

The sale of all species of salamanders is prohibited (VAC 15-360-60).

Chelydra serpentina, Common Snapping Turtles harvested from the wild in Virginia may be sold under the authorization of a Permit to Collect and Sell Snapping Turtles (VAC 15-369-30).

The importation, possession, and sale of albino specimens of native or naturalized amphibian and reptile species is not prohibited (VAC 15-30-30).

Certain species of captive bred native amphibians and reptiles may be bought, possessed, propagated, and sold under the authority of a Permit to Hold and Sell Certain Wildlife. The following native species may currently be propagated and sold with this captive breeder's permit (VAC 15-360-50):

Hyla cinerea [1]	Green Treefrog
Rana catesbeiana [1]	Bullfrog
Rana clamitans melanota [1]	Green Frog
Rana sphenocephala [2]	Southern Leopard Frog
Chelydra serpentina	Common Snapping Turtle
Elaphe guttata guttata [3]	Corn Snake
Lampropeltis calligaster rhombomaculata [3]	Mole Kingsnake
Lampropeltis getula getula [3]	Eastern Kingsnake

[1] May only be sold to bonafide research or educational institutions or processed for human consumption.
[2] Listed as *Rana utricularia* by Virginia. May only be sold to bonafide research or educational institutions or processed for human consumption.
[3] All snakes must be captive produced. The wholesale purchase of the above snakes is subject to the following maximum purchase size limits. Corn Snakes and Eastern Kingsnakes may not exceed 16 inches in length, Mole Kingsnakes may not exceed 12 inches in length. These size limits do not apply to retail sales of snakes.

Exotic Species

A permit is required to import, possess, or sell any non-native animal that may be detrimental to the native fish and wildlife resources of Virginia. Permits are currently required to import or possess the following non-native amphibian and reptile species and subspecies (VAC 15-30-40).

Bufo marinus	Giant Toad
Xenopus spp.	African Clawed Frogs
Ambystoma mavortium diaboli [1]	Gray Tiger Salamander
Ambystoma mavortium mavortium [1]	Barred Tiger Salamander
Ambystoma mavortium melanostictum [1]	Blotched Tiger Salamander
Crocodilians	Alligators and Crocodiles All species
Boiga irregularis	Brown Tree Snake

[1] All three taxa listed as subspecies of *Ambystoma tigrinum* by Virginia. *Ambystoma tigrinum* and *Ambystoma mavortium* are recognized as separate species in Collins (1997) with all former *tigrinum* subspecies reassigned to *Ambystoma mavortium*..

The sale of all species of salamanders, except non-native newts of the family Salamandridae, is prohibited (VAC 15-360-60).

All other non-native animals not specified as requiring a permit may be possessed and sold, provided they have been legally obtained and are not liberated within the borders of Virginia (VAC 15-30-40F).

License and Permit Information

Applications for any required permits, including the captive breeder's permit, may be obtained from the Virginia Department of Game and Inland Fisheries (address in Appendix I). Fees for these permits have not been set at the time of this writing.

CAPTIVE MAINTENANCE REGULATIONS

In addition to the restrictions on the possession of both native and exotic amphibians and reptiles included among the previous regulations, the following summarized statutes are also applicable to the captive maintenance of these animals.

It is unlawful to display, exhibit, handle, or use any poisonous or dangerous snake or reptile in such a manner as to endanger the life or health of any person (VC 18.2-313).

It is unlawful to keep any exotic or non-native reptile in any manner that will permit its escape or to knowingly allow a reptile to run at large (VC 29.1-569).

Captive Maintenance Regulations Review

The following is a brief review of Virginia's restrictions on the captive maintenance of amphibians and reptiles.

a. Endangered and threatened species may only be possessed by permit.
b. The possession of unprotected native amphibians and reptiles is limited to five of each species.
c. *Bufo marinus*, Giant Toads may be possessed by permit only.
d. *Xenopus* spp., Clawed Frogs may be possessed by permit only.
e. Permits are required to possess any species of crocodilian.
f. *Boiga irregularis*, Brown Tree Snakes may be possessed by permit only.

(b above see Native Wildlife Regulations).
(c through f above see Importation and Commercial Trade Regulations).

WASHINGTON

ENDANGERED, THREATENED, AND SPECIAL CONCERN SPECIES

Although the State of Washington does not have an official Endangered Species Act, the Washington Department of Fish and Wildlife lists various members of the state's fauna as endangered, threatened, sensitive, candidate, or monitor species. Animals included in the first three categories—endangered, threatened, or sensitive—are designated protected species, and their collection and possession without permit is prohibited as specified in the Revised Code of Washington (reference RCW 77-16-120).

The following amphibian and reptile species are included in the current (July 1993) list of legally protected wildlife of the State of Washington. Permits are required for all activities involving any of these species. In addition, U.S. Department of the Interior permits are required for any species included in the Federal Endangered Species List (see U.S. Endangered and Threatened Species).

Species	Common Name	Status
Plethodon larselli	Larch Mountain Salamander	Sensitive
Caretta caretta	Loggerhead Sea Turtle	Threatened
Chelonia mydas	Green Sea Turtle	Threatened
Chrysemys picta	Painted Turtle	Sensitive
Clemmys marmorata	Pacific Pond Turtle	Endangered
Dermochelys coriacea	Leatherback Sea Turtle	Endangered
Lepidochelys olivacea [1]	Pacific Ridley Sea Turtle	Threatened

[1] Although not officially included in Washington's list, this species is protected by the U.S. Endangered Species Act and may occasionally occur in the coastal waters of the state.

Protected Species Permit Information

Scientific permits allowing for the collection and possession of state protected wildlife for research or display purposes may be issued to qualified individuals and institutions. There is a $12 fee for a scientific permit, and a bond of up to $1,000 may be required on occasion. Applications and requirements for the scientific permit may be obtained from the Washington Department of Fish and Wildlife (address in Appendix I).

NATIVE WILDLIFE REGULATIONS

Restrictions on the collection and possession of amphibians and reptiles wild caught in Washington are specified in chapter 232 of the Washington Administrative Code (reference: WAC 232). The following is a summarization of these regulations.

With the exception of Bullfrogs (see Frogs below), a scientific permit is required to collect all native amphibians and reptiles from the wild in Washington (WAC 232-12-064).

Frogs

Rana catesbeiana, Bullfrogs are classified as game animals by the State of Washington, and as such a valid hunting license is required for their collection. The open season varies throughout the state. The daily bag limit is 10, and the possession limit is 20 frogs. Bullfrogs may be taken by the following methods: hand, hand held dip net, angling, spearing, or bow and arrow (WAC 232-12).

* *Rana catesbeiana* is not native to Washington and actually should be designated as deleterious exotic wildlife due to possible negative effects to wildlife species.

License and Permit Information

Scientific permits allowing for the collection of native amphibians and reptiles are available for a fee of $12 from the Washington Department of Fish and Wildlife (address in Appendix I). Hunting licenses are available from sporting goods and bait stores at an annual fee of $15 for residents and $150 for non-residents.

IMPORTATION AND COMMERCIAL TRADE REGULATIONS

Native Species

The following restriction on the sale of native animal species is included among the wildlife regulations of chapter 232 of the Washington Administrative Code.

Live wild animals, wild birds, or game fish held in captivity or their progeny or parts may not be sold or otherwise commercialized except as authorized (WAC 232-12-064.5).

* Whether this regulation applies to all specimens of native amphibians and reptiles regardless of their place of origin is unclear at this time.

Exotic Species

The only restrictions on the importation, possession, and sale of non-native amphibian and reptile species in Washington are included in the following summarized regulations.

Species designated as deleterious exotic wildlife may not be imported, possessed, propagated, sold, transferred, or released in Washington without a permit (reference WAC 232-12-017.2). The following species is the only amphibian or reptile included in the current deleterious exotic wildlife list.

>   *Xenopus laevis*   African Clawed Frog

The release of wild animals into the natural environment of Washington is prohibited except as authorized (RCW 77.16.150).

License and Permit Information

Permits allowing for the possession of prohibited deleterious wildlife may be issued to qualified individuals and institutions for purposes of legitimate scientific research or display. A complete list of permit conditions, including caging requirements and permit applications, may be obtained from the Washington Department of Fish and Wildlife (address in Appendix I).

CAPTIVE MAINTENANCE REGULATIONS

Restrictions on the possession of amphibians and reptiles are included among the regulations of the preceding sections. A brief review of these restrictions follows:

a. Permits are required to possess state protected species.

b. Permits may be required to possess unprotected native amphibians and reptiles.

c. *Rana catesbeiana*, Bullfrogs have a possession limit of 20 specimens. A valid hunting license may be required.

d. *Xenopus laevis*, African Clawed Frogs may not be possessed without permit.

e. No restrictions on the possession of other non-native amphibian and reptile species.

(b above see Native Wildlife Regulations and Importation and Commercial Trade Regulations).
(c above see Native Wildlife Regulations).
(d and e above see Importation and Commercial Trade Regulations).

Posted Sanctuary - Hopefully, signs like this one reflect the beginnings of a significant change in attitude regarding the ecological and aesthetic value of snakes, among both governmental wildlife agencies and private conservation organizations within the United States. Photograph courtesy of William B. Love.

WEST VIRGINIA

ENDANGERED, THREATENED, AND SPECIAL CONCERN SPECIES

West Virginia is one of the relatively few states which does not have individual state endangered species legislation, and the only native species officially designated as Endangered or Threatened are those included in the U.S. Department of the Interior's list of federally protected wildlife. Other published lists of state Species of Special Concern, such as the one developed and maintained by the West Virginia Non-Game Wildlife and Natural Heritage program, function as monitoring devices only and offer no specific legal protection for any listed species.

The following salamander is the only amphibian or reptile species native to West Virginia included in the current (January 1997) federal list of endangered and threatened species. Permits issued by the U.S. Department of the Interior are required for all activities involving this species. Scientific collecting permits issued by the West Virginia Division of Natural Resources are also required.

Species	Common Name	Status
Plethodon nettingi	Cheat Mountain Salamander	Threatened

Protected Species Permit Information

State scientific collecting permits authorizing the collection and/or possession of federally endangered and threatened species are issued to qualified individuals and institutions for legitimate research, educational, exhibition, or captive propagation purposes only. Federal permit requirements must be fulfilled before state permits will be issued (see U.S. Endangered and Threatened Species for federal permit information). There is no fee for state permits for scientific purposes. State scientific collecting permit applications may be obtained from the Wildlife Resources Section of the West Virginia Division of Natural Resources (address in Appendix I).

NATIVE WILDLIFE REGULATIONS

Restrictions on the collection and possession of native amphibians and reptiles wild caught in West Virginia are included among the state's general fish and wildlife legislation, as specified in chapter 20 of the West Virginia Code Annotated (reference: WV CA 20) or in title 47 of the West Virginia Code of State Rules (reference: WV CSR 47). In general, the collection and possession of terrestrial reptiles, including the Eastern Box Turtle, *Terrapene carolina*, is regulated separately from amphibians and aquatic turtles. The following is a summary of West Virginia's restrictions on the non-commercial collection and possession of native amphibians and reptiles wild caught in the state.

Salamanders

Salamanders may be taken year round by hand, seines six feet long by four feet deep or less, throw nets six feet in diameter or less, and minnow trap. The possession limit is 50 specimens in aggregate (all species combined). A valid fishing license is required (WV CA 20-2-27, and WV CSR 47-20-4 and 47-20-5).

Frogs

Frogs may be taken by legal fishing methods from the Saturday nearest June 15 to July 31. The daily bag limit is 10 and the possession limit is 20 frogs. There are no minimum size restrictions. A valid fishing license is required (WV CA 20-2-27 and WV CSR 47-20-4.11, 47-20-5.11 and 47-20-6).

* Although apparently designed to regulate the harvest of Bullfrogs, *Rana catesbeiana*, and Green Frogs, *Rana clamitans*, no species are specified among West Virginia's fish and wildlife regulations. As currently interpreted by the West Virginia Division of Natural Resources, the previous restrictions apply to collection and possession of all frog species.

Aquatic Turtles

Aquatic turtles may be taken by hand throughout the year. The open seasons for taking aquatic turtles by gigging, snagging, or snaring is from January 1 to May 15 and from July 15 to December 31. There is no minimum size requirement and the daily bag limit is 100 specimens. A valid fishing license is required (WV CA 20-2-27 and WV CSR 47-20-4.10, 47-20-5.10, 47-20-6 and 47-20-10).

* As currently interpreted by the West Virginia Division of Natural Resources all turtles native to the state, except the Eastern Box Turtle, *Terrapene carolina*, are considered aquatic species.

Snakes, Lizards and Terrestrial Turtles

Scientific collecting permits are required to collect and/or possess reptiles for scientific or propagation purposes (WV CA 20-2-50).

* As currently interpreted by the West Virginia Division of Natural Resources, scientific collecting permits are only required by individuals and institutions involved in actual research activities. No licenses are required to collect terrestrial amphibian or reptile species for non-commercial personal use purposes. Permits are required to possess live specimens in captivity, however (see Captive Maintenance Regulations).

License and Permit Information

West Virginia fishing licenses are available from numerous retail outlets including most bait and sporting goods stores. Annual fees for fishing licenses are $11 for residents and $25 for non-residents. Three-day non-resident fishing licenses are also available. In addition, West Virginia conservation stamps are required for all licensed fishermen and cost $3 for residents of the state and $5 for non-residents. Scientific collecting permits are issued free of charge. Applications for scientific collecting permits may be obtained from the West Virginia Division of Natural Resources Wildlife Resources Section (address in Appendix I).

IMPORTATION AND COMMERCIAL TRADE REGULATIONS

Native Species

Restrictions on the collection, importation, and possession of native amphibians and reptiles are included among the fish and wildlife legislation of the West Virginia Code Annotated and the Code of State Rules. In general, the sale of any native species wild caught within the state is prohibited except for salamanders. West Virginia's wildlife legislation contains commercial licensing provisions allowing for the sale of specimens of native amphibians and reptiles legally acquired outside of the state or produced in captivity. The following is a summarization of West Virginia's native species commercial trade restrictions.

It is unlawful to take, attempt to take, or possess from the wild any species of wildlife native to the state for commercial purposes unless otherwise authorized by license or permit (WV CSR 47 58-63-7.1).

Native amphibian and reptile species may be propagated, purchased, or sold under the authorization of an aquatic wildlife propagation license. All wildlife held at a licensed captive propagation facility must have been obtained from a licensed wildlife breeder, lawfully imported into West Virginia, or born at the captive propagation facility. Accurate records of all commercial transactions and of all specimens produced in captivity must be maintained (WV CA 20-2-47, 20-2-48 and WV CSR 47-23-1 to 47-23-8).

* Does not include the prohibited turtles of WV CSR 47-23-7.1 (see Turtles below).

Importation permits are required to import live wildlife or viable eggs into West Virginia. Veterinary certificates of inspection are also required (WV CA 20-2-13).

* As currently interpreted by the West Virginia Division of Natural Resources, importation permits are only required to import species native to the state.

Salamanders

Salamanders harvested from the wild within the State of West Virginia may be sold under the authorization of a commercial catch and sell bait dealer's license. The possession limit for salamanders taken for commercial purposes is 250 specimens in total of all species combined (total aggregate possession limit includes all specimens of crayfish, hellgrammites, and/or salamanders). Salamanders may be harvested commercially by cast nets of at least 1/4 inch mesh and three feet in diameter or less, dip nets of at least 1/4 inch mesh and 36 square feet in overall area or less, minnow traps with openings of one inch in diameter or less, or seines of at least 1/4 inch mesh and six feet long by four feet deep or less. Commercial buy and sell bait dealer's licenses are required to purchase salamanders for resale purposes (WV CA 20-2-55 and WV CSR 47-22-1 to 47-22-8).

Turtles

It is unlawful to catch, capture, sell, trade, take, kill, possess, export, or import the following turtles or their eggs for commercial purposes (WV CSR 47-23-7.1):

Apalone mutica mutica [1]	Midland Smooth Softshell Turtle
Apalone spinifera spinifera	Eastern Spiny Softshell Turtle
Chelydra serpentina	Common Snapping Turtle
Chrysemys picta marginata	Midland Painted Turtle
Chrysemys picta picta	Eastern Painted Turtle
Clemmys guttata	Spotted Turtle
Clemmys insculpta	Wood Turtle
Graptemys geographica	Common Map Turtle
Graptemys ouachitensis [2]	Ouachita Map Turtle
Pseudemys concinna concinna [3]	Eastern River Cooter
Pseudemys concinna hieroglyphica [4]	Hieroglyphic Turtle
Pseudemys rubriventris	Redbelly Turtle
Sternotherus odoratus	Common Musk Turtle [5]
Trachemys scripta elegans	Red-eared Slider

[1] Listed as *Apalone mutica* in the currently available West Virginia Division of Natural Resources' Regulation.
[2] Listed as *Graptemys pseudogeographica ouachitensis* in the currently available West Virginia Division of Natural Resources' Regulation.
[3] No subspecies listed in Collins (1997).
[4] No subspecies listed in Collins (1997). No longer considered a valid component of West Virginia's herpetofauna, this subspecies has not yet been deleted from currently available West Virginia Division of Natural Resources' Regulation.
[5] Listed as Stinkpot in the currently available West Virginia Division of Natural Resources' Regulation.

Exotic Species

The State of West Virginia does not currently regulate the importation, possession, or commercial trade of non-native amphibian and reptile species.

License and Permit Information

Commercial catch and sell bait dealer's licenses are available for a first time fee of $10 with renewal fees of $1 annually. Fees for commercial buy and sell bait dealer's and aquatic wildlife propagation licenses are $10 annually. Importation permits are issued free of charge. Veterinary certificates of inspection are obtained from within the state from which wildlife shipments originate. Further information on license requirements and license applications may be obtained from the Wildlife Resources Section of the West Virginia Division of Natural Resources (address in Appendix I).

CAPTIVE MAINTENANCE REGULATIONS

In addition to the restrictions on the captive possession of amphibians and reptiles included among the regulations of the preceding sections, two additional portions of West Virginia's wildlife legislation regulate the captive maintenance of these animals in captivity. These regulations are summarized below.

Permits are required to maintain native species of wildlife in captivity as pets, including specimens collected from the wild during the legal open season or acquired from a licensed commercial dealer (WV CA 20-2-51).

Permits are required to maintain amphibians and reptiles in captivity for display purposes at a roadside menagerie (WV CA 20-2-52).

License and Permit Information

Pet permits are available for a $2 application fee. Application fees for roadside menagerie permits are $25. Permit requirements and applications may be obtained from the West Virginia Department of Natural Resources (address in Appendix I).

Captive Maintenance Regulations Review

The following is a brief review of West Virginia's restrictions on the captive possession of amphibians and reptiles.

a. Federal and state permits are required to possess Plethodon nettingi.
b. Native salamanders have a possession limit of 50 specimens in total (all species combined). Pet permits are required. A valid fishing license may also be required.
c. Frogs have a possession limit of 20 specimens in total (all species combined). Pet permits are required. A valid fishing license may also be required.
d. Aquatic turtle species native to West Virginia have a possession limit of 100 per day. Pet permits are required. A valid fishing license may also be required.
e. Pet permits are required to possess other native reptile species.
f. No restrictions on the possession of non-native amphibian and reptile species.

(b, c and d above see Native Wildlife Regulations and Captive Maintenance Regulations).
(e above see Captive Maintenance Regulations).

* West Virginia is currently revising the state's amphibian and reptile legislation. When these revisions will be complete is uncertain at this time.

WISCONSIN

ENDANGERED, THREATENED, AND SPECIAL CONCERN SPECIES

The Wisconsin Department of Natural Resources lists various species of the state's flora and fauna as either threatened or endangered. All listed species are legally protected by the Wisconsin Endangered Species Act, as specified in Natural Resources legislation of chapters 27 and 29 of the Wisconsin Administrative Code (reference: WIAC NR 27.01-.06 and 29.41-5 and 6).

The following species are the amphibians and reptiles currently (July 1997) listed as threatened or endangered in Wisconsin. Endangered species permits are required for all activities involving any of these species.

Species	Common Name	Status
Acris crepitans	Blanchard's Cricket Frog	Endangered
Clemmys insculpta	Wood Turtle	Threatened
Emydoidea blandingii	Blanding's Turtle	Threatened
Terrapene ornata	Ornate Box Turtle	Endangered
Ophisaurus attenuatus	Slender Glass Lizard	Endangered
Regina septemvittata	Queen Snake	Endangered
Sistrurus catenatus	Eastern Massasauga	Endangered
Thamnophis butleri [1]	Butler's Garter Snake	Threatened
Thamnophis proximus	Western Ribbon Snake	Endangered
Thamnophis sauritus	Eastern Ribbon Snake	Endangered

[1] The listing of *Thamnophis butleri* as a threatened species has successfully passed all state legislative procedures and Butler's Garter Snake will become officially protected on July 1, 1997.

Protected Species Permit Information

Endangered Species permits allowing for the collection of endangered and threatened species for legitimate research purposes are issued to qualified individuals and institutions. Permits allowing for the possession of protected species for educational or propagation purposes are also issued on occasion. Requirements and applications for both permits may be obtained from the Wisconsin Department of Natural Resources (address in Appendix I).

NATIVE WILDLIFE REGULATIONS

Regulations on the collection and possession of amphibians and reptiles wild caught in Wisconsin are specified in the wildlife legislation of the Wisconsin Administrative Code (reference: WIAC) or in Wisconsin Statutes Annotated (reference: WSA). With the exception of the following restrictions, all native amphibians and reptiles not protected by the Wisconsin Endangered Species Act may be collected throughout the year with no possession limits (reference: WSA 29.48). A fishing or small game hunting license is required. The following is a summarization of Wisconsin's restrictions applicable to the non-commercial or recreational collection and possession of native amphibians and reptiles wild caught within the state.

Scientific collector's permits are required to collect amphibians and reptiles for research purposes (WSA 29.17).

* Applies to organized research activities only (i.e. museums, universities, etc.).

A valid small game hunting or fishing license is required to collect native amphibians and reptiles in Wisconsin (WSA 29.09).

Frogs

The open season for frogs is from the Saturday nearest May 1 to December 31. Frogs may not be taken by firearm (WIAC NR 19.27).

Rana catesbeiana, Bullfrogs may not be taken in Jefferson County at any time (WIAC NR 19.27-2a).

Turtles

The open season for turtles is from July 15 through November 30. Turtles may be taken by: hand, dip-net, hook and line, hooking, and by legal hoop net trap. No other trap types are allowed. Maximum number of traps allowed is 3 on inland waters and 10 on Iowa/Wisconsin and Minnesota/Wisconsin boundary waters. Turtles may not be taken by hook and line from designated trout streams during the closed season for trout. The daily bag and possession limit is 5 of each species and there are no minimum size requirements unless otherwise specified. A valid fishing or small game hunting license is required. On Iowa/Wisconsin and Minnesota/Wisconsin boundary waters either state's fishing licenses are considered valid (WIAC NR 19.275, NR 21, and NR 22).

* Does not include state threatened or endangered species.

Apalone spp., Softshell Turtles have a bag and possession limit of 3 specimens on inland waters. The bag and possession limit is 5 on Iowa/Wisconsin and Minnesota/Wisconsin boundary waters (WIAC NR 19.275, NR 21, and NR 22).

* No species specified by Wisconsin. It is uncertain if the bag and possession limit is 5 specimens of each species or 5 turtles in aggregate (all species combined) at this time.

Chelydra serpentina, Common Snapping Turtles have a bag and possession limit of 10 specimens on Iowa/ Wisconsin and Minnesota/Wisconsin boundary waters and 3 specimens on inland waters. Common Snapping Turtle size limits are 12 inches minimum to 16 inches maximum in carapace length. (WIAC NR 19.275, NR 21, and NR 22).

Turtle Hoop Trap Specifications

Traps must be designed of stretchable fabric (e.g. nylon) and must have a minimum mesh stretch of 6 inches. Wire mesh is not permitted. Each trap must have a metal tag bearing the name and address of the operator attached and visible above the water surface. Identified operators are the only individuals allowed to tend traps. Traps must be set with a minimum of two inches exposed above the water's surface. Turtle traps must be checked and emptied at least once each day (WIAC NR 19.275, NR 21, and NR 22).

License and Permit Information

Wisconsin Small Game hunting licenses are available from numerous retail outlets, including most sporting goods stores and bait shops. Annual fees for Small Game hunting licenses are $12.00 for residents and $70.00 for non-residents. Five day non-resident Small Game hunting licenses are also available at a cost of $40.00. Information on Scientific Collecting Permits and permit applications may be obtained from the Wisconsin Department of Natural Resources (address in Appendix I).

IMPORTATION AND COMMERCIAL TRADE REGULATIONS

Native Species

With the exception of the sale and use of frogs as fishing bait and the commercial harvest of turtles which requires a commercial fishing license, all native amphibians and reptiles may currently be harvested and sold without restriction (reference: WIS 29.48). Those portions of Wisconsin's wildlife legislation regulating the commercial collection and use of native amphibians and reptiles is summarized below.

Frogs

A bait dealer's license is required to commercially possess and sell frogs for use as bait (WIAC NR 29.137).

* Does not include state threatened or endangered species.

The use of frogs as bait on the Mississippi River for commercial fishing purposes is prohibited (WIAC NR 21.12).

Turtles

Turtles may be commercially harvested within specified bag limits by legal methods of taking turtle (see Native Wildlife Regulations). A commercial fishing license is required (WIAC NR 19.275, NR 21, and NR 22).

* Wisconsin is in the process of revising many of the state's regulations governing the collection and possession of native amphibians and reptiles. When these revisions will be completed is uncertain at this time.

Exotic Species

The State of Wisconsin does not currently restrict the importation, possession, and/or sale of any non-native amphibian or reptile.

* Wisconsin is currently considering a revision of the state's regulations governing the importation and possession of some non-native amphibian and reptile species. When this revision will be completed is uncertain at this time.

License and Permit Information

Bait dealers and commercial fishing license applications and requirements may be obtained from the Wisconsin Department of Natural Resources (address in Appendix I).

CAPTIVE MAINTENANCE REGULATIONS

With the exception of endangered or threatened species, the State of Wisconsin does not restrict the possession of native or non-native amphibian and reptile species. The following is a review of Wisconsin's current regulations concerning the captive maintenance of amphibians and reptiles.

a. Permits are required to possess endangered or threatened species.
b. Native species not protected as threatened or endangered may be possessed in unlimited numbers, unless otherwise specified.
c. The possession limit for native turtles is 5 specimens unless otherwise specified.
d. *Chelydra serpentina*, Common Snapping Turtles have a possession limit of 10 specimens.
e. No restrictions on the possession of non-native amphibians and reptiles.

(b, c, and d above see Native Wildlife Regulations).
(e above see Importation and Commercial Trade Regulations).

SINGLE ENTRANCE HOOP TRAP

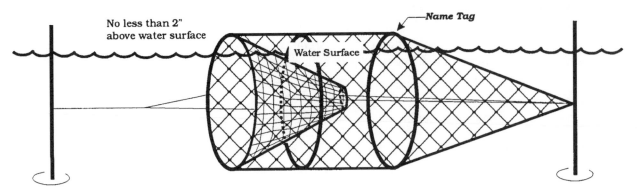

Turtle Trap - Diagrammatic representation of a single entrance hoop trap for turtles conforming to Wisconsin's legal specifications for these devices. Courtesy of the Wisconsin Department of Natural Resources.

Don't Murtle the Turtle - Hand-made signs, like this one from an Indian Reservation in the Upper Mississippi River Valley, are an indication of the concern many private individuals have regarding the survival of U.S. turtle populations. Photograph courtesy of Barney Oldfield.

WYOMING

ENDANGERED, THREATENED, AND SPECIAL CONCERN SPECIES

Along with North Dakota, Utah, and West Virginia, Wyoming is one of the few states that does not have individual state endangered species legislation and therefore no official list of state threatened or endangered species. Native species included in the U.S. Department of the Interior's list of endangered and threatened wildlife, however, are fully protected by the U.S. Endangered Species Act and are subject to all federal regulations and permit requirements.

The following species native to Wyoming is the only amphibian or reptile included in the current (January 1997) U.S. Department of the Interior list of threatened or endangered wildlife. Federal endangered species permits are required for all activities involving this species. In addition, permits issued by the Wyoming Game and Fish Department are required to collect or possess specimens of this animal in Wyoming.

Species	Common Name	Status
Bufo baxteri [1]	Wyoming Toad	Endangered

[1] Listed as *Bufo hemiophrys baxteri* by the U.S. Department of the Interior.

Protected Species Permit Information

Permits issued by the U.S. Department of the Interior are required for all activities involving Bufo hemiophrys baxteri, and these permits must be obtained before any state permits will be authorized. In general, federal permits will only be issued to qualified individuals for legitimate research, zoological, educational, or propagation purposes (see U.S. Endangered and Threatened Species for further information on federal permits). Requirements and applications for state permits may be obtained from the Wyoming Game and Fish Department (address in Appendix I).

NATIVE WILDLIFE REGULATIONS

Restrictions on the collection and possession of amphibians and reptiles, including specimens wild caught in the state, are included among the "Nongame Wildlife" regulation in chapter LII and in the "Regulation for the Importation, Possession, Confinement, Transportation, Sale and Disposition of Live Wildlife" in chapter X of the Wyoming Game and Fish Commission Regulations. The portions of Wyoming's wildlife legislation regulating the non-commercial collection and possession of native amphibians and reptiles wild caught within the state are summarized below.

The collection and possession of the following amphibian and reptile species wild caught within the State of Wyoming is prohibited without a scientific collecting permit (WY GFCR LII.11):

Bufo boreas boreas [1]	Boreal Toad
Bufo baxteri [2]	Wyoming Toad
Rana pretiosa	Spotted Frog
Rana sylvatica	Wood Frog
Crotalus viridis concolor	Midget Faded Rattlesnake
Lampropeltis triangulum multistriata [3]	Pale Milk Snake
Lichanura bottae [4]	Rubber Boa
Storeria occipitomaculata pahasapae [5]	Black Hills Redbelly Snake

1 Listed as *Bufo boreus boreus* by Wyoming.
2 Included in the U.S. list of federally protected wildlife. Listed as *Bufo hemiophrys baxteri* by Wyoming and the U.S. Department of the Interior.
3 Listed as *Lampropeltis triangulum multistrata* by Wyoming.
4 Listed as *Charina bottae* by Wyoming.
5 Listed as *Stoveria occipitomaculata pahasapae* by Wyoming.

* Whether or not permits are required to possess specimens of the above species lawfully acquired outside of Wyoming is uncertain at this time (see Importation and Commercial Trade Regulations).

All other amphibian and reptile species wild caught within the State of Wyoming may be collected and possessed for non-commercial, personal use purposes without restriction. Permits are not required (WY GFCR X.5c-i and LII.6).

Scientific permits issued by the Wyoming Game and Fish Department are required for all scientific research and/or educational collecting activities involving any native amphibian and reptile species within the State of Wyoming (WY GFCR X.5, LII.6 and .11 and WY GFCR XXXIII).

* Applies to organized collection and research activities such as those conducted by museums, universities, zoological institutions, and environmental agencies only.

License and Permit Information

Scientific permits authorizing the collection and/or possession of native amphibians and reptiles wild caught in the state may be issued to qualified individuals and institutions for legitimate research or educational purposes. There is no fee for scientific permits. Permit requirements and applications may be obtained from the Wyoming Game and Fish Department (address in Appendix I).

IMPORTATION AND COMMERCIAL TRADE REGULATIONS

Native Species

Restrictions on the collection and possession of native amphibians and reptiles wild caught within Wyoming for commercial purposes, and on the importation and possession of specimens of native species legally acquired outside of the state are included among the wildlife regulations of the Wyoming Game and Fish Commission. While the majority of these restrictions are specified in the general importation and possession regulations in chapter X of the Wyoming Game and Fish Commission Regulations, portions of the "Nongame Wildlife" legislation in chapter LII apply as well. Wyoming's restrictions on the importation and commercial possession of native amphibian and reptile species are summarized below.

Commercial permits are required to collect and/or possess native amphibians and reptiles wild caught within the State of Wyoming for commercial purposes (WY GFCR X.5c).

The following native amphibians and reptiles may not be imported into Wyoming without an importation/possession permit (WY GFCR X.5c-i and LVII.6):

Ambystoma mavortium mavortium [1]	Barred Tiger Salamander
Ambystoma mavortium melanostictum [2]	Blotched Tiger Salamander
Ambystoma mavortium nebulosum [2]	Utah Tiger Salamander
Ambystoma tigrinum	Tiger Salamander
Bufo cognatus	Great Plains Toad
Bufo woodhousii woodhousii [3]	Woodhouse's Toad

Pseudacris maculata [4]	Boreal Chorus Frog
Rana catesbeiana	Bullfrog
Rana pipiens	Northern Leopard Frog
Spea bombifrons [5]	Plains Spadefoot
Spea intermontana [6]	Great Basin Spadefoot
Apalone spinifera hartwegi [7]	Western Spiny Softshell Turtle
Chelydra serpentina serpentina	Common Snapping Turtle
Chrysemys picta belli	Western Painted Turtle
Terrapene ornata ornata	Ornate Box Turtle
Cnemidophorus sexlineatus viridis	Prairie Racerunner
Eumeces multivirgatus	Many-lined Skink
Holbrookia maculata maculata	Northern Earless Lizard
Phrynosoma douglassii brevirostre	Eastern Short-horned Lizard
Sceloporus graciosus graciosus	Northern Sagebrush Lizard
Sceloporus undulatus	Eastern Fence Lizard
Sceloporus undulatus elongatus	Northern Plateau Lizard
Sceloporus undulatus erythrocheilus	Red-lipped Prairie Lizard
Sceloporus undulatus garmani	Northern Prairie Lizard
Urosaurus ornatus wrighti [8]	Northern Tree Lizard
Coluber constrictor flaviventris	Eastern Yellowbelly Racer
Crotalus viridis viridis	Prairie Rattlesnake
Heterodon nasicus nasicus	Plains Hognose Snake
Liochlorophis vernalis [9]	Smooth Green Snake
Pituophis catenifer [10]	Gopher Snake
Pituophis catenifer deserticola [10]	Great Basin Gopher Snake
Pituophis catenifer sayi [10]	Bullsnake
Thamnophis elegans vagrans	Wandering Garter Snake
Thamnophis radix haydenii [2]	Western Plains Garter Snake
Thamnophis sirtalis	Common Garter Snake
Thamnophis sirtalis fitchi	Valley Garter Snake
Thamnophis sirtalis parietalis	Red-sided Garter Snake

WY

[1] Listed as *Ambystoma tigrinum movortium* by Wyoming. Both *mavortium* and *tigrinum* are recognized as valid Collins (1997).
[2] Listed as a subspecies of *Ambystoma tigrinum* by Wyoming.
[3] Listed as *Bufo woodhousei woodhousei* by Wyoming.
[4] Listed as *Pseudacris triseriata maculata* by Wyoming.
[5] Listed as *Scaphiopus bombifrons* by Wyoming.
[6] Listed as *Scaphiopus interomontanus* by Wyoming.
[7] Listed as *Trionyx spiniferus hartwegi* by Wyoming.
[8] Listed as *Urosaurus ornata wrighti* by Wyoming. No subspecies recognized in Collins (1997).
[9] Listed as *Opheodrys vernalis* by Wyoming.
[10] Listed as *Pituophis melanoleucas* by Wyoming.

* With the exception of the eight native species specified in section 11 of WY GFCR LII (see Native Wildlife Regulations), all of the amphibians and reptiles naturally occurring within the State of Wyoming are included in the preceding list. The exact legal status of specimens of the eight species listed in section 11 legally acquired outside of Wyoming is unclear at this time, as importation/possession permit requirements regarding these species are not specified in the wildlife legislation of the Wyoming Game and Fish Commission. Currently, the Wyoming Game and Fish Department's administrative policy is to require permits for these eight species.

Exotic Species

Wyoming has relatively few restrictions on the importation, possession, and commercial trade of non-native amphibian and reptile species. In general, all non-native amphibian and reptile species except one may be imported without restriction. These restrictions, included among the general importation regulations of the Wyoming Game and Fish Commission, are summarized below.

The release of any live wildlife into the natural environment of Wyoming without permit is prohibited (WY GFCR X.5b-i).

Prohibited Species

The importation and/or possession of the following non-native amphibian species is prohibited without permit (WF GFCR X.5e-ii):

Bufo hemiophrys   Manitoba Toad

Amphibians

All other non-native amphibians may be imported without restriction. Importation/possession permits and veterinary certificates of health are not required (WY GFCR X.5b-A).

Reptiles

Non-native reptile species may be imported without restriction. Importation/possession permits and veterinary certificates of health are not required (WY GFCR X.5b-E).

License and Permit Information

All applications for commercial collecting, importation, and/or possession permits are evaluated on an individual case by case basis. In general, importation/possession permits for specimens of native amphibians and reptiles legally obtained outside of Wyoming are issued without much complication, provided that all imported specimens are properly documented. Separate permits are required for each species to be imported. Permits authorizing the importation and possession of prohibited species such as Bufo hemiophrys are generally issued to recognized zoological, scientific, educational, or governmental organizations for legitimate research or exhibition purposes only. There are no application fees for any of the required permits of this section. Permit requirements and applications may be obtained from the Wyoming Game and Fish Department (address in Appendix I).

CAPTIVE MAINTENANCE REGULATIONS

Restrictions on the captive possession of both native and non-native amphibians and reptiles are included among the regulations of the preceding sections. The following is a brief review of these restrictions.

a. Federal and state permits are required to possess Bufo hemiophrys baxteri.
b. State permits are required to possess specimens of the following native amphibians and reptiles wild caught within Wyoming.

Bufo boreas boreas	Boreal Toad
Rana pretiosa	Spotted Frog
Rana sylvatica	Wood Frog
Crotalus viridis concolor	Midget Faded Rattlesnake
Lampropeltis triangulum multistriata	Pale Milk Snake
Lichanura bottae	Rubber Boa
Storeria occipitomaculata pahasapae	Black Hills Redbelly Snake

c. All other native species wild caught within the State of Wyoming may be possessed without permit.

d. Permits are required to possess imported specimens of native amphibians and reptiles.

e. Non-native *Bufo hemiophrys* may not be possessed without permit.

f. All other non-native amphibians may be possessed without restriction.

g. No restrictions on the possession of any non-native reptile.

(b and c above see Native Wildlife Regulations).
(d through g above see Importation and Commercial Trade Regulations).

Northern Leopard Frog, *Rana pipiens* - Like most amphibians and reptiles native to the state, Leopard Frogs captured within Wyoming may be possessed for non-commercial purposes without restriction. Specimens of Wyoming's native amphibian and reptile species lawfully obtained from outside the state, however, may not be imported or possessed in Wyoming without permit. Photograph by J.P. Levell.

APPENDIX I
STATE and FEDERAL REGULATORY AGENCIES

Government agency addresses for permit information and applications, special licenses, etc.

Alabama Department of Conservation and
    Natural Resources
Game and Fish Division
Law Enforcement Section
64 N. Union Street
Montgomery, AL 36130-1456

Alaska Department of Fish and Game
P.O. Box 25526
Juneau, AK 99802-5526

Arizona Game and Fish Department
Permits Coordinator
2221 W. Greenway Road
Phoenix, AZ 85023

Arkansas Game and Fish Commission
2 Natural Resources Drive
Little Rock, AR 72205

California Department of Fish and Game
Wildlife Protection Division
1416 Ninth St.
Sacramento, CA 95814

Colorado Department of Agriculture
State Veterinarian's Office
700 Kipling St., Suite 4000
Lakewood, CO 80215

Colorado Division of Wildlife
6060 Broadway
Denver, CO 80216

Connecticut Department of Environmental Protection
Wildlife Division
79 Elm Street
Hartford, CT 06102-5127

Delaware Department of Agriculture
2320 South Dupont Highway
Dover, DE 19901

Delaware Department of Natural Resources and
    Environmental Control
Division of Fish and Wildlife
Richardson and Robbins Building
89 Kings Highway
Dover, DE 19903

Florida Department of Environmental Protection
Office of Protected Species Management
3900 Commonwealth Boulevard
Tallahassee, FL 32399-3000

Florida Game and Fresh Water Fish Commission
620 South Meridian Street
Tallahassee, FL 32399-1600

Georgia Department of Natural Resources
Special Permit Unit
2070 U.S. Highway 278 S.E.
Social Circle, GA 30279

Hawaii Department of Agriculture
Plant Quarantine Branch
701 Ilalo Street
Honolulu, HI 96813-5524

Hawaii Department of Land and Natural Resources
1151 Punchbowl Street
Honolulu, HI 96813

Idaho Department of Fish and Game
600 S. Walnut Street, P.O. Box 25
Boise, ID 83707

Illinois Department of Natural Resources
Endangered Species Project Manager
524 S. Second St., Lincoln Tower Plaza
Springfield, IL 62701-1787

Indiana Department of Natural Resources
Division of Fish and Wildlife
Commercial License Clerk
Indiana Government Center South
402 W. Washington St. - Room W273
Indianapolis, IN 46204-2267

Iowa Department of Natural Resources
Wallace State Office Building
Des Moines, IA 50319-5145

Kansas Department of Wildlife and Parks
Route 2, Box 54A
Pratt, KS 67124-9599

Kentucky Department of Fish and Wildlife Resources
#1 Game Farm Road
Frankfort, KY 40601

Louisiana Department of Agriculture and Forestry
Post Office Box 631
Baton Rouge, LA 70821

Louisiana Department of Wildlife and Fisheries
Post Office Box 98000
Baton Rouge, LA 70898-9000

Maine Department of Inland Fisheries and Wildlife
State Station House 41
284 State Street
Augusta, ME 04333

Maryland Department of Natural Resources
Tidewater Administration, Fisheries Division
Tawes State Office Building C-2
Annapolis, MD 21401

Maryland Department of Natural Resources
Wildlife Division
Tawes State Office Building
580 Taylor Avenue
Annapolis, MD 21401

Massachusetts Division of Fisheries and Wildlife
100 Cambridge Street
Boston, MA 02202

Michigan Department of Agriculture
P.O. Box 30017
Lansing, MI 48909

Michigan Department of Natural Resources
Stevens T. Mason Building
Box 30028
Lansing, MI 48909

Minnesota Department of Natural Resources
Endangered Species Permit Coordinator
500 Lafayette Road
St. Paul, MN 55155-4001

Mississippi Department of Wildlife, Fisheries and Parks
Museum of Natural History
111 N. Jefferson St.
Jackson, MS 39202

Missouri Department of Conservation
2901 West Truman Boulevard
P.O. Box 180
Jefferson City, MO 65102-0180

Montana Department of Fish, Wildlife, and Parks
Law Enforcement Division
1420 E. Sixth Avenue
Helena, MT 59620

Nebraska Game and Parks Commission
2200 N. 33rd Street
P.O. Box 30370
Lincoln, NE 68503-0370

Nevada Division of Wildlife
P.O. Box 10678, 1100 Valley Road
Reno, NV 89520-0022

New Hampshire Fish and Game Department
2 Hazen Drive
Concord, NH 03301

New Jersey Department of Environmental Protection
and   Energy
Division of Fish, Game and Wildlife
CN 400
Trenton, N J 08625-0400

New Mexico Department of Game and Fish
Villagra Building
P.O. Box 25112
Sante Fe, NM 87504

New York State Department of Environmental
    Protection
Division of Fish and Wildlife
Special License Unit
50 Wolf Road
Albany, NY 12233

New York State Department of Environmental
    Protection
State University of New York
Building 40
Stoney Brook, NY 11794

North Carolina Wildlife Resources Commission
Archdale Building
513 N. Salisbury Street
Raleigh, NC 27611

North Dakota Game and Fish Department
100 North Bismarck Expressway
Bismarck, ND 58501-5095

Ohio Department of Natural Resources
Division of Wildlife
1840 Belcher Drive
Columbus, OH 43224-1329

Oklahoma Department of Wildlife Conservation
1801 North Lincoln Boulevard
Oklahoma City, OH 73105

Oregon Department of Agriculture
635 Capitol N.E.
Salem, OR 97310

Oregon Department of Fish and Wildlife
2501 SW First Ave., P.O. Box 59
Portland, OR 92707

Pennsylvania Fish and Boat Commission
Division of Fisheries Management
Herpetology and Endangered Species Coordinator
450 Robinson Lane
Bellefonte, PA 16823-9685

Rhode Island Department of Environmental
        Management
Division of Fish and Wildlife
Washington County Government Center
Wakefield, RI 02879

Rhode Island Division of Agriculture
22 Hayes Street
Providence, RI 02903

South Carolina Wildlife and Marine Resources
        Department
Rembert C. Dennis Building, P.O. Box 167
Columbia, SC 29202

South Carolina Department of Natural Resources
Alligator Control Program
Dennis Wildlife Center
P.P. Drawer 190
Bonneau, SC 29431

South Dakota Department of Game, Fish, and Parks
Foss Building
523 East Capitol
Pierre, SD 57501-3182

South Dakota Department of Game, Fish, and Parks
License Office
412 West Missouri
Pierre, SD 57501

Tennessee Wildlife Resources Agency
Ellington Agricultural Center
P.O. Box 40747
Nashville, TN 37204

Texas Parks and Wildlife Department
4200 Smith School Road
Austin, TX 78744

Utah Department of Agriculture
350 N. Redwood Road
Salt Lake City, UT 84116

Utah Department of Natural Resources
Division of Wildlife Resources
Wildlife Registration Office
1596 West North Temple
Salt Lake City, UT 84116

Vermont Fish and Game Department
Law Enforcement Division
103 South Main Street
Waterbury, VT 05676

Virginia Department of Game and Inland Fisheries
4010 West Broad Street
P.O. Box 11104
Richmond, VA 23230-1104

Washington Department of Fish and Wildlife
600 Capitol Way N.
Olympia, WA 98501-1091

West Virginia Department of Natural Resources
Division of Wildlife
P.O. Box 67
Elkins, WV 26241-0067

Wisconsin Department of Natural Resources
P.O. Box 7921
Madison, WI 53791-9414

Wyoming Game and Fish Department
5400 Bishop Boulevard
Cheyenne, WY 82006

Federal Agencies

U.S. Fish and Wildlife Service
Office of Management Authority
4401 N. Fairfax Dr., Room 432
Arlington, VA 22203

U.S. Fish and Wildlife Service
Region 1 Office
Eastside Federal Complex
911 N.E. 11th Avenue
Portland, OR 97232-4181

U.S. Fish and Wildlife Service
Region 2 Office
500 Gold Avenue S.W.
Albuquerque, NM 87103

U.S. Fish and Wildlife Service
Region 3 Office
Whipple Federal Bldg.
Fort Snelling, MN 55111-4506

U.S. Fish and Wildlife Service
Region 4 Office
1875 Century Center Boulevard
Atlanta, GA 30345-3301

U.S. Fish and Wildlife Service
Region 5 Office
300 Westgate Center Dr.
Hadley, MA 01035-9589

U.S. Fish and Wildlife Service
Region 6 Office
134 Union Boulevard
Lakewood, CO 80228

U.S. Fish and Wildlife Service
Region 7 Office
1011 East Tudor Road
Anchorage, AK 99503

U.S. Department of Health and Human Services
200 Independence Avenue S.W.
Washington, DC 20201

U.S. Food and Drug Administration
5600 Fishers Lane
Rockville, MD 20857

National Marine Fisheries Service
Silver Springs Metro Center 1
1335 East West Highway
Silver Springs, MD 20910

USFWS Regional District Map

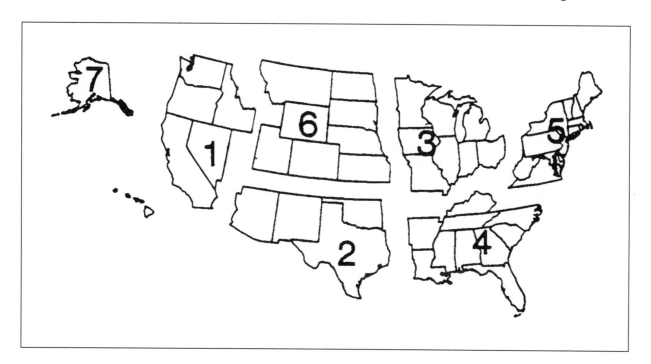

APPENDIX II
INDEX TO STATE PROTECTED SPECIES

The following taxonomic index provides an alphabetical listing of all North American amphibian and reptile species and subspecies fully protected (endangered, threatened, legally protected special concern species, etc.) at the state level of government. Subspecific designations are included when utilized by individual states. Each listed species and subspecies is followed by the standard U.S. Postal abbreviations for all states officially protecting that taxon. An asterisk (*) following the name of any taxa included in this index indicates a taxonomic designation differing from or not existing in the fourth edition of *Standard Common and Current Scientific Names for North American Amphibians and Reptiles* by Joseph T. Collins (1997).

To help facilitate the use of the species index, the following key to standard U.S. Postal Service State Abbreviations has been provided.

AK	Alaska	IL	Illinois	NC	North Carolina	SC	South Carolina
AL	Alabama	IN	Indiana	ND	North Dakota	SD	South Dakota
AR	Arkansas	KY	Kentucky	NE	Nebraska	TN	Tennessee
AZ	Arizona	KS	Kansas	NH	New Hampshire	TX	Texas
CA	California	LA	Louisiana	NJ	New Jersey	UT	Utah
CO	Colorado	MA	Massachusetts	NM	New Mexico	VA	Virginia
CT	Connecticut	MD	Maryland	NV	Nevada	VT	Vermont
DE	Delaware	ME	Maine	NY	New York	WA	Washington
FL	Florida	MI	Michigan	OH	Ohio	WI	Wisconsin
GA	Georgia	MN	Minnesota	OK	Oklahoma	WV	West Virginia
HI	Hawaii	MO	Missouri	OR	Oregon	WY	Wyoming
IA	Iowa	MS	Mississippi	PA	Pennsylvania		
ID	Idaho	MT	Montana	RI	Rhode Island		

Acris
  crepitans MN, NY, WI
        c. blanchardi MI
        c. crepitans NJ
Agkistrodon
  contortrix IA, MA
        c. mokasen NJ
  piscivorus IN
Alligator
  mississippiensis AR, FL, GA, LA, NC, OK
Ambystoma
  californiense CA
  cingulatum AL, GA, SC
  jeffersonianum MA, MD, NJ
  laterale CT, MA, NJ, OH
  mabeei VA
  macrodactylum
        m. croceum CA
  maculatum NJ
  mavortium
        m. melanostictum OR
  opacum MA, MI, NJ

  platineum * IL, NJ
  talpoideum NC, TN
  texanum MI
  tigrinum DE, MD, NY
        t. tigrinum * NJ, NC, VA
  tremblayi * NJ
Amphiuma
  pholeter GA
Aneides
  aeneus AL, GA, IN, MD, MS, NC, OH, PA
  ferreus OR
  flavipunctatus OR
  hardii NM
Anniella
  pulchra
        p. nigra CA
Anolis
  carolinensis TN
Apalone
  spinifera MD, NC, NJ, VT
Ascaphus
  truei CA, OR

Arizona
  elegans KS
  occidentalis
        o. eburnata UT
Batrachoseps
  aridus CA
  attenuatus OR
  campi CA
  simatus CA
  stebbensi CA
  wrightorum OR
Bufo
  alvarius CA, NM
  baxteri WY
  boreas NM, OR
        b. boreas CO, ID, UT
  canorus CA
  debilis
        d. debilis KS
        d. insidior KS
  exsul CA
  houstonensis TX

microscaphus CA
> m. microscaphus * UT

punctatus KS

woodhousii OR

Callisaurus

draconoides
> d. rhodostictus UT

Caretta

caretta CA, CT, DE, FL, GA, HI, LA, MA, MD, ME, MS, NC, NJ, NY, RI, OR, SC, TX, VA, WA

Carphophis

amoenus IA, MA
> a. amoenus NJ

Cemophora

coccinea IN, MD, TX
> c. copei NJ

Chelonia

mydas AK, CA, CT, DE, FL, GA, HI, LA, MA, MD, MS, NC, NJ, NY, RI, OR, SC, TX, VA, WA

Chrysemys

picta WA
> p. bellii OR
> p. marginata NJ

Clemmys

guttata GA, IL, IN, MA, ME, MI, NH, NJ, RI, VT

insculpta CT, IA, MA, MI, MN, NH, NJ, NY, RI, WI, VA

marmorata CA, ID, OR, WA

muhlenbergii CT, DE, GA, MA, NC, NJ, NY, PA, RI, SC, TN, VA

Clonophis

kirtlandii IL, IN, MI, PA

Cnemidophorus

burti NM

dixoni NM

hyperythrus CA

Coleonyx

reticulatus TX

switaki CA

variegatus
> v. utahensis UT

Coluber

constrictor ME
> c. constrictor NJ

Coniophanes

imperialis TX

Contia

tenuis OR

Crocodylus

acutus FL

Crotalus

cerastes
> c. cerastes UT

horridus CT, IL, IN, KS, MA, MD, MN, NH, NJ, NY, OH, RI, TX, VT
> h. atricaudatus * VA

lepidus AZ
> l. lepidus NM

mitchellii UT

pricei AZ

scutulatus UT

viridis IA, UT

willardi AZ, NM

Crotaphytus

bicinctores ID, OR

reticulatus TX

Cryptobranchus

alleganiensis AL, GA, IL, IN, MD, NC, OH, TN

Deirochelys

reticularia
> r. miaria MO
> r. reticularia VA

Dermochelys

coriacea AK, CA, CT, DE, FL, GA, HI, LA, MA, MD, ME, MS, NC, NJ, NY, OR, RI, SC, TX, VA, WA

Desmognathus

aeneus TN

fuscus IL

monticola AL

quadramaculatus TN

welteri TN

wrighti TN

Diadophis

punctatus ID
> p. acricus FL
> p. edwardsii NJ
> p. punctatus NJ

Dicamptodon

copei OR

Dipsosaurus

dorsalis
> d. dorsalis UT

Drymarchon

corais TX
> c. couperi AL, FL, GA, MS, SC

Drymobius

margaritiferus TX

Elaphe

emoryi IL, UT

gloydi MI

guttata
> g. guttata * FL, NJ

obsoleta MA
> o. obsoleta MI, NJ

vulpina
> v. vulpina * MO

Elgaria

panamintina CA

Emydoidea

blandingii IN, MA, ME, MI, MN, MO, NH, NY, SD, WI

Eretmochelys

imbricata CA, FL, DE, GA, HI, LA, MA, MD, MS, NC, NJ, NY, RI, SC, TX, VA

Eumeces

anthracinus MD, SC

callicephalus NM

egregius
> e. egregius FL
> e. lividus FL

fasciatus CT, NJ, VT

laticeps KS

obsoletus IA

Eurycea

bislineata
> b. bislineata * NJ

junaluska NC, TN

longicauda NC
> l. longicauda NJ
> l. melanopleura KS

lucifuga KS, MS, OH

multiplicata
> m. griseogaster KS

nana TX

quadridigitata NC

tridentifera TX

Farancia

erytrogramma MD, MS

Gambelia

sila CA

wislizenii OR

Gastrophryne

carolinensis KS, MD

olivacea NM

Gopherus

agassizii AZ, CA, NV, UT

berlandieri TX

polyphemus AL, FL, GA, LA, MS, SC

Graptemys
> *barbouri* AL, GA
> *flavimaculata* MS
> *geographica* GA, KS, MD, NJ
> *nigrinoda* MS
> *oculifera* LA, MS
> *pseudogeographica* SD
> *pulchra* AL, GA

Gyrinophilus
> *palleucus* AL, TN
> *porphyriticus* CT, MA, MS
>> *p. porphyriticus* NJ

Haideotriton
> *wallacei* FL, GA

Heloderma
> *suspectum* AZ, NM, NV,
>> *s. cinctum* CA, UT

Hemidactylium
> *scutatum* IL, IN, MA, NC, NJ, TN

Heterodon
> *nasicus* IA, IL, KS
> *platirhinos* KS, NJ, SD
> *simus* AL, MS

Hydromantes
> *brunus* CA
> *platycephalus* CA
> *shastae* CA

Hyla
> *andersonii* AL, FL, NJ, SC
> *chrysoscelis* DE, NJ
> *gratiosa* DE, MD, TN, VA
> *regilla* UT
> *versicolor* NJ

Hypopachus
> *variolosus* TX

Hypsiglena
> *torquata*
>> *t. jani* KS

Kinosternon
> *baurii* FL
> *flavescens* IA, IL
>> *f. flavescens* MO
>> *f. spooneri* MO
> *hirtipes*
>> *h. murrayi* TX
> *sonoriense* CA
> *subrubrum* IN, NY
>> *s. subrubrum* NJ

Lampropeltis
> *getula* IA, OR
>> *g. californiae* UT
>> *g. getula* NJ
>> *g. sticticeps* * NC

> *pyromelana*
>> *p. infralabialis* * UT
> *triangulum*
>> *t. taylori* UT
>> *t. triangulum* NJ
> *zonata* OR
>> *z. pulchra* CA

Lepidochelys
> *kempii* CT, DE, FL, GA, LA, MA, MD, ME, MS, NC, NJ, NY, RI, SC, TX, VA
> *olivacea* CA, HI, OR, WA

Leptodactylus
> *labialis* TX

Leptodeira
> *septentrionalis* TX

Leptotyphlops
> *dulcis*
>> *d. dissectus* KS
> *humilis*
>> *h. utahensis* UT

Lichanura
> *bottae* CA

Liochlorophis
> *vernalis* IA, IN, MO, NC
>> *v. blanchardi* * TX
>> *V. vernalis* * NJ

Macrochelys
> *temminckii* AL, GA, IL, IN, KS, TN, TX

Malaclemys
> *terrapin* MA, NC, RI
>> *t. pileata* AL

Masticophis
> *flagellum* IL
>> *f. flagellum* AL
>> *f. ruddocki* CA
> *lateralis*
>> *l. euryxanthus* CA

Necturus
> *lewisi* NC
> *maculosus* IA, MD, NC

Neoseps
> *reynoldsi* FL

Nerodia
> *clarkii*
>> *c. clarkii* AL
>> *c. taeniata* FL
> *cyclopion* IL, TN
>> *c. cyclopion* * MO
> *erythrogaster* IA, IN, NM
>> *e. neglecta* MI, OH
> *fasciata* IL
> *harteri* TX

> *paucimaculata* TX
> *rhombifer* IA
> *sipedon*
>> *s. sipedon* NJ
>> *s. williamengelsi* NC

Notophthalmus
> *meridionalis* TX
> *perstriatus* GA
> *viridescens* IA
>> *v. louisianensis* KS

Opheodrys
> *aestivus* NJ, PA

Ophisaurus
> *attenuatus* IA, WI
>> *a. longicaudus* TN
> *mimicus* NC
> *ventralis* VA

Phaeognathus
> *hubrichti* AL

Pituophis
> *melanoleucus*
>> *m. lodingi* AL, MS
>> *m. melanoleucus* NC, NJ, TN
>> *m. mugitus* AL
> *ruthveni* TX

Plethodon
> *cinereus*
>> *c. cinereus* * NJ
> *dorsalis* NC
> *elongatus* CA, OR
> *glutinosus* CT
>> *g. glutinosus* * NJ
> *idahoensis* ID
> *larselli* OR, WA
> *longicrus* * NC
> *neomexicanus* NM
> *nettingi* WV
> *petraeus* GA
> *shenandoah* VA
> *stormi* CA, OR
> *websteri* SC
> *wehrlei* MD, NC, TN
> *welleri* NC, TN

Phrynosoma
> *coronatum* CA, TX
> *douglassii* NE, OR
>> *d. hernandesi* TX
> *mcallii* AZ, CA
> *platyrhinos* OR

Phyllodactylus
> *nocticolus* CA

Pseudacris
> *brachyphona* MD, NC

clarkii NM
crucifer
      c. crucifer KS, NJ
feriarum NJ
kalmi NJ, PA
streckeri IL
      s. streckeri * KS
triseriata VT

Pseudemys
alabamensis AL
concinna IL, IN
gorzugi NM
rubriventris NJ, MA, PA
      r. sp. * MS

Pseudobranchus
striatus SC

Pseudotriton
montanus PA
      m. montanus NJ
ruber IN
      r. ruber NJ

Rana
areolata IA, IN
      a. circulosa KS
aurora CA, OR
blairi AZ
boylii CA, OR
capito
      c. aesopus FL
      c. capito NC
      c. sevosa AL, FL, MS
cascadae CA, OR
chiricahuensis AZ
clamitans
      c. melanota KS
heckscheri NC
muscosa CA
okaloosae FL
onca AZ, UT
palustris NJ
pipiens AZ, ID, OR, UT
pretiosa CA, ID, OR, UT
sphenocephala PA
      s. utricularia NJ
subaquavocalis AZ*
sylvatica CO, NJ
tarahumarae AZ
virgatipes MD, NJ
yavapaiensis AZ, CA, NM, UT

Regina
septemvittata NJ, WI

Rhinocheilus
lecontei ID
      l. tessellatus KS

Rhinophrynus
dorsalis TX

Rhyacotriton
cascadae OR
kezeri OR
olympicus CA
variegatus OR

Sauromalus
obesus
      o. multiforaminatus UT
      o. obesus UT

Scaphiopus
holbrookii CT, MA, OH
      h. holbrookii * NJ

Sceloporus
arenicolous NM
scalaris * NM

Scincella
lateralis NJ

Senticolis
triaspis NM

Siren
lacertina MD
sp. * TX

Sistrurus
catenatus AZ, IA, IL, IN, MN,
    NY, PA, WI
      c. catenatus MI, MO
miliarius
      m. streckeri TN

Smilisca
baudinii TX

Sonora
semiannulata ID, OR

Spea
hammondii CA

Sternotherus
depressus AL
minor
      m. peltifer NC
odoratus IA, NJ

Stilosoma
extenuatum FL

Storeria
dekayi
      d. dekayi NJ
      d. victa FL
occipitomaculata
      o. occipitomaculata KS,
    NJ

Tantilla
coronata IN
cucullata TX
oolitica FL

Terrapene
carolina MA, ME, NY, RI
      c. carolina MI, NH, NJ
ornata IA, IN, WI

Thamnophis
butleri IN, WI
eques NM
gigas CA
hammondii CA
marcianus
      m. marcianus KS
proximus NM, WI
radix
      r. radix * OH
rufipunctatus NM
sauritus IL, WI
      s. sackenii FL
sirtalis
      s. tetrataenia * CA

Trachemys
scripta
      s. elegans NJ

Trimorphodon
biscutatus
      b. lambda UT
      b. vilkinsonii TX

Tropidoclonion
lineatum SD

Typhlomolge
rathbuni TX
robusta TX

Typhlotriton
spelaeus KS

Uma
inornata * CA

Virginia
striatula KS
pulchra MD
valeriae IA
      v. elegans KS
      v. valeriae NJ

Xantusia
henshawi CA
riversiana CA
vigilis
      v. utahensis UT
      v. vigilis UT

Herpetological Literature Cited and Selected Bibliography

Allen, William B. 1988. *State Lists of Endangered and Threatened Species of Reptiles and Amphibians and Laws and Regulations Covering Collecting of Reptiles and Amphibians in Each State*, 3rd edition. Privately Printed, Pittsburgh Zoo. Pittsburgh, PA.

Ashton, R. E. Jr. et. al. 1976. *Endangered and Threatened Amphibians and Reptiles in the United States.* Society for the Study of Amphibians and Reptiles, Herpetological Circular No. 5.

Ashton, R. E. Jr., and Ashton, P. S. 1985-1988. *Handbook of Reptiles and Amphibians of Florida*, 3 Volumes. Windward Publ. Miami, FL.

Banks, Richard C., McDiarmid, Roy W., and Gardner, Alfred L. 1987. *Checklist of Vertebrates of the United States, the U.S. Territories, and Canada.* U.S. Dept. Interior, Res. Publ. 166. Washington, DC.

Barbour, Roger W. 1971. *Amphibians and Reptiles of Kentucky.* Univ. Press of Kentucky. Lexington, KY.

Baxter, G. T. and Stone, M. D. 1985. *Amphibians and Reptiles of Wyoming*, 2nd edition. Wyoming Fish and Game Dept. Cheyenne, WY.

Black, J. H. and Sievert, G. 1989. *A Field Guide to the Amphibians of Oklahoma.* Oklahoma Dept. Wildlife Cons. Oklahoma City, OK.

Collins, Joseph T. 1990. *Standard Common and Current Scientific Names for North American Amphibians and Reptiles*, 3rd Edition. Society for the Study of Amphibians and Reptiles, Herpetological Circular No. 19. Lawrence, KS.

Collins, Joseph T. 1993. *Amphibians and Reptiles in Kansas*, 3rd edition. Univ. of Kansas. Lawrence, KS.

Collins, Joseph T. 1997. *Standard Common and Current Scientific Names for North American Amphibians and Reptiles*, 4th Edition. Society for the Study of Amphibians and Reptiles, Herpetological Circular No. 25. Lawrence, KS.

Conant, Roger. 1951. *The Reptiles of Ohio*, 2nd Edition. American Midland Naturalist. Notre Dame, IN.

Conant, Roger and Collins, Joseph T. 1991. *A Field Guide to Reptiles and Amphibians of Eastern and Central North America*, 3rd Edition. Houghton Mifflin Co. Boston, MA.

Christensen, J. L. and Burken, R. R. 1978. *The Endangered and Uncommon Reptiles and Amphibians of Iowa.* Iowa Aca. Sci. Cedar Falls, IA.

Czajka, Adrian F. and Nickerson, Max A. 1974. *State Regulations for Collecting Reptiles and Amphibians.* Milwaukee Public Museum, Spec. Publ. Bio. and Geo. No. L. Milwaukee, WI.

DeGraaf, R. M. and Rudis, D. D. 1983. *Amphibians and Reptiles of New England.* Univ. of Massachusetts Press. Amherst, MA.

de Klemm, Cyrille. 1993. *Guidelines for Legislation to Implement CITES.* IUCN Environmental Policy and Law Paper No. 26. IUCN. Gland, Switzerland.

Degenhardt, W. G., Painter, C. W., and Price, A. H. 1996. *Amphibians & Reptiles of New Mexico.* Univ. of New Mexico Press. Albuquerque, NM.

Denny, Guy L. 1990. *Ohio's Amphibians.* Ohio Department of Natural Resources.

Denny, Guy L. 1990. *Ohio's Reptiles.* Ohio Department of Natural Resources.

Dowling, H. G. 1957. *A Review of the Amphibians and Reptiles of Arkansas.* Univ. Arkansas Mus. Occ. Pap. No. 3. Fayetteville, AR.

Dundee, H. A. and Rossman, D. A. 1989. *The Amphibians and Reptiles of Louisiana.* Louisiana St. Univ. Press. Baton Rouge, LA.

Ernst, Carl H. and Barbour, Roger W. 1989. *Turtles of the World.* Smithsonian Institution Press. Washington, D.C.

Fishbeck, D. W. and Underhill, J. C. 1959. *A Check List of the Amphibians and Reptiles of South Dakota.* Proc. South Dakota Aca. Sci. Vermillion, SD.

Fowlie, J. A. 1965. *The Snakes of Arizona.* Azul Quinta Press. Fallbrook, CA.

Frank, Norman and Ramus, Erica. 1994. *State, Federal, and C.I.T.E.S. Regulations for Herpetologists*. NG Publ. Inc. Pottsville, PA.

Frank, Norman and Ramus, Erica. 1995. *A Complete Guide to Scientific and Common Names of Reptiles and Amphibians of the World.* NG Publ. Inc. Pottsville, PA.

Funderbunk, S. 1985. *Herps and Federal Wildlife Permits*. In: 8th International Herpetological Symposium on Captive Propagation and Husbandry. Zoological Consortium Inc. Thurmont, MD.

Garrett, J. M. and Barker, D. G. 1987. *A Field Guide to Reptiles and Amphibians of Texas*. Texas Monthly Press. Austin, TX.

George, Susan M., et. al. 1996. *Saving Biodiversity: A Status Report on State Laws, Policies and Programs*. Defenders of Wildlife. Washington, DC.

Green, Bayard N. and Pauley, Thomas K. 1987. *Amphibians and Reptiles in West Virginia*. University of Pittsburgh Press. Pittsburgh, PA.

Groves, Craig. 1994. *Idaho's Amphibians & Reptiles: Description, Habitat & Ecology.* Idaho Department of Fish and Game Nongame Leaflet 7. Boise, ID.

Hammerson, Geoffrey A. 1982. *Amphibians and Reptiles in Colorado*. Colorado Division of Wildlife. Denver, CO.

Harding, James H. and Holman, J. Alan. 1990. *Michigan Turtles and Lizards: A Field Guide and Pocket Reference.* Michigan State University. East Lansing, MI.

Harding, James H. and Holman, J. Alan. 1992. *Michigan Frogs, Toads, and Salamanders: A Field Guide and Pocket Reference*. Michigan State University. East Lansing, MI.

Hoberg, Ted and Gause, Cully. 1992. *Reptiles & Amphibians of North Dakota*. North Dakota Outdoors LV(1). Bismark, ND.

Hodge, Robert P. 1976. *Amphibians & Reptiles in Alaska, the Yukon, and Northwest Territories*. Alaska Northwest Publ. Co. Anchorage, AK.

Holman, J. Alan, Harding, James H., Hensley, Marvin M., and Dudderar, Glenn R. 1989. *Michigan Snakes: A Field Guide and Pocket Reference*. Michigan State University. East Lansing, MI.

Hunter, M. L. Jr., Albright, J. and Arbuckle, J (editors). 1992. *The Amphibians and Reptiles of Maine*. Maine Agri. Exp. Stat. Bull. No. 838.

Johnson, Tom R. 1987. *The Amphibians and Reptiles of Missouri*. Missouri Dept. Conservation. Jefferson City, MO.

Kelly, H. A. 1936. *Snakes of Maryland*. Nat. Hist. Soc. of Maryland. Baltimore, MD.

King, F. Wayne and Burke, Russell L. (editors). 1989. *Crocodilian, Tuatara, and Turtle Species of the World: A Taxonomic and Geographic Reference*. Association of Systematic Collections. Washington, DC.

Klemens, M. W. 1993. *Amphibians and Reptiles of Connecticut and Adjacent Regions*. St. Geol. and Nat. Hist. Sur. of Conn. Bull. No. 112.

Lang, Jeffrey W. and Karns, Daryl. 1988. *Amphibians and Reptiles*. In: Coffin, B. and Pfannmuller, L. (editors). 1988. *Minnesota's Endangered Flora and Fauna.* Univ. of Minnesota Press. Minneapolis, MN.

Lazell, James D., Jr. 1976. *This Broken Archipelago - Cape Cod and the Islands, Amphibians and Reptiles*. Demeter Press. New York, New York.

Levell, John P. 1995. *A Field Guide to Reptiles and the Law*, 1st edition. Serpent's Tale Natural History Books. Excelsior, MN.

Linder, A. D. and Fichter, E. 1991 (1977). *The Amphibians and Reptiles of Idaho*. Idaho State Univ. Press. Pocatello, ID.

Liner, Ernest A. 1994. *Scientific and Common Names for the Amphibians and Reptiles of Mexico in Spanish and English.* Society for the Study of Amphibians and Reptiles, Herpetological Circular No. 23. Lawrence, KS.

Lohoefener, R. and Altig, R. 1983. *Mississippi Herpetology*. Mississippi St. Univ. Res. Center Bull. No. 1. Mississippi State, MS.

Lynch, J. D. 1985. *Annotated Checklist of the Amphibians and Reptiles of Nebraska*. Trans. Nebraska Aca. Sci. Vol. 13. Lincoln, NE.

Martof, B. S., Palmer, W. M., Bailey, J. R., and Harrison, J. R. 1980. *Amphibians and Reptiles of the Carolinas and Virginia*. Univ. of North Carolina Press. Chapel Hill, NC.

McCoy, C.J. 1982. *Amphibians and Reptiles in Pennsylvania*. Carnegie Mus. Nat. Hist. Spec. Publ. No. 6. Pittsburgh, PA.

McDiarmid, Roy W. et. al. (editors) 1995. *Reptiles and Amphibians*. In: LaRoe, Edward T. et. al. (editors). *Our Living Resources: A Report to the Nation on the Distribution, Abundance, and Health of U.S. Plants, Animals, and Ecosystems*. U.S. Dept. Interior, National Biological Service. Washington, DC.

McKeown, Sean. 1996. *A Field Guide to Reptiles and Amphibians in the Hawaiian Islands*. Diamond Head Publ. Co. Los Osos, CA.

Minton, Sherman A. Jr. 1972. *Amphibians and Reptiles of Indiana*. Indiana Academy of Sciences, Monograph No. 3. Indianapolis, IN.

Moler, P. E. (ed.) 1992. *Rare and Endangered Biota of Florida — Vol. III Amphibians and Reptiles*. Univ. of Florida Press. Gainesville, FL.

Mitchell, Joseph C. 1994. *The Reptiles of Virginia*. Smithsonian Institution Press. Washington, DC.

Musgrave, R. S. and Stein, M. A. 1995. *State Wildlife Laws Handbook*. Government Institutes, Inc. Albuquerque, NM.

Mount, Robert H. 1975. *The Reptiles and Amphibians of Alabama*. Auburn University Press. Auburn, AL.

Nussbaum, R. A., Brodie, E. D., and Storm, R. M. 1983. *Amphibians and Reptiles of the Pacific Northwest*. Univ. of Idaho Press. Moscow, ID.

Oldfield, B. and Moriarty, J. J. 1994. *Amphibians and Reptiles Native to Minnesota*. Univ. of Minnesota Press. Minneapolis, MN.

Over, William H. 1923. *Amphibians and Reptiles of South Dakota*. South Dakota Geological and Natural History Survey Bulletin 12. Vermillion, SD.

Palmer, W. H., and Braswell, A. L. 1995. *Reptiles of North Carolina*. Univ. of North Carolina Press. Chapel Hill, NC.

Peters, James A. 1964. *Dictionary of Herpetology*. Hafner Publ. Co. New York, NY.

Pritchard, Peter C. H. 1979. *Encyclopedia of Turtles*. T.F.H. Publications, Inc. Neptune City, NJ.

Sievert, G. and Sievert, L. 1988. *A Field Guide to the Reptiles of Oklahoma*. Oklahoma Dept. Wildlife Cons. Oklahoma City, OK.

Schmidt, Karl P. 1953. *A Check List of North American Amphibians and Reptiles*, 6th Edition. American Society of Ichthyologists and Herpetologists.

Sinclair, R. W. and Ferguson, R. B. 1965. *Amphibians and Reptiles in Tennessee*. Tennessee Game and Fish Comm. Nashville, TN.

Smith, Philip W. 1961. *The Amphibians and Reptiles of Illinois*. Illinois Natural History Survey, Vol. 28 Art. 1. Urbana, IL.

Stebbins, R. C. 1985. *A Field Guide to Western Amphibians and Reptiles*, 2nd edition. Houghton Mifflin Co. Boston, MA.

Szaro, Robert C., et. al. (editors). 1988. *Management of Amphibians, Reptiles, and Small Mammals in North America:Proceedings of a Symposium, July 19-21, 1988. Flagstaff, Arizona*. U.S. Dept. Agri. Forest Service Gen. Tech. Rep. RM-166.

Tenant, A. 1984. *The Snakes of Texas*. Texas Monthly Press. Austin, TX.

Tyning, Thomas F. (editor). 1997. *Status and Conservation of Turtles of the North Eastern United States: A Symposium*. Serpent's Tale Natural History Books. Lanesboro, MN.

Vogt, R. C. 1981. *Natural History of Amphibians and Reptiles of Wisconsin*. Milwaukee Public Mus. Milwaukee, WI.

Wells-Mikota, Susan K. 1993. *Wildlife Laws, Regulations, and Policies*. In: Fowler, M.E. (editor). *Zoo & Wild Animal Medicine: Current Therapy 3*. W.B. Saunders Co. Philadelphia, PA.

Wheeler, G. C., and Wheeler, J. 1966. *The Amphibians and Reptiles of North Dakota*. Univ. of North Dakota Press. Grand Forks, ND.

Zug, George R. 1993. *Herpetology: An Introductory Biology of Amphibians and Reptiles*. Academic Press, Inc. San Diego, CA.